Restorative Justice

Restorative Justice
Theoretical foundations

**Edited by Elmar G. M. Weitekamp
and Hans-Jürgen Kerner**

WILLAN
PUBLISHING

Published by

Willan Publishing
Culmcott House
Mill Street, Uffculme
Cullompton, Devon
EX15 3AT, UK
Tel: +44(0)1884 840337
Fax: +44(0)1884 840251
e-mail: info@willanpublishing.co.uk
website: www.willanpublishing.co.uk

Published simultaneously in the USA and Canada by

Willan Publishing
c/o ISBS, 5824 N.E. Hassalo St,
Portland, Oregon 97213-3644, USA
Tel: +001(0)503 287 3093
Fax: +001(0)503 280 8832
e-mail: info@isbs.com
website: www.isbs.com

First published 2002

ISBN 1-903240-83-2 (paper)
ISBN 1-903240-72-7 (cased)

British Library Cataloguing-in-Publication Data

A catalogue record for this book is available from the British Library

Printed by T.J. International, Padstow, Cornwall
Project management by Deer Park Productions
Typeset by GCS, Leighton Buzzard, Beds.

Contents

List of figures and tables   vii

Notes on contributors   xi

Preface   xix

1   **The shape of things to come: a framework for
thinking about a restorative justice system**
Daniel W. Van Ness   **1**

2   **Journey to belonging**
Howard Zehr   **21**

3   **Restorative justice and the politics of decolonization**
Chris Cunneen   **32**

4   **Justified criticism, misunderstanding, or important steps
on the road to acceptance?**
Martin Wright and Guy Masters   **50**

5   **From community to dominion: in search of social values
for restorative justice**
Lode Walgrave   **71**

6 Deconstructing restoration: the promise of restorative justice
   George Pavlich   90

7 Restorative justice theory validation
   Paul McCold and Ted Wachtel   110

8 Restorative justice and the future of diversion and
   informal social control
   Gordon Bazemore and Colleen McLeod   143

9 Restorative conferencing for juveniles in the United States:
   prevalence, process and practice
   Mara Schiff and Gordon Bazemore   177

10 Restorative justice for children: in need of procedural
   safeguards and standards
   Christian Eliaerts and Els Dumortier   204

11 From the 'sword' to dialogue: towards a 'dialectic'
   basis for penal mediation
   Grazia Mannozzi   224

12 Punishment, guilt and spirit in restorative justice:
   an essay in legal and religious anthropology
   Robert E. Mackay   247

13 The role of shame, guilt and remorse in restorative
   justice processes for young people
   Gabrielle Maxwell and Allison Morris   267

14 Peacemaking and community harmony: lessons (and
   admonitions) from the Navajo peacemaking courts
   L. Thomas Winfree Jr.   285

15 From philosophical abstraction to restorative action,
   from senseless retribution to meaningful restitution:
   just deserts and restorative justice revisited
   Ezzat A. Fattah   308

16 Restorative justice: present prospects and future directions
   Elmar G. M. Weitekamp   322

Index   339

List of figures and tables

I. Figures:

Figure 7.1   Social discipline window   113

Figure 7.2   Stakeholders in restorative justice   115

Figure 7.3   Restorative practices typology   116

Figure 7.4   Percentage of victim satisfaction by programme
             and category   128

Figure 7.5   Percentage of victim fairness by programme and
             category   130

Figure 7.6   Percentage of offender satisfaction by programme
             and category   132

Figure 7.7   Percentage of offender fairness by programme
             and category   134

Figure 7.8   Weighted totals by category of practice   135

Figure 7.9   Offender fairness by victim satisfaction by programme
            (with weighted category averages)   136

Figure 9.1   Percentage of states reporting restorative conferencing
            programmes as of January 2001   181

Figure 9.2   Number and type of restorative conferencing
            programmes in the US as of January 2001   183

Figure 9.3   Variety of restorative conferencing programmes by
            state among nine leading states as of January 2001   184

Figure 11.1 Drawing based on 'Justitia thront über König und
            Bettler' (1566) by Justinus Gobber, cf. Kissel 1984, 110   225

Figure 11.2 Drawing based on Roman coins: (A) 'Justice' (Age of
            Tiberius); (B) 'Equity' (Age of Vespasian); (C) 'Equity'
            (Age of Marcus Aurelius), cf. Jacob 1994, 220   225

Figure 11.3 Drawing based on 'Stanza della Segnatura in Vaticano'
            (1508–1511) by Raphael, cf. Kissel 1984, 37   226

Figure 11.4 Drawing based on 'Die Gerechtigkeit mit Kranich'
            (1495) by Albrecht Dürer, cf. Kissel 1984, 43   227

Figure 11.5 Drawing based on 'La Justice', attributed to
            Domenico Beccafumi (1486–1551); cf. Jacob 1994, 224   244

II. Tables:

Table 1.1   Encounter   8

Table 1.2   Amends   8

Table 1.3   Reintegration   9

Table 1.4   Inclusion   10

Table 1.5   Fully restorative system   11

Table 1.6   Moderately restorative system   12

Table 1.7   Minimally restorative system   13

Table 1.8   Basic models of restorative justice   16

Table 7.1   Victim satisfaction by category of practice (excluding US public and victims)   121

Table 7.2   Victim fairness by category of practice (exluding US victims)   122

Table 7.3   Offender satisfaction by category of practice (excluding US victims)   123

Table 7.4   Offender fairness by category of practice (excluding US victims)   124

Table 7.5   Programme participant samples   126

Table 7.6   Victim satisfaction by category of practice   129

Table 7.7   Victim fairness by category of practice   131

Table 7.8   Offender satisfaction by category of practice   133

Table 7.9   Offender fairness by category of practice   135

Table 8.1   Emerging restorative justice theories of intervention   158

Table 9.1   Per cent of total programmes that report accepting programmes at several points in case process   188

Table 9.2   Average number of people present at the conference   189

Table 9.3   The importance of repairing harm by actual achievement of goals   191

Table 9.4   The importance of victim participation by actual achievement of goals   191

Table 9.5   The importance of victim satisfaction by actual achievement of goals   192

Table 9.6   The importance of offender reintegration by actual
             achievement of goals   193

Table 9.7   The importance of holding offenders accountable by
             achievement of goals   193

Table 9.8   The importance of community involvement by actual
             achievement of goals   194

Table 9.9   The importance of building local community capacity
             to respond to crime by actual achievement of goals   194

Table 14.1. Sovereignty in Euro-Western development and
             Aboriginal North American tradition   290

Notes on contributors

Gordon Bazemore is currently Professor of Criminology and Criminal Justice and Director of the Community Justice Institute at Florida Atlantic University. His recent publications appear in *Justice Quarterly*, *Youth and Society, Crime and Delinquency*, and *The Annals of the American Academy of Political and Social Sciences, The Justice System Journal*, and the *International Journal of Victimology*. Dr Bazemore has completed two books, *Restorative Juvenile Justice: Repairing the Harm of Youth Crime* (co-edited with Lode Walgrave) (Criminal Justice Press) and *Restorative and Community Justice: Cultivating Common Ground for Victims, Communities and Offenders* (co-edited with Mara Schiff) (Anderson Publishing). He is currently Principal Investigator of a national study of restorative justice conferencing funded by the National Institute of Justice and the Robert Wood Johnson Foundation, and a national action research project funded by the Office of Juvenile Justice and Delinquency Prevention to pilot restorative justice reform in several juvenile court jurisdictions.

Chris Cunneen is Associate Professor and teaches criminology at the University of Sydney Law School. He is also Director of the Institute of Criminology, University of Sydney. He has published widely in the area of juvenile justice, policing, restorative justice and indigenous issues including a number of books on issues such as juvenile justice (*Juvenile Justice. An Australian Perspective*, Oxford University Press, 1995); on indigenous legal issues (*Indigenous People and the Law in Australia*, Butterworths, 1995); hate crime (*Faces of Hate*, Federation Press, 1997) and policing (*Conflict, Politics and Crime*, Allen and Unwin, 2001).

Els Dumortier is Scientific Researcher at the Free University of Brussels (VUB). She graduated in Law (1995) and Criminology (1997). She has published in the fields of Juvenile Justice and Juvenile Criminology. She is preparing a PhD dissertation on the topic of 'Juvenile Judges and Legal Rights for Juvenile Delinquents in the 20th Century'.

Christian Eliaerts is Professor of Criminology and Head of the Department of Criminology at the Free University of Brussels (VUB). He received his Dr Juris (1969) and his Ph.D. in Criminology (1977) from the Free University of Brussels (VUB). He was Dean of the Faculty of Law. His teaching and research concentrate on the fields of (juvenile) criminology, rights of children, (community) policing and criminal policy.

Ezzat A. Fattah is the founder of the School of Criminology at Simon Fraser University in Vancouver, Canada, where he is an Emeritus Professor. He is the author, co-author, editor and co-editor of over a dozen books and has published over ten dozen book chapters, articles, and papers in scholarly journals. He is one of the pioneers in victimology, having published in the discipline as early as 1966, and is a strong proponent of restorative justice. Among his recent books are: *Criminology, Past, Present and Future*; *Understanding Criminal Victimization*; *Towards a Critical Victimology*; *The Plight of Crime Victims in Modern Society*; and *From Crime Policy to Victim Policy*. He is a Fellow of the Royal Society of Canada, Doctor *honoris causa* from the University of Liège, Belgium, and is an elected member of the Board of Directors of the International Society of Criminology.

Grazia Mannozzi is Professor of Commercial Criminal Law (Faculty of Law of Como, University of Insubria, Italy). In her research activity, she has mainly focused on the sentencing system, also from a comparative perspective (her main publication in this field is *Razionalità e 'giustizia' nella commisurazione della pena. Il Just Desert Model e il nuovo sentencing nordamericano* (Rationality and 'justice' in the proportionalization of punishment. The Just Desert Model and the new sentencing in North America), Padua, 1996). She is also interested in restorative justice, on which she has published a series of articles. She is one of the signatories of the '*Declaration of Leuven on the Advisability of Promoting the Restorative Approach to Juvenile Crime*'. She has also collaborated with the representatives of the four International Associations (AIDP, SIC, FIP, SIPDS) in drafting the proposed '*Recommendations to the United Nations for the Tenth UN Congress on the Prevention of Crime and Treatment of Offenders*' (Vienna 2000). Since May 2000 she has been charged by the Italian 'Consiglio Superiore della Magistratura' with the criminal justice training of Italian judges and prosecutors. Since January 2002 she has also worked as honorary judge at the Tribunale di Sorveglianza of Venezia (Court for the Enforcement of Sentences of Venice).

Gabrielle Maxwell is a psychologist and criminologist. She is Senior Research Fellow and Acting Director of the Crime and Justice Research Centre at Victoria University of Wellington, Wellington, New Zealand. Previous posts have been with the Office of the Commissioner for Children, the Department for Justice and the University of Otago. Currently, much of Dr Maxwell's research has focused on restorative justice and the New Zealand youth justice system in particular. Other recent work has focused on family violence, crime prevention and children's rights.

Robert Mackay is a Lecturer in Social Work at the University of Dundee, Scotland, UK. He is Chair of the UK Restorative Justice Consortium (RJC) and Secretary of the European Forum for Victim–Offender Mediation and Restorative Justice. He set up and managed Scotland's first adult pre-prosecution adult victim–offender mediation scheme. He has subsequently published theoretical work in restorative justice and has undertaken empirical research in neighbourhood mediation. He has also done work on standards and principles for restorative justice practice with the RJC.

Guy Masters is currently a Postgraduate Research Fellow at the Centre for Restorative Justice, Australian National University. He was awarded his PhD in 1998 from Lancaster University (UK), after completeing a thesis exploring the links between restorative justice, reintegrative shaming and discipline in Japanese schools. Since then he has held a number of research, policy and practice posts in relation to restorative justice, and has published widely on the topic. He considers his main contributions to the field to include producing national guidance on developing restorative practice in youth justice on behalf of the National Youth Justice Board for England and Wales, and the edited book *Group Conferencing: Restorative Justice In Action* (with Annie Roberts, 2000).

Paul McCold is the Director of Research for the International Institute for Restorative Practices, Bethlehem, PA, where he is currently developing university curriculum materials on restorative justice as well as conducting research on a variety of restorative practices. Paul represents the Friends World Committee on Consultation of the Religious Society of Friends at the Alliance of Non-Governmental Organizations (NGOs) on Crime Prevention and Criminal Justice (NY), and was a member of the Alliance's Working Party on Restorative Justice from 1995–2000.

Colleen McLeod is a graduate student in the School of Criminology and Criminal Justice at Florida Atlantic University. Her interests include restorative community justice, juvenile justice, and conflict analysis and resolution. Colleen is currently working on a national restorative conferencing project with Dr Gordon Bazemore and Dr Mara Schiff. She is also collaborating with Dr Sean Byrne from the Department of Conflict Analysis and Resolution at Nova Southeastern University on a research project looking at young people's attitudes towards conflict, violence and peacemaking in four ethnic conflict zones.

Allison Morris was, until recently, Professor of Criminology at the Institute of Criminology, Victoria University of Wellington, Wellington, New Zealand. Before that, she was a lecturer in criminology at the Institute of Criminology, University of Cambridge, and in the Faculty of Law, University of Edinburgh. She has carried out research on women's prisons, youth justice systems, violence against women and restorative justice.

George Pavlich is a Professor in the Department of Sociology at the University of Alberta, Canada. He is the author of several articles in critical criminology, governance, restorative justice and the sociology of law. His books include *Justice Fragmented: Mediating Community Disputes Under Postmodern Conditions* (Routledge, 1996), *Critique and Radical Discourses on Crime* (Ashgate, 2000) and a recent co-edited collection (with Gary Wickham) *Rethinking Law, Society and Governance: Foucault's Bequest* (Hart Publishing, 2001).

Mara Schiff is currently Associate Professor of Criminology and Criminal Justice at Florida Atlantic University. She has worked for a variety of government, academic and non-profit organizations, concentrating on criminal justice policy planning and research since 1981. From 1989 to 1993 she served as Research Director in the Program Planning Unit in the New York City Office of the Deputy Mayor for Public Safety. She received her

PhD in Public Administration from New York University in 1992. Her research and publications are in restorative and community justice, substance abuse and juvenile justice. Her articles have appeared in *The Justice System Journal*, *Criminal Justice Review* and *Western Criminology Review*. She has also completed an edited volume (with Dr Gordon Bazemore) on *Restorative Community Justice: Repairing Harm and Transforming Communities* (Anderson Publishers, 2001). She is currently completing work on two major grants (from the National Institute of Justice and the Robert Wood Johnson Foundation) examining restorative conferencing for youth in the United States. In addition, she is involved in a variety of community-based projects to promote and implement restorative justice locally through victim–offender dialogue and conferencing, delinquency prevention and other community-justice initiatives.

Daniel W. Van Ness is Executive Director of the International Center for Justice and Reconciliation (ICJR), based in Washington DC. He has been involved in restorative justice for 20 years, as an advocate, teacher, programme designer and writer. Dan is the author of a number of articles and several books on restorative justice, including *Restoring Justice*, (2nd edition, co-authored with Karen Strong). He is the general editor of a comprehensive website on the topic, 'Restorative Justice Online' (www.restorativejustice.org). ICJR is a programme of Prison Fellowship International, an association of 95 national NGOs mobilizing volunteers for prison visitation and other criminal justice activity.

Ted Wachtel is the President of the International Institute for Restorative Practices, a non-profit organization which includes Real Justice, SaferSanerSchools, Good Company and Family Power, programmes dedicated to training, consulting and research in restorative practices for schools, workplaces and families. Ted also founded the Community Service Foundation (CSF) and Buxmont Academy, which work restoratively with troubled and delinquent youth in south-eastern Pennsylvania. In 1982, Ted co-authored the book *Toughlove*, a bestseller for parents of troubled adolescents. CSF served as the sponsoring agency for the Toughlove programme, which established parent support groups throughout North America and abroad.

Lode Walgrave is Professor of Criminology at the Katholieke Universiteit Leuven, Belgium, and Director of the Research Group on Youth Criminology. He is also the Chair of the International Network for Research on Restorative Justice for Juveniles. He has recently (co)edited or written several volumes, book chapters and articles on Restorative Justice.

Elmar G. M. Weitekamp is Professor of Criminology, Victimology and Restorative Justice at the Katholieke Universiteit Leuven, Belgium, and Distinguished adjunct Professor of Sociology at the Central China Normal University in Wuhan, People's Republic of China. He is a member of the Executive Board of the World Society of Criminology and Co-director of the Postgraduate Courses in Victimology, Victim Assistance and Criminal Justice in Dubrovnik, Croatia. His primary research and writing interests are restorative justice, longitudinal research, comparative criminology and victimology, and youth violence.

L. Thomas Winfree Jr., is Professor of Criminal Justice at New Mexico State University in Las Cruces, New Mexico, USA. He earned the PhD degree in sociology in 1976 at the University of Montana, and has previously held faculty appointments at the University of New Mexico, East Texas State University and Louisiana State University. He is the author or co-author of over 80 refereed journal articles and book chapters, as well as six books. His primary research and writing interests are in criminological theory, delinquency and policing.

Martin Wright was Director of the Howard League for Penal Reform, policy officer of Victim Support and a founder member of Mediation UK. He is a Visiting Research Fellow at the School of Legal Studies, University of Sussex, and a board member of the European Forum for Victim/Offender Mediation and Restorative Justice. His books include *Making Good: Prisons, Punishment and Beyond* (1982), *Justice for Victims and Offenders: A Restorative Response to Crime* (2nd edn 1996), and *Restoring Respect for Justice* (1999).

Howard Zehr joined the graduate Conflict Transformation Program at Eastern Mennonite University in 1996 as Professor of Sociology and Restorative Justice and is currently serving as Interim Director of the programme. Prior to that he served for 19 years as director of the Mennonite Central Committee, US Office on Crime and Justice. He received his BA from Morehouse College (Atlanta, GA), his MA from the University of Chicago and his PhD from Rutgers University. From 1978–97 he taught humanities and history at Talladega College in Alabama. Zehr's book, *Changing Lenses: A New Focus for Crime and Justice*, has been a foundational work in the growing restorative justice movement. In their recent book *Restoring Justice*, Dan Van Ness and Karen Heederks Strong cite him as the 'grandfather of restorative justice'. As a result, he lectures and consults internationally on restorative justice and the victim offender conferencing programmes, which he helped to pioneer. Other publications include *Crime and the Development of Modern Society* (1976), *Doing Life: Reflections of Men and Women Serving Life Sentences* (1996) and, most recently, *Transcending: Reflections of Crime Victims* (2001).

He has also worked professionally as a photographer and photo-journalist, both in North America and internationally. His primary interest currently is in the use of photography and interviews for documentary work.

Preface

This book brings together a number of the leading authorities on restorative justice in order to explore the theoretical foundations underlying this rapidly expanding movement. It reflects new thinking about restorative justice philosophy, and the ways in which new models have been applied to juveniles, adults, corporate crime, family violence and to cases of extreme violence. The chapters in this book have been developed from papers and discussions at the Fourth International Conference on Restorative Justice for Juveniles, which was held in Tübingen on October 1–4, 2000 to address 'Restorative Justice as a Challenge for the New Millennium'. This event was part of a series of conferences arranged by the members of the International Network for Restorative Justice for Juveniles. Their purpose is to bring together academics, policy makers and practitioners to discuss specific topical issues relating to restorative justice, and to develop ideas about its further expansion in as many juvenile justice and criminal justice systems in the world as possible.

The chapters in this book cover a wide range of fundamental questions about how the core essence of restorative justice is to be determined, how conceptual pitfalls could be avoided, and how traditional models of peacemaking and healing as developed in traditional societies over the centuries are to be integrated in the justice systems of late modern societies. *Daniel Van Ness* starts with a conceptual 'framework for thinking' about how a true restorative justice system might be configured, and how we might assess the restorative character of a given system of justice that incorporates restorative as well as other values. *Howard Zehr* then turns our attention to the individual level by dealing with the 'challenging but rather risky assignment' of exploring in the same space the 'journey to belonging' that victims as well as offenders must take. *Chris Cunneen* explores in his chapter the intersection between decolonization and restorative justice as a general issue of concern, influenced specifically by the way restorative justice programmes have been introduced in Australia over the last decade. *Martin Wright* and *Guy Masters* add another perspective by starting with the notion that it is useful for restorative justice to see how it is perceived elsewhere, that it needs constructive criticism so that it can attempt to answer it, be it by modifying the paradigm or the way it is usually presented, or by showing that the criticisms are based on the assumptions of the old paradigm and are thus inappropriate to the new one.

Lode Walgrave argues in his chapter that the widely used 'community' notion in the restorative justice movement is not useful for theory and perhaps even dangerous to poorly thought out systemic practice. Restorative justice theory should instead, he contends, 'unpack' the social values from their 'community container', and find a way to combine these values with the principles of a democratic constitutional state. The notion of 'dominion' is proposed as a possible key. *George Pavlich* adds important insights on the promise of restorative justice with the perspective of 'deconstructing restoration'. In his chapter he offers an overview of some important themes that underscore two of restorative justice's key promises, to initiate a form of justice that discards the state's 'repressive' or 'rehabilitative' responses to crime, and to nurture harmonious communities that embrace restorative justice practices.

Paul McCold and *Ted Wachtel* start with the notion that the evolution of restorative justice has been a process of discovery rather than invention. The near simultaneous discovery of restorative processes in far-flung corners of the globe from wholly independent sources indicates for them that practice continues to lead theory as a physics of social transformation reveals itself. The purpose of their chapter is to show that if these emerging restorative justice practices are to improve and if others are to learn from their discovery, then the social sciences should and actually can play an important role by providing description, theory and evaluation. *Gordon Bazemore* and *Colleen McLeod* argue that, for the most part, restorative justice advocates have not yet taken a position on the practical and theoretical issues of social control, and have yet to address the future of informalism in juvenile justice, or the related issues of formal system expansion. Based on a critique of the diversion experience in the US as a case study, they develop a concept for a restorative intervention theory and practice aimed at building community social capital by mobilizing and empowering informal mechanisms of social control and social support.

Mara Schiff and *Gordon Bazemore* deal in detail with community-based, informal decision-making alternatives to court and other adversarial processes for dealing with youthful offending considered to have 'proliferated' across the US since the late 1980s and early 1990s. The purpose of their chapter is to present relevant information from a national study recently completed, designed to answer some of the basic questions about 'restorative conferencing' in the United States, its prevalence, process and practice. *Christian Eliaerts* and *Els Dumortier* then turn our attention to a related issue of 'necessary concern': that the claimed informalism and the lack of rules within restorative justice might easily lead to practices not sufficiently respectful of some fundamental basic human rights, or to non-restorative justice practices masqueraded as restorative justice. There is seen a strong need of procedural safeguards and standards.

Grazia Mannozzi refers in her chapter to the idea of justice as reflected in its allegoric personification. The constant symbols in traditional iconography are considered to be 'the scales' and 'the sword', exhibited by Justice as a female figure, at times blindfolded. According to a recent interpretation of Roman and Christian iconography, this portrayal may refer back to an idea of justice as 'mediation' between divine, absolute and inexorable law, and the 'fallible' conduct of man on earth. The author shows, along this line of thinking, a way from the sword to dialogue, conceiving of a 'dialectic' basis for penal mediation. *Robert Mackay* adds further insights to this problem by arguing in his paper that anthropology, including historical studies of ancient law and religion, provides a number of challenges for proponents of restorative justice. His findings in sources of legal anthropology from different eras and places seem to suggest that 'restorative' practices and attitudes can co-exist with rather strong currents of punitiveness and violence in society, and often incorporate, for example, strong religious elements relating to sacrifice.

Gabrielle Maxwell and *Allison Morris* review in their chapter some examples of linguistic deconstruction of the notions of shame, guilt and remorse before turning to some examples of empirical findings on these emotions. Based on these general approaches they focus then on the role of shame in the criminal justice process by examining Braithwaite's theoretical analyses of shame and shaming, and then the research findings on the role of shame, guilt and remorse in family group conferences. *L. Thomas Winfree Jr.* starts with the notion that proponents of restorative justice cite existing programmes and practices with deep roots in long-standing Western and non-Western cultural traditions. Others are said to ground their descriptions of restorative justice programmes in native or indigenous cultures. One of the most interesting responses to such programmes derives from the cultural practices of Aboriginal peoples. In his chapter, the author explores one telling example in depth: the Navajo peacemaking courts, and the lessons and admonitions one can draw from their way of peacemaking and reaching community harmony. *Ezzat A. Fattah* adds some fundamental criminal policy thoughts. He considers the current criminal justice system as but another piece of archaic and antiquated institutions, a vestige of a bygone era. This is also reflected in the dominant paradigms developed over the centuries, for example, the abstract, philosophical goals of expiation, atonement and retribution. The author argues for the necessity of gearing the criminal justice system toward the achievement of social objectives such as reconciliation, restoration, reparation and reintegration. Particular attention is paid to challenge the 'just deserts' model as developed mainly in the US and the Scandinavian countries during the last decades.

Finally *Elmar G. M. Weitekamp* focuses his chapter on some paradoxes, problems and promises of restorative justice, where the movement stands at present, and where it might be able to go in the years to come. Restorative justice is considered to be an umbrella term for all sorts of ways to undo the wrong caused by crimes or offences. They all focus on losses, repair the damage inflicted, seek satisfied parties and view the victim as the central player in the whole process. They bear a strong potential to overcome the old concepts and responses to crime, such as the rehabilitative and retributive ones, which seemingly no longer work appropriately.

As conference organisers and editors we were lucky and happy to have with us a number of persons highly dedicated to the task of making our endeavours a success. We would like to mention in particular Beatrice Lunkenbein and Maria Pessiu. Carsten Brombach and Ulrike Höschle deserve special thanks for helping to refine the final text of the chapters, in linguistic as well as in technical respects.

Elmar G. M. Weitekamp
Hans-Jürgen Kerner

Chapter 1

The shape of things to come: a framework for thinking about a restorative justice system

Daniel W. Van Ness[1]

In the spring of 2002, during the meeting of the United Nations Commission on Crime Prevention and Criminal Justice, 40 countries joined the government of Canada in sponsoring a resolution on restorative justice. The Commission adopted the resolution, as did the Economic and Social Council a few months later. The resolution directs the Secretary General to circulate its annexe – draft elements of a set of basic principles on the use of restorative justice – and convene an expert committee to review responses concerning whether principles such as these should be adopted by the UN.

The sheer number of countries sponsoring this resolution was remarkable, suggesting substantial interest on the part of governments in the potential of restorative justice. This interest is also reflected in new domestic legislation and practices in both juvenile and adult justice systems. Sentencing reform legislation adopted in Canada five years ago has been interpreted by that nation's Supreme Court as having the purposes of 'reducing the use of prison and expanding the use of restorative justice principles in sentencing.'[2]

The Youth Justice Act, recently proposed in South Africa, incorporates restorative justice principles and practices in that country's response to juvenile crime. Provisions of Austria's Juvenile Justice Act of 1988 have been used to divert young offenders into mediation programmes in that country. Its Criminal Procedural Law Amendment of 1999, which goes into effect this year, does the same for adult offenders.[3] Young offenders appearing in English or Welsh youth courts for the first time will now receive a mandatory referral order under the Youth Justice and Criminal Evidence Act enacted in 1999. The legislation specifically mentions mediation as one possible outcome under the referral order, and the Labour government has described this an introduction of restorative justice into youth justice.[4]

What is happening here? Clearly there is significant governmental interest in restorative justice, and some are adopting reforms to implement restorative features. But what will those changes amount to? Can we look to Canada, South Africa, Austria or England and Wales and declare that they now have restorative systems? I suspect that restorative justice advocates in those countries would be hesitant to do that. On the other hand, those nations have taken significant and important moves in the direction of restorative justice.

For more than ten years writers have speculated on how a restorative justice system might be configured. But with the growing activity by governments towards incorporating restorative principles, this work has a new immediacy. What are the components of a restorative justice system? How might we assess the restorative character of a system that incorporates restorative as well as other values? These are questions I would like to begin exploring in this chapter.

To do that I will draw on three principles and four values of restorative justice that Karen Strong and I proposed several years ago.[5] The three principles are:

(1) justice requires that we work to restore victims, offenders and communities who have been injured by crime;
(2) victims, offenders and communities should have opportunities for active involvement in the restorative justice process as early and as fully as possible;
(3) in promoting justice, the government is responsible for preserving order and the community for establishing peace.

The four values are encounter, amends, reintegration and inclusion.

The values are logically related to the first two principles, since those address the purpose and the participants in restorative justice processes. I will focus on those values in the discussion in the initial part of this chapter on the components of a restorative justice system. The third principle has to do with the construction of that system and will be considered later in this chapter, where I suggest models for a restorative system.

What are the components of a restorative justice system?

In considering the components of a possible restorative system, it would be helpful to begin by examining the four values in more detail.

Encounter

Restorative justice theory developed out of the early experience of Howard Zehr and others with what they called victim–offender reconciliation programmes. These programmes – now usually called victim–offender mediation or dialogue programmes – have been joined by conferencing and circles as ways of bringing together the offender, the victim and community members who have also been touched by the crime, the victim or the offender. While not all restorative programmes involve encounters, the importance of this feature of restorative justice is substantial, and clearly influences restorative programmes.

The key elements of these encounters are:

- *meeting*: the parties often meet in person, although in some circumstances the meeting is conducted with a third party, a surrogate;

- *narrative*: the people who come talk about what happened, how it affected them, and how to address the harm done;

- *emotion*: this interaction is different from that of a court, with its emphasis on rationality; in encounters, emotion is viewed as contributing to understanding, rather than impeding it;

- *understanding*: the parties come to better understand each other, the crime, the harm caused by the crime, and how to make things right;

- *agreement*: when the parties have been able to explore the personal, material and moral/spiritual repercussions of the crime, they design an agreement that is specific to their situation and is practical.

These five elements are not all of the same kind. We might cluster the middle three into a category called *communication* and then prioritize the elements with this result: the three components of encounter are the meeting, the communication that takes place at the meeting, and the resulting agreement.

Amends

Encounter has to do with the most distinctive restorative process. Amends has to do with its most distinctive outcome: the wrongdoer takes steps to make amends for his or her crime in tangible ways. Restitution is certainly one way that this can be done, but there are others as well. In fact, when we reflect on the agreements reached during encounters, we notice four key elements when offenders make amends to their victims.

- *Apology*: a genuine apology, when offered by someone who has not been forced to do it, is a significant way of making amends. It is an acknowledgement of wrongdoing and places the offender in the powerless position of waiting to find out whether the victim will accept that apology.

- *Changed behaviour*: another way to make amends is to agree not to do it again, or to take steps that make it less likely that the offender will do it again. The changed behaviour that emerges from encounters often involves things like returning to school, getting a job, receiving counselling for substance-abuse problems, and so on.

- *Restitution*: this is probably the most obvious way to make amends. It involves paying the victim, although it can also be done by returning property or by providing in-kind services.

- *Generosity*: this element might seem surprising at first, but it is not all that rare. It involves the offender agreeing to go beyond a strictly proportionate response of restitution to something more. This might be expressed by offering to do free work for an agency selected by the victim, or in some other way.

I should note that these outcomes have been features of rehabilitative and retributive programmes as well. However, these become components of *amends* in a restorative programme or system when they are the result of the parties' agreement about what the offender will do to make things right. In other words, the obligation is voluntarily undertaken by the offender rather than being imposed by a court.[6]

These elements might be consolidated by conflating 'changed behaviour' and 'generosity' into a general component we could call 'change'. This would permit a ranking of the components as follows: apology is followed by restitution and then by the change that reinforces and demonstrates that the apology was sincere.

Reintegration

A fundamental value of restorative justice is that both victim and offender be reintegrated into their communities as whole, contributing members of those communities. Both victims and offenders can suffer stigmatization, and reintegration is therefore necessary. The reintegration process has three key elements.

- *Respect*: when a person rejoins the community it should not be as a member of a lesser class of individuals, but as a member in full standing. The work of John Braithwaite on reintegrative shaming reminds us that the alternative to reintegration is stigmatization, when the shame is never lifted. Reintegration means that beyond – and more profound than – any shame the offender feels is a fundamental respect by others for the offender. This same respect needs to be shown to the victim.

- *Material assistance*: crime produces real injuries, and sometimes the criminal justice process causes even more. Both victim and offender will experience these injuries, and they may need material assistance in overcoming them. For example, burglary victims may need help repairing a door or window, or in cleaning up the crime scene. Released prisoners often need help finding a place to live.

- *Moral/spiritual direction*: but the assistance needed is often not simply material. Crime can produce emotional and moral or spiritual crises in both the victim and offender. A growing body of recent research from the US shows that offenders who become involved in religious programmes have significantly lower recidivism rates than those who do not.[7]

Once again we might cluster the two forms of assistance, leaving the components of *respect* followed by *assistance*.

Inclusion

The most important restorative value, I suggest, is inclusion. By inclusion I mean giving the victim, offender and affected community the opportunity to participate meaningfully in the subsequent justice process. This means more than a token offer to observe or to make a statement. It means giving those parties the opportunity to participate as fully as they wish. There are three key elements.

- *Invitation*: whoever is responsible for the justice process issues an invitation to the affected parties to participate

- *Acknowledgement of interests*: the kind of participation offered in contemporary criminal justice processes essentially involves serving the interests of the prosecution or defence. The victim may participate, but as a witness for the prosecution. The offender may participate, but that involvement will be limited by her lawyer's trial strategies. These individuals have their own interests, and genuine inclusion invites them to pursue those interests as part of the process.

- *Acceptance of alternative approaches*: this means that different approaches may be needed than those offered by contemporary criminal justice – approaches such as mediation, conferencing, circles and other forms of encounter, or restitution, apology and the other forms of amends. The willingness to accept or adopt new approaches to responding to crime demonstrates that the invitation to participate was genuine and deep.

The reason for suggesting that inclusion is the most important of the four values has to do with Nils Christie's observation that the State has stolen their crime from the victim and offender.[8] Inclusion reminds us that this theft is always a possibility, one that can be perpetrated even by restorative justice advocates who may feel that they know best what the parties need. Inclusion is the way that we make sure that whatever legitimate interests the State may have in the crime, and it does have some, these do not become the only focus of the processes established. It reminds us that, in spite of our motivations in creating processes, those processes may serve to exclude even when that was not our intention.

For this reason, I believe that we must think of all the elements of encounter as a bundle of equally important components. All need to be present in a fully restorative response.

These, then, would be the components of a restorative system:

meeting of the parties;
communication between the parties;
agreement by the parties;
apology by the offender;
restitution to the victim;
change in the offender's behaviour;
respect shown to all the parties;
assistance provided to any party that needs it; and
inclusion of the parties.

Assessing the restorative character of a system

If, for the sake of argument, we accept these values and elements as the components of a restorative system, it is obvious that a system that includes all the components would be considered fully restorative.

If none of them were present, then we would have no problem in saying that the system was not restorative. But what if some of those values are reflected but not others? Or they are only partially present? Or present in only part of the system? We certainly cannot label the system 'restorative' because certain restorative values, practices or programmes are present, but by the same token we cannot say that it is not restorative in any way.

Perhaps we need to think of a range of options in describing the restorative character of a system. For example, we could call a system 'fully restorative' when these components are sufficiently predominant and competing values are sufficiently subordinate that the processes and outcomes of the system are highly restorative. A system in which these values and components are less predominant will be less restorative.

It seems clear that an encounter that yields only an agreement (say, through a form of shuttle diplomacy) will be less restorative than one that involves a meeting and an agreement. An encounter with a meeting and an agreement will have a more restorative character than an encounter that involves only communication (by exchange of letters, for example) but no meeting or agreement.

In fact, we could construct a series of options related to the value of encounter that would not only include these elements, but elements of criminal justice that run counter to this value (see Table 1.1). The most complete encounter is one that involves all the elements. The next most complete is one in which there is a meeting as well as communication. This is a situation in which the parties are not able to agree on a response, but in which each has been able to tell their stories, express emotion and come to understand one another. The third cell addresses situations in which there is a meeting, but the discussion focuses on the negotiation of an agreement. This meeting will probably be relatively short, and the more relational effects of the crime will not be addressed. The fourth cell describes situations in which the parties do not meet directly, but communicate indirectly their stories and emotions and as a result come to understanding and an agreement. In some cases of incest, for example, any interaction between the victim and the offender is conducted through writing rather than in person, due to the victim's vulnerability to the offender. The next cell describes such an indirect encounter that fails to reach an agreement, but in which the parties are able to tell their stories, express emotion and achieve a degree of understanding. The next cell covers the situation in which an agreement is reached, but no other elements of encounter occur. This possibility will arise in situations where a probation officer or other person contacts both parties to negotiate an agreement. Little else about the crime and its effects will be exchanged. The next cell describes situations in which neither party has any contact and there is no agreement, which is the most likely circumstance under contemporary criminal justice processes. The final category addresses situations in which the parties are kept apart, either for reasons of individual or public safety or to serve the trial interests of the prosecution or defence.

Table 1.1 Encounter

Meeting, communication and agreement
Meeting and communication
Meeting and agreement
Communication and agreement
Communication
Agreement
No elements of encounter
Separation of parties

Table 1.2 presents a similar range of options related to amends. The most expansive way of making amends will involve apology, restitution and the constellation of changed behaviour and generosity. The next most complete form involves an apology and restitution. In this situation the offender was able to address the past but not the future. The next cell describes those situations in which the offender apologizes and changes. This might occur when there is no actual damage to the victim, when the victim's damages are covered in some other way (such as through insurance) or when the offender is unable to pay restitution. The fourth cell depicts a situation where there is restitution and change. An example of this would be when the offender and victim negotiate both restitution payments and additional community service by the offender at an agency selected by the victim. The next cell describes those situations in which an apology is all that is offered by the offender. It may be all that the victim wants, or it could be that for some reason the offender is unable or fails to

Table 1.2 Amends

Apology, restitution and change
Apology and restitution
Apology and change
Restitution and change
Apology
Restitution
Change
No amends/new harm

Table 1.3   Reintegration

Respect and assistance
Respect
Assistance
Indifference to either victim or offender
Indifference to both victim and offender
Stigmatization or isolation of either victim or offender
Stigmatization or isolation of both victim and offender
Safety obtained through separation of offender from victim and/or community

do more. The sixth cell describes the times when restitution is the only amends made. The seventh cell depicts situations in which the offender changes, but there is no apology or restitution. In the final cell, nothing related to amends takes place or new harm is inflicted, a common result in contemporary criminal justice.

Table 1.3 reviews different ways in which parties might be reintegrated into the community. The optimal response is for them to be shown respect and given the material, moral and spiritual assistance they need. The next cell describes situations in which they are shown respect but do not receive the assistance that they need. This might be done, for example, in removal of legal impediments on the offender following conviction, such as giving the offender the right to vote. The third cell describes a situation in which assistance is offered, but the process is not respectful; it may be degrading or dehumanizing to the individual. The fourth and fifth cells describe a community response of neglect – indifference to the needs of one or both of the parties. The sixth and seventh cells move to a community posture that stigmatizes or alienates one or both of the parties. This might be done through formal procedures or more likely through informal communication of shame and rejection. The final cell describes those times when an offender is removed from the community entirely, making reintegration impossible in the short run and more difficult in the future.

Table 1.4 shows the range of responses to the value of inclusion. I suggested earlier that only the first cell is acceptable in a restorative system. It involves an invitation, acknowledgement of the interests of the parties and acceptance of alternative approaches so that the parties may be fully involved. This is preferable to an invitation to participate in a process that does not acknowledge their interests or permit alternatives. It is also preferable to a kind of paternalistic response in which experts determine the party's interests and create ways to address those, but the parties

Table 1.4   Inclusion

Invitation, acknowledgement of interests and acceptance of alternative approaches
Invitation and acknowledgement of interests
Invitation
Permission to participate in traditional ways
No interest in participation of parties
Prevention of parties who wish to do so from participating
Prevention of parties who wish to do so from observing
Coercion of unwilling parties to serve state or defence interests

themselves are not invited to that discussion. The next cell describes situations where parties are allowed to participate if they wish, but it is not at all clear why their participation is relevant in the context. An example is the victim impact statement offered at sentencing when there is no clarity about how judges should use the statement. Lesser options are listed below that, with the least inclusive posture being to coerce involvement in a process that serves the interests of the prosecution or defence.

These continuums, when consolidated, suggest a way of assessing the restorative character of a particular case, a programme or a system. When evaluating the handling of a particular *case* or of a *programme,* the question will be whether the response was as restorative as possible under the circumstances. It may be, for example, that the particular offender has never been identified. This means that a meeting is not possible, although it may be possible for the victim to meet with surrogate offenders and thereby tell her story, express emotion and gain some understanding of the offender. Furthermore, the victim will not receive amends from the offender. However, a restorative response will ensure that there is sufficient material, moral and spiritual support to help the victim recover her losses.

The restorative character of a *system* seems to reflect two features. The first has to do with its aspirations as reflected in programmes and resources. How far up these charts does the system aspire to go? Or to ask a somewhat different question, at what level is it willing to settle? The second evaluation criterion has to do with the number of people given access to the restorative system: is this approach offered to every person or to a select few? The more people given access to the restorative approach, the more restorative the system will be.

The following three tables deal with the first factor, the level to which the system aspires. Table 1.5 shows a fully restorative system in which all elements of each of the four values are available. Not all parties will avail themselves of these features because particular circumstances may make that unnecessary or impossible. But all features are offered. If such a system makes this offer to all parties, there is no difficulty with describing the system as fully restorative.

Table 1.5 Fully restorative system

Meeting, communication and agreement	Apology, restitution and change	Respect and assistance	Invitation, acknowledgement of interests and acceptance of alternative approaches
Meeting and communication	Apology and restitution	Respect	Invitation and acknowledgement of interests
Meeting and agreement	Apology and change	Assistance	Invitation
Communication and agreement	Restitution and change	Indifference to either victim or offender	Permission to participate in traditional ways
Communication	Apology	Indifference to both victim and offender	No interest in participation of parties
Agreement	Restitution	Stigmatization or isolation of either victim or offender	Prevention of parties who wish to do so from participating
No encounter elements	Change	Stigmatization or isolation of both victim and offender	Prevention of parties who wish to do so from observing
Separation of parties	No amends/ new harm	Safety obtained through separation of offender from victim and/or community	Coercion of unwilling parties to serve state or defence interests

Table 1.6 Moderately restorative system

Meeting, communication and agreement	Apology, restitution and change	Respect and assistance	Invitation, acknowledgement of interests and acceptance of alternative approaches
Meeting and communication	Apology and restitution	Respect	Invitation and acknowledgement of interests
Meeting and agreement	Apology and change	Assistance	Invitation
Communication and agreement	Restitution and change	Indifference to either victim or offender	Permission to participate in traditional ways
Communication	Apology	Indifference to both victim and offender	No interest in participation of parties
Agreement	Restitution	Stigmatization or isolation of either victim or offender	Prevention of parties who wish to do so from participating
No encounter elements	Change	Stigmatization or isolation of both victim and offender	Prevention of parties who wish to do so from observing
Separation of parties	No amends/ new harm	Safety obtained through separation of offender from victim and/or community	Coercion of unwilling parties to serve state or defence interests

Table 1.6 describes a system that aspires to something less. In this system, the relational elements of crime and justice are reflected in its commitment to offering parties the opportunity to meet, the expectation that amends involve something more than restitution or community service, and the recognition that the parties deserve respect as they reintegrate. This system would not accept, for example, a streamlined negotiation process conducted by probation officers to reach restitution

Table 1.7   Minimally restorative system

Meeting, communication and agreement	Apology, restitution and change	Respect and assistance	Invitation, acknowledgement of interests and acceptance of alternative approaches
Meeting and communication	Apology and restitution	Respect	Invitation and acknowledgement of interests
Meeting and agreement	Apology and change	Assistance	Invitation
Communication and agreement	Restitution and change	Indifference to either victim or offender	Permission to participate in traditional ways
Communication	Apology	Indifference to both victim and offender	No interest in participation of parties
Agreement	Restitution	Stigmatization or isolation of either victim or offender	Prevention of parties who wish to do so from participating
No encounter elements	Change	Stigmatization or isolation of both victim and offender	Prevention of parties who wish to do so from observing
Separation of parties	No amends/ new harm	Safety obtained through separation of offender from victim and/or community	Coercion of unwilling parties to serve state or defence interests

agreements quickly without giving the victim and offender the chance to meet. Provided that these services are offered to all victims and offenders, we would call this a moderately restorative system.

Table 1.7 depicts the minimum to which a system could aspire and still claim to be restorative in any way. In this approach the relational elements of crime are not pursued, but material and financial costs of crime are taken seriously. This system is reparative in nature, but its respect for the value of inclusion moves it into the category of 'restorative'.

Models of restorative justice systems

What might a restorative justice system look like, particularly as it would relate to the contemporary criminal justice system? One way of thinking about this question is to consider ways in which restorative programmes have intersected with the justice system.

One way has been to find discrete problems or opportunities that cannot be adequately addressed by contemporary criminal justice, and use that occasion to fashion a restorative response.[9] One example of this is the work of Dennis Wittman and others in Genesee County, New York. This programme operates out of the sheriff's office and organizes community service, community reparations, reconciliation, victim assistance, pre-sentence diversion, intervention in child abuse situations, victim-directed sentencing and other programmes. It has grown to this scale only after years of operation; it started in 1980 as a relatively modest diversion programme. By asking questions about larger dimensions of justice, by recognizing the needs of the particular victims, offenders and community members in that county, and by being willing to take responsible risks, the programme has become an intriguing and stimulating model of a restorative response to crime.[10]

A second approach has been to create restorative programmes that are essentially outside the criminal justice system. This is the approach adopted by Ron Claassen and his colleagues involved with the Fresno Victim–Offender Reconciliation Program in California. For nearly twenty years, Fresno VORP has administered an entirely community-based and -funded encounter programme. The only connection with the justice system on these cases was that it accepted referrals from juvenile and adult justice officials. After demonstrating the effectiveness of this approach over many years, officials in the justice system became interested in learning more about restorative justice principles and values. In conjunction with the Center for Peacemaking and Conflict Studies and Fresno Pacific University, Ron has designed a series of training sessions called 'Implementing Restorative Justice Principles In Your Agency'. The sessions include basic and advanced courses in restorative justice as well as a course in implementation strategies.[11]

A third relationship involves identifying stages or decision points in the criminal justice process that, because of their history or structure, may be amenable to restorative practices. There are a number of possibilities here. For example, when they were developed, juries were intended to be a community voice in the criminal justice process.[12] Their conduct and deliberations might be made more restorative by having them hold their discussion in the presence of the victim and defendant,[13] seeking ways to increase the diversity of the persons on the jury,[14] and encouraging juries to ask questions of witnesses, lawyers and the judge.[15]

Terry O'Connell took this approach in Wagga Wagga, New South Wales. Because of community-oriented police leadership there, O'Connell (who was a sergeant in the police force) was permitted to adapt the family group conferencing model from New Zealand for use by police officers dealing with juvenile offenders. Typically, officers decided whether to warn the young person (called 'cautioning') or send them to juvenile courts. O'Connell used this window of discretion to devise an approach to cautioning that could be conducted by police, rather than social welfare workers or community volunteers. Restorative practices were incorporated directly into a particular point in the formal justice system.[16]

A fourth relationship involves adding restorative outcomes (as opposed to processes) to the justice system itself. Restitution could become a sentencing option for judges, for example, as could community service. Paroling authorities and probation agencies could assume responsibility for collecting restitution or overseeing community service. While this approach has none of the benefits of restorative processes (such as the opportunity for encounter and all the aspects of amends aside from restitution), it would provide reparative benefits to the victim and community.

This is the approach taken by some community service programmes in Belgium. There an organization called BAS![17] accepts referrals of minors whom the juvenile court has sentenced to do community service. The rationale is that only an adjudication process adequately protects the legal rights of the minor and overcomes the problem of disparity, but that at the conclusion of that process, restorative outcomes should be available. Community service becomes another judicial sentencing option, considered restorative because its focus is on having the offender repair the harm (in this case symbolically) rather than on punishment or rehabilitation of the minor. This approach is used in other parts of continental Europe as well.[18]

These four approaches may reflect diverse intermediate strategies for achieving a system model or they may stem from different conceptions of what a restorative system will look like. For example, the first three relationships could be part of a strategy to achieve a unified system that is fully restorative. The strategy would be to demonstrate the superiority of restorative justice by developing restorative programmes in discrete parts of the justice system, or by operating outside it and hence influencing the criminal justice system to become restorative.

But a unified, fully restorative system is only one system model. Table

Table 1.8 Basic models of restorative justice

Stages	Unified model	Dual track model	Safety net	Hybrid model

1.8 presents four basic models, the first of which is a unified, fully restorative system, which would be brought about either by the conversion of criminal justice to restorative purposes and values, or by its replacement by a restorative system.

A second model is what has been called the dual-track model, in which the criminal justice and restorative justice systems operate side-by-side with occasional cooperation.[19] This model assumes that both approaches are necessary for practical if not theoretical reasons. Independence of restorative programmes from the criminal justice system would be seen as normative and not merely strategic.

A third model is a variation on those two, oriented toward a unified system but concluding that vestiges of the criminal justice system will also be needed as a safety net when the restorative approach cannot work (for example, when guilt is an issue).[20]

The fourth model is a hybrid model, with parts of the system exhibiting strong restorative values and other parts reflecting contemporary criminal justice values. An example of this is when the typical adversarial process applies until sentencing, and then a restorative approach is taken. In this hybrid model, both restorative and contemporary features make up part of the normative process.[21]

The unified model is simple: the restorative system is the only option. It is capable of handling all eventualities, including for example situations in which parties refuse to participate voluntarily. The dual track model incorporates both a restorative and criminal justice system, each operationally independent of the other. There may be bridges between them in order to permit participants to move from one to the other when they choose. There could also be other more permanent forms of cooperation such as joint projects around particular areas of interest or concern. The safety net model assumes that the restorative response will predominate, but that a significant (although smaller) criminal justice response will also be needed for such matters as determining guilt when that is disputed. The hybrid model limits restorative justice to the sanctioning phase and therefore does not include restorative features at other junctures.

Each of these models has significant theoretical implications that need to be developed further. It will be important to explore the political philosophy underlying them, and the cultural contexts that might lead proponents to advocate one or the other. However, we might gain direction from the third principle of restorative justice, mentioned earlier in this article: 'In promoting justice, the government is responsible for preserving order and the community for establishing peace.' *Order* in the context of a restorative system has two applications. First, it involves ensuring order within communities, which means that coercive power, to the extent it is needed, would be applied or overseen closely by the government. Second, it implies responsibility for maintaining an orderly system. This would entail oversight of the entire process to ensure effective coordination between the formal and informal, community and justice, system. Oversight, however, is not the same as determination. The decision about how the system will operate must, in a restorative framework, be a mutual decision involving all the parties. Once that decision is made, the coordination of it might be a governmental responsibility.

Conclusion

Restorative justice programmes and thinking have now expanded throughout the world. This expansion shows no sign of letting up, and while there is always need for caution in making claims about a restorative future, there does seem to be evidence that the future of justice will at least include restorative elements.

One way of tracking the progress of restorative justice within a system is to use a framework such as the one we have proposed to assess the restorative character of the system. The availability of restorative programmes is only one indicator; far more important is the importance given to those programmes in actual usage. In restorative systems, the values and principles of restorative justice sufficiently predominate and competing values and principles are sufficiently subordinate that the system's processes and outcomes are highly restorative.

Notes

1. This paper is adapted from *Restoring Justice* (2nd edn) by Daniel W. Van Ness and Karen Heetderks Strong (Cincinnati, OH: Anderson Publishing Co, 2002) and from a paper presented at the BARJ Train the Trainers Seminar, 19 May 2001, Jupiter, FL, USA.
2. *R. v. Wells* (2000) S.C.J. No. 11 at 382.
3. See Pelikan, C. (2000) 'Victim–offender mediation in Austria', in *Victim–Offender Mediation in Europe: Making Restorative Justice Work* The European Forum for Victim–Offender Mediation and Restorative Justice (ed.), Leuven, Belgium: Leuven University Press, pp. 125–152.
4. See Liebmann, M. and Masters, G. (2000) 'Victim–offender mediation in the UK' in *Victim–Offender Mediation in Europe: Making Restorative Justice Work* The European Forum for Victim–Offender Mediation and Restorative Justice (ed.), Leuven, Belgium: Leuven University Press, pp. 337–369.
5. D. W. Van Ness and Strong (1997) *Restoring Justice* (Cincinnati, OH: Anderson Publishing, 1997). The wording of the principles and values are changing somewhat in the second edition of the book; I am using the more recent wording.
6. The term 'voluntary' must be used advisedly, since the offender's decision to undertake the responsibility may be made in the context of other more onerous alternatives. However, offenders do not have such choices in either retributive or rehabilitative systems, and it is because there is choice in a restorative system that I describe this as a voluntary assumption of the elements of amends.
7. See for example, Byron R. Johnson, David B. Larson and Timothy C. Pitts (1997) 'Religious Programs, Institutional adjustment, and recidivism among former inmates in Prison Fellowship Programs', *Justice Quarterly*, 14(1), March 1997, Academy of Criminal Justice Sciences.
8. Nils Christie (1977) 'Conflict as property', *British Journal of Criminology*, 17(1): 1–14.
9. Martin Wright has proposed a similar approach: In the transitional phase there would, as we have seen, be tension with the traditional retributive philosophy of the courts. A vital key to progress would be to remove this dichotomy by encouraging the courts to move towards a restorative philosophy. Initially this might be done in relation to juvenile offenders; it could be extended to adults whose crime arose out of a relationship, and then to crimes by adult strangers. Finally the legislature could set the seal on the changeover. There would then no longer be two or even three principles pulling in different directions.
   Martin Wright, 'Victim–Offender Mediation as a Step Towards a Restorative System of Justice,' in Heinz Messmer and Hans-Uwe Otto (eds), *Restorative Justice on Trial*. Dordrecht, The Netherlands: Kluwer Academic Publisher, 1992, p. 535.
10. For more information, contact Dennis Wittman, Genesee Sheriff's Office, County Building 1, Batavia, NY 14020.

11. For more information on this and other projects, see www.fresno.edu/pacs/rjp.html (August 31, 2000).
12. Daniel W. Van Ness (1998) 'Preserving a community voice: The case for half-and-half juries in racially-charged criminal cases', *John Marshal Law Review* 28: 1.
13. Herman Bianchi (1994) *Justice as Sanctuary: Toward a New System of Crime Control*. Bloomington: Indiana University Press, p. 96.
14. Van Ness, supra note 12.
15. George P. Fletcher (1995) *With Justice for Some: Victims' Rights in Criminal Trials*. New York: Addison-Wesley Publishing Company, pp. 250–251.
16. Terry O'Connell, 'From Wagga Wagga to Minnesota,' paper presented at 'Conferencing: A New Response to Wrongdoing,' August 6–8, 1988, Minneapolis, Minnesota. Paper available at www.realjustice.org/Pages/mn98papers/nacc_oco.html (August 31, 2000).
17. BAS! stands for Begeleidingskienst voor Alternatieve Sancties or Counselling Service for Alternative Sanctions. In addition to its community service programme, BAS! also runs a mediation programme. Christian Eliaerts, Els Dumortier and Rachel Vanderhaegen (1998) 'Critical assessment of community service and mediation for juvenile offenders in Brussels: A discussion of the Project BAS!' in Lode Walgrave (ed.), *Restorative Justice for Juveniles: Potentialities, Risks and Problems*. Leuven, Belgium: Leuven University Press, pp. 351–356.
18. See for example the description of Italian practice in Carlo Enrico Paliero and Grazia Mannozi (1998) 'Criminal conflicts involving minors: Problems and perspectives of victim–offender Mediation', in Lode Walgrafe (ed.), *Restorative Justice for Juveniles: Potentialities, Risks and Problems*. Leuven, Belgium: Leuven University Press, pp. 317–334.
19. Herman Bianchi commends having two tracks (although he does not distinguish between what we are calling the dual track model and the safety net model) for two reasons. First, it will reassure those who fear violence that the familiar criminal justice process is available and hence it undercuts one objection to the development of a more restorative process. Second, the existence of two systems, side by side, increases the likelihood that each will limit the power of the other. He observes that the presence of conflict resolution mechanisms will not prevent individuals from attempting to abuse power: 'One of the disputing parties, either plaintiff or defendant, might, if motivated by human malice, consider the abuse of power as a workable reality… . If two systems keep an eye on one another, they can keep each other in order' (Bianchi, supra note 13). Martin Wright adds that this permits opportunities for experimentation in the restorative track with the possibility of adoption later by the criminal justice system. (Wright, supra note 4, at 535.)
20. Ibid.
21. Martin Wright frames the issue somewhat differently. He suggests that there is an 'authoritarian' restorative justice, which is characterized by decision making by courts and other criminal justice authorities. The restorative

features are incorporated into the justice system, and probably feature restitution, with mediation seen (if at all) as a way to arrive at restitution. 'Restorative' sanctions such as restitution and community service are likely to be viewed as punitive, and it is not likely to be important whether the offender offers reparation or provides it because of an order to do so. This authoritarian restorative justice is essentially the hybrid model presented here.

The alternative is 'democratic' restorative justice, which is located as much as possible in the community rather than not in the justice system. The victim, offender and community members make the decisions. Persuasion and empowerment are used as alternatives to coercion (although coercion may be needed as a last resort). Mediation will be administered by non-profit organizations rather than government agencies. The focus will be on benefiting both the victim and the offender, not one party alone. Democratic restorative justice would lend itself to any of the other three models I have described. Martin Wright, 'Restorative justice: for whose benefit?' in *Victim–Offender Mediation in Europe: Making Restorative Justice Work*, The European Forum for Victim–Offender Mediation and Restorative Justice (ed.), (Leuven, Belgium: Leuven University Press, 2000).

Chapter 2

Journey to belonging

Howard Zehr

Recently I was given a challenging but rather risky assignment: to explore in the same space the 'journey to belonging' that victims as well as offenders must take. I found the assignment a fruitful challenge and so I am going to pursue that topic again, but I must begin with two warnings. Some of you may find it problematic, even offensive, to address both at the same time, and especially so to assume there might be parallels or even intersections in the two journeys. And at least some of what I have to say here should be understood as exploratory and suggestive rather than conclusive. I am on a journey here, too.

This topic and title (Journey to Belonging) implies that alienation as well as its opposite – belonging – are central issues for both those who offend and those who are offended against. The journey metaphor also suggests that the goal – belonging – requires a search or a process and that belonging is not simply binary – you do or you do not – but rather might fall on a continuum.

Paradoxically, perhaps, the journey to belonging often involves a journey to identity – the two are deeply intertwined, like a double helix. Identity is defined in relationship to others; in Michelle Fine's (1994) words, it requires us to 'work the self-other hyphen.'

These concurrent journeys – the journey to belonging and the journey to identity – are journeys we all (not just victims and offenders) must make, and then remake. We make this journey as we move from childhood to adulthood, and sometimes we make parts of it again as we go through the stages of our lives. But when we experience insecure or traumatic or other life-changing situations, we often have to make these journeys anew, almost as if we were starting over.

Such journeys may be made along safe and healthy routes, but they can also be made along routes that are unhealthy. Racism, extreme nationalism, delinquent gangs, the conflicts we have seen in Northern Ireland or the former Yugoslavia, the process of 'othering' that we do when we label offenders as outsiders – these are some of the sidetracks which occur when our desperate need to belong is resolved in unhealthy ways.

To explore this journey, I suggest we use the lenses of tragedy and of trauma. When we use more common shorthand terms like 'crime', we trigger a host of stereotypes and assumptions that condition the subsequent dialogue. What they have in common, however, is an experience of tragedy. The lens of tragedy may allow us to explore this reality with more empathy and understanding. In fact, psychiatrist James Gilligan – whose important book, *Violence: Reflections on a National Epidemic* (1996) I will cite again later – argues that the perspectives on tragedy applied in the domains of literature and drama sometimes provide more helpful frameworks than do psychological approaches.

I will use the second concept – trauma – a bit loosely, as a continuum extending from very high levels of ordinary stress on one end to traumatic and post-traumatic stress on the other. Such trauma is a core experience of both victims and offenders. That victims of crime experience trauma is widely recognized – although the trauma of so-called 'minor' crime is often overlooked. What is less understood is that offenders often experience forms of trauma as well, both as a precursor to their offences and as a result of their experience of 'justice'. Much violence may actually be a re-enactment of trauma that was experienced earlier but not responded to adequately. Unfortunately, society tends to respond by delivering more trauma in the form of imprisonment. Prisons, in fact, are some of the most powerful trauma factories I can imagine. While these realities must not be used to excuse, they do help to understand and they must be addressed.

Several years ago I completed a book based on interviews with and photographs of men and women who were serving actual life sentences as a result of having participated in the taking of a life (Zehr 1996). More recently I completed a similar project with survivors of severe violence (Zehr 2001). My dialogues with those who have offended and those who have been offended against have convinced me that issues of belonging – of connection and disconnection – are intimately connected both to the *causes* of trauma and also to the *transcendence* of trauma. A core element of the trauma is disconnection and the road to transcendence of this trauma is through re-connection.

All of this suggests, at minimum, that the journey to belonging may encompass a number of 'legs' or stretches along a route that often twists and turns, looping back on itself like a mountain road. Given my brief timeframe, I want to briefly explore only a few of these legs.

Journey toward meaning

Listen now to the words of Penny Beerntsen, attacked as she jogged on the beach, dragged into the woods, raped and beaten and left for dead.

> You have to reconfigure your world. It's like a jigsaw puzzle where there's more than one way to put the pieces together. Maybe that's part of the reordering. I used to think there was one way. There was logic in the world and there was one way that things fit together, and when they didn't fit that way, the world was out of alignment. But now I think it's like the piece doesn't fit real good here but it feels important to me that it might fit somewhere else. The key is trying to find where that piece of the puzzle fits.

Like many of the victims and survivors I have interviewed, Penny describes a world knocked out of alignment, a logic destroyed. One victim has described his experience as 'a profoundly political state in which the world has gone wrong, in which you feel isolated from the broader community by the inarticulable extremity of experience' (Shappiro 1995).

In this disordering lies one of the primary roots of trauma. When we become victims, the experience calls into question our most fundamental assumptions about who we are, who we can trust, and what kind of world we live in. These include our assumptions about the orderliness of the world, our sense of autonomy or personal control, and our sense of relatedness – where we fit in a web of social relationships. Our lives rest on these three pillars. We built these pillars as we built our lives, from childhood to adulthood, and now they have been knocked out from under us. The core trauma of victimization might be called the 'three ds' – disorder, disempowerment and disconnection. The journey from trauma to healing thus may mean revisiting issues we thought were long settled: empowerment, order and connection.

Paradoxically, perhaps, offenders must travel a parallel road. I am convinced that offending behaviour often arises out of unhealthy ways of coming to terms with these same 'pillars' of autonomy, order and relatedness. For a variety of reasons – one of which is trauma experienced as children – we may construct a world in which we establish a sense of autonomy by domination over others, an order based on violence and force, and a sense of relatedness rooted in distrust of others and kinship with fellow 'outsiders'. As with victims, the journey to healing for offenders means re-constituting these pillars, often in new ways. For offenders as well as victims, until these issues are settled, we cannot belong; for offenders as well as victims, the process of settling these issues is a journey to belonging. Since it involves relationships with others, the journey cannot be made alone.

To put it in other terms, trauma involves the destruction of meaning; transcendence of trauma involves the recreation of meaning. It is no accident that both victims and offenders who are on healing journeys have mentioned to me that Viktor Frankel's book entitled *Man's Search for Meaning* (1984), based on his experience in the holocaust, was important for them. Tom Martin, who is spending his entire life in prison because of a murder he committed, put it like this:

> A thinking man wants each day to matter. Maybe that's one of the dilemmas. Too many of us think in here. So you face each day, not by saying, 'How do I just struggle through?' but 'What can I do to make something of this day?

Penny Beerntsen, the survivor who I quoted previously, describes the journey with a metaphor reminiscent of the looping mountain road image I used earlier:

> It's like an S-curve chain … where the links don't go all the way around but hook on to one another. At first I thought it was serendipity, all these different events happening, and they all seemed to be connected, and now it really seems like it's Providence. It's like you start at the bottom – that's not how you build a chain, but this is how I image it – there's a curve, and you can't see what's at the end of that link. There are obstacles along the way. Then you get to the end, and Wow!, there's another link there. And you keep going.

Our identities are embedded in our stories, so the recreation of meaning requires the 're-storying' of our lives. Those who created the Truth and Reconciliation Commission in South Africa recognized that healing comes by facing one's past, coming to terms with it, drawing boundaries around it, incorporating experiences of hurt and wrongdoing into a new story. Repressed memories are dangerous; painful experiences cannot be denied but must be incorporated into who we are. Sharon Wiggins was sentenced to death for a crime committed at age thirteen or fourteen, and is now serving a life sentence. She knows she cannot deny her violent and tragic past:

> I have a hard time believing I am the same person who came to prison 27 years ago. But I realize that if it were not for those experiences, I would not be the person I am today. So I hold on to that part of my past in order to recognize this part of me now.

Earlier this year I met Khallil Osiris, an ex-offender who had spent many years in prison. He had completed a master's degree and was now living successfully on the outside. Under his shirt he was wearing his prison tee shirt with his stencilled inmate number – so that he would not forget where and who he had been.

As we shall see shortly, for victims as well as offenders this involves not only retelling their stories but transforming these stories of humiliation and shame into stories of dignity and courage. This process has a public as well as a private dimension; that's why Judith Lewis Herman, in her seminal book *Trauma and Recovery* (1992), prefers the term 'testimony.' Stories are shaped in the telling and retelling; they need compassionate listeners to hear and to validate their 'truths'.

Journey toward judgement

For both victims and offenders, the journey toward meaning requires them to make moral judgements about what happened and their responsibility in it. Like it or not, they often find themselves struggling to understand and explain what happened in order to take an appropriate level of responsibility. Victims tend to blame themselves, taking far too much responsibility for what happened. For them, a key need is to be vindicated: this includes acknowledgement that a wrong was done to them and recognition that someone else is responsible, they are not ultimately to blame. Yet as Herman (1992) has pointed out, most victims do not find it realistic to be totally absolved of all responsibility for what happened and/or how they responded to the trauma. Rather, the process of recovery requires locating an appropriate spot for themselves on the continuum between total responsibility and total blamelessness.

The same can be said for offenders who are on a healing path; they too must acknowledge those hurtful things that were done to them while at the same time taking responsibility for the hurt they have caused. Health does not lie in relying on the traumas of one's past to explain away responsibility for wrongdoing, but neither is health possible without acknowledging and validating the harm that was experienced. As Gilligan (1996) and others have pointed out, most offenders have been victims or believe themselves to have been victims; most violence is a response to a perceived violation. According to Gilligan, violence – like the criminal justice system itself – is an effort to undo injustice. This sense of victimization may not be a valid excuse for their victimization of others, but neither can it simply be ignored as if it did not exist or did not play a role. The journey for meaning requires moral judgements, and here apology and forgiveness may play important roles.

Journey toward honour

As I have suggested above, the journey to meaning incorporates another journey, the journey toward honour and respect, and that brings us to the topic of shame and its close cousin, humiliation.[1] These are relational phenomena, experienced only in relationship to others, so this journey too is intricately intertwined with the journey to belonging.

Since the publication of John Braithwaite's important book, *Crime, Shame and Reintegration* (1990), the topic of shame has become highly controversial within restorative justice circles. Many fear its misuse; they worry that what people will learn is not that shame must be removed, but that it should be imposed – that shame will be used as a verb rather than a noun. Others, like my friend Rosemary Rowlands from the First Nations community in northern Canada, argue that their people have been so distorted by shame that they cannot imagine a positive use of the concept. Yet, while acknowledging the legitimacy of these concerns, I am convinced that it is essential to explore this old and universal theme.

Those of us enmeshed in contemporary western culture are used to hearing the concepts of humiliation and honour applied to cultures and eras distant from our own. However, I am coming to believe that they continue to operate in powerful but often subterranean ways. In fact, I want to test a hypothesis with you: that they provide an important lens for understanding crime, justice and the responses of victims.

I am intrigued by the role of shame and humiliation and the search for their opposites – honour and respect – in (1) the origins of offending behaviour, (2) the ways offenders experience justice, (3) the trauma of victimization and (4) the ways victims experience justice. I am convinced by Gilligan's (1996) argument that shame – along with the desire to avoid, remove or transform shame – motivates much if not all violence. I suspect that shame – along with the desire to avoid, remove or transform shame – is a crucial component of victims' trauma and thus drives and shapes their needs for justice. Unfortunately, I also have no doubt that justice as we know it often does little to remove or transform shame, for either offender or victim. In fact, the process of justice often increases shame and humiliation for all parties. The result: offenders may re-offend and victims may demand vengeance.

If it is true, as Gilligan (1996) and Braithwaite (1989) suggest, that shame and the desire to remove it motivates much crime, then our prescription for crime is bizarre: we impose more shame, stigmatizing offenders in ways that begin to define their identities and encourages them to join other 'outsiders' in delinquent subcultures. Guilt and shame become a self-perpetuating cycle, feeding one another. In fact, psychiatrist Gilligan argues that punishment decreases the sense of guilt while at the same time accentuating shame, the very motor which drives offending behaviour!

The dynamics of shame also help to explain why shame is ultimately ineffective as a deterrent to those at the fringes of society such as racist groups or paramilitaries: it feeds into shame/rage cycles and forces those who are ostracized to come together more urgently. It often strengthens the very phenomenon we hope to discourage. I remember vividly the reflections of a participant in one of my courses, a former paramilitary ex-prisoner in Northern Ireland: it was not shame that caused him to change – indeed, efforts at shame had strengthened his resolve and his solidarity with his compatriots – but rather it was a new vision of meaning and belonging.

The experience of shame and humiliation is a thread that runs through victims' experiences as well, and the struggle to remove or transform it is a central element in the journey to heal and belong. Why? One reason is that in western society, which values power and autonomy, it is shameful to be overpowered by others. When we are victimized, our status is lowered. We are humiliated by that event but also often by the ways that we respond to that event – the things we did or did not do at the time, the ways it affects us afterwards. Shame is further heaped on us when our versions of what happened are not validated by others and when we are forced to keep our experiences secret.

But I have suspected that there is another layer to this as well. Ellen Halbert was brutally attacked in her bedroom by an enraged man in a Ninja suit who had hidden in her attic all night. When I interviewed her recently, she tied the sense of shame felt by victims to the fingers of blame pointed not only by others but by oneself. Here we connect to what I said earlier: recovery involves moral judgements set in stories of resilience, validated by others.

Whether we have victimized or have been victimized, the journey from brokenness and isolation to transcendence and belonging requires us to re-narrate our stories so that they are no longer just about shame and humiliation but ultimately about dignity and triumph. Questions of meaning, honour and responsibility are all part of this journey.

Journey toward vindication

The process of justice can contribute to or detract from this journey in a variety of ways. I want to explore just one of justice's important functions: vindication.

William Ian Miller (1993) has argued a sense of reciprocity is deeply imbedded in our psyches and cultures: we have an inherent drive to pay back what we owe and to be paid back what is owed to us, both the good and the evil. The exchange of gifts and the need to reciprocate honour and shame are closely related. 'The failure to reciprocate,' he says, 'unless convincingly excused, draws down our accounts of esteem and self-esteem.' (p. x) He goes on to show that honour and humiliation are ultimately tied to this concept of reciprocity. I would suggest that this need for reciprocity, for a righting of the balance of honour and humiliation, is tied to the need for vindication.

If Gilligan is right, violence itself is often driven by a need to reciprocate, to vindicate oneself, by replacing humiliation with honour. Similarly, the criminal justice response to this behaviour may be seen as an effort to achieve this reciprocity. A motivating force in both violence and in justice, in other words, is a drive for vindication. Crime and justice both may be viewed as reciprocal systems for the exchange of humiliation and honour.

My work with victims suggests that the need for vindication is indeed one of the most basic needs that victims experience; it is one of the central demands that they make of a justice system. I will go out a limb, in fact, and argue that this need for vindication is more basic and instinctual than the need for revenge; revenge, rather, is but one among a number of ways that one can seek vindication.

What the victimizer has done, in effect, is to take his or her own shame and transfer it to the one victimized, lowering them in the process. When victims seek vindication from justice, in part they are seeking reciprocity through the removal of this shame and humiliation. By denouncing the wrong and establishing appropriate responsibility, the justice process should contribute to this. However, if we vindicate the victim by simply transferring that shame back to the offender, we are repeating and intensifying the cycle. In order to progress on their journeys, both victim and offender need ways to replace their humiliation with honour and respect. Shame and humiliation must at least be removed and ideally be transformed. This does not easily happen within the retributive framework of our criminal justice systems.

Retribution or restoration?

I have often drawn a sharp contrast between this retributive framework and a more restorative approach to justice. But hold on here: both Conrad Brunk (2001) and Charles Barton (1999) have argued that in theory, retribution and restoration may not be the polar opposites that we often assume. In fact, they have much in common and we do all of us a disservice when we ignore these connections. A primary focus of both concepts is to vindicate through reciprocity; where they differ is in what effectively will right the balance.

Both retributive and restorative theories of justice acknowledge a basic moral intuition that a balance has been thrown off by the wrongdoing. Consequently, the victim deserves something and the offender owes something. Both argue that there must be a proportional relationship between the act and the response. Where they differ is on the currency that will right the balance or acknowledge that reciprocity. Retributive theory argues pain will restore a sense of reciprocity, but the dynamics of shame and of trauma help explain why this so often fails to achieve what is wished for either victim or offender. Retribution as punishment seeks to vindicate and reciprocate, but is often counterproductive. Restorative justice theory, on the other hand, argues that what truly vindicates is acknowledgement of victims' harms and needs combined with an active effort to encourage offenders to take responsibility, make right the wrongs and address the causes of their behaviour. By addressing this need for vindication in a positive way, restorative justice has the potential to affirm both victim and offender and help them transform their stories.

I have used here the language of humiliation and honour. Parenthetically, I might note that that we could also use the language of disrespect and respect. The journey to belonging is also a journey from disrespect to respect.

My friend Hal Pepinsky recently sent me a paper (forthcoming) he had written in which he concluded, 'Shame is my prime suspect for what makes us punitive.' If he is right, then this journey to belonging is not just for victims and offenders but for all of us.

In the world of criminal justice, prison walls are overwhelming realities. Within these walls of concrete and razor ribbon we keep people locked up out of fear, pointing fingers of blame and shame, guarding others from them. But the outer walls of prison are mirrored by inner prisons. Within each prisoner – and within each victim – and indeed within each of one us – there are parts of ourselves that we keep locked up in segregation, pointing fingers of blame and shame, guarding these parts from others. All of us have traumas; all of us have inner wounds, parts of our personalities that we hide. We are apt to sentence these parts to life without parole. We all need healing.

I have referred to two concepts of justice – retributive and restorative. Kathleen Denison (1991), who leads healing workshops in prison, has argued that these two approaches to justice in fact mirror inner world views. The retributive approach to justice reflects walls that have been not addressed; the restorative approach is only possible when our wounds and traumas have been acknowledged. The outer world reflects the inner world. If we do not deal with our traumas, we are prone to re-enact them. If our inner world is governed by fear, so is our worldview. If we maintain these inner walls, we cannot truly feel we belong.

How do we remove these walls? The biblical story of marching around the walls of Jericho, blowing horns until they fell, sounds dramatic but may be a tad impractical for many of us. Breaking them down seems too violent. Indeed, this must be gentle work: we have to remove these walls tenderly, as articulated by the prophet Isaiah, speaking of the Suffering Servant: '… a bruised reed he will not break, and a dimly burning wick he will not quench; he will faithfully bring forth justice.' The key is not in silencing the pain, building walls and posting guards but in giving voice to our pain, telling our truths; the solution is in what long-time peace advocate Eloise Boulding calls 'prophetic listening' to one another.

Crime is a symbol of our woundedness and alienation. So also is the retributive approach to justice. The outer reality mirrors the inner reality. Only love and compassion can remove these walls. Only when these walls are addressed will we reach our destination. Only then will we belong.

Notes

1. I will use the terms shame and humiliation somewhat loosely and interchangeably. However, while they are in the same family of emotions, there are actually significant differences between the two. See Miller (1993).

References

Barton, C. (1999) *Getting Even: Revenge as a Form of Justice*. Chicago, IL: Open Court.

Braithwaite, J. (1989) *Crime, Shame and Reintegration*. Cambridge, UK: Cambridge University Press.

Brunk, C. (2001) *Restorative Justice and the Philosophical Theories of Criminal Punishment*. In M. L. Hadley (ed.) *The Spiritual Roots of Restorative Justice*. Albany, New York: State University of New York Press.

Denison, K. (1991) Restorative Justice in Ourselves, New Perspectives on Crime and Justice, Occasional Paper No. 11. Akron, PA, Mennonite Central Committee.

Fine, M. (1994) *Working the Hyphens*. In N. Denzin and Y. Lincoln (eds) *Handbook of Qualitative Research*. Thousand Oaks, CA: Sage.

Frankel, V. *Man's Search for Meaning*. New York: Pocket Books.

Gilligan, J. (1996) *Violence: Reflections on a National Epidemic*. New York: Random House.

Herman, J. L. (1992) *Trauma and Recovery: The Aftermath of Violence – From Domestic Abuse to Political Terror*. New York: Basic Books.

Miller, W. I. (1993) *Humiliation*. Ithaca, New York: Cornell University Press.

Pepinsky, H. (forthcoming) Shame and Punishment, Democracy and Anger. In *Postmodern Criminology*.

Shappiro, B. (1995) 'One Violent Crime', *The Nation*, 3 April 1995: 444–52.

Zehr, H. (1996) *Doing Life: Reflections of Men and Women Serving Life Sentences*. Intercourse, PA: Good Books.

Zehr, H. (2001) *Transcending: Reflections of Crime Victims*. Intercourse, PA: Good Books.

Chapter 3

Restorative justice and the politics of decolonization

Chris Cunneen

Introduction

This chapter explores the intersections between decolonization and restorative justice. Perhaps the major reason for considering this relationship is that restorative justice has drawn on and connected itself with justice processes among colonized peoples, particularly indigenous peoples in Australia, New Zealand, Canada and the United States. A second reason for analysing this relationship is that it may cast light on a range of issues that are relevant to restorative justice beyond its relationship with colonized and minority groups. In other words, how the restorative justice 'movement' deals with minority and indigenous rights also speaks to the extent to which restorative justice might be considered a progressive political and social movement.

My interest in these issues arises from a concern that has developed over the last decade with the way restorative justice programmes have been introduced in Australia. I have detailed these concerns more fully elsewhere (Cunneen 1997). All Australian states and territories have introduced some type of conferencing programme for juveniles either as limited pilot programmes or within a broader legislative juvenile justice framework (see Daly 2000a for a recent overview). I am sympathetic to the aspirations of restorative justice. However I am not sympathetic to a political naiveté on the part of some proponents of restorative justice when it comes to considering the impact of these programmes on indigenous peoples, nor am I sympathetic to the trivialization of indigenous culture and law in the name of universalizing claims about restorative justice (see also Blagg 1997, 1998; Daly 2000b). It is within this context that this chapter has developed.

There are three themes that underpin this discussion. The first deals with the interrelationship between knowledge and power and the implications of the knowledge/power relationship to decolonization and postcolonialism. The second refers to globalization and the link between this process and restorative justice. Finally, the chapter explores the connections between decolonization and restorative justice.

Foucault, when questioning Enlightenment thought, drew attention to the role of decolonization in posing the issue of what entitles the West – 'its culture, its science, its social organisation and finally its rationality itself, to be able to claim universal validity'. And he poses the question: 'was this not a mirror image associated with economic domination and political hegemony?' (cited in Young 1990: 9). More generally, Foucault argued that knowledge is constructed according to a discursive field that creates a representation of the object of knowledge, its constitution and its limits. In his famous study of Orientalism, Said (1978) takes this as the starting point for considering the complex set of representations which were fabricated and which for the West became the 'Orient' and determined the West's understanding of 'it'. Both Said and Foucault draw attention to the deep articulation of knowledge with power within the colonial construction of truth. Said in particular discusses the connections between imperialism and the universalizing knowledge of the West and its construction of the Other. Orientalism demonstrates above all the complicity of academic forms of knowledge with institutions of power. Orientalism has also provided a fruitful avenue of analysis of the way restorative justice has come to construct indigenous justice mechanisms devoid of political and historical context. Blagg in particular has utilized this approach in a number of articles on restorative justice (Blagg 1997, 1998, 2001).

A second area of interest is globalization. Globalization can be understood as a process occurring through various formations: for example, as economic relations, cultural relations, political relations, legal relations. All of these layers are of relevance to restorative justice. In a recent paper concerning globalization and (sexual) identity, sociologist Bob Connell discusses how 'locally situated lives are … powerfully influenced by geopolitical struggles, global markets, multinational corporations, labor migration, [and] transnational media' (Connell 1998: 7). We need to incorporate these ideas on globalization into our theories about how masculinity and femininity is analysed. According to Connell, 'with the collapse of Soviet communism, the decline of postcolonial socialism, and the ascendancy of the new right in Europe and North America, world politics is more and more organized around the needs of transnational capital and the creation of global markets' (Connell 1998: 15). Connell is primarily concerned with the relationship between the analysis of masculine and feminine identity in the context of globalization. However, what is important for those of us concerned with restorative justice is the potential theoretical links and insights which can be drawn between globalization and subjectivity. Subjectivity and identity go to the heart of issues raised by restorative justice, particularly claims about restoration, the functions of punishment and the impact on offenders and victims. Again this has been particularly important in the way restorative justice narratives have constructed images of indigenous subjectivities. What it is to be a 'victim' or an 'offender' is often understood as uncomplicated and homogeneous categories of self. There are no ontological complexities and the globalizing assumption is that we all subjectively experience these categories in identical or, at least, similar ways.

Theories about globalization also alert us to the fact that we need to situate the growing interest in restorative justice somewhere within the shifting boundaries of relations between the First World/Third World, the colonized and the colonizer. This is particularly the case when much restorative justice talk presents *itself* within the context of the Other, as the alternative narrative on justice; as something outside the justice paradigms of retribution, deterrence and rehabilitation. As Daly (2000a) has noted, proponents paint restorative justice as the list of 'good' things, in contrast to retributivist or rehabilitation models of justice. Yet, restorative justice has been as much a globalizing force as traditional western legal forms. The potential to overrun traditional indigenous and localized custom and law is as real with restorative justice as it is with models built on retributivism or rehabilitation. Thus one point of discussion has been whether restorative justice is indeed contrary to retributivist or rehabilitation models of justice or can combine elements of these approaches (Daly and Immarigeon 1998). Another point of discussion needs to be whether restorative justice, as it is conceptualized in the West, runs the risk as a globalizing force of trampling over local custom, and crushing the very thing it claims to be.

Thirdly, the notion of 'decolonization' needs addressing. Decolonization has a number of interrelated meanings, and there are least three different ways we can think of the concept. It can refer simply to a historical epoch of the post-1945 period marking the collapse of European imperialism and the movement towards independence of former colonial states. Secondly, in the case of white settler democracies like Australia,

Canada or New Zealand, decolonization might refer to the growing recognition of the rights of indigenous peoples vis-á-vis the colonial state. Without stretching the concept, we might also include the current move in former Eastern European states to reconsider their positions outside of the domination of Soviet communism. In all the above cases, decolonization can refer to the need to 'rethink' institutions outside of the context of colonization; decolonization implies the potential of postcolonialism. This point has particular relevance to restorative justice given that, historically, the institutions of the criminal justice system have been so instrumental in the colonial project of delegitimizing the social institutions and political aspirations of colonized peoples.

In this context it is worth considering what many colonial subjects have referred to as the need for a 'decolonization of the mind'. It was the issue that Franz Fanon and Jean-Paul Sartre were addressing forty years ago in the classic anti-colonial text *The Wretched of the Earth*. European systems of thought are also a creation, an outcome, an affect of the colonial Other. Fanon notes that 'Europe is literally the creation of the Third World' (Fanon 1967: 81). And Sartre, 'For we in Europe too are being decolonized … that is to say that the settler which is in every one of us is being savagely rooted out' (Sartre 1967: 21).

Decolonization requires a shift in the way we think about the impact of colonization on subjectivity and more broadly on societies and their peoples. A decolonization of the mind requires a re-imagining of the possibilities. There is a clear resonance here with restorative justice as an alternative to the existing criminal justice system – and the need to rethink justice institutions. As will become evident in this paper, however, such a relationship between decolonization and restorative justice is fraught with various difficulties. However, the relationship between restorative justice and decolonization is fundamental to whether we see restorative justice as a critical force for destructuring existing justice processes, for opening up old boundaries and creating different, new justice spaces which are potentially less oppressive. It is these difficulties which form much of the substance of this chapter.

Spatial forms and colonial and post-colonial identities

I want to begin by considering spatial forms. Through the notion of space we can explore the intersection between the physical world and social world, how both are constructed by particular relations and how justice systems play a part in their regulation. In particular the 'racialization' of space through the criminal justice system and its interconnectedness with ideas about community and governance are important in the context of colonization. What does 'community' mean and how does it relate to, for example, racial and ethnic minorities in post-colonial cities or to distinct indigenous peoples within predominately European 'settler' states? How do distinct cultural or ethnic groups who are political minorities within a nation state create new social spaces and reconstruct community on their own terms through new mechanisms of policing and order maintenance? Importantly, how are restorative justice processes interacting with, and being conditioned by, indigenous forms of social control?

Some of the discussion on policing and the criminal justice system has argued that social space is a *modality* or medium through which racial subordination is constructed and naturalized (see for example Keith 1993: 209). Thus the process of criminalization is symbiotically connected to racialization. Minority groups are subordinated through policing, regulation and subsequent criminalization around their position in social spaces. Policing and the criminal justice system has a determining role in actually constituting social groups as threats and in reproducing a society built on racialized boundaries. In Keith's (1993: 193) terms, 'the process of criminalisation itself now constitutes a significant racialising discourse'. We see the effect of the intersection between racialization and criminalization in public space through the use of new public order legislation in many countries which is aimed at young people and which impacts particularly on minority and indigenous youth: move-on powers, expanded police search powers, and so forth. A critical question is whether restorative justice actually challenges the racializing practices of the criminal justice system or simply reconfirms the power of a bifurcated and discriminatory justice system.

Social space is at least partially constructed by the dominant interests in society. Of particular concern to us here are the power relationships of the state exercised through particular legal forms. Spatial forms express and implement a variety of power relationships: we referred to racializing practices above; others include class and gender. Spatial forms are produced by human action and express and perform the interests of dominant social groups. However, social space is also earmarked by resistance (Soja 1985: 15). In other words, social space is an arena of contestation. It is an arena of contest both in a literal sense between, for example, young people and police, as well as an arena of struggle in the area of public policy and law reform. What then if the introduction of restorative justice programmes occurs within a new 'moralism' towards young people which criminalizes difference and imposes public 'civility' through criminal coercion? (Crawford, forthcoming).

Space is also a gendered reality and some of the most profound spatial differences which have impacted upon the administration of the criminal justice system have revolved around definitions of 'public' and 'private'. Yet the differences between public and private which allowed for the failure to protect majority women in the domestic sphere never held in quite the same way for minority or colonized women. Notions of a private sphere of social relations has always been denied colonized peoples. Indeed the colonial 'problem' was often defined as a problem of the visibility of minorities within 'public' places. Yet the family life of the colonized was also highly regulated in a very public way through relationships of slavery or on reserves, missions and settlements subjected to specific governmental control. The social visibility of colonized and minority women has been policed in a way which has brought them into the criminal justice system in a manner very different from majority women.

I return to the issue of gender later in this chapter. For now the question can be asked, where does restorative justice sit with these issues of social space? Is it aimed at deconstructing or decentring exploitative relationships or does it reinforce existing unequal power relationships? This is the question that has been asked by critical commentators, perhaps more prosaically, for some time: Is restorative justice about the restoration of the status quo complete with inequalities, with racism, sexism and exploitation? Or does it aspire to be *politically* transformative?

Globalization

Globalization is also relevant to a discussion of spatial forms, particularly given the impact on regions, rural areas and cities, and new levels of conflict of arising from these changes. The work of Zygmunt Bauman is useful here. According to Bauman (1998: 2), 'globalizing processes lack the commonly assumed unity of effects … Globalisation divides as much as it unites; it divides as it unites'. People on the 'receiving end' of globalization are increasingly subject to segregation, separation and exclusion.

Findlay (1999) has discussed the globalization of preferred models of modernization and urbanization. In this context, globalization increasingly demands a *form* of relations which include a capitalist mode of commodity production, the prioritization of industrial development and a developed state surveillance techniques among other changes. Issues such as high levels of unemployment particularly among young people and the move to urban centres in developing countries may be the result of specific policies which prioritize specific forms of capitalist economic development. In other words, the changing spatial patterns of cities and regions are the outcome of globalized economic policies which also may well be criminogenic. Globalizing forces are creating new spatial forms and new environments which in themselves may lead to the greater incidence of crime.

Again we can ask where restorative justice sits within these globalizing tendencies. Particularly when criminalization increasingly becomes the preferred response of states which effectively give up on autonomous economic policy as a precondition for joining the 'New World Order'. As Bauman (1998: 5) notes, the 'existiential insecurity brought about by the process of globalisation tends to be reduced to the apparently straight-forward issue of "law and order".' The nation state itself becomes 'a simple security-service for the mega-companies' administering affairs on their behalf (Bauman 1998: 66). Does restorative justice provide an effective critique of these tendencies, or does it simply present itself as a more effective and efficient form of crime control?

Space and community

Space and community for colonized peoples have also been profoundly affected by specific colonial policies of removing and concentrating different tribal and language groups in different areas to suit the interests of imperial powers. In white settler countries like Australia, many con-temporary indigenous communities have been constructed through the forcible removal and relocation of different indigenous groups. Com-munities have developed from missions, station camps, reserves and other concentrations of people which arose as a result of colonial government policies. One example from Australia is illustrative: by the early twentieth century the Cherbourg Aboriginal community in Queensland was constituted by 28 different linguistic groups living on the one settlement (Cunneen 2001). The point to be made is not that these 'communities' are necessarily dysfunctional because of their history, but rather that the reality of community is a profoundly political and historical construction. Colonial policies were directly responsible for constructing community in the interests of the colonizers. 'Community' is not a natural process.

The criminal justice system has been inextricably linked with con-structing notions of consensus and citizenship on the one side, and disorder and criminality on the other. One of the effects of colonization has been that particular racial and ethnic groups have been linked to criminality, and have been defined as being outside the community and the nation. Specifically within the criminal justice system these are the offenders who, for whatever reasons (recidivist, uncooperative, hard-core, etc), become ineligible for restorative justice practices. What may occur, and there is considerable evidence to support the proposition in Australia (Cunneen 1997), is that justice systems may bifurcate along boundaries whereby those most marginalized receive the most punitive outcomes. In such a scenario restorative justice practices may simply legitimize existing inequalities.

As part of the racialization/criminalization process, minorities are redefined as criminals, and thus seen as devoid of social and political legitimacy. Integral to this view of consensus and citizenship is the concept of 'community'. Maintaining social order is defined as being in the community interest. It is well established now that 'community' is a concept which is highly problematic in restorative justice (as in other areas of social and legal policy) not least because of the definitional problems associated with the term. The way in which particular geographical or social groups are designated as forming 'communities' has a direct impact on the implementation of policy – whether we are discussing community policing or restorative justice sanctions such as 'conferencing' and so forth.

At a policy level 'community' may be seen as a 'spray-on solution' to fix any number of social problems (Bryson and Mowbray 1981), while at the ideological level 'community' may provide a powerful device in de-legitimizing and criminalizing the activities of particular groups. 'Community' is based on a notion of social harmony, a view of the world which is seen as conflict free. Within the ideology of community, gross inequality, persecution and intolerance are carefully forgotten. The 'real' community is seen only in terms of harmonious co-operation between free individuals. Under the rubric of the community, conflictual social relations derived from the effects of colonization are made to disappear, they are effectively made invisible. Indeed, relations between groups of people which may involve the exercise of power, oppression and exploitation are deemed non-existent or illegitimate. The notion of 'community' also has a particular historical irony in the colonial context given that so much of the colonial process was concerned with the disruption, dismantling and destruction of pre-existing indigenous 'communities' in the interests of imperial demands for land, labour and resources, and imperial religious ideologies.

More than a decade and a half ago, Stan Cohen made some well known and important points about community in his book *Visions of Social Control*. He argued that 'the rhetorical quest for community … has come to dominate Western crime-control discourse in the last few decades' (1985: 116) and that the emphasis on 'community-based' programmes can be seen to be an extension of state power. Such policies are 'sponsored, financed, rationalised, staffed and evaluated by state-employed personnel. It is unlikely that [the same forces] which destroyed the traditional community – bureaucracy, professionalization, centralisation, rationalisation – can now be used to reverse the process' (Cohen 1985: 123).

For these reasons Cohen argued that community-based strategies represent an increase in public regulation, rather than the reverse. While such a process may not be as linear or as all-encompassing as Cohen conceived of it in the mid 1980s, his critique still demands our attention. When governments develop state-authorized policies of 'restorative justice', one must question the power relations implicit and explicit in these processes. And this questioning is even more important where these policies are aimed at the poor and marginalized, or even said to derive from the traditional customs of dispossessed peoples.

There have been various critiques of 'community': as attempts to deal with the crises of capitalist societies; as penetration of the state through the community; and so on. One of the most perceptive critiques for our current purposes is that of Pavlich (2001) who argues that 'community' is also fundamentally about *exclusion*. 'The promise of community's free and uncoerced collective association is offset by a tendency to shore up limits, fortify a given identity, and rely on exclusion to secure self-preservation' (Pavlich 2001: 3). And indeed there are those communitarians who would use the criminal justice system as a response to the outsider. In particular see Pavlich's critique of DiJulio who advocates a zero tolerance policing approach to 'community-sapping disorders' (Pavlich 2001; DiJulio 1998). Such a vision of community is only a short step away from the 'gated' community of the wealthy excluding the poor; the community of interest generated by power and prestige. And in many scenarios that power and prestige has been generated by and in opposition to colonized minorities, or to ethnic minorities relocated by the demands of global capital. In these cases, the 'community' spills over into cultural and racial purity, xenophobia and racism. Indeed it is the argument that Bauman (1998) advances: 'an integral part of the globalizing processes is progressive spatial segregation, separation and exclusion' (1998: 3). It is the most homogenous of communities in terms of ethnicity, race or class which are most intolerant and with the most 'hysterical, paranoiac concern with law and order' (1998: 47).

If restorative justice is tied to these patterns of exclusion in the name of 'community' then there is little doubt that it will directly contribute to the further oppression of minority groups and will contribute to xenophobia and racism. Far from opening up new areas of justice, restorative justice practice will be used to close, to limit and to exclude.

Decolonization and gender

Colonial processes have had a profoundly gendered nature: colonial policy was never gender neutral. It relied on differing intervention strategies that were dependent on factors such as the sex, the age and the 'colour' of the subject. Some of these processes were explicitly gendered either in their intent or outcomes. The exploitation, abuse and rape of colonized women was a feature of the colonial process. Colonial policies developed extensive classificatory procedures and strategies based on 'race' for controlling subjects depending on whether they were 'half caste', 'quarter caste', and so on. These strategies also differentiated between males and females, children and adults. For example, at various times the forced removal of indigenous children from their families also involved a targeted strategy of removing pubescent girls to welfare institutions and circumventing the child-bearing capacities of native peoples (NISATSIC 1997).

The gendered nature of the colonial project has lead to what some have referred to as 'deep colonising effects' (Rose 1996). These effects have valorized men's knowledge over women's knowledge and have altered the balance of gender relations. Western legal traditions continue to impact on and change gender relations in indigenous societies. For example, these issues can been seen in laws regulating heritage protection and land rights where men's knowledge is treated as universal and women's knowledge is considered particular and sectional – and often excluded from the legal process because it is seen as 'partial'.

In terms of restorative justice, such changes have had and continue to have an impact in the area of criminal law and domestic violence. The long term gendered impact of colonization has not been well understood and there is often inadequate attention paid to the voices of indigenous women (Zellerer and Cunneen 2001). The realignment of gender interests impacts on the ability of indigenous and minority women to develop and utilize restorative justice mechanisms. It stills seems there is little understanding of the complexity of the way gendered patterns of knowledge and culture have shifted with the external interference of colonial political and legal power. There is no a priori reason to suspect that restorative justice practices will privilege or indeed give a voice to women *against* dominant trends to silence women. This factor is further complicated in relation to minority women who are situated within a different social and economic space to majority women.[1]

Creating a new space for postcolonial justice

Blagg (1998) discusses the need to open up and imagine new pathways and meeting places between indigenous people and the institutions of the colonizer – a point where dialogue can take place. He refers to this as the 'liminal spaces' where dialogue can be generated, where hybridity and cultural difference can be accepted. It is a place where we accept that what is often taken for granted as normal and unproblematic is a landscape at present imbued with the institutions of the colonizer – a landscape where the cultural artefacts of the colonizers are held to be universal. In this context, decolonization is not only about changing institutions, it also requires a decolonization of the mind and of our imagination; a rethinking of possibilities.

What is demanded here is the creation of new spaces where indigenous or minority communities can formulate and activate processes that derive from their own particular traditions and conditions. Should we be surprised if indigenous peoples are sceptical about imposed forms of restorative justice? In line with this, indigenous or minority resistance should not only be seen as a negative response to colonial power. It is also fundamentally *productive* in its struggle to open up new spaces, new areas for indigenous or minority control. Resistance is integral to processes of decolonization. In this sense resistance is also central to creating new spaces for the exercise of post-colonial self-determination – even if it is relatively small scale and operating within the interstitial points of the formal dominant criminal justice system. For example, a significant body of research indicates that Aboriginal communities attempt to (or in some jurisdictions do) exert greater control over the nature and style of justice within their own lands and communities. And in many cases where Aboriginal community justice initiatives have flourished there have been successes in reducing levels of arrests and detention, as well as improvements in the maintenance of social harmony. The success of these programmes has been acknowledged as deriving from active Aboriginal community involvement in identifying problems and developing solutions (for example, the NISATSIC 1997).

Opening up dialogue within institutionalized patterns of unequal power is always difficult. It is clear that the domain of the colonized has continued to not only survive but develop in many places even if at a subterranean level below the formal criminal justice system of the dominant power. These subterranean spaces continue to be defended and where possible extended. In contrast, governance through policing, criminal justice and the broad spectrum of government policy and programmes tends to circumscribe and delimit the struggle for autonomy. In his discussions on governmentality, O'Malley (1996) notes that these can also be seen as government rule and indigenous resistance. However, he makes clear that the relationship between resistance and rule can be reflexive and productive, 'if resistance and rule actively engage with each other, then rule is at least potentially destabilised and subjected to a transformational politics' (O'Malley 1996: 12). In this regard, if we see restorative justice as being truly 'transformative' justice then we should be celebrating resistance, even where that resistance may involve avoidance of restorative justice practices which are externally-sponsored and imposed.

According to O'Malley, state programmes and policies (or *technologies*) which allow 'government at a distance' have been attractive and have included 'community-based' processes. These have involved apparent indigenous forms of control where they are seen as complementary to the broader aims of government. The attempt is usually made to appropriate certain aspects of indigenous forms of governance and to ignore others. Some forms of indigenous governance are selected as appropriate, while others are seen as irrelevant or inappropriate. The selective and ahistorical claims that restorative justice practitioners have made about indigenous social control conforming with the principles of restorative justice, while conveniently ignoring others, are now legend (Blagg 1997; Cunneen 1997; Daly 2000b).

The domain of the colonized

A significant part of the success of indigenous justice initiatives is also related to the ongoing forms of indigenous governance which have been maintained in the domain of the colonized, despite the formal authority of colonial power. Various writers[2] have used the notion of the 'Aboriginal domain' to refer to the social, political and cultural space of Aboriginal people, the space where the dominant social and cultural life, and the language of the colonized has been maintained. The 'Aboriginal domain' provides a point of resistance to colonizing processes, a way of insulating minority cultural, social and political space from the European domain. The Aboriginal maintenance of control over their domain occurs in spite of the formal control of European authority. Built on interpersonal relations around kinship, gender, age and knowledge, indigenous governance may pose considerable challenges to western bureaucratic forms of decision-making. Structures of decision-making are tied to social life, and social life for some indigenous peoples may involve a lack of distinction between public and private/familial domains and the existence of diffuse social boundaries.

Non-colonial decision-making may survive because it is also seen as 'less important' by those who define power within legal–bureaucratic structures. Sutton notes that decision-making and the relative autonomy of Aboriginal people may appear to be concentrated in areas constructed by Europeans as part of the 'private' domain such as entertainment, sport, religion and ceremonial life. Yet it may be these areas which provide the focal point 'on which the Aboriginal public, political and economic life is lived out ... they are not a side show, they might be core activities for people and core activities for whole communities' (quoted in Rowse 1992: 21). Restorative justice seeks to harness the importance of civil society to the practice of doing justice and, in this regard, could be seen as sympathetic to the domain of decision-making that lies outside the legal–bureaucratic parameters of the state. Yet it is also apparent that when we discuss restorative justice as it is exemplified in practices such as family group conferencing in New Zealand, or community conferencing in Australia, or sentencing circles in Canada, then the practices are in the main state-sponsored and state-controlled.

Conclusion: the quest for restorative justice

How can notions of restorative justice be brought into line with issues arising from a demand for decolonization, for a collapsing of the categories of colonizer and colonized? One of the great dangers is that restorative justice may simply dissolve into a process of maintaining neo-colonial relations. Nations such as Canada, New Zealand and Australia have moved to respond to the political demands of indigenous people by *indigenizing* existing justice systems. Indigenization refers to the process of involving indigenous people and organizations in the delivery of existing or modified services and programmes. Havemann (1988) developed the notion of the 'indigenisation of social control' in the Canadian context where he argued that the recruitment of indigenous people to enforce the laws of the colonial state masks the coercive nature of the state, relies essentially on a model of integration into colonial legal relations, and is likely to impede the processes of self-determination (Havemann 1988: 71–100). Using the development of family group conferences as an example, Maori writer, Juan Tauri (1998) has argued that indigenization of the criminal justice system is not the same as self-determination. If the outcome of restorative justice practices is the further integration of colonized peoples into the dominant legal system, then we surely cannot claim for restorative justice that it is socially and politically transformative or a radical alternative to existing justice practices.

There has been a widespread policy imperative in Australia, Canada and New Zealand to achieve greater involvement of colonized peoples in various aspects of policing and sanctioning. Some of this has occurred within the context of restorative justice and a greater apparent recognition of the contribution indigenous people can make to a justice system that has broader legitimacy. However, much of the change, at least in Australia, has also been superficial, relying on grossly simplistic notions of indigenous society and providing little in the transfer of power from the formal criminal justice system to indigenous communities (Cunneen 1997; Blagg 1997, 1998). The lack of statutory authority for indigenous decision-making has allowed tokenism to flourish. Indeed, some of the changes, while represented as an increase in indigenous community involvement, may represent further extensions of state power into indigenous communities.

One might raise similar questions about the growth of circle sentencing in Canada. While there is no doubt that the circle sentencing process has enabled greater participation of indigenous Canadians in the formal sentencing processes of the criminal justice system, there is doubt about the extent to which it represents a shift in power relations. Judges are still exercising a judicial function and have an obligation to impose a 'fit and proper' sentence within the sentencing guidelines of the Canadian Criminal Code. It is not surprising that tension remains between the participants of the circle and the function which the judge must perform (Green 1998). While circle sentencing can been seen as an innovative response to the problem of sentencing in indigenous communities, it is still very much trapped within the confines of the Canadian justice system.

A related issue can be seen in Findlay (1999) in his discussion of western legal forms and customary law. Findlay looks at punishment in the context of the intersection between globalized forms of penalty and local contexts of control. In the first instance he makes the important point that 'in most cultures crimes are dealt with informally, or through non-state instrumentalities' (1999: 194). In the formalized western criminal justice system penalty focuses on individual guilt, in many custom-based systems penalty is attached to communal responsibility. In developing nations this conflict between penalty is played out in the justice system. However, pre-eminence is given to western legal forms. Findlay notes that, indeed, western legal forms, including penalty, are seen as being in the vanguard of policies 'designed to annex and overrule indigenous cultures' (1999: 205).

The conceptualization of 'customary law' adds weight to the pre-eminence of western legal forms. 'Custom' becomes circumscribed within the framework of the 'formal' legal system. Custom might be recognized, it might be considered, it might be given a place, but it is always as Other and as inferior. As Findlay notes, 'the trend in post-colonial states has been to reduce custom to the realm of mitigation and sentence within the criminal jurisdiction ... this puts custom obligation outside central considerations of liability and legality' (1999: 209).

It seems there needs to be much more precise and analytical thinking about the relationship of restorative justice to indigenous and minority mechanisms of resolving crime and conflict. Daly and Immarigeon (1998) note that there has been substantial confusion and caricature in terms of theories of punishment and restorative justice – particularly around rigid and misleading dichotomies of retribution, rehabilitation and restorative justice. One could add to this the confusion about the relationship between restorative justice and the variety of indigenous mechanisms of control and punishment. Many of the 'links' drawn between restorative justice and indigenous mechanisms of social control rely on a parody of the complexities of indigenous cultures – a parody that demeans people's cultures and historical experiences and makes finding a common ground between indigenous peoples and restorative justice proponents even more difficult.

Daly and Immarigeon (1998) also note that discussion of restorative justice reaches into long standing debates about the nature and purpose of punishment, and about the relationship between the citizen, state and community. I would add to this that it raises issues in relation to the nature of decolonization and criminal justice responses within a postcolonial framework. The difficulties between restorative justice and indigenous peoples are emblematic of the broader problem restorative justice faces with working with minority and colonized groups. Through the nineteenth and much of the twentieth century, colonized peoples were denied citizenship rights. Nation building exercises were conducted without the inclusion of minorities. In a negative sense, the category of 'native' was central to the institutional definition and development of citizenship. For example, in Australia to be a 'native' was to be a member of an exclusionary category of people removed from citizenship on the basis of 'race'. The exclusion of colonized peoples went to the very heart of the idea of who could be a citizen, of who could be part of the 'nation'.

This chapter argues that many of the contemporary practices of the criminal justice system can be traced through the history of colonization. Indeed, the distinct nature of the relationship between the justice system and indigenous people and the over-representation of indigenous people in the criminal justice system is symptomatic of the failure to decolonize justice institutions. Thus the question which needs to be addressed is how do we go about the process of *decolonizing* justice institutions and does restorative justice provide us with this opportunity?

It is important to explore the *possibilities* of restorative justice, and to *rethink* key concepts in the light of decolonization. At a broad level, this rethinking is necessary to respond to the demands of 'differential citizenship' (Havemann 1999: 472). This represents a new notion of citizenship based on collective rights for peoples (self-determination), as well as the traditional individual rights associated with liberal notions of citizenship and human rights. Collective rights for peoples are embodied in the principle of self-determination, yet individual rights are also still important – particularly those rights relating to freedom from arbitrary state intervention and freedom from racial discrimination.

The challenge of the post-colonial is to indicate the limits of Western ethnocentricity, to decentre and displace the norms of western knowledge, and to question the assumptions of justice – in its various 'traditional' and 'restorative' forms. Restorative justice exists within the global marketplace of criminal justice ideas, indeed it can be seen in this context as a force for globalization, as much as 'traditional' western mechanisms of crime control and punishment. Yet one of the ironies or paradoxes of its place in the global marketplace of criminal justice policies is its claim to an indigenous pre-modern authenticity.[3]

The political outcomes of this paradox can be seen exemplified in Australia. Australia has some form of conferencing operating in all State and Territory jurisdictions. Along with New Zealand, Australia is regularly held out as example of restorative justice programmes in action. Yet during 1999 and 2000, the Australian Government was criticized by no less than four United Nations human rights monitoring bodies for possible breaches of the International Covenant on Civil and Political Rights, the Convention on the Rights of the Child, the International Covenant on Economic, Social and Cultural Rights and the Convention Against Torture. All criticisms were partly based on the operation of 'three strikes' mandatory sentencing legislation for juveniles.

How can this be? The answer can be found in the increasingly bifurcated justice systems where restorative justice practices are used for more minor offences and more punitive punishment including mandatory imprisonment is used for those defined as repeat or serious offenders. However, this bifurcation is not simply along the basis of legal categories. It also occurs along racialized boundaries – which is hardly surprising given the role of the justice system in maintaining social inequality. Thus one political irony is that at the very time restorative justice is aligning itself with what it perceives to be indigenous mechanisms of resolving disputes and conflict, indigenous and minority youth in practice are facing the harshest outcomes available from the traditional criminal justice system. To actually understand how these paradoxes have arisen requires an analysis that draws the links between the criminal justice and colonial practices. For restorative justice to achieve its goals as being politically transformative, it needs to be part of the struggle for effective decolonization.

Notes

1. An irony here is the presentation of restorative justice as being a 'feminine' ethic. See Daly 2000b for discussion.
2. In the Australian context, see Keen 1989, Rowse 1992 and Trigger 1992.
3. Daly (2000b) discusses this in the context of a 'myth of origin'.

References

Bauman, Z. (1998) *Globalization. The Human Consequences*. New York: Columbia University Press.

Blagg, H. (1997) 'A Just Measure of Shame'. *British Journal of Criminology*, 37(4).

Blagg, H. (1998) 'Restorative Visions and Restorative Justice Practices: Conferencing, ceremony and reconciliation in Australia', *Current Issues in Criminal Justice*, 10(1).

Blagg, H. (2001) 'Aboriginal Youth and Restorative Justice: Critical Notes from the Frontier' in A. Morris and G. Maxwell (eds) *Restorative Juvenile Justice*. Hart Publishing, Oxford.

Bryson, L. and Mowbray, M. (1981) 'Community: The Spray-On Solution', *Australian Journal of Social Issues*, 16: 244–56.

Cohen, S. (1985) *Visions of Social Control*. Cambridge: Polity Press.

Connell, R. W. (1998) 'Masculinities and Globalisation', *Men and Masculinities*, 1(1): 3–23.

Crawford, A. (forthcoming) 'Joined-Up but Fragmented: Contradiction, Ambiguity and Ambivalence at the Heart of New Labour's "Third Way"' in R. Matthews and J. Pitt (eds) *Crime Prevention, Disorder and Community Safety: A New Agenda?* Routledge, London.

Cunneen, C. (1997) 'Community Conferencing and the Fiction of Indigenous control', *Australian and New Zealand Journal of Criminology*, 30(3): 292–311.

Cunneen, C. (2001) *Conflict, Politics and Crime. Aboriginal Communities and the Police*. Sydney: Allen and Unwin.

Daly, K. (2000a) 'Restorative Justice in Diverse and Unequal Societies', *Law in Context*, 17(1): 167–90.

Daly, K. (2000b) 'Restorative Justice: The Real Story'. Paper presented to the Scottish Criminology Conference, Edinburgh, 21–22 September 2000.

Daly, K. and Immarigeon, R. (1998) 'The Past, Present and Future of Restorative Justice: Some Critical Reflections', *Contemporary Justice Review*, 1(1): 21–45.

DiJulio, J. J. (1998) 'Inner-city Crime: What the Federal Government Should Do' in A. Etzioni (ed.) *The Essential Communitarian Reader*. Lanham, MD: Rowman and Littlefield.

Fanon, F. (1967) *The Wretched of the Earth*. Harmondsworth: Penguin.

Findlay, M. (1999) *The Globalisation of Crime. Understanding Transitional Relationships in Context*. Cambridge: Cambridge University Press.

Green, R. G. (1998) *Justice in Aboriginal Communities. Sentencing Alternatives*. Saskatoon, Canada: Purich Publishing.

Havemann, P. (1988) 'The Indigenisation of Social Control in Canada' in B. Morse, and G. Woodman (eds) *Indigenous Law and the State*. Dordrecht: Foris Publications.

Havemann, P. (1999) 'Indigenous Peoples, the State and the Challenge Differentiated Citizenship' in Havemann, P. (ed.) *Indigenous Peoples in Australia, Canada and New Zealand*. Auckland: Oxford University Press.

Keen, I. (1989) 'Aboriginal governance' in J. C. Altman (ed.) *Emergent Inequalities in Aboriginal Australia*. Sydney: University of Sydney.

Keith, M. (1993) 'From Punishment to Discipline' in M. Cross and M. Keith (eds) *Racism, The City and The State*. London: Routledge.

NISATSIC (1997) 'Bringing Them Home', Report of the National Inquiry into the Separation of Aboriginal and Torres Strait Islander Children from Their Families. Sydney: HREOC.

O'Malley, P. (1996) 'Indigenous Governance', *Economy and Society*, 25(3): 310–326.

Pavlich, G. (2001) 'The Force of Community' in H. Strang and J. Braithwaite (eds) *Restorative Justice and Civil Society*. Melbourne: Cambridge University Press.

Rose, D. B. (1996) 'Land Rights and Deep Colonising: The Erasure of Women', *Aboriginal Law Bulletin*, 3(85): 6–14.

Rowse, T. (1992) *Remote Possibilities, The Aboriginal Domain and the Administrative Imagination*. North Australia Research Unit, Australian National University, Darwin.

Said, E. (1978) *Orientalism, Western Representations of the Orient*. London: Routledge and Kegan Paul.

Sartre, J.-P. (1967) 'Preface' in F. Fanon *The Wretched of the Earth*. Harmondsworth: Penguin.

Soja, E. (1985) 'The Spatiality of Social Life: Towards a Transformative Retheorisation' in D. Gregory and J. Urry (eds) *Social Relations and Spatial Structures*. London: Macmillan.

Tauri, J. (1998) 'Family Group Conferencing: A Case Study of the Indigenisation of New Zealand's Justice System', *Current Issues in Criminal Justice*, 10(2).

Trigger, D. (1992) *Whitefella Comin*. Melbourne: Cambridge University Press.

Young, R. (1990) *White Mythologies. Writing History and the West*. London: Routledge.

Zellerer, E. and Cunneen, C. (2001) in G. Bazemore and M. Schiff (eds). *Community and Restorative Justice: Cultivating the Common Ground*. Cincinnati, OH: Anderson Press.

Chapter 4

Justified criticism, misunderstanding, or important steps on the road to acceptance?

Martin Wright and Guy Masters

Since restorative justice, in its modern incarnation, is more than twenty-one years old, we can say that, if it has not come of age, then it is certainly coming of age, and so ought to be able to withstand criticism. The restorative justice[1] movement is fortunate to have some candid friends; there are also some commentators who criticize a version of restorative justice which, if it happens, represents poor practice, or which we believe represents misunderstanding. This may be because critics are making unwarranted assumptions about what actually happens; or they may be generalizing from a particular piece of bad practice which advocates of restorative justice would be equally unhappy with; but they may also identify some potential traps, which we would want to guard against, or into which the restorative justice movement may have already stumbled. This chapter will examine two recent commentaries upon restorative justice. We have chosen one, from the United Kingdom, which focuses on victims' concerns (Reeves and Mulley 2000); the other, American, paper comes from an offender-based, due process perspective (Delgado 2000). As well as looking at individual comments, we will try to assess the background of the authors' standpoints, and the implications of these commentaries about the development of restorative justice as a paradigm.

It is useful for restorative justice to see how it is perceived elsewhere; we believe that at this stage of its development it needs constructive criticisms, so that it can attempt to answer them, in some cases by modifying the paradigm or the way it is presented, in others by showing that the criticisms are based on the assumptions of the old paradigm, and are inappropriate to the new one. Restorative justice has come a long way; it must take account of such concerns if it is to move from the margins to the mainstream.

England and Wales: a victim assistance perspective

Reeves and Mulley's (2000) (references in this section will be to Reeves and Mulley (2000) unless otherwise stated) paper is based on an address by Dame Helen Reeves, chief executive of Victim Support, to a conference in York, England, in 1998 (Reeves 1998). Dame Helen Reeves, who has always been cautiously supportive of restorative justice (see Reeves 1989), was speaking when the Crime and Disorder Bill had just appeared, and its likely impact on victims was unknown; unsurprisingly she is clearly giving a signal to the government that the new law should take proper account of victims, and not be merely a new way to deal with offenders. Reeves and Mulley point to the large number of people who are burgled, some 500,000 of whom are contacted in England and Wales each year by Victim Support. There will be general agreement when they say that for these victims, most of whose offenders will never be caught, Victim Support offers practical and emotional help, and is restorative in nature. They refer to the victims' right to make their own decisions (p. 127); 'Approaching victims to participate in restorative justice initiatives can be very liberating in that it allows victims of crime to confront the offender and to have their say' (p. 139).

The authors rightly raise a number of criticisms of some practices that may be carried out in the name of restorative justice, and point to the safeguards required to guard against this. They note that in case victims feel that they *'ought'* to participate in the new provisions for the treatment of young offenders (authors' italics), 'obviously, the way this choice is put to them will be of vital importance, and [police] officers will need to be trained for this role.' They also comment that 'a stated aim of the Crime and Disorder Act is to speed up the youth justice process. Yet, if victims are to be increasingly involved … they will need sufficient time to consider their options or seek advice, [otherwise] some may end up feeling bulldozed into co-operating' (p. 139). Further, some restorative justice initiatives are indeed victim-focused, but 'the measures in the Crime and Disorder Act will need to attract sufficient resources to ensure that they are of a high quality'. These are all points regularly also made by supporters of restorative justice, and all we ask is that it is poor, or poorly resourced, practice that is criticized, and not restorative justice itself.

Reeves and Mulley (2000:138) set out the five principles propounded by Victim Support (1995). The first is the right to compensation, and there is some evidence (Northamptonshire ARB 1992) that it is more likely to be paid in full when it has been agreed on by the victim and the offender. Second, protection: safety is a primary consideration in deciding whether direct mediation is appropriate, and research suggests that victims who have taken part in mediation are less afraid of re-victimization (Umbreit and Roberts 1996, Table F-1). Third, victims have a right to services, and victim/offender mediation is a service. Fourth, they have a right to information and explanation: the criminal justice system has never been good at this, and although in England the Witness Support Service has done much to fill the gap, victims are still not fully informed about decisions and the reasons for them (*Independent*, 23.5.2000). In mediation, by contrast, the procedure is explained. The fifth principle is that victims should have 'freedom from the burden of decisions relating to the offender'. There are good reasons why victims should not have a say in sentencing an offender to punishment (see for example the case *H. M. Advocate* v *McKenzie* 1990). But it seems entirely appropriate for victims to be able to express their view when it comes to deciding compensation and reparation, as distinct from punishment, especially when reparation is taken to include the process of mediation itself. If done well, this would not place on victims any responsibility for what is required of the offender, they are simply offered an opportunity to participate voluntarily, which they should not feel under any pressure to accept.

There is a need for absolute clarity about the aims of any process that victims are invited to be a part of (pp. 142–4). If there are any other objectives besides those of helping the victim, such as re-education of the offender, then these must be relayed honestly to victims, many of whom, the research evidence suggests (see Marshall and Merry 1990), would be pleased to support them. Time must be taken to communicate all intentions accurately to all those concerned, and the relevant agencies must receive training to help them to do so. There will still be a need for the specific work of Victim Support. There is an enormous motivation, and opportunity, for change, and all those working with victims of crime have a duty to turn it into a new reality. Those working for restorative justice would certainly endorse that, and hope to work with Victim Support and others to achieve it.

Criticisms of restorative justice

At one point, Reeves and Mulley (2000) appear to criticize the very idea of offering restorative justice to victims, on the grounds that although such an approach can be 'liberating' (as quoted above), 'it could be experienced as an additional burden in the form of unwanted contact with, or even responsibility for, the offender.' Victims 'may feel guilty if they choose not to participate and yet anxious if they do' (p. 139). This is true of any involvement of victims in the criminal justice system. Victims have to decide whether to report the crime in the first place. They have to decide whether to ask for compensation, and if so how much. As stated, what is needed is good practice in contacting victims and explaining what mediation offers them. The same considerations apply to the 'victim personal statements' introduced in October 2001 (evaluated by Morgan and Sanders 1999). It is true that there are a small number of people who object to receiving unsolicited offers of help from Victim Support. With regard to the anxiety that victims may feel if they participate in some restorative process, it is true that they (and offenders) may feel apprehensive before a meeting, but they can pull out at any time, or opt for indirect mediation with no face-to-face meeting; and of those who do go through with it, the great majority say they would do it again and recommend it to others (Marshall and Merry 1990; Umbreit and Roberts 1996). If it is done well, then victims should not be under any impression that a refusal to take part will make things worse for the offender, by affecting the sentence, because the offender can be offered the chance to make amends through reparation to the community instead (Wright 1984).

Reeves and Mulley (2000) appear concerned that government support for assisting victims may become limited to funding restorative justice initiatives, which are limited to cases where an offender has been detected, and so might use scarce resources that will thus 'distract from the provision of more general support' to victims (p. 138–9). In the early days, Victim Support made a principled decision not to divert its energies towards victim/offender mediation for this reason (Reeves 1989: 44–7). We would agree with Reeves and Mulley (2000) that too few resources are currently made available for the provision of either comprehensive victim assistance, or restorative justice, and would not wish to see their funding diverted into restorative justice projects. Rather, we would hope that both will be recognized as worthwhile in their own right, and adequately funded. When basic restorative processes are used to divert cases from the criminal justice system, then the costs of prosecution, court and the implementation of the sentence can be saved (Dignan 1990: 42–7), and ideally, re-directed. However, it has to be recognized that human and financial resources are limited, and arranging full mediations and conferences is time-consuming; one solution is that they should be limited to cases where victims have been seriously affected, with seriousness defined in terms of the effect on the victim, rather than the legal category of the offence or the point in the system reached by a particular offender.[2]

Putting restorative justice into practice

Early victim/offender mediation projects have been criticized for 'placing the interests of offenders at centre stage and for not paying enough attention to the interests of victims' (p. 139). However, these criticisms date from 1988 and 1989 (Davis *et al.* 1988; Young 1989), and good practice has taken account of them. It is a fear however, that some of those now introducing measures labelled 'restorative' are unaware of the experience of the 1980s and 90s; and these lessons may have to be re-learnt. It would be profitable if Victim Support and restorative justice advocates were to combine efforts to get the message across to practitioners.

We strongly agree with Reeves and Mulley's (2000) next point, that 'the measures in the Crime and Disorder Act will need to attract sufficient resources to ensure that they are of a high quality rather than a mere paper exercise which only pays lip service to the views of victims' (p. 139). This we believe is a very real danger, regarding political action, which also applies to the provisions aimed at meeting the needs of offenders. Allison Morris and her colleagues have consistently warned about this in New Zealand (see for example Morris *et al.* 1996: 231), and Kate Akester has reinforced the point (Akester 2000: 77). In addition to support for victims, it is vital to have the resources to train facilitators and run conferences properly, and to enable the offender to meet the reparative commitments made in the mediation or conference. Otherwise offenders, or the concept of restorative justice, will be blamed for shortcomings in its realization.

A procedural problem is that if victims are consulted in a perfunctory way, the process may be damaging to them (p. 139); likewise if ex-pectations are raised and then thwarted. Here again restorative justice advocates can make common cause with Victim Support. The Crime and Disorder Act contains a potential design fault, in that victims are asked to suggest what reparation they want *before* having had the opportunity to communicate with the offender. This is exacerbated by the pressure to speed up the process, and hence to ask victims to make decisions before they have had time to reflect and to discuss with their families. However, the Youth Justice Board's practice standards do not *prevent* mediation from being arranged previously. The YJB's guidance on restorative justice does recognize that the process should take account of the victim's needs, and recommends allowing four weeks for this. Some courts and Youth Offenders Teams (YOTs)[3] in England appear to have read the Act as requiring that the form the reparation will take must be specified, and that the victim has to consent; but in fact the Act (section 67) says only that the victim must be named when the reparation involves him or her directly.

An American critique: the offender's concerns

For a second example of a recent critique of restorative justice let us turn to the *Stanford Law Review*, which recently contained some criticisms with which advocates of restorative justice will feel uncomfortable (Delgado 2000). The author starts with a good summary of restorative justice and its claims, including some of the flaws in the adversarial process which it believes it avoids; such as over-using prison, making victims re-live their ordeals, and treating them as mere providers of testimony. Restorative justice enables both parties to talk things over and agree on an appropriate solution. Its use is extending, not only in numbers but in the seriousness of the cases it handles.

However, there are problematic issues. The first mentioned by Delgado (p. 759–60) is consistency. He concedes that the traditional system falls short, but it does at least aim at consistency, whereas the victim and offender, experiencing victim/offender mediation probably for the first time, lack a 'metric' on which to base the appropriate punishment. This misses the essence of restorative justice in several ways. Firstly, it does not recognize that communication between victim and offender is at least as important in restorative justice as any tangible outcome. Secondly, the outcome is not 'punishment', which means the infliction of pain for its own sake (Christie 1982) and hence making things worse, but reparation, which means attempting to make things right. Thirdly, the existing system not only fails to achieve consistency and proportionality but cannot possibly do so (Wright 1999: ch. 5–6). Most important of all, restorative justice aims to reach a conclusion which is satisfactory to a particular victim and offender, which need bear no relation to what is appropriate for any others who may appear similarly placed: 'The notion of uniformity of reparations and of all responses being proportionate to the offence is contrary to the nature of the [restorative] system' (Akester 2000: 31).[4] However, although a corrective is needed to the vain attempt to grade punishments according to the precise seriousness of the offence (Wright 1999: ch. 6), fairness dictates that the reparation should not be excessive, even if a contrite offender agrees to it. At the other end of the scale there have been cases where both victims and offenders had a sense of unfairness when they agreed that, say, an apology was sufficient, but the court (in accordance with the Act) insisted that even so the offender should do some community service in addition. This is another example of retributive thinking undermining the restorative ideal.[5]

Delgado (2000) returns to the subject of punishment and its 'traditional goals' deterrence, rehabilitation, increased social safety and retribution (pp. 761, 763). No evidence is offered that it achieves these goals (not surprisingly, because research findings are mixed to say the least) but Delgado claims that if mediation achieves them it is only as a by-product. He says that it leaves society's need [sic] for retribution or vengeance unsatisfied; advocates of restorative justice would question whether such a need exists, or if it does, their experience is that it is at least matched by the desire to see good come out of the harm caused by the offence. Restorative justice does not aim at general deterrence, although there is always the fear of being caught, and possibly the fear of meeting one's victim when a greater number of potential offenders are aware of victim/offender mediation. Nor does it aim primarily at rehabilitation. Rather, it is (in its ideal form) a process in which offenders are made aware of the harm they have caused, which can lead to remorse and apology, and hence often to a change of attitude. This can be reinforced when the victim is understanding or even forgiving.

The place of general deterrence in the restorative justice paradigm is taken by a focused crime reduction strategy (Wright 1999: 190, 197); as Akester (2000: 29) puts it, 'Some co-ordinators [of victim/offender mediation services] are becoming more proactive, and encouraging community and government bodies to examine trends and patterns, so that preventive measures to minimize offending may be taken'.

Victim/offender mediation, according to Delgado (2000), 'casts the victim in the role of sentencer, holding the power of judgment over the offender' (p. 762). This is not what the process should be like. Firstly it should be a process; often the outcome is only a symbol, setting the seal on the interaction that has taken place. There have been cases where the victim has pressed for too much compensation, in relation to the harm done or the offender's ability to pay; mediators should guard against this and take steps to prevent it.

Another type of criticism simply does not square with the doctrine of restorative justice as it is preached. Delgado states that 'the mediator frequently advises the offender that he will be referred back to the court system for trial if he and the victim cannot reach a restitution agreement' (p. 760, citing Brown 1994) and that 'the judge will take his lack of co-operation into account at the time of sentencing'; he offers no evidence for the second of these statements. Failure to reach agreement could be because the victim, rather than the offender, is being unhelpful; mediators should observe both neutrality and confidentiality, not judging whether either party was unreasonable, and telling the court only that agreement was not reached, without disclosing the content of the discussion. It is possible that such practices are employed in some places in the United States, in which case Delgado's concerns are justified and the practice should be overhauled.

As regards victims, Delgado (2000) alleges that 'Mediation *may* disserve victims by pressuring them to forgive offenders before they are psychologically ready to do so', and that 'Mediators *may* intimate that victims are being obstructionist or emotionally immature [if they refuse to put aside their anger and distrust]' (p. 762, emphasis added). Here again, he is relying not on empirical evidence but on the already-quoted article by a law professor (Brown 1994: 1273–6); and Brown in turn offers no evidence, saying only that 'V O M's emphasis on "reconciliation" [her quotation marks] may [that word again!] inhibit victims' expressions of anger and pressure them to forgive their offenders' (p. 1274). If this is a correct account of some American practice, it probably reflects the church-based roots of much victim/offender mediation in that country. In Britain, where the motivation has come more from a social-work philosophy, mediators have generally taken more care to avoid suggesting that the victim *ought* to forgive. There is the suggestion instead that the process of victim/offender communication *may* enable victims to forgive; they are fortunate if they can do so, but in no way to be reproached if they cannot.

Mediators should be trained not even to think that victims *ought* to forgive or put aside their anger, let alone express such thoughts to the victim. It is of course possible that some of them do. The first place for any effort to avoid such undesirable practices is clearly in training, and training programmes should include this issue. Secondly, day-to-day practice should be monitored; one of the advantages of mediating in pairs is that a co-mediator can intervene if his or her colleague shows signs of making such errors, and/or point it out during the evaluation afterwards. Client satisfaction surveys should give victims an opportunity to say whether they felt any such unwelcome pressures. Certainly it is hoped that the interaction will be cathartic for victims, leading to an offender's expression of remorse, which may then help the victim to be more understanding; but there should be no question of blame if this does not take place. Much evaluation on these lines has already taken place; mediation has been subjected to more searching empirical scrutiny than the legal process, despite the claim (quoted by Brown[6] from another law professor that 'in practice there is much room for the expression of anger

... in a formal constrained way through the ritualized behaviour of the lawyers' (Brown: 1276). In a way Brown is right: the legal process does encourage victims (and readers and viewers of the media) to feel angry, but the only way it offers of assuaging the anger is by punishing the offender, which can lead to further anger if the punishment does not appear to match the victim's suffering. Mediation invites the parties to forsake the battlefield and to honour the casualties by working towards understanding, and reparation where appropriate. If it leads to atonement and forgiveness, most people would regard that as a bonus, but no one should be reproached, least of all by a mediator, if they cannot find forgiveness in their hearts.

Brown makes some valid points. She concedes that 'In some respects the V O M movement is consistent with various strands of the victims' rights movement' (p. 1274), and rightly points out that 'a victim's recovery in the wake of a crime is a delicate process' (Brown: 1273). She states that 'V O M promises healing and reconciliation that many victims desire' (p. 1274); she might have added, however, in support of her sceptical stance, that mediators should beware of making offers which they cannot guarantee to fulfil, and that many victims take part in mediation as a civic duty because they hope to exercise a good influence on the offender. Healing for the victim and education of the offender are both *possibilities* for the victim, but should not be presented as *expectations*, because that could lead to disillusionment[7] (Reeves and Mulley 2000: 142–3). In England there have been many expressions of concern that the Crime and Disorder Act 1998, and accompanying ministerial pressure to speed up the justice process, does put pressure on victims to make snap decisions about whether to take part in mediation – in some pilot projects, even over the telephone – or, often, results in victims not being consulted at all.

Another allegation is that 'Offenders are urged to be forthcoming and admit what they did, yet often what they say is admissible against them in court if the case is returned' (Reeves and Mulley 2000: 763). In some English schemes they have to admit guilt before being referred for mediation, but the same applies to other forms of diversion such as a police warning; in others mediation is not suggested until they have pleaded guilty in court. An alternative method is used in continental Europe and New Zealand: the accused is only required 'not to deny' the alleged act. This means that he or she acknowledges having done something which can be discussed with the complainant, but if the matter is not resolved, he or she can go to court having admitted only that; any defence (such as provocation or honest mistake) can still be put forward.

At this point Delgado is again relying on Brown (1994: 1288–90). Brown points out, correctly, that although mediators claim privilege for the contents of mediation, this is not guaranteed by statute (in the United States, and the same is true of the United Kingdom); also that even if mediators would not testify, there is nothing to stop victims passing on to the prosecution lawyer admissions made during a mediation which proved to be unsuccessful. These might not be admissible as evidence themselves, but they could suggest to the prosecution new lines of enquiry.

Reinforcing the status quo?

Delgado's (2000) picture of the process appears to be something like this. Offences (assumed to be property offences) are committed by young offenders, often from ethnic minorities, against middle-class victims. They agree to a mediation process run by middle-class mediators, who guide the process towards repayment of the amount stolen out of the young offender's meagre earnings, or to 'community service' which turns out to be a menial task such as sweeping the parks in the leafy suburbs where the victims and the mediators live. This, like their previous examples, may be a correct description of some American practice, and England is not immune to it – the example of repairing canals on which affluent people enjoy taking water-borne holidays has been quoted – and it sometimes seems as if that is the model which some politicians actually want to introduce. In general, however, it is our impression that organizers of reparation projects in England are alert to the requirements of good equal-opportunities practice.

Thus it is stated that 'In most cases, a vengeful victim and a middle-class mediator will gang up on a young, minority offender, exact the expected apology, and negotiate an agreement to pay back what she has taken from the victim by deducting portions of her earnings from her minimum-wage job' (p. 764). Delgado offers no evidence for this assertion. It is of course possible, and it is not a desirable outcome. But reports of actual mediations show that victims are often understanding rather than vengeful: Marshall and Merry (1990: 157) even found that almost all offenders considered that their victims had been either reasonable or demonstrably sympathetic; victims often come from the same background as the offender; and they are often satisfied by receiving an apology, token compensation, or by the offender's offer to work for a charitable cause. We do need to bear in mind, however, that the reason so many researchers have found victims to be sympathetic may be that the unsympathetic ones are screened out. What does restorative justice offer the vengeful victim? Some may become less vengeful after the passage of time, and perhaps after having discussions with mediation workers; for others, there remains the still-retributive criminal justice system.

As for the middle-class-ness of mediators, this is possible, especially when they are full-time professionally qualified people; but part of the restorative ideal is that mediators (whether volunteers or sessionally paid) should come from as wide a range of backgrounds as offenders. Many mediation services aim at finding a pair of mediators who each share some characteristic, such as ethnicity, with either the victim or the offender, though this is not always attainable. Delgado rightly says that there should be more mediators from minority groups (p. 774).

It is claimed that 'Mediation treats the *victim* respectfully, according him the status of an end-in-himself, while the offender is treated as a thing to be managed, shamed, and conditioned' (p. 765, italics in original). This too, if it happens, is directly contrary to the training which mediators commonly receive in England; the concept of neutrality is explained in terms of respecting the human being, while not condoning the act: 'hating the sin but loving the sinner'. The victim/offender mediation movement, it is alleged, believes it can balance inequalities, but is apt not to do so. This is admittedly not easy; partly it is a matter of training, partly of recruitment of mediators; and if people on low incomes cannot afford the time to volunteer as mediators, there is a case for offering a sessional fee.

Researchers are also criticized for asking the victim whether he or she felt better afterwards, while merely asking offenders whether they completed their work order and whether they recidivated (Delgado 2000: 765–6). Marshall and Merry (1990: 154ff.) asked offenders quite a lot more, and Coates and Gehm (1989: 253–6) also asked if they were satisfied with the mediation experience (83 per cent were). Umbreit also asked offenders about their assessment: 87 per cent were satisfied, and 89 per cent felt the process was fair. He does quote a few, however, who felt that victims were 'ripping them off' (Umbreit 1994: ch. 6). In Australia, Sherman and Strang (1998) asked offenders a battery of questions, not only about their chances of re-offending but also about mediation, their feelings about the police – and about themselves. Maxwell and Morris (1999), perhaps writing too late for Delgado to have seen their report, also asked about the factors he is interested in: significant deficits in early life, poverty, inadequate parental support, frequent changes of school, bullying and abuse. This charge of Delgado's, therefore, does not stand up.

In England the boot is, if anything, on the other foot: there have been constant criticisms of victim/offender mediation for 'using' the victim in the interests of rehabilitating the offender, especially during the 1980s (Davis 1992), and suggestions that the new legislation and its accompanying research, with its heavy emphasis on recidivism rather than on victim satisfaction, is failing to learn from that early experience.

If reparation takes the form of community service, there is an issue about what this should consist of. Delgado (2000) thinks there is a danger that this will come close to 'prison labor gangs' (p. 769). In England the tendency has been for community service to be directed towards people in need, either in person or in institutions such as hospitals; even so, community service projects which employ groups of offenders with no personal contact with beneficiaries have been nicknamed 'chain gangs' by probation officers who share these concerns. There is another concern, not mentioned by Delgado: the guidance accompanying the Crime and Disorder Act in England lays down that the work should be directly related to the crime (though admittedly it only says 'if possible' – Home Office 1998, paragraph 6.12). One of the hackneyed examples given is that vandals should be made to clean off graffiti. Apart from the health and safety problems of requiring inexperienced young people to handle dangerous chemicals, this misses an important point. As Delgado rightly says, most young offenders have little self-esteem (p. 765). The community service projects which deserve five-star grading are those which treat the young person decently, develop skills and raise self-esteem; not infrequently he or she responds by continuing voluntarily after completing the compulsory hours. Gill McIvor's (1992) work on community service found that work which was clearly productive and enabled offenders to socialize with the people benefiting from the work was most successful.

It must be conceded that work of this kind is more difficult to organize for the very short periods prescribed in sanctions such as the new English reparation orders (maximum 24 hours). The longer established community service orders, introduced in 1972, can last up to 240 hours, and there is a strong feeling that the Home Secretary is quite wrong to devalue this idealism by renaming this sanction 'community punishment orders' (in the Criminal Justice and Court Services Act 2000). It would however be wrong to be dogmatic about this; often graffiti can be dealt with by applying a coat of paint, and the young offenders can see the sense of having to do it, provided it is presented to them as reparation and not mere punishment. It depends on having the right relationship with their supervisor.

Victims often use mediation sessions to tell the offender about the disturbance he has caused in their lives; but Delgado asks whether the victim in turn should not have to learn about the offender's background and neighbourhood, to prompt recognition of their common humanity (p. 768). When the emphasis is placed on dialogue, and not merely on restitution of property, the offender is indeed given the chance, in a well-run mediation session, to 'tell it like it is' from his or her point of view. There is a danger that this may sound like making excuses; but it can and does give victims more knowledge of the background of the offence, and can lead to greater understanding of the offender's conduct. Hence the victim becomes more willing to accept reparation, and the offender, sensing the victim's empathy, to offer it. Once again, stereotypes must be avoided: many victims, or members of their family and peer group, have themselves been offenders, and are all the more keen to persuade 'their' offender not to make the same mistakes.

Delgado's picture of a poor person stealing from an affluent one, being required to repay the money, and thus leaving the society as unequal as ever, has been recognized before, although it has admittedly not featured prominently in the debate. A small survey (quoted by Delgado 2000: 763–4) among mediation co-ordinators and legal practitioners in the United States and Canada in 1984 asked, among other things, whether respondents agreed or disagreed with the statement: 'In those cases where a poor offender is required to pay back an affluent victim, mediation reinforces the unequal distribution of property.' Only one agreed and said it had been a concern of his. Some argued in effect that even in an unequal society, theft is not an acceptable way of redistributing property, and two people pointed out that jailing offenders reinforces the unequal status quo at least as much as reparation does. Delgado suggests that 'the middle-class mediator, the victim, or society at large might well feel shame or remorse over the conditions that led to the offender's predicament (p. 764) and, again assuming that victims are middle-class, that victims might be required to be taken on 'a bus tour of the offender's neighborhood and learn something about the circumstances in which he lives' (p. 768). In the survey just quoted, hardly anyone had considered whether any 'middle-class or affluent victims' might 'significantly change their attitude to social policy, or their life-style, as a result of meeting an offender' Wright 1996: 130). But as Delgado says (p. 765), 'A forty-five minute meeting is unlikely to have a lasting effect if the offender is released to her neighborhood and teenage peer group immediately afterwards', and a similar comment might be made about victims. Indeed those victims whose background is very like that of the offenders might well be very keen on restoring the status quo. Nevertheless, at least one study found that about one third of victims and offenders felt that their attitudes had changed, and 'the common refrain was, "We see them now as real people"' (Coates 1985, quoted by Wright 1996: 130–1).

Do restorative justice procedures lack formal safeguards?

If the offender accepts an informal process, Delgado states, he or she waives important constitutional rights such as confronting witnesses, being represented by counsel, avoiding self-incrimination, trial by jury, and the right to appeal. Mediation takes place early in the criminal process when he is unaware of the evidence against him or the range of possible defences (p. 760–1). Confronting witnesses, however, does not arise, because mediation does not take place if the offender denies the act. The process is a voluntary one; admittedly, as with most diversion services, the offender has an apparent inducement to take part, because the outcome is perceived as less severe; but facing the victim is also difficult, for different (and probably better) reasons. In good mediation practice it is made clear to the offender that he or she can exercise the right to choose a court trial at any time before an agreement is reached. This, combined with the oversight which courts should exercise over the process, should be equivalent to a right to appeal. As regards the evidence against the offenders, if they deny any involvement, they should clearly plead not guilty and go to court. If they did it but think they can get away with denying it, or escaping on a legal technicality, that is understandable when the outcome is likely to be punishment; the New Zealand experience is, however, that when the outcome is a constructive one, for them and the victim, the culture of challenging 'the system' to prove it is replaced by one where there is much more willingness to set the record straight and make a fresh start. This is surely in everyone's interests, including the offender's.

The other aspect of guilt is the intention, the *mens rea*; if the mediation does not reach a satisfactory conclusion, this part of the accused's defence remains, as has been mentioned above. Under the Crime and Disorder Act the problems with diversion are only possible with reprimands and final warnings. Other cases are dealt with by the court after conviction, and here the problem is a different one: that courts, still using the old way of thinking, use punishment in combination with restorative measures rather than as a replacement; or as a sanction for not complying with, for example, a reparation order. As with many innovations, old ideas are very deep-rooted, and the result can be that heavier sanctions are imposed on a larger number of offenders.

It is true, however, that this procedure involves important choices. The stereotypical legal process is one in which the young accused, in the intimidating formality of the courtroom, remains passive and says nothing, while the defence lawyer looks for procedural loopholes, tries to destroy the credibility of prosecution witnesses by crafty cross-examination, and if he fails to secure an acquittal, presents a plea in mitigation of punishment including a hard-luck story about the defendant and often trying to put some blame on the victim. Mediation rightly encourages the offender to take an active part, by facing the effects of his actions on the victim, while also giving him or her the opportunity to express remorse and suggest how to make amends. But at several points in the process, as we have seen, the young person (who in England may be as young as ten) is given the right to make significant decisions; he or she should be aware of the right (for example to pull out of mediation) and have guidance as to the effects of doing so. Brown (1994: 1289–90) points to the need of a young person for legal guidance, and criticizes mediation services which, anxious that lawyers' adversarial approach might jeopardize the reconciling atmosphere of the mediation process, want to forbid counsel to attend the mediation. Delgado implies that the only way to safeguard the offender by providing a lawyer is to revert to the formality of the court, where 'the flag, the robes, and the judge sitting on high remind everyone of the principles of fairness, equal treatment, and every person receiving his day in court' (Delgado: 766). He admits later on, however, that courts fall far short of these ideals (p. 771–2). Once again it appears that New Zealand has pointed the way: youth advocates, funded by the courts, are available, but they are imbued with restorative principles so that they do not introduce adversarial conflicts, but facilitate the process and support the young people by explaining the process, negotiating appropriate reductions in charges with the police, and clarifying matters. As in some other countries, however, Akester (2000) points out that they are not available at the pre-court stage when the young people are dealt with by the police. This would be a further desirable safeguard, and it may be raised in the courts when the European Convention on Human Rights becomes part of British law on 2 October 2000[8] although in a non-punitive, reparative system it is not so vital (Akester 2000: 30–1; see also comments on New South Wales pp. 44–5, and England and Wales pp. 69, 76).

There are two ways in which mediation, like other forms of diversion, could make matters worse for offenders. One is 'net-widening': bringing minor offenders into the system who would otherwise have been dealt with informally (Delgado: 761–2). In some places this tendency has indeed been seen; others have guarded against it by excluding the less serious cases – not least because of the expenditure of time required to set up mediations and especially conferences. A related problem is that when offenders fail to comply with a reparation agreement, they may, in a system that is still basically punitive, be imprisoned for an offence which would otherwise not have merited a custodial punishment.

It should be mentioned that Delgado's article has a sting in the tail, where it points to the many failings of the conventional justice system, especially in its treatment of minorities, so that, at least in white-dominated regions of the United States, persons subject to prejudice might be better off with victim/offender mediation – which, however, should take steps to ensure that it lives up to its professed ideals.

Discussion

It seems reasonable to assume that both these sets of criticisms reflect their origins. Reeves and Mulley work for an organization which arranges for volunteers to visit victims; they are naturally concerned at asking too much of volunteers, and it would not be surprising if they were also apprehensive about the possibility that the government might try to fund mediation out of the money at present allocated to victim support, in the belief that it would thus get 'two for the price of one'. This would clearly not be in the interests of the quality of service offered in either way.

Delgado's and Brown's American background, on the other hand, is imbued with concepts of due process and just deserts. Restorative justice needs to take note of both of these, but not to be ruled by them. Due process does require that the accused, especially juveniles, should have access to legal advice before making significant decisions, but the need is less acute, firstly, where it is a question of diversion, because in some systems this leaves the offender with no criminal record once the reparation is completed; and secondly, where the outcome is reparation rather than punishment. To be required to do something valuable is less of an imposition than to be subjected to punishment. Nevertheless, mediation like anything else can be done badly; the minimum require-ment is proper standards (including equal opportunities, confidentiality, impartiality, and a complaints procedure with mediation (of course!) built in), training and practical (not necessarily professional) accreditation of mediators, with supervision and support.

As for just deserts, several writers have pointed out that restorative justice is not based on proportionality, because ideally each victim and offender reach an outcome with which both are content; but it is possible for a reparation agreement to be disproportionately large or small. Both victims and offenders can feel aggrieved when courts overrule their agreements, so restorative justice has to balance the requirements of fairness with the principle of participants' autonomy, in addition to im-posing non-punitive restraining measures if these are needed for the protection of the public.

In this chapter we have focused on individual criticisms of victim/ offender mediation. We hope this will be a stage towards designing a 'restorative justice system'. Victim Support would be an essential part of such an integrated system: victims' and offenders' rights would be safeguarded; so criticisms that, for example, victim/offender mediation does not look after victims whose offender has not been caught, or that offenders are not given access to legal advice, would no longer apply.

These examples show that we need to hold on to some of the issues which the conventional paradigm addresses; but the new paradigm must find its own way of dealing with them. Advocates of restorative justice see it as not merely a few new programmes to be incorporated into the system; but at present that seems to be exactly how many politicians do see it. We need to show that it is, as Howard Zehr pointed out in *Changing Lenses* (1995), as different from retributive justice as Copernican astronomy from its Ptolemaic predecessor. People have an accepted way of looking at things, but it becomes apparent that some observed phenomena do not fit this accepted theory. On the assumption that planets moved round the earth, they appeared to be moving backwards. Attempts were made to fit this into the geocentric theory by assuming that they moved in smaller orbits within the larger orbit, called 'epicycles'. Other scientists, like Galileo, Kepler and Newton, made new discoveries, and at last the conclusion was unavoidable: the earth went round the sun (Zehr 1995: 89–92 and Zehr 1998).

Zehr quotes Thomas Kuhn's *Structure of Scientific Revolutions* (1970), and this provides a helpful framework to follow what is going on in the theory of justice. Although Kuhn is writing about scientific researchers, much of his description applies also to the practitioners who, through their training, are imbued with the established theories of their day. Research is fitted into the existing conceptual boxes, and subversive novelties are suppressed; for example, it may be difficult to publish a revolutionary article in a peer-reviewed journal, because the reviewers adhere to the old paradigm. A new paradigm, Kuhn says, arises when there is awareness of anomalies in the conventional one; some anomalies are serious enough to be described as a crisis, and there is certainly a crisis when over eight million people are held in prisons world wide, and many (especially prison governors) would agree that in most cases the use of imprisonment is an admission of failure to find a better way of dealing with offenders. So, says Kuhn, as with political revolutions, there is a growing sense among at least some of those in the field that existing institutions no longer adequately meet the problems. But a crisis provides a welcome opportunity to 're-tool'.

The new paradigm succeeds in solving some of the problems of the old, but not all; some 'mopping up' is needed. But no theory ever solves all the puzzles: if any and every failure to fit were a ground for rejection of the theory, all theories ought to be rejected, Kuhn asserts. So if some of the criticisms by Reeves and Mulley and Delgado are valid, that does not mean that restorative justice should be dismissed; the new paradigm forces re-appraisal and must itself be clarified, and residual ambiguities removed. This is the stage which restorative justice has reached.

A new paradigm inspires new journals and organizations, and gains a place in the curriculum, so that it can attract the next generation's practitioners. They recognize that the new paradigm works better, is more suitable, simpler and more elegant. The task of the supporters of the new paradigm is the need to improve it, explore its possibilities, and show what it would be like to belong to a community guided by it.

Kuhn's view is undoubtedly adversarial (not a favourite word among mediators); he claims, controversially, that assimilation of a new theory must demand rejection of the old. But Howard Zehr says in the introduction to the Russian edition of *Changing Lenses* (1998: 12–13):

> In this book I tried to present two models of justice: the retributive ('legalistic') and the restorative, as mutually exclusive systems. Although such an approach clearly helps to demonstrate the differences, I now understand that it is too naïve, unrealistic, and even not entirely honest. To-day I incline to think that justice should include elements of both systems, taking into account not only the inadequacies but also the merits of the legalistic model.

Kuhn does concede that it is a question of proving not which is correct, but which fits the facts better. And he has a warning for innovators: their paradigm may itself lead to professionalization, an esoteric vocabulary, restriction of vision and resistance to further paradigm change. It may not be helpful to assume that there is one full, objective truth.

Notes

1. The main method of implementing restorative justice that will be referred to in this chapter is victim/offender mediation, which will also be used as a general term including victim/offender conferencing, except where the latter method is specifically meant.
2. By 'basic restorative process' we mean for example restorative cautions, in which a police officer or victim support worker brings home to an offender, or a group of offenders, the effects of their actions on victims. 'Full mediation or conferencing' involves a meeting with the offender, the victim, perhaps their

families, and a facilitator for a more in-depth exploration of the offence and its consequences.

3. These are interdisciplinary teams established throughout England and Wales to administer youth justice services and crime reduction strategies.

4. Mika has made a similar point: 'Fairness is assured, not by uniformity of outcomes, but through provision of necessary support and opportunities to all parties and avoidance of discrimination based on ethnicity, class and sex' (Mika 1999: 12).

5. The point is well illustrated by the New Zealand case of *Clotworthy* (R. v. Clotworthy (1998) 15 CRNZ 651 CA, quoted by Morris and Young 2000; see also Boyack 1999). Mr Clotworthy inflicted severe stab wounds on his victim. The latter did not want him to be sent to prison – he had done time himself, and said that it would achieve nothing for Mr Clotworthy or for himself. Instead, he wanted $15,000 to pay for cosmetic surgery on an 'embarrassing scar'. The court made a compensation order accordingly, with a suspended prison sentence and 200 hours of community work. But the Court of Appeal, in the name of deterrence, replaced this with a four-year sentence of immediate imprisonment and compensation of $5,000. Braithwaite (2002: 147) comments that 'The victim got neither his act of grace nor the money for the cosmetic surgery. He subsequently committed suicide for reasons unknown.'

6. Brown is quoting from a long article in *Yale Law Journal* (Grillo 1991, who in turn quotes earlier work by Delgado) which relates to family mediation. Although the author is in favour of mediation, she warns that some received wisdom of mediators, about treating both sides equally, focusing on the future rather than the past, and so on, could be gravely unfair to the weaker party, who is often the woman.

7. Just as expectations that a victim's personal statement will affect sentencing might not be realized (see above).

8. Under the Human Rights Act 1998.

References

Akester, K. (2000) *Restoring Youth Justice: New Directions in Domestic and International Law and Practice.* Available from Justice, 59 Carter Lane, London EC4V 5AQ. London: Justice.

Boyack, J. (1999) 'How sayest the Court of Appeal?' in H. Bowen and J. Consedine (eds). *Restorative Justice: contemporary themes and practice.* Lyttelton, NZ: Ploughshares.

Braithwaite, J. (2002) *Restorative justice and responsive regulation.* New York: Oxford University Press.

Brown, J. G. (1994) 'The Use of Mediation to Resolve Criminal Cases: A Critique', *Emory Law Journal*, 43: 1247–1309.

Christie, N. (1982) *Limits to Pain.* Oxford: Martin, Robertson.

Coates, R. B. (1985) *Victim Meets Offender: An Evaluation of Victim/Offender Reconciliation Programs.* Valparaiso: PACT Institute of Justice.

Coates, R. B. and Gehm, J. (1989) 'An Empirical Assessment' in M. Wright and B. Galaway (eds) *Mediation and Criminal Justice: Victims, Offenders and Community*. London: Sage.

Criminal Justice and Court Services Act (2000), Great Britain, Parliament.

Davis, G. (1992) *Making Amends*. London: Routledge.

Davis, G., Boucherat, J. and Watson, D. (1988) 'Reparation in the Service of Diversion: The Subordination of a Good Idea', *Howard Journal*, 27(2): 127–34.

Delgado, R. (2000) 'Goodbye to Hammurabi: Analyzing the Atavistic Appeal of Restorative Justice', *Stanford Law Review*, 52: 751–75.

Dignan, J. (1990) *Repairing the Damage: An Evaluation of an Experimental Reparation Scheme in Kettering, Northamptonshire*. Centre for Criminological and Legal Research, University of Sheffield. Sheffield, UK: University of Sheffield.

Grillo, T. (1991) 'The Mediation Alternative: Process Dangers for Women', *Yale Law Journal*, 100: 1545–610.

H. M. Advocate v McKenzie (1990) High Court of Justiciary, Scotland, *Scots Law Times*, January 12, 1990, 28–33, at 33 G-H.

Home Office (1998) *The Reparation Order: Draft Guidance Document*. London: Home Office.

Kuhn, T. (1970) *The Structure of Scientific Revolutions*. Chicago: University of Chicago Press.

McIvor, G. (1992) *Sentenced to Serve: The Operation and Impact of Community Service by Offenders*. Aldershot, UK : Avebury.

Marshall, T. and Merry, S. (1990) *Crime and Accountability: Victim/Offender Mediation in Practice*. London: HMSO.

Maxwell, G. and Morris, A. (1999) *Understanding Reoffending*. Wellington, New Zealand: Institute of Criminology, Victoria University of Wellington.

Mika, H. (1999) 'A Restorative Framework of Community Justice Practice: The Critical Road Ahead' in NIACRO, *Reflections on Community Restorative Justice*. Available from NIACRO, 169 Ormeau Road, Belfast BT7 1SQ, Belfast, UK: NIACRO.

Morgan, R. and Sanders, A. (1999) *The Uses of Victim Statements*. London: Home Office Research Development and Statistics Directorate, Information and Publications Group.

Morris, A. and Young, W. (2000) 'Reforming criminal justice: the potential of restorative justice' in H. Strang and J. Braithwaite, eds. *Restorative justice: philosophy and practice*. Aldershot: Ashgate.

Morris, A, Maxwell, G., Hudson, J. and Galaway, B. (1996) 'Concluding Thoughts', in J. Hudson, A. Morris, G. Maxwell and B. Galaway (eds) *Family Group Conferences: Perspectives on Policy and Practice*. Leichardt, NSW: Federation Press; Monsey, NY: Willow Tree Press.

Northamptonshire Adult Reparation Bureau (1992) *Annual Report 1992*.

Reeves, H. (1989) 'The Victim Support Perspective' in M. Wright and B. Galaway (eds) *Mediation and Criminal Justice: Victims, Offenders and Community*. London: Sage.

Reeves, H. (1998) 'Restorative Justice.' *Magistrate*, February: 13.

Reeves, H. and Mulley, K. (2000) 'The New Status of Victims in the UK: Threats and Opportunities' in A. Crawford and J. Goodey (eds) *Integrating a Victim Perspective within Criminal Justice: International Debates.* Aldershot, UK: Ashgate.

Sherman, L. W. and Strang, H. (1998) (Papers 1–4), *The Reintegrative Shaming Experiments (RISE) for Restorative Community Policing.* Law Program, Research School of Social Sciences, Institute of Advanced Studies, Australian National University.

Umbreit, M. S. (1994) *Victim Meets Offender: The Impact of Restorative Justice and Mediation.* Monsey, NY: Criminal Justice Press.

Umbreit, M. S. and Roberts, A. W. (1996) *Mediation of Criminal Conflict in England: An Assessment of Services in Coventry and Leeds.* St Paul, MN: Centre for Restorative Justice and Mediation, University of Minnesota.

Victim Support (1995) *The Rights of Victims of Crime: A Policy Paper.* London: Victim Support.

Wright, M. (1984) *In the Interests of the Community: A Review of the Literature on Community Service Orders.* Department of Social Administration: University of Birmingham.

Wright, M. (1996) *Justice of Victims and Offenders: A Restorative Response to Crime* (2nd edn). Winchester: Waterside Press.

Wright, M. (1999) *Restoring Respect for Justice.* Winchester: Waterside Press.

Young, R. (1989) 'Reparation as Mitigation.' *Criminal Law Review*, 463–72.

Zehr, H. (1995) *Changing Lenses: A New Focus for Crime and Justice* (2nd edn). Scottdale, PA: Herald Press.

Zehr, H. (1998) *Vosstanovital'naya Pravosudie* ('Restorative Justice': Russian translation of *Changing Lenses*). Moscow: Sudebno-Pravovaya Reforma (Judicial and Legal Reform).

Chapter 5

From community to dominion: in search of social values for restorative justice

Lode Walgrave

'As long as we continue to use the term "community" in a loose and imprecise way, the restorative justice theoretical development cannot proceed in any coherent way', McCold writes (1999: 26). This statement, which is representative of a large part of the restorative justice literature, presupposes two elements. First, that it would actually be possible to define 'community' concretely and precisely, and, second, that this definition would be crucial for developing a coherent theory of restorative justice. This chapter will challenge both presuppositions. I shall argue that the notion of 'community' is not useful for theory and even dangerous for poorly thought out systemic practice. Instead, restorative justice theorizing should unpack the social values from their 'community container', and find a way to combine these values with the principles of a democratic constitutional state. The notion of 'dominion', put forward by Braithwaite and Pettit (1990), is proposed as a possible key to find this way.

The central position of community in restorative justice thinking

The notion of community undeniably occupies a central position in restorative justice thinking (Bazemore and Schiff 2001). Community is then advanced as the social environment of informal interactions based on spontaneous human understanding, as opposed to the formal institutionalized society ('the government' or 'the state') with its rules and rigid communication channels. Revalorizing the informal community, restorationists claim, is the crucial plus value of the restorative approach to crime.

The central position of community in restorative justice thinking is understandable. At first glance, there seems even to be an intrinsic link between restorative justice thinking and practice, and an 'idea' of community.

Community and the weakness of retributive justice

Historical studies suggest that the early 'acephalous' collectivities dealt with norm transgression in a restorative way (Weitekamp 1999). They did so in order to safeguard cooperation and peace (in fact to preserve their 'community') through restitution or compensation for the victim and reintegration of the offender. This was probably a pragmatic attitude, because such small communities needed every man in the battle for life with the elements of nature, and could not afford conflict nor the exclusion of available manpower. Other studies indicate that the first written codes were basically oriented at reparation and restoring community life (Van Ness and Heetderks Strong 1997). The re-emergence of restorative justice in recent decades has been greatly stimulated by the same concern for the quality of social life; as a reaction to individualism and fragmentation in our (post)modern societies, communitarians plead for the revitalization of local communities to provide the fertile soil for informal mutual support and control (Etzioni 1995).

Based partly on a notion of social justice and partly on concerns for quality of human relations, critical criminology and other critical studies concluded that existing criminal justice systems did not bring more safety in society nor relief for the victims, and that they did not favour reintegration of the offenders (van Swaaningen 1997). Instead, it was said, we should 'give back the crime conflict to its owners' (Christie 1977) and provide opportunities for resolving the problems as they are experienced by those involved, in their own terms and in their own ways. Many turned their attention to experiments which were close to what is now called 'restorative practices', encouraged by dissatisfaction with the rigid, alienating justice system. Many active communities of different kinds inspired and oriented this shift. Indigenous movements demanded the right to resolve crime in their own way, which was basically community- and restoration-oriented (Jaccoud 1998; Griffiths and Corrado 1999). Active religious movements understood the disastrous impact of formal justice interventions for community life, and developed practices and visions in which forgiveness and restoration play a crucial role (Zehr 1990;

Gehm 1992). Communities thus obviously play an important role in the re-emergence and the flourishing of restorative justice, as a practice and as a movement; moreover, these community-based practices appear to yield observable and beneficial results (Pranis 2001; McCold 1996; Braithwaite 1999).

Finally, also from the point of view of principles, it seems to be difficult to uncouple community from restorative justice. The priority given to restoring the harm caused by a crime inevitably focuses the attention also on the social unrest, threat and other harm suffered by the community. It seems obvious, then, that the living community is more directly victimized by the occurrence of an offence than the state.

Community and restorative justice therefore look like forming an inseparable couple (Pranis and Bazemore 2000). Restorative interventions require a minimum of 'community': victim and offender must at least feel a common interest in settling the aftermath of the crime through constructive dialogue and reparation. But restorative justice is also a way to preserve community life, and to prevent it from shifting downwards towards alienation.

Developing restorative justice

However, when trying to conceptualize the 'idea' of community, problems arise, which are often hard to resolve. Advanced restorative justice practitioners appear to be able to determine 'intuitively' the community which is affected by a concrete crime and to 'sense' whom they should invite to participate in the process. Such intuition may be satisfactory, and even crucial in practice. But restorative justice is now leaving its experimental stage to evolve towards being an integrated recognized practice, even if this brings with it the danger of too routinized 'fast food' intervention (Umbreit 1999). In order to avoid deterioration, good normative theory on restorative justice must be developed, and checking the practice according to the principles of constitutional democracy is necessary. It then appears that the more restorative justice reflection goes beyond practice and aims at developing a coherent theory, the more community is hard to define and to theorize. Transcending the (very constructive and instructive) inspiration of practitioners to build workable theoretical concepts clearly reveals the weaknesses of the notion of community. Trying to develop a fully-fledged systemic restorative response to criminality comes up against the unresolvable fluidity of the notion, and thus the impossibility of its use in even a minimally formalized system.

Problems with the notion of community

Several points of criticism are advanced from within and from outside the restorative justice paradigm.[1]

Community is not an ontological given, but a socio-ethical ideal

As a reaction to post-modern phenomena like atomization, fragmentation in society and egocentrism in individuals, communitarians plead for the revival of community (Bell 1993; Etzioni 1995). Community is then 'a place in which people know and care for one another ...' (Etzioni 1995: 31), but it is also emphasized that 'community is *not* a place' (McCold and Wachtel 1997: 3; Marshall 1994: 248). It is 'a web of affect-laden relationships ... and a measure of commitment to a set of shared values ...' (Etzioni 1996: 127) or a set of 'dense networks of individual interdependencies with strong cultural commitments to mutuality of obligations' (Braithwaite 1989: 85). We all belong to several such communal networks or webs, differing in content and in intensity (Braithwaite 1993; Bell 1993). The degree and the way in which such networks or webs are stakeholders in a restorative process also are different (Van Ness and Heetderks Strong 1997; McCold 1999).

But the problem still remains to set the limits. A good theoretical concept must deal with a well-delimited series of phenomena, and capture its common essence. Even if community is not a territorial space, it must at least be an 'area', delimited mentally, structurally or territorially. What finally remains is that the limits of community are mental: what community is and is not is decided by subjective feelings. Community is defined by a feeling of 'we-ness' (Etzioni 1995: 31), a 'sense of community' (Marshall 1994; McCold and Wachtel 1997), a 'perception of connectedness' (McCold and Wachtel 1997: 2), involving an 'existential commitment ...' (Charvet 1995: 173). Community 'is subjective in that the ascription to community membership or social identity is personal and does not necessarily carry any fixed or external attributes of membership' (Crawford and Clear 2001: 135).

Community appears to be more like a dimension in behaviour, a mental area, a psychological topic, rather than a set of characteristics of given collectivities.[2] Therefore, communitarianism may drive practitioners and socio-ethical movements. Communitarianism may even be a useful concept for indicating a specific psychological attitude, and I hereby confirm my own communitarianism. Community is, however, too vague a concept to characterize and delimit adequately as a part of the social reality, providing handles to come to grips with it scientifically. Nowhere is community defined in a concrete way, even when explicit attempts are made to cope with the criticism of non-definition (as in Schiff and Bazemore 2001: 311–14). Community is the utopia of communitarians, for whom community is 'the antidote to the *fin de siècle* crisis of modernity' (Crawford 1997: 148), or a mirage of what we are craving for in the desert of fragmentation and individualism, but which we cannot really make concrete.

Lack of clarity on the position of community in the process

Community plays several different roles in restorative justice. (1) Sometimes, community is described as the extension of both offender and victim. In group conferencing, for example, both are supported by their 'community of care' (Braithwaite and Daly 1994). This is not the community as a 'third party' on its own, but a private 'community' which will meet another private 'community'. (2) Community is often presented as a tool: independently from these private support groups, a more basic common 'community' must provide the adequate social context needed for good restorative practice through 'reintegrative shaming', for example (Braithwaite 1989; Karp and Walther 2001). (3) Community is also advanced as a party with a stake in the process: besides the victim and his private community, larger communities may be a secondary victim which has suffered its own harm through social unrest or threat, which must also be addressed by the restorative process (McCold 1999). (4) Finally, community is often also presented as a goal of restorative practices: appealing systematically to participatory processes for settling conflicts may contribute to the building of communities through healing social relationships (Van Ness and Heetderks Strong 1997) and enhancing feelings of security (Guarino-Ghezzi and Klein 1999).

The role of community is, however, very often not defined precisely, and community as an extension, as a tool, as a stakeholder and as a goal are mixed up without distinction (Crawford and Clear 2001). It is true, of course, that these functions actually can be partly interdependent in practice: private communities may feel victimized by one of their members' offending, and group together to reach a constructive solution for the incident; an active community may be victimized by an offence in its midst and undertake a restorative process in order to preserve the quality of community life. Nevertheless, this is different to the identification of community as the 'niche' of mutual respect and solidarity, being available to seek constructive solutions to conflicts, or the presentation of community as an ideal form of collective life, pursuing organized, systematically restorative, responses to crime.

The limited availability of community

In particular, the supposed general availability of community for restorative justice practice is highly problematic. Building on communities for developing restorative responses to crime, as many do, presupposes that a community really exists, and this is not self-evident (Crawford 1995). In modern western societies, communities as defined above are often not available, especially not in the cities (Braithwaite 1993; Crawford 1996). It is difficult to mobilize 'community' in the settlement of a street robbery where victim and offender live many kilometres from each other and belong to completely different social networks. And even if both do live in the same area, 'How can we then thrust towards neighborhoods a task that presupposes they are highly alive?' (Christie 1977: 12)[3]. Christie admitted in 1977 that he only had weak arguments in response to this sceptical question, and there is no reason to believe that things have changed since then. Of course, local networks of shared values and mutual solidarity do exist and function ('The death is not complete', Christie 1977: 12), but it is difficult to generalize from this. Most crimes occur in non community-like social settings, and the resolution of these crimes will also have to be found in such settings.

Risks of exclusivism

Leaving 'community' as the loose concept it is exposes it to possible misuses and excesses. Although it may seem to be laudable to seek communities of free individuals, based on mutual understandings, support and control, this may yield potential dangers which are insufficiently recognized. Communities are not 'good' *per se*. The supposed 'niche' of community may appear to be a hotbed of suffocating social control inside, and exclusivism towards those outside.

In the 1970s, young people struggled to free themselves from their 'communities', which they felt were parochial areas of moralistic social control, curtailing their autonomy and creativity (van Swaaningen 1997). These dangers still exist. In the name of 'community', people are still subjected to unreasonable control, local stigmatization and exclusion (Crawford 1997). 'These communities can be, and often are, pockets of intolerance and prejudice' (Crawford and Clear 2001: 137). Local communities often support repressive police forces and judges, and vote for punitive politicians. True, the rejection of community in the seventies may have tipped the scales too far in the opposite direction, contributing strongly to the current dominance of individualism and fragmentation in society. But that does not mean that we should foster nostalgia and return to the 'good old days'. Community, which 'had once been rejected as a constraint' cannot now simply be 'hailed as the enabling capacity' (Bauman 1995, in van Swaaningen 1997: 207).

A community may develop exclusivist tendencies towards the outside. Defining community as an ontological category needs to distinguish between the inside-community and the outside, sometimes fatally. The sharing of values and other social goods is limited to those who are considered to belong to the community. Those who do not are excluded from it, and are often even considered to be a threat. Conflicts between communities are enhanced, and may become violent struggles based on territories, ethnicity or religion. On the nation scale, excesses lead to nationalism and racism. In the past and in the present, those responsible for perpetrating genocide claimed to be preserving the purity and harmony in the community of a nation. As Pavlich writes, 'community' contains 'the seeds of parochialism which can lead ... to atrocious totalitarian exclusions' (Pavlich 2001: 58).

From community to communitarianism in a democratic state

Unpacking the communitarian ideals

Being sceptical about the notion of community is not to reject the ideals promoted by most communitarians: social unity, a form of harmonious living together, with citizens assuming responsibility, based on mutual respect and solidarity. But do we need the concept of community for promoting that? Can we not promote these ideals without running the risks of exclusionary excesses that seem to be linked with 'community'?

Maybe we should not stick to the idea of a community as an ontological 'area', delimited mentally, structurally or territorially, as a necessary condition for achieving harmonious living together. Instead of an area, we should promote the socio-ethical attitudes and functions themselves: mutual respect, solidarity and taking responsibility, which are not the monopoly or privilege of a given 'area' defined by 'community'. ... there is no necessary reason for the privileged association which now exists between the new communitarian images of community and the spirit of spontaneous collective solidarity' (Pavlich 2001: 67).

Most communitarians in fact promote ethics and values, not areas. In restorative justice the word 'community' is like an icon, covering the informal, interdependent, respectful social environment, wherein exchanges can take place, aimed at restoring the victim's harm, reintegrating the offender and healing relations within community (Van Ness and Heetderks Strong 1997). The word 'community' appears as a container for ethics and social values, not a factual given. Rather than using the 'abusable' container we should name the values.

It is true that this spirit, or these socio-ethical attitudes, are activated more spontaneously towards members of what we subjectively define as 'our community'. It is easy to understand, but it is not the ideal situation. It is not the 'normative' end. In order to avoid exclusionary aberrations, such mental communities have to be subjected to control.

The need for inclusion in the democratic state

Here is where the need for an overarching legal principle, able to accommodate possible anomalies, comes to the fore. This need is almost generally accepted: '... restorative community justice should never be viewed as something that happens independent of the formal system' (Bazemore and Umbreit 1995: 20). For Braithwaite and Parker also, 'contestability under the rule of law' is a way to avoid possible dangers of restorative justice (Braithwaite and Parker 1999: 109f). However, accepting that whatever 'community' there is should function in accordance with the 'formal system' inevitably entails the need to come to grips legally with that 'community'. And here another weakness of the community concept becomes apparent.

Problems exist with identifying the concrete community with a stake in a real crime and with the way in which it will be involved in the process (representation, role); with controlling the power balance within the so-called community process; with ensuring that the outcome of the process is 'reasonable' in relation to the seriousness of the offence and the guilt of the offender, etc. If we 'shield' communities from any state-based legal control, these problems are unresolvable. If we accept some legal control, minimal 'hard' definitions of community are needed, and it is highly questionable whether these can be made.

It is sometimes argued that free participation of stakeholders in the process proves that they feel their membership of community, and that free agreements express the participants' feelings of reasonableness. This is not self-evident. Uncontrolled communities may exert subtle and less subtle pressure and abuses of power, which can only be avoided through external check of powers and balances.[4] Moreover, the majority of crimes cannot be dealt with through free participation, but needs coercive intervention, and here also the responses should be maximally restorative (Walgrave 2000). It is hard to find a place for the loosely defined 'community' in the procedure. The basic problem is in fact that, as we have shown above, 'community' is a mental category, which does not allow for legal categorizing.

The often-suggested opposition between community, the life-world with its full richness of shared traditions and supporting relationships, and formal society, with its rules and powers, is a caricature. Habermas, for example, recognizes the problematic relation between the real life-world and the criminal justice system, but that does not 'lead him to oppose the role systems play in the life-world *per se*, nor to a rejection of the criminal justice system' (van Swaaningen 1997: 207). Rather, an alternative vision of law is advanced 'as an institution of procedurally guaranteed dispute settlement,' while promoting 'communicative action within the life-world' (ibid). Braithwaite and Parker (1999) present a model of 'checking and balancing law and community', in which 'the rule of law percolates down into restorative justice' and 'restorative justice percolates up into the rule of law' (1999: 115–121).

But the legal framework we need cannot be opposed to community. On the contrary, the idea that community assures peace through offering healing and reintegration, and society assures order through redress and legal safeguards (Van Ness and Heetderks Strong 1997), is only tenable if it is based on socio-ethical premises of respect and global solidarity and overarched by strong legal principles. Besides its intuitive pragmatism, adhering to the notion of community seems to be rather a handicap than a central issue in the development of restorative justice theory and a fully-fledged restorative justice system.

Challenges for restorative justice

Two challenges emerge from these reflections for developing a normative restorative justice theory that could provide a basis for policy and research.

(1) Restorative justice must build upon the ethics and social values it promotes, and explain its possible superiority in comparison with social responses to crime which are not primarily restoration-oriented. (2) It must reflect more on the way restorative practice and policy can be built into the principles of a constitutional democracy.

Ethics in restorative justice

Two ethical questions on restorative justice are (1) whether restorative justice promotes ethics and social values which are different from the other social responses, and/or (2) whether restorative justice offers a better strategy to achieve the same social values than the other social responses.

Defining the goal of restorative justice is simple: it aims at restoration. The question then is whether restoration as the primary goal would be superior to rehabilitation or reintegration (as in the rehabilitative juvenile justice systems), or maintaining morality (as in the retributive penal justice systems). Does restoration have a plus value because it serves ethically higher goals, or because it is a more efficient way to achieve the same goals?

The ethics of restorative justice

Let us now do an exercise, and try to find out what are in fact the basic ethics behind aiming at restoration. Why do restorative justice advocates pretend that their justice option is preferable to both the punitive and the rehabilitative option in doing justice? Based on the first section of this chapter, we can tentatively advance the proposition that 'community', including all the valued characteristics it supposes, is the central value which drives restorationists. But, as argued above, 'community' as a concept is not strong enough to serve as a reliable cornerstone in building a normative theory. However, while rejecting community as an ontological area, we considered communitarianism as a possibly useful concept for indicating a socio-ethical movement.

Could communitarian ethics underpin restorative justice? The communitarians are dreaming of a collectivity of unity and harmony, which would draw its strength not from threat, coercion and fear, but from motivation of its members, based on trust, participation and mutual support. A collectivity which aims at this utopia will promote socio-ethical attitudes which serve it. Tentatively, I would hypothesize three such attitudes and behavioural guidelines: respect, solidarity and taking responsibility.

Respect is an ethical attitude which recognizes the intrinsic value of the other. Respect for humans implies the recognition of the intrinsic value of a human being. This is why respecting 'human dignity' is considered to be a basic obligation for all social institutions.

Solidarity presupposes more commitment than respect, because solidarity includes a form of companionship and reciprocity of support. Companionship allows for empathy and mutual trust, and it is therefore most visible in the attitudes towards those in trouble. Contrary to community rhetoric, which locates solidarity within the scope of a community, solidarity is now not limited by a given 'area', but is a general ethical value: '... this spirit of solidarity may be regarded as a forever-elusive promise of unpremeditated collective togetherness.' (Pavlich 2001: 67).

Responsibility links the person to his acts and its consequences. Responsibility confronts the self with its own actions. Taking responsibility is an active form of responding autonomously to the obligations created by social life, which is, in communitarian ethics, oriented towards solidarity.

Other ethical guidelines may be superfluous if these three valuable attitudes were to be achieved. I am not sure, for example, that 'justice' is a value on its own, because I suspect that the need for 'justice' as a separate value would disappear if all citizens would assume responsibility based on respect and solidarity for each other.[5]

At first glance, advancing respect, solidarity and responsibility as basics in a communitarian philosophy underpinning restorative justice may seem to be cheap rhetoric. Don't we all value such ethical attitudes?

The ethics of retributive justice

Do we really all value such ethical attitudes? As an exercise, let us compare the ethics described above with the ethics which may orient retributive justice, as presented by Andrew von Hirsch (1993).[6]

Respect does not dominate in retributionism. Respect for the victim is absent, because she/he is not included in the retributionist world view. Retributionism is focused on the offender. Considering the offender as a conscious moral agent, and to treat him in a just (deserts) way, seems to recognize him as a human being, and as a citizen with guaranteed rights. But the respect is not complete. The offender is not respected as a whole person with their own interests and interpretations, including the possible willingness to make up for their misbehaviour. The offender ultimately has to be submitted to a just-deserts punishment. In fact, once the crime has been committed, respect for the person is abandoned. She/he is seen as a moral agent to be considered guilty; no attempt is made to find a constructive response to the harm caused to quality of life. This is clearly different from restorative justice. All parties with a stake in the offence are respected as humans and as citizens, which becomes apparent through the invitation to express what they have to say and to participate in the quest for a socially constructive solution.

Is solidarity an ethical attitude in retributionism? Such a value cannot be seen in retributionism. The punitive response does not aim to support the victim in trouble, but to punish the offender, very often hampering reparation. In restorative justice, solidarity with the victim is evident, whilst solidarity with the offender remains. The offender is not excluded, but is encouraged to make reparation for the conduct, in order to preserve his/her position as an integrated member of the collectivity.

Responsibility certainly is present in retributionism. The offender is held responsible by being obliged to respond autonomously to the obligation created by the misconduct, but again, the responsibility is incomplete: the offender is being held responsible for bearing the negative consequences of their behaviour, but not for contributing to finding a constructive solution to the problems created by their behaviour. It is limited to a passive, backward-looking responsibility (Braithwaite and Roche 2001). The victim, again, is not considered responsible for anything, except maybe in reporting the criminal act and in giving evidence at a trial. Retributionism in fact seems to burden the (agents of the) criminal justice system with the heaviest responsibility, to censure prohibited behaviour, and to impose proportionate punishments. Contrary to retributive justice, restorative justice extends the responsibility of the offender to 'active responsibility' (Braithwaite and Roche 2001), including the obligation to contribute to the reparation of the harm caused. The victim is encouraged, but not obliged, to take a general citizens' responsibility to search for peace-promoting solutions of a conflict. Restorative justice also stands for responsible (informal and formal) collectivities, bound by obligations to search for socially constructive responses within the rules of law.

This superficial exercise, of course, needs to be deepened and extended, but it may be sufficient to demonstrate that restorative justice favours social and ethical attitudes like respect, solidarity and taking responsibility to a greater extent than does retributive justice, and that it is therefore more likely to contribute constructively to social life and relations.

Inserting communitarianism into constitutional democracy

As mentioned above, we cannot just depend on ethical attitudes and principles to guide a collectivity. We need coercive rules for when these principles are not spontaneously implemented, certainly in existing fragmented and individualistic societies. In fact, there is a need for a model that allows a constructive combination of a significant space for informal processes based on high socio-ethical attitudes with legal rules and powers to check formally respect for these rules. These rules also should be maximally based on the same socio-ethics.

The republican theory of criminal justice

It is worthwhile exploring the potential of Braithwaite and Pettit's republican theory of criminal justice (Braithwaite and Pettit 1990; Braithwaite and Parker 1999). This theory calls 'for a formalism that empowers and constitutionalises informalism' (Braithwaite and Daly 1994: 198). The theory also allows for a 'rule of law' that 'percolates down into restorative justice' and 'restorative justice' that 'percolates up into the rule of law' (1999: 115–121).

The republican theory of criminal justice is built on the concept of 'dominion'.[7] One can summarize the several observations on the concept by defining dominion as 'the set of assured rights and freedoms'. It is the mental and social territory of which we freely dispose, and which is guaranteed by the state and the social environment. Of crucial importance is the assurance of rights and freedoms. 'I know that I have rights, and I know that the others know it, and I trust that they will respect it.' It is only then that I will fully enjoy my mental and social territory. In this assurance of rights and freedoms lies the crucial distinction from the liberal concept of 'freedom as non-interference'. In such a concept, 'the other' is a rival in the struggle for freedom. In the republican view, 'the other' is an ally in trying to extend and mutually assure dominion as a collective good. The dominion concept could make the tensions just described between informal processing and formal rights manageable in a credible and useful manner.

The pursuit of dominion

A good state, Braithwaite and Pettit say, is one which promotes dominion for its citizens. This makes it clear that dominion is not a priori delimited and that it is considered a value, not just a factual given. It is the central value which underpins the normative republican theory of criminal justice. The state must seek to extend and deepen dominion by promoting equality through more democracy, good education, equitable socio-economic policy, welfare policy and the like. Crime is primarily defined as an intrusion into dominion, and criminal justice must act to repair it. When a crime has occurred, the state must play its defensive role, and strive for restoring dominion through criminal justice (Walgrave 2000b).

But dominion is not only a value, it is at the same time also a factual given. Basing the concept on 'rights and freedoms', dominion allows for a delimitation, a 'hard core' from which principles and enforceable legal rules can be deduced. Braithwaite and Pettit (1990) include three criteria in the definition of their objective, and deduce four constraints in the pursuit of 'dominion'. Together these elements constitute a normative theory on criminal justice.

An example may illustrate how the theory can integrate the interest of promoting informal processes with the need for formal controls. According to the republican theory, criminal justice must strive for achievable goals (repairing the intruded dominion), and is bound by the constraint of parsimony in using its coercive and punitive power. The meaning of parsimony is close to that of satiability, but it is more restricting. We can eat until full satiation, but we can parsimoniously do with less to survive. Satiability restricts the possible coercive intervention by imposing an upper limit. Parsimony actually limits the coercive intervention to what is strictly needed. Its prescription is: 'If in doubt, do less.' That can be less than would be acceptable according to the satiability requirement.

The satiability/parsimony couple is close to the retributionist issue of proportionality, in that both limit the quantum of intervention permissible. There is, however, a crucial difference. Satiability obliges the setting of an upper limit, as required by the proportionality principle in retributive justice. Parsimony, however, excludes the setting of a lower limit, as would be required by the same principle. On the contrary, the parsimony constraint requires an active involvement to search for non-coercive ways to restore dominion. For reasons of parsimony, the opportunities for non-coercive restorative processes are of crucial importance. The more voluntary restorative processes can lead to satisfying and balanced outcomes, the less appeal to the coercive judicial system will be needed and thus the more the parsimony principle will be realized. A fully-fledged restorative justice system should fulfil its parsimony obligation by leaving space for, or by diverting to, voluntary processes, wherein victim, offender and collective life together can seek an agreed settlement of the aftermath of a crime that maximally restores the dominion injured.[8]

The legal foundations of dominion also make it territorially limited, which can make 'dominion' as vulnerable to exclusionary tendencies as was indicated earlier with regard to 'community'. Citizens in ancient Rome (Braithwaite and Pettit explicitly refer to the Roman *libertas* to explain dominion) excluded non-Romans from their *libertas*. Rights and freedoms are for citizens only, which may exclude non-citizens. This might indeed be a problem, as can be observed in exclusivist attitudes of states against immigrants and economic fugitives. On the other hand, however, there is a movement toward internationalization of citizenship, as is apparent through the United Nations Declaration of Human Rights and its implementation by international courts in The Hague, Arusha, etc.

Finally, dominion is also a subjective concept. As mentioned earlier, a key to understanding it is the assurance of rights and freedoms, and being assured is a subjective feeling. I can be assured of my dominion only if I have some trust in my fellow citizens and in the state, that they will take my rights and freedoms seriously. My assurance rests upon my reliance on the state's and the citizens' respect for me and their solidarity with me.

If a crime occurs, public intervention is not needed primarily to put right the balance of benefits and burdens, nor to re-confirm morality. Public intervention is needed especially to communicate to the victim and to the public that the authorities do take dominion seriously. Intrusion in the dominion of one citizen must be responded to, to assure the victim and the public of their rights and freedoms, and thus to complete their set of rights and freedoms into being a fully-fledged dominion. Victims of crime do not only depend on the formal public responses to it; they must also be supported informally by their fellow citizens. This formal and informal support will enhance the subjective assurance of rights and freedoms, which is crucial to enjoying them to the full. This 'subjective aspect' of dominion refers to a social context close to the setting claimed by communitarians: a setting based on respect, solidarity and responsibility.

Conclusion

We have distanced ourselves from the concept of 'community' as an ontological concept, because it appears to be too vague to be useful in scientific and legal constructs, and because it holds serious risks of social anomalies. Instead, we advanced communitarianism as the label for a socio-ethical movement oriented towards a utopian collectivity driven by its members taking responsibility based on mutual respect and solidarity.

This utopian ideal has to be built into the rule of law. The concept of 'dominion' seems to offer the opportunity to combine the crucial elements of both 'communitarianism' and 'legal society'. The set of rights and freedoms refers to the state, the organized society, which defines them and organizes their enforcement and safeguarding. The assurance, however, is a subjective element. Much better than 'community', 'dominion' clearly displays the interdependency of the state and the social values promoted by most communitarians, and it avoids the risks of exclusionary anomalies. If there were no state, there would be no rights, and one would depend on the goodwill of others or on one's own power to compete with others and to oppress them. If there was only the state, there would be no trust, and 'the other' would be considered as a rival, a threat to one's own territory. Such a state would deteriorate into anarchy or tyranny.

For 'Making Democracy Work' (Putnam 1993), we need to rely on social capital, defined by Putnam as 'features of social organization such as trust, norms and networks, that can improve the efficiency of society by facilitating coordinated actions' (1993: 167). Trust is the crucial element. Putnam does not limit trust to 'thick trust' based on strong ties with family, friends and close neighbours,[9] because of their possible exclusionary side effects. On the contrary, the strongest social capital for effectively functioning societies lies in a generalized trust based on weak ties with social organizations and with the generalized 'other'. It is the assurance included in Braithwaite and Pettit's concept of 'dominion'. We should explore this further.

Notes

1. It is probably not coincidental that the most confirmed promoters of the concept of community, as opposed to that of the state, are found in the United States, while most scepticism is expressed in Europe (see also van Swaaningen 1997). Many Americans seem to view their state as a bureaucratic taxing machine, an opponent of their freedom, located at an unbridgeable distance from real life. The state institutions of education, medical care, and social services are reduced. Communities, based on religion, territory or ethnicity, partly fulfill this lack of provisions. Many communities indeed express solidarity among their members. That may explain why Americans foster the idea of community as opposed to 'government' or 'state', and are less sensitive to the absence and/ or exclusionary anomalies of communities in many places. In Europe, by contrast, the state is supposed to be more the emanation of community or the community of communities. Though Europeans are also sensitive to bureaucratic and formalist excesses, they do not give up this basic idea, and try to correct the anomalies in the state's functioning. Not that Europeans love paying taxes, but they basically consider it as a contribution to the collectivity. The state is not an opponent, but a tool to be improved. Though the distinction between 'Gemeinschaft' and 'Gesellschaft' was put forward by a German sociologist, community is less of an issue in European debates because its distinction from the state is not evident.
2. The term 'collectivity' is used to refer to groups of humans as neutrally as possible.
3. In crimes like tax fraud, it seems rather the organized state, and not a local community, which is victimized.
4. The possibility of external checks by court of the Family Group Conferences is included in the most advanced restorative system, the New Zealand Children, Young Persons and their Families' Act (1989).
5. I do not include peace, either, because conflict may be very constructive in social life if it is embedded in a context of mutual respect, solidarity and taking responsibility.
6. At first glance, this comparison may seem to be unjustified. Contrary to restorative justice, which is clearly a consequentionalist theory, retributivism is a deontological theory, which grounds criminal justice not on the useful consequences it yields, but on principles of justice and fairness. Deontological theories of punishment do not refer to goals in the functioning of criminal justice. However, with many others, I do think that a purely deontological theory is impossible. A deontological model can only be argued for on the basis of the values it defends (morality, for example). As a consequence, deontological theories implicitly declare the defence of the values as being the goal of the justice system. After all, if the criminal justice system is not supposed to at least defend some values, we would do better to abolish this very expensive pain- causing machine.
7. In later publications, 'dominion' has been renamed as 'freedom as non-domination'. It may make it easier to oppose it to the liberal concept typified as

'freedom as non-interference', but I do not see any other advantage in complicating the wording to indicate the central concept. I will therefore stick to the 'old' name, 'dominion'.

8. In *Censure and Sanctions* (1993), von Hirsch and Ashworth address serious critiques of the dominion concept ('Dominion and Censure', ch. 3). I must confine myself to a brief comment here. One of the basic critiques is that the republican theory does not provide a good base for a decremental strategy with regard to punishment (despite Braithwaite and Pettit's claim). This criticism may be justified, but is not relevant here. The republican theory is wrong not to question the criminal justice system as basically a 'punishing machine', while the a priori option for punishing crime is in itself a wrong choice for repairing dominion. The theory should in fact be reoriented as a republican theory of restorative justice. In view of the constructive claims of restorative justice, there is no need for a decremental strategy on restorative justice. Another critique is that censure cannot operate independently from severity of sanction, which is suggested by the republican theory. There are two answers here: first, that the sanction should not be punitive, but may also be restorative; second, that the severity of censure is but one of the elements in 'restorative sentencing'. Other elements will be the degree of guilt (as in retributive justice), and the restorative benefits (parsimoniously imposed – or accepted – sanctions will be much more restorative).

9. Deontological theories of punishment deny any goal to the functioning of criminal justice. It could therefore seem to be unjustified to try to compare restorative justice and penal justice according to the social values they promote. However, as indicated in endnote 6, I think that a purely deontological theory is impossible.

References

Baumann, Z. (1995) 'The Strangers of Consumer Era: From the Welfare State to Prison', *Tijdschrift voor Criminologie*, 37(3): 210–18.

Bazemore, G. and Schiff, M. (eds) (2001) *Restorative Community Justice. Repairing Harm and Transforming Communities*. Cincinnati, OH: Anderson.

Bazemore, G. and Umbreit, M. (1995) 'Rethinking the Sanctioning Function in Juvenile Court: Retributive or Restorative Responses to Youth Crime', *Crime and Delinquency*, 41(3): 296–316.

Bell, D. (1993) *Communitarianism and its Critics*. Oxford: Clarendon.

Braithwaite, J. (1993) 'Shame and Modernity', *The British Journal of Criminology*, 33(1): 1–18.

Braithwaite, J. (1989) *Crime, Shame and Reintegration*. Cambridge: Cambridge University Press.

Braithwaite, J. (1999) 'Restorative Justice: Assessing Optimistic and Pessimistic Accounts' in M. Tonry (ed.) *Crime and Justice: A Review of Research*, 25. Chicago: University of Chicago Press.

Braithwaite, J. and Daly, K. (1994) 'Masculinities, Violence and Communitarian

Control' in T. Newburn and E. Stanko (eds) *Just Boys Doing Business? Men, Masculinities and Crime*. London: Routledge.

Braithwaite, J. and Pettit, P. (1990) *Not Just Desert. A Republican Theory of Criminal Justice*. Oxford: Oxford University Press.

Braithwaite, J. and Parker, C. (1999) 'Restorative Justice is Republican Justice' in G. Bazemore and L. Walgrave (eds) *Restorative Juvenile Justice: Repairing the Harm by Youth Crime*. Monsey: Criminal Justice Press.

Braithwaite, J. and Roche, D. (2001) 'Responsibility and Restorative Justice' in G. Bazemore and M. Schiff (eds) *Restorative Community Justice. Repairing Harm and Transforming Communities*. Cincinnati: Anderson.

Charvet, J. (1995) *The Idea of an Ethical Community*. New York/London: Cornell University Press.

Christie, N. (1977) 'Conflicts as Properties', *British Journal of Criminology*, 1: 1–14.

Crawford, A. (1995) 'Appeals to Community and Crime Prevention', *Crime, Law and Social Change*, 22: 97–126.

Crawford, A. (1996) 'The Spirit of Community: Rights, Responsibilites and the Communitarian Agenda', *Journal of Law and Society*, 2(23): 247–62.

Crawford, A. (1997) *The Local Governance of Crime. Appeals to Community and Partnerships*. Oxford: Clarendon, Studies in Criminology.

Crawford, A. and Clear, T. (2001) 'Community Justice: Transforming Communities Through Restorative Justice?' in G. Bazemore and M. Schiff (eds) *Restorative Community Justice. Repairing Harm and Transforming Communities*. Cincinnati: Anderson.

Etzioni, A. (1995) *The Spirit of Community. Rights, Responsabilities and the Communitarian Agenda*. London: Fontana Press.

Etzioni, A. (1996) *The New Golden Rule. Community and Morality in a Democratic Society*. New York: Basic Books.

Gehm, J. (1992) 'The Function of Forgivenness in the Criminal Justice System' in H. Messmer and H. U. Otto, *Restorative Justice on Trial. Pitfalls and Potentials of Victim–Offender Mediation. International Research Perspectives*. Dordrecht: Kluwer Academic Publishers.

Griffiths, T. and Corrado, R. (1999) 'Implementing Restorative Youth Justice: A Case Study in Community Justice and the Dynamics of Reform' in G. Bazemore and L. Walgrave (eds) *Restorative Juvenile Justice. Repairing the Harm by Youth Crime*. Monsey, New York: Criminal Justice Press.

Guarino-Ghezzi, S. and Klein (1999) 'Protecting Community. The Public Safety Role in a Restorative Juvenile Justice' in G. Bazemore and L. Walgrave (eds), *Restorative Juvenile Justice. Repairing the Harm by Youth Crime Exploring*. Monsey, New York: Criminal Justice Press.

Jaccoud, M. (1998) 'Restoring Justice in Native Communities in Canada' in L. Walgrave (ed.), *Restorative Justice for Juveniles. Potentialities, Risks and Problems for Research*. Leuven: Leuven University Press.

Karp, D. and Walther, L. (2001) 'Community Reparative Boards in Vermont' in G. Bazemore and M. Schiff (eds) *Restorative Community Justice. Repairing Harm and Transforming Communities*. Cincinnati: Anderson.

Marshall, T. (1994) 'Grassroots Initiatives Towards Restorative Justice: The New

Paradigm?' in A. Duff *et al*. (eds) *Penal Theory and Practice. Tradition and Innovation in Criminal Justice*. Manchester: University Press.

McCold P. and Wachtel, T. (1997) *Community is Not a Place*. Paper presented at the International Conference on Justice without Violence, Albany, June 5–6, available at www.realjustice.org/pages/albany.html

McCold, P. (1996) 'Restorative Justice and the Role of Community' in B. Galaway and J. Hudson (eds) *Restorative Justice: International Perspectives*. Amsterdam/Monsey: Kugler/Criminal Justice Press.

McCold, P. (1999) 'Toward a Holistic Vision of Restorative Justice: A Reply to Walgrave', presentation at the 4th International Conference on Restorative Justice for Juveniles, Leuven, 24–27 October 1999. In *Contemporary Justice Review* 3(4): 357–414.

Pavlich, G. (2001) 'The Force of Community' in H. Strang and J. Braithwaite (eds) *Restorative Justice and Civil Society*. Cambridge: Cambridge University Press.

Pranis, K. (2001) 'Restorative Justice, Social Justice, and the Empowerment of Marginalized Populations' in G. Bazemore and M. Schiff (eds) *Restorative Community Justice. Repairing Harm and Transforming Communities*. Cincinnati: Anderson.

Pranis, K. and Bazemore, G. (2000) *Engaging the Community in the Response to Youth Crime: A Restorative Justice Approach*. Washington, DC: Department of Justice OJDP.

Putnam, (1993) *Making Democracy Work: Civic Traditions in Modern Italy*. Princeton: Princeton University Press.

Schiff, M. and Bazemore, G. (2001) 'Dangers and Opportunities of Restorative Community Justice: A Response to Critics' in G. Bazemore and M. Schiff (eds) *Restorative Community Justice. Repairing Harm and Transforming Communities*. Cincinnati, OH: Anderson.

Umbreit, M. (1999) 'Avoiding the McDonaldization of Victim–Offender Mediation' in G. Bazemore and L. Walgrave (eds), *Restorative Juvenile Justice. Repairing the Harm by Youth Crime Exploring*. Monsey, New York: Criminal Justice Press.

Van Ness, D. and Heetderks Strong, K. (1997) *Restoring Justice*. Cincinnati: Anderson.

van Swaaningen, R. (1997) *Critical Criminology. A Vision from Europe*. London: Sage.

von Hirsch, A. (1993) *Censure and Sanctions*. Oxford: Clarendon.

Walgrave, L. (2000) 'How Pure Can a Maximalist Approach to Restorative Justice Remain? Or Can a Purist Model of Restorative Justice become Maximalist?', *Contemporary Justice Review*, 3(4): 415–31.

Walgrave, L. (2000b) 'Restorative Justice and the Republican Theory of Criminal Justice. An Exercise in Normative Theorizing on Restorative Justice' in J. Braithwaite and H. Strang (eds) *Restorative Justice: From Philosophy to Practice*. Dartmouth: Ashgate.

Weitekamp, E. (1999) 'History of Restorative Justice' in G. Bazemore and L. Walgrave (eds) *Exploring Restorative Justice for Juveniles*. Monsey, New York: Criminal Justice Press.

Zehr, H. (1990) *Changing Lenses: A New Focus for Crime and Justice*. Scottsdale: Herald Press.

Chapter 6

Deconstructing restoration: the promise of restorative justice

George Pavlich

Restorative justice is a concept whose time has come. Many, regardless of political persuasion, see in it the makings of a viable panacea.[1] Conservative thinkers find solace in restorative justice's emphasis on the plight of victims, the family, offender responsibilities, cost savings, administrative efficiencies, etc. Many too are attracted by communitarian utopias that herald a return to mythically conceived communities, harmoniously gracing the days of yore (DiJulio Jr 1998; Etzioni 1998; Dignan and Cavadino 1996). The more liberally inclined are enticed by its promise to deal with offenders and the community without relying – in the first instance – on retributive and coercive punishments (see Galaway and Hudson 1996). Other advocates champion its attempts to deal with the emotional deprivations and scars left on victims by 'criminal' behaviours (Cragg 1992). Reformers are enticed by images of social and community transformation, and see restorative justice as possibly leading to 'transformative' justice (Morris R. 2000; Cooley 1999; Bush and Folger 1994). If such endorsements highlight the wide appeal of restorative justice, they also signal its disparate discourses, programmes, institutions and procedures.[2]

A personal experience of having a car stolen by a 15-year-old youth in New Zealand confirmed the official blessing there conferred to restorative justice in the youth justice terrain. After being apprehended, the youth precipitated much activity in the name of restorative justice. As a result, I found myself speaking on the telephone to a youth justice co-ordinator seeking a date for a family group conference (FGC). He boldly pointed to the virtues of the process, and my important role – as victim – therein. In response to one of my questions, he spoke of the FGC as a complement to the state's justice system but one that defers to the offender's family, the victim and the community in general. There was a note of politely resigned patience as I pursued my questioning; I was told to expect a voluntary process that allowed me to have my say as a victim (which, he emphasized, is not possible in courtroom settings). As well, he assured me, there were benefits to being part of a community process aimed at restoring and healing relationships. In his circles, I gathered, evoking the authority of restorative justice was sufficient to silence further questions into the underlying rationales of the FGCs. My own ambivalence about the promises of such justice surfaced around its assumption that I wanted to repair a harm (beyond having my vehicle returned), had a 'relationship' with the offender that needed to be restored, and was a member of a common set of relations – an amorphous 'community' which required my active participation for the benefit of all concerned. Nevertheless, the idea of restorative justice has tapped into a rich vein, evoking considerable political, cultural, religious and common sense appeal (see Cooley 1999; Walgrave 1998).

But what precisely are we to understand by restorative justice, and more specifically how might one assess its promise? Responding to the question is no easy task, given the exponential growth of diverse discourses in the area. Even so, in this chapter, I shall offer an overview of some important themes that underscore two of restorative justice's key promises; namely, to (i) initiate a form of justice that discards the state's 'repressive' or 'rehabilitative' responses to crime, and (ii) to nurture harmonious communities that embrace restorative – rather than the state's legal – justice practices. I point to certain paradoxes and dangers in the ways that the promise of justice and community are enunciated by influential restorative justice discourses. This discussion leads me to review both justice and community through deconstructionist lenses, and to consider restorative justice as a way of challenging, continuously, any given calculation of justice and collective solidarity. My endeavour bears traces of Derridean deconstruction in the sense that its overriding approach is one of opening up concepts rather than closing them off as necessary, immutable or inevitable decrees (See Derrida 1976, 1997). But deconstruction is not destruction; it is one way of coming to grips with the radical contingency, and paradox, of any discourse that speaks now about what might come.

Intimations of restorative justice

The broad appeal of restorative justice is, no doubt, related to the ambiguity of its formulation. Indeed, as at least one author discovered, it is very difficult to achieve anything like a clear consensus on the concept's meaning (McCold 1998a; 1998b). There is good reason for this: to narrow its meaning would open the concept to specific challenge, thus risking the popularity that its equivocation affords. Nevertheless, there are several privileged signs in the discourse through which protagonists espouse restorative justice. To begin with, as with most enunciations of what something is – claims to presence – advocates explicitly refer to what it is not. Presence is enunciated by absence, as it were, and that is why many key restorative justice texts specify what they stand against. Zehr's (1990) influential text, for example, explicitly describes restorative justice as a radical shift of perspectives, a change of 'lenses' from those used by conventional state justice practices. Equally, the *leitmotiv* recurs in various bids that pit restorative justice against the poverty of existing criminal justice frameworks (e.g., Bazemore and Walgrave 1999; Bazemore 1998; Zehr 1995, 1990).

This rhetorical strategy has a rich genealogy, descending as it does from earlier promises of community justice (Shonholtz 1988/89; Abel 1982), popular justice (Merry and Milner 1993), victim–offender reconciliation (e.g., Umbreit et al 1994, 1995), community mediation (Pavlich 1996a), and the quest for, as Auerbach (1983) puts it, 'justice without law'.[3] From this lineage, restorative justice emerged as an *alternative* to two dominant crime control perspectives framed by classical and positivist criminology (see Bazemore 1998; Bazemore and Umbreit 1995; Zehr 1990). It does not approach crime through legally-defined guilt, and so rejects both criminology's classical legislative images of crime as a violation of law and the consequent 'just-deserts' model that belies neo-conservative calls to 'get tough on crime' (see Pavlich and Ratner 1996). At the same time, restorative justice advocates embrace neither the rehabilitative, correctional, emphasis of liberal 'welfare' justice, nor its positivist foundations (Braithwaite 1999: 8; see Pfohl 1994). This welfare image of justice calls for treatment that has included such horrors as social defence and correction through sterilization, genocide and the like, but its main impact has been to encourage classification-based, rehabilitative, treatment-orientated, correctional efforts in prisons (see Cullen and Gilbert 1982). Most often, the individual is targeted as the source of the problem, requiring remedial attention from criminal justice agencies. The victim and community tend to be tangential to the main thrust of both philosophies.

By contrast, restorative justice is positioned as an alternative form of justice far older than professional, legal justice (Bazemore 1998; Braithwaite 1999, 1998; Zehr 1995; etc.). It focuses practical attention on the harms caused by an offending (criminal) act, emphasizing the victim, the offender and the community rather than centring itself around abstracted laws (Zehr 1990). Justice emerges not as Thrasymachus' will of the strong, as a metaphysical Platonic virtue, or retributive 'just deserts'; rather, it is cast in terms of resolving conflict.

> Justice means achieving a situation in which the conduct or action of individuals is considered to be fair, right and appropriate for the given circumstances ... Justice is then, bound up with responses to conflict (Cooley 1999: 14).

Conflict is said to exist when, 'the actions of one individual or group are defined by another as inappropriate and therefore meriting some response' (Cooley 1999: 3). Some conflicts produce significant harm for parties, while others do not; but all provide an opportunity for social actors to reflect on appropriate behaviour, and to accept or revise collective norms. More left-leaning analysts thus detect a 'transformative' potential in conflict and the possibility of its leading to a more 'just society' (Cooley 1999: 4; see also Sullivan and Tifft 1998). However, for the most part, restorative justice discourses simply promise a justice that is tied to effectively resolving local conflict:

> Our sense of justice and injustice is aroused when we face situations of conflict. Our sense of justice is affirmed when we are able to resolve conflict to our satisfaction (Cooley 1999: 4).

Hence the promise of justice is a by-product of practices that resolve conflict in specific contexts. This promise can be understood on at least three levels (see Braithwaite 1998: 331 ff). First, at a 'micro' (grassroots) level, restorative justice promises to heal the effects of harmful conflicts on both individuals and communities (Putney 1997). The aim here is to 'restore', 'replenish' and 'heal' the damage done by harmful acts, using inclusive (integrative), non-stigmatizing and non-coercive procedures. Many restorative justice programmes, therefore, focus on restoring victims' trust in given communities by addressing their fears, concerns, losses, images of what needs to be done, and so on. At the same time, restorative procedures encourage offenders to confront their wrongful actions, understand the pain inflicted on victims and rectify these through physical restitutions and/or community obligations (e.g., 'reintegrative shaming' rather than retributive punishment, public humiliation, or individually prescribed treatments – see Braithwaite 1989). The processes also try to 'repair' the lost dignity of offenders and involve 'the community' as meaningfully as possible. At this level, restorative justice cannot address structural injustices:

> It settles for the procedural requirement that parties talk until they feel that harmony has been restored on the basis of discussion of all the injustices they see as relevant to the case (Braithwaite 1998: 329–330).

Secondly, at a 'medium' level, restorative justice enlists and develops supportive community agencies, including churches, community organizations, non-governmental organizations, and the like. It advocates broader institutional supports for its micro operations, mainly through communitarian reforms (Etzioni 1998), or community development frameworks (See Merry and Milner 1993). Thirdly, a 'macro' dimension strives for harmonious, peaceful and functional communities to revitalize democratic institutions and empower members to exercise political freedoms. Protagonists of community justice initiatives have long advocated strengthening communities as the public backbone of viable civil societies that involve the 'people' in viable democracies.[4] Communitarians elaborate upon this by calling for 'the community' to complement, if not replace, many aspects of state control (see Pavlich 2001). Braithwaite (1998, 1999) echoes the goal in context, by calling for restorative justice to develop institutions of a 'deliberative democracy' where individuals and communities deliberate responsibly on the harms of crime.[5]

Although brief, these key aspects of restorative justice discourse imply at least two legitimating promises. These promises are articulated in various ways, but one could viably use Braithwaite's (1999) useful synopsis of restorative justice as an illustrative reference point. First, there is the promise of a 'deliberative' *justice* – beyond the law's justice – focused on processes that restore relationships between disputants, offenders, victims and communities involved with a given conflict (or criminal) situation. As he puts it,

> Restorative Justice is deliberative justice; it is about people deliberating over the consequences of crime, and how to deal with them and prevent their recurrence (Braithwaite 1998: 329).

Secondly, restorative justice processes promise strong *communities* of civil society. Embracing this pledge is wider one: functional communities help to institute a thriving and free democracy. Thus, for Braithwaite,

> If we take restorative justice seriously, it involves a very different way of thinking about traditional notions such as deterrence, re-habilitation, incapacitation, and crime prevention. It also means transformed foundations of criminal jurisprudence and of our notions of freedom, democracy, and community (1999: 2).

The two promises also coincide: restorative justice entails an alternative form of justice capable of developing sustainable communities. There are several potential dangers in such seemingly innocuous promises; but they provide an opening for thinking about different images of restorative justice.

Promises of popular justice beyond law

The basic problem is of course whether we consider restorative justice as merely a series of techniques which are to be integrated into the existing systems of penal or re-educative responses to crime, or if restorative justice has to become a fully fledged alternative which should in the longer term replace maximally the existing systems (Walgrave 1997: 12). Walgrave's statement alludes to a paradox surrounding the promise of justice within restorative justice discourses: on the one hand, advocates claim legitimacy by promising 'maximal' transformations of current justice systems; on the other, they defer to closed principles of justice that – by virtue of their homologies with existing criminal justice formulations – do not permit such 'maximal' replacements. The paradox is encompassed by the ambiguity of the term 'restoration'. Restoration can connote ideas of 'replenishment', and even 'refurbishment' (thereby suggesting degrees of change); equally it often refers to 'reinstatement', 'return' (as in returning to the way things were before) when used by conservative programmes. The contradictory meanings often curtail restorative justice's promise to create *alternative* processes that revitalize democratic patterns of association. How so?

As noted, much restorative justice discourse centres on social change, and claiming to provide alternatives to professional courtroom justice (i.e., with its costly, time-consuming, inefficient, alienating, etc., processes that frequently escalate conflict). Walgrave's statement notes the prospect of 'maximally' replacing legal institutions with those that adhere to 'restoring' or 'healing' principles.[6] This maximal replacement would extend over philosophies and institutions (e.g. Nicholl 2000; Umbreit

1994). Rhetorically, at least, this commits restorative justice protagonists to fairly significant transformations of the legal *status quo*, and demands reforms that empower individuals and communities to assume responsibility for conflict (see Bush and Folger 1994). There are various conceptions of the changes to be made, including those centred on spiritual fellowship, the redressing of harm, communitarian quests for empowered moral communities, as well as political calls for viable civil societies and democracies (Braithwaite 1999). Despite their differences, all see restorative justice as an alternative vision and practice of justice – restorative justice, in other words, is concerned with changes to the communities currently associated with professional legal justice.

At the same time, however, many protagonists view restorative justice as a way of redressing wrongs, as defined from within a given *status quo*. For instance, reflecting a common enough theme in the discourse, Cooley argues that restorative justice proceeds from the basic premise that, 'the most effective response to conflict is to repair the harm done by the wrongful act' (1999: 5). Furthermore, he notes,

> Restorative justice approaches turn on the existence of a wrong. Restorative justice begins with the premise that a wrong has occurred. Restorative justice works well within the criminal justice system because the criminal law provides a ready-made list of wrongs and an easily identifiable wrongdoer … For restorative justice, because the culpability of the wrongdoer is taken for granted, determining what happened is important only to address the wrong (1999: 38).

Although raised to ponder whether restorative justice is suited to civil jurisdictions, Cooley's statement could equally be used for another purpose; namely, to signal just how much restorative justice's promise of alternative frameworks of justice is compromised by a dogged allegiance to (mostly individual) conceptions of wrong, or harm-doing. That is, if restorative justice is premised simply on repairing wrongs as enunciated from given contexts, then how can it accommodate calls for significant social change? Viewing restorative justice as a slave to contextual definitions of wrong commits adherents to the assumption that restorative justice's main purpose is to redress wrongful acts. Missing in this logic is, for instance, the possibility that certain kinds of conflict may well be needed to spearhead important social changes (e.g., to totalitarian contexts). What, asks someone like Morris (1995), about the harms that produce the sometimes tragic lives of offenders? Can a justice tied to wrongdoing adequately challenge existing criminal justice institutions, or is it merely an extension of criminal law? Many have pointed to the net-widening dangers of restorative justice (see Levrant *et al.* 1999) and community justice (Cohen 1985), but there is also the danger of a self-imposed limitation that would mark restorative justice as a mere complement to state justice, as a way to mop up its overt failures. The latter radically reverses the spirit of restorative justice's promise to provide a 'maximal' replacement to law's crime and punishment model.

In sum, responding to individual harms within communities through narrowly conceived restorative justice practices (e.g. FGC, mediation, conciliation, etc.) restricts what sorts of change is possible. For instance, can restorative justice significantly challenge the 'norms' that define 'harm' in a given context, or challenge the idea of harm when enunciated exclusively in individual/community terms? And if it cannot do this, then is restorative justice really all that different from the criminal justice systems it seeks to 'maximally' replace? In what sense does it breathe life into alternatives that promise an actively lived justice? Concentrating effort on local harms leads protagonists to develop political arenas (FGCs) to contain, isolate and thwart the very conflict that might otherwise en-courage broader political resistance to oppressive collective domination. Restorative justice may avoid the state's emphasis on legal guilt, but it still assumes that some wrong *has* occurred, that there is a responsible offender and a receiving victim/community. Adjudication is replaced with consensus-seeking restorative devices that seek peaceable agreements to narrowly defined 'problems' (e.g., individual harm – see Bazemore 1998).

In the process, many legal assumptions and objectives are replicated: placing culpability for harm on individuals (or groups); serving reasonable, law-abiding individuals in communities; seeking communal order by resolving particular conflicts (as opposed to dealing with wider power structures); focusing conflict resolution process on micro cases; etc. Restorative justice practices may differ (e.g. mediation versus adjudication), but the fundamental continuities between the assumptions of existing criminal justice and restorative justice initiatives are trans-parent. Very often, restorative justice (even if inadvertently) replicates the very thought systems it was supposed to eschew. That is why, perhaps, its promises do not so much carve out new conceptual horizons of justice but delineate what restorative justice is not (i.e., it is not repressive, not reactive, reparative, distributive, etc.). One might say that the basis for conceiving restorative justice lies in current criminal justice provisions, indicating a mutually constitutive relation between restorative justice and state law (Pavlich 1996a; Fitzpatrick 1988).

Adding to this, and following some of Foucault's precepts, various authors have argued that medieval 'law and sovereign' models of power survived in modern societies through the support of disciplinary powers designed to create normal individuals in society.[7] It may be that under postmodern conditions, law and discipline are increasingly subjected to governmental priorities, such as the rise of restorative justice's attempts to restore selves to peaceful, harmonious and secure communities (Pavlich 2000). In any case, opposing restorative justice with the law is all too often a deceptive ruse. The homologies, mutual constitutions and common assumptions shared by these are far greater than their differences. Advocates who see restorative justice as a logical complement of liberal legal assumptions readily concede the point; but that concession comes at the cost of diluting restorative justice's promise to nurture fundamental alternatives.[8] As such, one could argue that law's justice is not restorative justice's opponent. Instead, both legal and restorative justice fall on the side of liberal and/or communitarian images of justice; in turn, both could be situated against a deconstructive vision of justice as a promise that endlessly invites its own recalculation.

Derrida (1992) and Lyotard and Thébaud (1985) elaborate upon the possibility of such an open-ended notion of justice.[9] One need not agree with their approaches to underscore the basic point: it is possible to conceptualize justice beyond the common assumptions of either legal or restorative justice. Indicating what such a formulation might mean, Derrida insists that justice does not exist as such; it is never present, an absolute entity, a reality or even a definable ideal to which our institutions might strive. Justice instead implies,

> non-gathering, dissociation, heterogeneity, non-identity with itself, endless inadequation, infinite transcendence. That is why the call to justice is never, never fully answered. That is why no one can say 'I am just'. If someone tells you 'I am just,' you can be sure that he or she is wrong, because being just is not a matter of theoretical determination (Derrida 1997: 17).

If anything, justice is an incalculable, non-definable 'there being' that forever calls us from the mists of the future. Its promise is always on the way, always to come, always beyond what is presently calculated. Justice thus emerges as an incalculable promise requiring calculations in its name; law and restorative justice are two such calculations, but neither is ever entirely just, for justice always extends beyond any particular reckoning. As such, justice is – if it is anything – but a promise that calls us to calculate in its name, realizing that no formulation/practice can ever embrace it entirely.

This suggests the value of approaching restorative justice with a sense of disquiet, with vigilance to the inevitable dangers of any calculations of justice and remaining open to other possible computations. The latter implies a welcoming of otherness, of claims and formulations outside the ambit of given conceptions of the just. Derrida (1992) notes the importance of remaining forever open to the other, to the future, preventing any image of justice declaring itself as a necessary event, as unquestionably better than any other. In the illusory comforts of such decrees reside the atrocities of totalitarian social formations. So, one may insist upon a primary responsibility to what lies outside, what is other to, a given calculation of the just. This view implies a sense of justice that welcomes alterity, never portraying the present as necessary; any given present is always constituted by its connection with the 'other'. It also views justice as involving a constant reflection and recalculation of present limit formations, opening up to democratic practices that are themselves always open (Derrida 1994, 1997).

Promises of community versus hospitability

Central to Restorative Justice is recognition of the community, rather than criminal justice agencies, as the prime site of control (New Zealand, Ministry of Justice 1995: 1).

If by community one implies, as is often the case, a harmonious group, consensus, and fundamental agreement beneath phenomena of discord or war, then I do not believe in it very much and I sense in it as much threat as promise (Derrida 1995: 355).

Restorative justice's promise to develop/restore/replenish harmonious, peaceful, warm community relations is closely tied to the legitimizing rationales of the discourse. So too are its calls to return justice to the community. I have elsewhere echoed Derrida's concerns about promises that centre on the 'community' (Pavlich 2001, 1996b). Appeals to homogeneous, consensual and unified images of community harbour serious dangers marked by identity through exclusion. For instance, the assumption of harm to be restored is always issued from within a given community, and responsibility for that definition is mostly placed upon self-defined members – not to 'others' at the margins of (and so constituting) that identity formation. This argument rests on the view that a universal community, one that includes everybody, cannot be specified – quite literally, it is meaningless (Young 1990). Communities always have members and outsiders; the ability to identify a community rests on the assumption of insiders who are somehow not the same as its images of the stranger, the other, the offender, etc. (Bauman 1997).

This basic definitional requirement of community, for all its warm connotations, involves a responsibility to the like, effectively fortifying them from the unalike. The unity (*unum*), being with (*com*), the identity, the common, is made present through successful exclusions that brace limits, specify boundaries.[10] It is perhaps not surprising that community should be related to the Latin *municeps* (from whence we have 'municipal') that referred to those who were citizens of a Roman city (the *municipium*), but not permitted to be magistrates. Restorative justice's community is like the citizen, who serves the state, but not as a sanctioned official. The walled city keeps strangers outside through the coercions of law's empires, but the community operates through limits carved by its own double-edged sword, its fist in the velvet glove. This is community's secret, the secret of its subtle identification through exclusion. The dark side remains so long as a community does not face the continuous threat of a totalitarian refusal; namely, refusing to accept responsibility for the excluded others that enable specific community identities to be limited as a real, instituted present.

But let me be clear on this score. The promise of community is not necessarily totalitarian, nor something to be denounced out of hand. My point is just that a blind quest to develop communities at all costs is not an unequivocal good, devoid of severe dangers. Rather the threat of totalitarian closures around specific community identities can never be guarded against so long as one heralds, as do many advocates of restorative justice, the (peaceful, secure, harmonious, etc.) community as panacea for the ills of contemporary state law. The quest for a closed identity that defines a given community and its harms involves closures around specific limits. Furthermore, this should not deceive us: such a community identity does not stand in necessary opposition to the state and its legal justice. As Agamben insightfully notes,

> the state can recognise any claim for identity… What the state cannot tolerate in any way, however, is that the singularities form a community without affirming identity, that humans co-belong without any representable condition of belonging (1993: 86).

Agamben's point suggests an interesting alternative to the quest for a closed, identifiable community that can serve state justice, perhaps especially because it claims to oppose the state. He notes a way of calculating collective solidarity without resorting to the definitional closures of specific community images, or indeed those suggested by allied

conceptions of 'society'. To be blunt, it may be possible to calculate promises of collective solidarity via meaning horizons beyond the ambit of
state justice; perhaps by resisting the tendency to close off (unify) limits
and to relentlessly open up particular instances of community. One could,
furthermore, calculate collective solidarity differently by using the
limitations of restorative justice's community promise to indicate new
languages of open resistance to governance centred on closed (community, etc.) identifications.

Derrida alludes to the possibility in this passage:

> There is doubtless this irrepressible desire for 'community' to form
> but also for it to know its limit – and for its limit to be its *opening*.
> Once it thinks it has understood, taken in, interpreted, *kept* the text,
> then something of this latter, something in it that is altogether *other*
> escapes or resists the community, it appeals for another community,
> it does not let itself be totally interiorised in the memory of a present
> community. The experience of mourning and promise that institutes
> that community but also forbids it from collecting itself, this
> experience stores in itself the reserve of another community that will
> sign, otherwise, completely new contracts. (Derrida 1995: 355).

I interpret this statement in context thus: the very processes of
instantiating a community (such as those advocated through restorative
justice) always involve a dual mourning of past limits, and the promise of
new ones. Hence, one could read restorative justice's critique of law's
failures and the universality of restorative justice as 'mourning' for a
timeless 'justice without law' (e.g., Braithwaite 1998, 1999; Auerbach 1983).
At the same time, promises of an alternative justice, community and
democracy herald new patterns of solidarity. In the interstice between the
mourning and the promise, through which specific community identities
are pursued, lies the impossibility of ever fully closing off a given
calculation of community. The very process of identifying the limits of
community, of specifying what it is not, its promise, etc., opens the
floodgates of doubt, uncertainty – hence the ambiguity, ambivalence and
ethereality of the communities to which restorative justice is addressed.
The inability to specify 'community' is not a failure on the part of
restorative justice advocates; on the contrary, it is the source of their
deliverance. Indeed, this supposed failure brings community limits to the
fore, presenting an opening from whence new images of solidarity may be
countenanced and promised. This relentless opening up of limits
disallows the 'community' from collecting itself into a totalitarian unity, a

fortified exclusivity; it always calls for an escape to *other* calculations of collective solidarity.

Perhaps restorative justice's promise of community could be seen as succeeding through its failure to define and fortify the limits of community absolutely. But this is more a matter of circumstance than design, because the approach does not actively ward off the totalitarian dangers inherent to all discourses that champion descriptive closure, and try to eliminate indecision. One could attempt calculations of collective solidarity through images of community that endorse uncertainty, and explicitly disallow fixed closures. Corlett (1989), for example, provides a lengthy analysis of the possibilities of seeking, as its title conveys, a *Community Without Unity*. Nancy (1991), too, explores various ways of calculating community as an open (and therefore inoperative) frontier of possibility, as one always on guard against the totalitarian dangers attendant upon attempts to close off particular limits as necessary, ordered, etc. Without discounting the value of these attempts to calculate collective solidarity through open images of community, I still wonder whether another concept – less tarnished with the brushstrokes of fascist totalities – might better serve such calculations.

And what candidate concept do I have in mind? Perhaps images of collective solidarity could be rephrased through one that is usefully addressed in Derrida (e.g., 1999; 2000), namely *hospitality*. I suggest this possibility because it invites us to calculate collective solidarity without implying that the host gives up an identity, and yet emphasizes a responsibility to the other as guest, the terms of which must always be negotiated in specific contexts. Etymologically, the term derives from the Latin *hospitale* that connotes 'place where guests are received' (Ayto 1990: 287). The host is one who receives guests in such a place. In this place too, unlike community, hospitality calls for an approach to others not centred on closing off identities to include or exclude; instead it intimates a welcoming, an invitation to the other to cross the threshold of place, a *domus* perhaps. This gesture simultaneously opens the limit of that threshold to otherness and accepts an undecided negotiation of the terms of the host relationship. It extends an invitation to the stranger at various levels, from the guest in my home, to the negotiations of host countries for refugees, immigrants, and so on (Barkan 2000).

It is important to stress that as a host one does not give up having and maintaining levels of control over the place where guests are received. No doubt, to welcome is to remain open to the means by which mastery over place is negotiated, even to allow for the dissociation of mastery as presently understood. It cannot require a gathering of limits, an eternal closing of place that demands strangers to play by set rules, or risk eternal exclusion. Hospitality, instead, opens these limits without requiring the host to relinquish the 'place' of his or her identity. It requires that the host be at 'home' with the other, welcoming the other that is to come, to a future that does not settle within boundaries closed off as necessary by past incarnations of the place where guests have been received (Derrida 1999: 18–21). Indeed, for a host to give up mastery over this place is to go beyond the limits of what it is to be a host, to exceed the limited mandate of hospitality. Hospitality is limited to that degree.

This introduces a productive tension at the heart of hospitality: to limit its welcome reduces the extent of the hospitality on offer, but to allow for unlimited hospitality is to cede being a host (see Derrida 2000: 77–83). The tension is reflected, as Ayto indicates (1990: 287), in the way 'host' has always contained traces of its opposite. That is, the word host derives from the Indo-European *ghostis* (stranger), the Greek *xenos* (guest, stranger – as in 'xenophobia') and the Latin *hostis* (stranger, enemy – as in 'hostility'). The welcoming host who invites the stranger is built upon footings of the hostile warrior who sees the stranger as enemy (*hostilis*) and who has power of the place where the stranger is met (*pets, potis, potes*). Through this tension, one comes to see that:

> The *hospes* is someone who has the power to host someone, so that neither the alterity (*hostis*) of the stranger, nor the power (*potentia*) of the host is annulled by the hospitality (Caputo 1997: 110)

Hospitality is then negotiated through the undecided 'place' where the host invites, welcomes and meets the other. The meeting at that place is always undecided, and so never settled, fixed or closed in advance for all time. Calculating collective solidarity in this way is without end – hospitality's promise is never wholly present. In exploring Levinas' work, Derrida too notes that while we do calculate hospitality in finite instances,

> hospitality is infinite or it is not at all; it is granted upon the welcoming of the idea of infinity, and thus of the unconditional…
> (1999: 48)

Such tensions paralyse one from ever fully attaining hospitality, for to host without any constraint is to yield hospitality to some other arena (asceticism, sainthood?); and yet to host with constraint is to limit the welcome that might be expected from unrestrained hospitality. This inability to secure hospitality within stable limits, to fix its identity, provides a basis for understanding its promise. That is, hospitality's promise gestures beyond given claims to being hospitable. It never actually exists, is never fully there in a given instance. It is a promise that never ceases to call forth, beckon, from impossible futures, or futures that cannot be contemplated within current limits. Like justice described above, hospitality never 'is'; its presence, if that is what it is (for it may be but an elusive experience) is a promise that beckons from the murky outlines of the 'to come'. Its call is to welcome others without yielding mastery over the place where the gathering takes place, *and* without annulling, denying, the alterity that constitutes those who gather. Hospitality's open-ended negotiation allows us to calculate collective solidarity without gathering fixed unities (say community). This stance aligns rather well with restorative justice's call for a deliberative, and hence open, justice that gives expression to the spirit of another open term: democracy.

Openings ...

Not wishing to collect the above into the bindings of a fixed summary, and so reverse its dissociated spirit, I shall instead call for restorative justice to echo its early promise to gaze past what is, towards new calculations of how to be just. This opening gesture might be continuously evoked, always seeking unexpressed possibilities beyond a given present – in the process its sends forth the elusive promise of justice, and invites multiple calculations in its name. As well, restorative justice could incorporate notions of hospitality, rather than community, to direct host and other responsibilities, without assuming fixed (necessary) patterns of being. If both promises endorse a sustained uncertainty, they also intimate opening gestures that welcome what is to come, that embrace – rather than annul – other possibilities, inconceivable within present realities. Out of undecidable spaces that release 'the impossible' one might hospitably replenish restorative justice's promise to face up to, and beyond, present calculations of the just.

Notes

1. The term is frequently bandied about in various discourses, from the enunciations of criminological circles, sentencing forums and young offender regimes to the brainstorm meetings of criminal justice agencies. Many politicians, eager to be seen to be doing something about a variously defined 'crime problem', embrace restorative justice enthusiastically. In New Zealand, for example, restorative justice has since 1989 been officially approved as a favoured initial technique for governing young offenders (See Akester 2000:

25–36, and New Zealand Ministry of Justice 1995). Religious leaders, many involved in pioneering the concept, herald its spiritual promise as a humane and defensible way to heal the social harms witnessed in the course of their ecumenical duties (Consedine 1995; Van Ness *et al.* 1989). Some judges and lawyers, implicated in the shortcomings of state–legal institutions, see value in supplementing justice beyond that provided by Themis, with adversarial, congested and alienating courtrooms (e.g., British Columbia 1998; Brown and McElrea 1993). As well, community workers and communitarians see restorative justice's potential value for democratic empowerment and ownership of local conflict (Merry and Milner 1993).

2. As noted, there are state-sanctioned family group conferences (FGCs) in New Zealand (Bazemore 1998; Morris and Young 1989), and equivalents in Wagga Wagga (Australia – Braithwaite 1998), the NGO efforts in Canberra, the healing or sentencing circles of Canada, the many different 'community' or 'neighbourhood' victim–offender reconciliation efforts, and mediation programmes in the USA (Kurki 1999; Bazemore *et al.* 1997), Britain (Akester 2000) and Europe (Akester 2000; Walgrave 1998). See generally, Galaway and Hudson (1996).

3. The promise to develop alternative forms of dispute resolution (ADR) institutions was also related to the work of legal anthropologists and sociologists of law, who – in effect – questioned western legal claims to have uniquely advanced, progressive legal systems (see Starr 1989; Roberts 1979). This preliminary deconstruction of western jurisprudential hegemony opened the way for prominent debates on popular, and socialist, justice that rose to prominence in the 1970s and 1980s (see Pavlich 1996b; Marshal 1995). The complexities of these debates defies simple enunciation here, but suffice it to say that they established the key bases for attempts to recalculate justice beyond law's institutions on the strength of promises to resolve what contemporaneous criminal justice practices could not.

4. See my review in Pavlich (1996a); see also Strang and Braithwaite (2001) and Shonholtz (1988/89).

5. As well, one could note the connections between some aspects of restorative justice discourse and the abolitionist perspective in criminology, as thoughtfully enunciated by Mathiesen (1998).

6. Relating to this point, some aspects of the discourse claim that restorative justice is not so much a philosophy as a framework for specific practices (Braithwaite 1999; Cooley 1999: 19; Zehr 1992, etc.). In my view, however, it seems somewhat disingenuous to claim that restorative justice offers alternate principles and visions of justice, as well as a series of guides on how to live justly, and then claiming that this is not a philosophy or theory. Restorative justice's formulate expressly arranges signs into a discourse that give meaning to particular practices, advocating one view of the world rather than another – this constitutes, at the very least, the rudiments of a philosophy of justice.

7. See Pavlich (1996a, 1996b), Fitzpatrick (1988), Matthews (1988) and Foucault (1977).

8. Related to this point, Braithwaite (1999: 93) accepts the claim that law and restorative justice are mutually constituted, but fails to then recognize that this acceptance compromises the claims to alternation that he uses to legitimate the concept.
9. See also Pavlich (1996a: ch. 2).
10. Caputo (1997: 108) notes the relevance of the related *communio* and its intimations of defending and fortification – from *munis*, defence, fortification and *com*, common, etc.

References

Abel, R. L. (1982) *The Politics of Informal Justice, Vol. I*. New York: Academic Press.

Agamben, G. (1993) *The Coming Community*. Tr. Hardt, M. Minneapolis, MS: University of Minnesota Press.

Akester, K. (2000) *Restoring Youth Justice: New Directions in Domestic and International Law and Practice*. London: Justice.

Auerbach, J. S. (1983) *Justice without Law?* New York: Oxford University Press.

Ayto, J. (1990) *Dictionary of Word Origins*. London: Bloomsbury.

Barkan, E. (2000) *The Guilt of Nations: Restitution and Negotiating Historical Injustices*. New York: Norton.

Bauman, Z. (1997) *Postmodernity and its Discontents*. Cambridge: Polity.

Bazemore, G. (1998) 'Restorative Justice and Earned Redemption: Communities, Victims, and Offender Reintegration', *American Behavioral Scientist*, 41: 768–813.

Bazemore, S. G., Pranis, K. and Umbreit, M. Balanced and Restorative Justice Project, and United States. Office of Juvenile Justice and Delinquency Prevention (1997). *Balanced and Restorative Justice for Juveniles: A Framework for Juvenile Justice in the 21st Century*. Washington, DC: Office of Juvenile Justice and Delinquency Prevention.

Bazemore, G. and Umbreit, M. (1995) 'Rethinking the Sanctioning Function in Juvenile Court: Retributive or Restorative Responses to Youth Crime', *Crime and Delinquency*, 41: 296–316.

Bazemore, S. G., Walgrave, L. and International Network for Research on Restorative Justice for Juveniles (1999) *Restorative Juvenile Justice: Repairing the Harm of Youth Crime*. Monsey, NY: Criminal Justice Press, Willow Tree Press.

Braithwaite, J. (1989) *Crime, Shame and Reintegration*. Cambridge: Cambridge University Press.

Braithwaite, J. (1998) 'Restorative Justice' in *The Handbook of Crime and Punishment* M. Tonry (ed.). New York: Oxford University Press.

Braithwaite, J. (1999) 'Restorative Justice: Assessing Optimistic and Pessimistic Accounts', *Crime and Justice*, 25: 1–127.

British Columbia. Ministry of Attorney General. (1998). *A Restorative Justice Framework: British Columbia Justice Reform*. Victoria, BC: British Columbia Ministry of Attorney General.

Brown, B. J., McElrea, F. W. M. and Legal Research Foundation (University of Auckland) (1993) *The Youth Court in New Zealand: A New Model of Justice: Four Papers*. Auckland, NZ: Legal Research Foundation.

Bush, R. and Folger, J. (1994) *The Promise of Mediation: Responding to Conflict Through Empowerment*. San Francisco, CA: Jossey-Bass.

Caputo, J. D. (1997) *Deconstruction in a Nutshell: A Conversation with Jacques Derrida*. New York: Fordham University Press.

Cohen, S. (1985) *Visions of Social Control: Crime, Punishment, and Classification*. Oxford: Polity.

Consedine, J. (1995) *Restorative Justice: Healing the Effects of Crime*. Lyttelton, NZ: Ploughshares Publications.

Cooley, D. and Law Commission of Canada (1999) *From Restorative Justice to Transformative Justice: Discussion Paper*. Ottawa: Law Commission of Canada.

Corlett, W. (1989) *Community without Unity: A Politics of Derridian Extravagance*. Durham, NC: Duke University Press.

Cragg, W. (1992) *The Practice of Punishment: Towards a Theory of Restorative Justice*. London: Routledge.

Critchley, S. (1992) *The Ethics of Deconstruction: Derrida and Levinas*. Oxford, UK: Blackwell.

Cullen, F. T. and Gilbert, K. E. (1982) *Reaffirming Rehabilitation*. Cincinnati, OH: Anderson.

Derrida, J. (1976) *Of Grammatology*. Baltimore, MD: Johns Hopkins University Press.

Derrida, J. (1992) 'The Force of Law: The Mystical Foundation of Authority' in *Deconstruction and the Possibility of Justice* D. Cornell, M. Rosenfeld, D. Carlson and B. N. Carlson (eds). New York: Routledge.

Derrida, J. (1994) *Specters of Marx: The State of the Debt, the Work of Mourning, and the New International*. New York: Routledge.

Derrida, J. (1995) *Points …: Interviews, 1974–1994*. Stanford, CA: Stanford University Press.

Derrida, J. (1997) 'Roundtable' in *Deconstruction in a Nutshell: a Conversation with Jacques Derrida* J. D. Caputo (ed.). New York: Fordham University Press.

Derrida, J. (1999) *Adieu to Emmanuel Levinas*. Stanford, CA: Stanford University Press.

Derrida, J. (2000) *Of Hospitality: Anne Dufourmantalle invites Jacques Derrida to Respond*. Stanford, CA: Stanford University Press.

Dignan, J. and Cavadino, M. (1996) 'Towards a Framework for Conceptualising and Evaluating Models of Criminal Justice from a Victim's Perspective', *International Review of Victimology*, 4: 153–82.

DiJulio Jr, John. J. (1998) 'Inner-City Crime: What the Federal Government Should Do' in *The Essential Communitarian Reader* A. Etzioni (ed.). Lanham, MD: Rowman and Littlefield.

Etzioni, A. (1998). 'The Essential Communitarian Reader.' Pp. xxxix, 323. Lanham, MD: Rowman and Littlefield.

Fitzpatrick, P. (1988) 'The Rise and Rise of Informal Justice.' Pp. 214 in *Informal Justice?*, R. Matthews (ed.). London, Newbury Park: Sage.

Foucault, M. (1977) *Discipline and Punish: The Birth of the Prison*. New York: Pantheon Books.

Galaway, B. and Hudson, J. (1996) *Restorative Justice: International Perspectives*. Monsey, NY: Criminal Justice Press.

Kurki, L. (1999) *Incorporating Restorative and Community Justice into American Sentencing and Corrections*. Washington, DC: US Department of Justice Office of Justice Programs National Institute of Justice.

Levrant, S., Cullen, F. T., Fulton, B., and Wozniak, J. F. (1999) 'Reconsidering Restorative Justice: The Corruption of Benevolence Revisited?', *Crime and Delinquency*, 45: 3–27.

Lyotard, J. F. and Thébaud, J.-L. (1985) *Just Gaming*. Minneapolis, MS: University of Minnesota Press.

Marshall, T. F. (1995) 'Restorative Justice on Trial in Britain', *Mediation Quarterly*, 12: 217–231.

Mathiesen, T. (1998) 'Towards the 21st Century – Abolition, an Impossible Dream?', *Humanity and Society*, 22: 4–22.

Matthews, R. (1988) 'Informal Justice?' in *Sage Contemporary Criminology*. London, Newbury Park: Sage.

McCold, P. (1998a) *Restorative Justice: An Annotated Bibliography*. New York: Criminal Justice Press.

McCold, P. (1998b) 'Restorative Justice: Variations on a Theme' in *Restorative Justice for Juveniles: Potentialities, Risks, and Problems for Research* L. Walgrave (ed.). Leuven: Leuven University Press.

Merry, S. E. and Milner, N. A. (1993) *The Possibility of Popular Justice: A Case Study of Community Mediation in the United States*. Ann Arbor, MI: University of Michigan Press.

Morris, A. and Young, W. (1987) *Juvenile Justice in New Zealand: Policy and Practice*. Wellington, NZ: Institute of Criminology Victoria University of Wellington.

Morris, R. (1995) 'Not Enough!', *Mediation Quarterly*, 12: 285–291.

Morris, R. (2000) *Stories of Transformative Justice*. Toronto: Canadian Scholars' Press.

Nancy, J.-L. (1991) *The Inoperative Community*. Minneapolis, MN: University of Minnesota Press.

New Zealand. Ministry of Justice (1995) *Restorative Justice: A Discussion Paper*. Wellington, NZ: Ministry of Justice.

Nicholl, C. G. (2000) *Toolbox for Implementing Restorative Justice and Advancing Community Policing: A Guidebook Prepared for the Office of Community Oriented Policing Services, U.S. Department of Justice*. Washington, D.C. (1100 Vermont Avenue, NW, Washington 20530): United States Department of Justice, Office of Community Oriented Policing Services and National Victim Center (US).

Pavlich, G. (1996a) *Justice Fragmented: Mediating Community Disputes under Postmodern Conditions*. London: Routledge.

Pavlich, G. (1996b) 'The Power of Community Mediation: Government and Formation of Self', *Law and Society Review*, 30: 101–127.

Pavlich, G. (2000) *Critique and Radical Discourses on Crime*. Aldershot: Ashgate/ Dartmouth.

Pavlich, G. (2001) 'The Force of Community' in *Restorative Justice and Civil Society* H. Strang and J. Braithwaite (eds). Cambridge: Cambridge University Press.

Pavlich, G. and Ratner, R. S. (1996) 'Justice and the Postmodern' in *Critical Theory, Poststructuralism and the Scoial Context* M. Peters, J. Marshall and S. Webster (eds). Palmerston North: Dunmore Press.

Pfohl, S. J. (1994) *Images of Deviance and Social Control: A Sociological History*. New York: McGraw-Hill.

Roberts, S. (1979) *Order and Dispute: An Introduction to Legal Anthropology*. New York: St. Martin's Press.

Shonholtz, R. (1988/89) 'Community as Peacemaker: Making Neighborhood Justice Work', *Current Municipal Problems*, 15: 291–330.

Starr, J. and Fishburne Collier, J. (1989) *History and Power in the Study of Law: New Directions in Legal Anthropology*. Ithaca, NY: Cornell University Press.

Strang, H. and Braithwaite, J. (eds) (2001) *Restorative Justice and Civil Society*. Cambridge: Cambridge University Press.

Sullivan, D. and Tifft, L. (1998) 'The Transformative and Economic Dimensions of Restorative Justice', *Humanity and Society*, 22: 38–54.

Umbreit, M., Coates, R. B. and Kalanj, B. (1994) *Victim Meets Offender: The Impact of Restorative Justice and Mediation*. Monsey, NY: Criminal Justice Press.

Umbreit, M. S. (1995) 'The Development and Impact of Victim–Offender Mediation in the United States', *Mediation Quarterly*, 12: 263–76.

Van Ness, D. W., Crawford, T. and Justice Fellowship (1989) *Restorative Justice*. Washington: Justice Fellowship.

Walgrave, L. (1998) 'Restorative Justice for Juveniles: Potentialities, Risks, and Problems for Research' in *Samenleving, Criminaliteit and Strafrechtspleging, 12*. Leuven: Leuven University Press.

Young, I. M. (1990) 'The Ideal of Community and the Politics of Difference' in *Feminism/Postmodernism* L. J. Nicholson (ed.). New York: Routledge.

Zehr, H. (1990) *Changing Lenses: A New Focus for Crime and Justice*. Scottdale, PA: Herald Press.

Zehr, H. (1995) 'Justice Paradigm Shift? Values and Visions in the Reform Process', *Mediation Quarterly*, 12: 207–216.

Chapter 7

Restorative justice theory validation

Paul McCold and Ted Wachtel

The evolution of restorative justice has been a process of discovery rather than invention (McCold 2000). Practice continues to lead theory as a physics of social transformation reveals itself. The near simultaneous discovery of restorative processes in far-flung corners of the globe from wholly independent sources supports this view (see McCold 1996; Weitekamp 1999). For example, family group conferences (FGCs) in New Zealand and sentencing circles in Canada arose during the late 1980s, both based on indigenous people's needs and practices, after the previous decade's development of victim–offender mediation (VOM) and victim–offender reconciliation programs (VORP). But if these emerging restorative justice practices are to improve and if others are to learn from their discovery, then the social sciences can play an important role by providing description, theory and evaluation.

Assertions about what constitutes good practice should be tested before they are proposed as standards or imposed in legislation. Without the guidance of research, a mythology develops around the use of restorative practices based merely on personal or political preferences. For example, police have been prohibited from conducting restorative conferences in some jurisdictions despite favourable evaluation results (Moore 1995). Even while positive empirical evidence continues to accumulate world-wide in support of police-facilitated conferences (McCold 1999), in New South Wales, Australia, for example, unproven generalizations and turf issues have precluded police from doing conferencing as part of their job. The scientific method, not mythology and politics, should guide standards of good practice.

The scientific method should also play a critical role in the development of a valid restorative justice theory. Social science is in the business of proposing and testing theoretical concepts to explain and predict social processes (Babbie 1995). We have proposed a set of concepts which can provide the basis for a generalizable theory of restorative justice (McCold 2000; Wachtel and McCold 2000). If these proposed concepts are to be more than mere teaching tools, they must be tested for validity within a social science framework. As a beginning to such a process, this paper attempts to test the validity of one of the major hypotheses derived from this theory of restorative justice using the currently available research.

Concepts are the building blocks of theory. Theory is the structure that explains the relationship among the concepts. Propositions are conclusions drawn about the relationships among concepts. Finally, hypotheses are specific predictions about empirical reality, derived from the propositions (Babbie 1995: 49). If these predictions are not supported by objective measurements, the theory is in doubt. Theories which are not falsifiable, that is, which are incapable of being tested and potentially shown to be untrue, are not scientific and are merely conjecture or statements of belief (Babbie 1995: 26).

There have been a number of attempts to define the key restorative justice concepts necessary for theory construction, particularly the term 'restorative justice' itself, although there is no clear consensus yet (McCold 1998a). We have encouraged the adoption of Marshall's (1996) definition which requires that the stakeholders, those directly affected by a crime, be involved in a process where they determine the outcome in order for that process to be called 'restorative' (McCold 1998b, Declaration of Leuven 1998). We also agree with Bazemore and Walgrave (1999: 48) that the goal of the reparation of harm is a necessary element in the definition of restorative justice.

Simply put, restorative justice is a process involving the direct stakeholders in determining how best to repair the harm done by offending behaviour. This definition raises as many issues as it resolves because it introduces the undefined concepts of 'direct stakeholders', 'determine', 'repair the harm', and 'offending behaviour'. The next section of this chapter presents one theoretical explanation of the meaning of and relationship between these concepts.

A theory of restorative justice

We propose a theory of restorative justice that has three distinct but connected causal structures: the Social Discipline Window (Wachtel 2000a, 2000b; Wachtel and McCold 2000), Stakeholder Needs (McCold 1996, 2000) and Restorative Practices Typology (McCold 2000).

Social discipline window

Every part of society faces choices in deciding how to maintain social discipline, whether it be parents raising children, teachers in a classroom, employers supervising employees, or justice systems responding to criminal offences. Until recently, most Western societies seem to assume that punishment is the only effective way to discipline those who misbehave. Most people seem to think that if those in authority do not punish, that is, if they do not inflict at least some pain or suffering on those who violate society's rules, then they are by definition being permissive and evading their social responsibilities.

But one can identify other social discipline choices when one looks at the interplay of two continuums, control and support, which comprise the Social Discipline Window. 'Control' is defined as the act of exercising restraint or directing influence over others (Black 1990: 329). Clear limit-setting and diligent enforcement of behavioural standards characterize high social control. Vague or weak behavioural standards and lax or non-existent efforts to regulate behaviour characterize low social control. 'Support' is defined as the provision of services intended to nurture the individual (Black 1990: 1070). Active provision of services and assistance and concern for individual well-being characterize high support. Lack of encouragement and minimal provision for physical and emotional needs characterize low support.

For simplicity, these continuums are limited to the extremes of 'high' or 'low.' In Figure 7.1, a high or low level of control is combined with a high or low level of support to reveal four general approaches to social discipline and the regulation of behaviour. We call these four approaches or policy models *punitive, permissive, neglectful* and *restorative.*

The punitive approach (upper left of Figure 7.1) is comprised of high degrees of control but little individual support or nurture. This approach has also been called authoritarian, stigmatizing or retributive. The permissive approach (lower right of Figure 7.1) is comprised of low control and high support, a scarcity of limit-setting and an abundance of nurturing. In criminal justice policy, this approach to social discipline has also been called therapeutic or rehabilitative and has a tendency to protect or shield people from the natural and logical consequences of wrongdoing. An absence of both limit-setting and nurturing is neglectful (lower left of Figure 7.1), characterized by indifference or passivity in response to misbehaviour or wrongdoing.

The fourth possibility is restorative (upper right of Figure 7.1). Building on the aforementioned definition, we describe restorative justice as a process where those primarily affected by an incident of wrongdoing come together to share their feelings, describe how they were affected and develop a plan to repair the harm done or prevent a reoccurrence (McCold 1996, 2000). The essence of the restorative approach is a collaborative problem-solving approach to social discipline intended to reintegrate individuals and repair the affected communities. Restorative responses to wrongdoing simultaneously exercise high control and high support, confronting and disapproving of wrongdoing while supporting and acknowledging the intrinsic worth of the wrongdoer.

Four key words serve as a shorthand method to help distinguish the four approaches contained in the social discipline window: NOT, FOR, TO and WITH. If one were to be neglectful, one would NOT do anything in response to offending behaviour. If permissive, one would do everything FOR the offender and ask little in return, making excuses for the

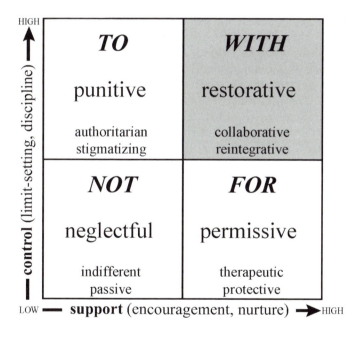

Figure 7.1. Social Discipline Window

wrongdoing. If punitive, one would respond by doing things TO the offender, admonishing and punishing. Responding in a restorative manner requires that one work WITH the offender and engage that person directly in the process of accountability. A critical element of this restorative approach is that, whenever possible, WITH implies including all of the stakeholders in the process – victims, family, friends and community – anyone who has been affected by the offender's behaviour.

Stakeholder needs

The second causal structure of our theory of restorative justice, Stakeholder Needs, relates the injuries caused by offending behaviour to the specific social responsibilities required to meet those needs. This causal structure distinguishes the interests of the direct stakeholders, those most affected by a specific offence, from those indirectly affected as shown in Figure 7.2.

The principals, victims and offenders, are the most directly affected, while their family and friends who comprise their 'community of care' are also directly affected. Then there are indirect stakeholders who live nearby or who live in the wider society. The injuries, needs and obligations of direct stakeholders are different than those of the indirect stakeholders.

All of the direct stakeholders need an opportunity to express their feelings and have a say in how to repair the harm. Victims are injured by the loss of control they experience as a result of the offence. Victims need to regain a sense of personal power (Zehr 1990). This empowerment is what transforms victims into survivors. Offenders damage their relationships with their own community of care by betraying trust. To regain that trust, they need to be empowered to take responsibility for their wrongdoing (Fatic 1995). The community of care, those who have an emotional connection with a victim or offender (Wachtel 2000a), such as parents, spouses, other family members, teachers, employers and others, meet their individual needs by ensuring that something be done about the wrong, that the wrongfulness be acknowledged, that constructive steps are being taken to prevent further offending, and that victims and offenders be reintegrated into their communities (McCold 2000).

The indirect stakeholders, those who not are emotionally connected to the principals but who live nearby or are members or officials of government, religious, social or business organizations whose area of responsibility includes the place or people affected by the incident, must not steal the conflict by usurping the responsibilities of those directly affected (Christie 1977). These indirect stakeholders have a responsibility to support and facilitate processes in which the direct stakeholders determine for themselves the outcome of the case (McCold 1996). Such

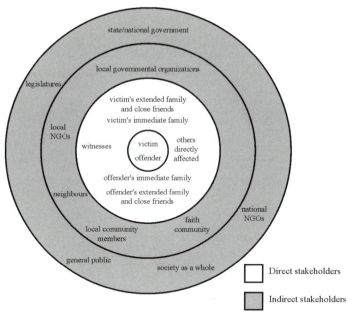

Figure 7.2. Stakeholders in restorative justice

processes will reintegrate both victim and offenders, build problem-solving communities and strengthen civil society (Braithwaite 1999, Braithwaite and Strang 2000).

Restorative Practices Typology

The direct stakeholders in restorative justice are victims, offenders and their communities of care. The degree to which all three are involved in meaningful emotional exchange and decision-making is the degree to which any form of social discipline can be termed fully 'restorative'. These three sets of direct stakeholders are represented by the two innermost circles in Figure 7.3. The very process of interacting is critical to meeting stakeholders' emotional needs. The emotional exchange necessary for meeting the needs of all those directly affected cannot occur with only one set of stakeholders participating (McCold 2000). The most restorative processes involve the active participation of all three sets of direct stakeholders. Where social discipline approaches deal with only one group of direct stakeholder needs without involvement of the other direct stakeholders, such as with crime compensation for victims, the process is 'partly restorative'. Where a process like victim–offender mediation includes the principal stakeholders but excludes their communities of care, the process is 'mostly restorative'. Only when all three sets of direct stakeholders are involved, such as in conferences or circles, is a process 'fully restorative'.

The Social Discipline Window (Wachtel and McCold 2000) structure assumes that the transformation of conflict into cooperation requires the involvement of offenders and others. The Stakeholder Needs structure assumes that restorative transformation is caused by empowering those directly affected to freely express their feelings and influence the outcome (McCold 2000, Wachtel 2000a). The Restorative Practices Typology assumes that participation of all direct stakeholders is required to address all stakeholders' needs (McCold 2000).

Testing theory validity

It is one thing to propose a theory, but quite another to validate it. Those who propose a theory should demonstrate at least some empirical support for it. The proposed theory of restorative justice easily generates a number of hypotheses capable of being tested and falsified. Because the scientific method does not support or prove theories, validation is achieved by a process of elimination – trying to disprove or falsify those hypotheses which underlie the theory.

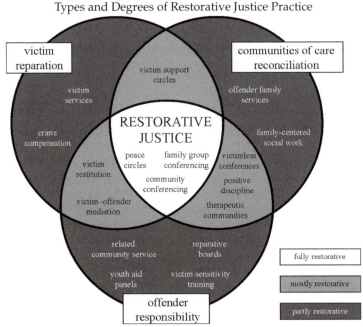

Types and Degrees of Restorative Justice Practice

Figure 7.3. Restorative practices typology

We have identified four major theoretical hypotheses derived from the definitional and conceptual structures proposed. They are:

- the 'transformation' hypothesis: testing restorative outcomes;

- the 'collaboration' hypothesis: testing the Social Discipline Window;

- the 'empowerment' hypothesis: testing Stakeholder Needs;

- the 'involvement' hypothesis: testing the Restorative Practices Typology.

Defining restorative justice as a process to address and repair the injuries caused by a given crime includes a supposition that restorative outcomes have a transformative dimension: transforming victims into survivors, conflict into cooperation, shame into pride, and individuals into community (Nathanson 1992, 1998; Tomkins 1995; Moore 1996; Braithwaite 1999). In order to validate the transformation hypothesis, there need to be better ways to assess the outcomes from restorative processes. This will constitute a major part of the work of restorative justice research over the next decade.

Explicit in the Social Discipline Window is a diagonal dimension running from neglect to restorative which we call the 'collaboration' dimension. Social discipline which is done 'to' offenders, and approaches which are done 'for' offenders are both fundamentally disrespectful of the individual (Nelsen 1996). Responses to misbehaviour which are simultaneously high on social control and high on social support require the active collaboration of the offender, since healing in relationships and new learning are voluntary and cooperative processes (Claassen 1995). Testing the validity of the collaboration hypothesis would be relatively easy, but may be unnecessary. There is already a wealth of empirical support which says that engaging stakeholders in determining solutions produces better outcomes than non-restorative approaches (Wachtel and McCold 2000).

Implicit in the Stakeholder Needs structure is the dimension of 'empowerment'. Those directly affected by harmful behaviour must be part of the solution to regain their sense of autonomy. Outcomes fashioned by the direct stakeholders commit them to the agreement and may be the essential element in the high compliance rates for offenders reported by restorative justice programmes. Further testing of the empowerment hypotheses is still necessary.

Finally, the Restorative Practices Typology asserts that outcomes from partly, mostly and fully restorative practices should be progressively better, on average, in an ascending order, as they become more restorative, and that all restorative practices should produce better outcomes than non-restorative practices. This ordinal assumption about restorative practices assumes the social dimension which we call 'involvement'. The involvement hypothesis is that practices which involve more sets of stakeholders will produce outcomes which are more restorative, more empowering, and more transformative. The next section of this paper provides one test of the validity of this theoretical structure.

A partial test of the involvement hypothesis

Empirical social science is a messy business because measuring human behaviour is challenging and complex. Variation in the subject of study is necessary to compare differences and is the essence of quantitative statistics. Yet variations within and between programme types often make results seem less than dramatic, if not downright ambiguous. No programmes implement perfect model protocols and any single programme's outcomes can be affected by a host of factors. In criminal justice research these factors include differences like seriousness of cases, age of offenders, involvement of the victim or unusual individuals.

The difficulty in comparing restorative practices is that they are used in a wide variety of settings with a wide variety of offences. For example, how can mediation of violent adult crimes be compared with conferencing of truancy offences in a middle school? Are they not like apples and oranges, not comparable? In truth, each restorative programme and facilitated process and offender and victim is unique. Nonetheless, only by comparison can it be learned what practices work best under what circumstances.

We propose a simple methodology which capitalizes on the differences in restorative programmes to make inferential conclusions. While one cannot legitimately contrast a violent adult mediation with a truancy conference, one can discern patterns by comparing ten of each type of case. Also, ten mediations will be more representative of this restorative practice than any single case. Assuming restorative programmes are relatively internally consistent with respect to the type of case and kind of practice, programme averages are good measures of that category of practice. Ten oranges are more representative of oranges than one orange is likely to be. Of course, 100 oranges are even more representative and 1,000 even more so. The larger the sample size the more accurately any single average is a measure of oranges or apples.

Since programme evaluations report averages across case types, these aggregate data are readily available from the published literature. Each programme represents an independent sample of some larger population.

By comparing independent sample means, the law of averages says the mean of means will more precisely reflect the true mean than any single average. Thus, comparing averages of ten samples of apples with ten samples of oranges will be a powerful test of the differences between them.

If the Restorative Practices Typology is correct, comparing the means on the same set of measures across different programmes should reveal the ordinal relationships predicted by the involvement hypothesis. The more samples of each category of programme, the more precisely the mean of means represents the 'true' value. The more means available – the more samples of a kind of programme – the more readily any patterns of difference will emerge. By using aggregate measures, one does not require hundreds of programme averages to be statistically rigorous.

The validity of the Restorative Practices Typology rests upon the ordinal relationships predicted, that is, the greater the number of the three direct stakeholder groups involved in a justice process, the more restorative the outcome. A full empirical test would include samples from all four categories of practice in the Typology;

(1) non-restorative (existing system),

(2) involving one set of direct stakeholders,

(3) involving two sets of direct stakeholders, and

(4) involving all three sets of direct stakeholders.

The null hypothesis is that the 'restorativeness' of justice programmes varies as much within categories of practice as between categories of practice. If that is so, then the typology and theory are not supported.

We need to operationalize the dependent variable by defining the restorative outcome measures for this hypothesis test. A set of standard questions have been developing as commonly-used restorative programme measures. Chief among these are those that ask the victim and the offender if they were satisfied by the way the case was handled and whether they thought the process was fair. Good programme evaluations also include non-restorative comparison groups who are asked these same questions. For purposes of this hypothesis test, we define 'restorativeness' as the percentage of victims who report being satisfied by the process and the percentage of offenders who report they were treated fairly.

In this chapter the test is limited, because data is available for only three of the four possible categories of practice: non-restorative programmes, programmes which involve two sets of stakeholders, and programmes which involve all three sets of stakeholders. Nonetheless this should still provide a sufficient test of theory validity.

Subjects

Data were collected from published programme evaluation studies (see Tables 7.1–4) where victims and offenders were surveyed regarding their overall satisfaction and sense of fairness (see programme participant samples, Table 7.5). Comparison group surveys of victims and offenders from studies reporting these results constitute the non-restorative programmes. A large representative survey of the general public is also included in the charts to provide a comparative base-line.

Only those participant surveys with sample sizes of more than five were included in the analysis. Comparison group survey results from the Indianapolis programme were excluded because nearly one third of this group were referred to VOM programmes and were thus received a mixture of partly and non-restorative treatments.

Measures of restorativeness

Measures of restorativeness were established according to

(1) the percentage of victims and offenders expressing satisfaction with the way their case was handled,

(2) the percentage of victims and offenders rating the processing of their case as fair, and

(3) the balance of ratings between victims and their offenders.

Programme evaluations using forced choice responses (i.e., without a middle category) were collapsed into satisfied–not satisfied and fair–not fair. For evaluations using 5- or 7-point scales, satisfaction or fairness was assumed only for scores above the midpoint (e.g., 4–5 or 5–7).

Hypothesis: Rating$_{CONFERENCE}$ > Rating$_{VOM}$ > Rating$_{NOT}$
On average, participants will rate fully restorative programmes (conferences) as more satisfying and fair than mostly restorative programmes (victim–offender mediation) and both as more satisfying and fair than non-restorative (traditional justice system).

Null hypotheses: Rating$_{CONFERENCE}$ = Rating$_{VOM}$ = Rating$_{NOT}$
(1) There are no differences in victim satisfaction or offender sense of fairness between categories of practice; or the differences within categories are greater than between categories of practice.

(2) The differences between categories of practice are ordered differently than predicted.

Table 7.1. Victim satisfaction

Fully restorative practices				
	No. of victims			
Programme	% satisfied	total	satisfied	not satisfied
RISE p.property CGC	70%	40	28	12
RISE violent CGC	74%	26	19	7
Ipswich FGC	90%	40	36	4
Indianapolis CGC	92%	42	39	3
Logan FGC	94%	42	40	3
RCMP CGC	94%	62	58	4
Bethlehem property CGC	95%	40	38	2
Minnesota 12-site CGC	95%	166	158	8
Virginia 4-site CGC	100%	8	8	0
Bethlehem violent CGC	100%	12	12	0
Wagga Wagga CGC	100%	6	6	0
Weighted	91,3%	484	442	42
Unweighted	91,3%			

Mostly restorative practices				
	No. of victims			
Programme	% satisfied	total	satisfied	not satisfied
Albuquerque VOM	57%	40	23	17
Langley VOM	58%	38	22	16
Orange VOM	59%	27	16	11
England 2-site VOM	62%	19	12	7
Santa Clara VOM	77%	39	30	9
Winnipeg VOM	82%	88	72	16
Oakland VOM	83%	42	35	7
Ottawa VOM	85%	41	35	6
Minneapolis VOM	85%	80	68	12
Santa Barbara VOM	86%	21	18	3
Calgary VOM	86%	7	6	1
Austin VOM	88%	38	33	5
Los Angeles VOM	98%	133	130	3
Weighted	81,6%	613	500	113
Unweighted	77,4%			

Non-restorative practices				
	No. of victims			
Programme	% satisfied	total	satisfied	not satisfied
Winnipeg referred	41%	74	30	44
Albuquerque referred	42%	33	14	19
Albuquerque nonreferred	46%	25	12	14
RISE p.property nonreferred	47%	62	29	33
Ottawa referred	52%	21	11	10
Oakland nonreferred	56%	10	6	4
Langley referred	57%	37	21	16
RISE violent nonreferred	58%	27	16	11
Minneapolis nonreferred	61%	72	44	28
Oakland referred	63%	19	12	7
Minneapolis referred	64%	51	33	18
Bethlehem viol. referred	72%	18	13	5
Bethlehem prop. referred	75%	12	9	3
Bethlehem viol. nonreferred	77%	14	11	3
Bethlehem prop. nonreferred	80%	20	16	4
Weighted	55,6%	495	275	220
Unweighted	59,4%			
U.S. 9-state Victims	48%	483	232	251
U.S. 9-state Public	16%	4015	642	3373

Table 7.2. Victim fairness

Fully restorative practices

Programme	No. of victims			
	% fair	total	fair	not fair
RISE violent CGC	77%	31	24	7
Bethlehem violent CGC	92%	12	11	1
Logan FGC	94%	42	39	3
Ipswich FGC	94%	40	37	2
RCMP CGC	97%	62	60	2
RISE p.property CGC	97%	51	50	1
Bethlehem property CGC	98%	40	39	1
Virginia 4-site CGC	100%	8	8	0
Minnesota 12-site CGC	100%	166	166	0
Weighted	96,1%	452	434	18
Unweighted	94,2%			

Mostly restorative practices

Programme	No. of victims			
	% fair	total	fair	not fair
Calgary VOM	43%	7	3	4
England 2-site VOM	59%	19	11	8
Langley VOM	63%	38	24	14
Orange VOM	68%	27	18	9
Albuquerque VOM	72%	40	29	11
Oakland VOM	78%	42	33	9
Sonoma VOM	78%	9	7	2
Winnipeg VOM	86%	88	76	12
Ottawa VOM	88%	41	36	5
Austin VOM	88%	38	33	5
Minneapolis VOM	89%	80	71	9
Santa Babara VOM	90%	21	19	2
Los Angeles VOM	100%	133	133	0
Weighted	84,7%	583	494	89
Unweighted	77,2%			

Non-restorative practices

Programme	No. of victims			
	% fair	total	fair	not fair
Winnipeg referred	40%	74	29	45
Ottawa referred	42%	21	9	12
Langley referred	49%	37	18	19
Oakland referred	50%	19	10	10
Albuquerque referred	52%	33	17	16
Minneapolis referred	54%	51	28	23
Oakland nonreferred	56%	10	6	4
Albuquerque nonreferred	63%	25	16	9
Minneapolis nonreferred	63%	72	45	27
Bethlehem viol. nonreferred	71%	14	10	4
Bethlehem viol. referred	75%	16	12	4
Bethlehem prop. nonreferred	84%	20	17	3
Bethlehem prop. referred	90%	12	11	1
Weighted	56,2%	406	228	178
Unweighted	60,7%			
U.S. 9-state Victims	37%	483	179	304

Table 7.3. Offender satisfaction

Fully restorative practices					Mostly restorative practices					Non-restorative practices				
	No. of offenders					No. of offenders					No. of offenders			
Programme	% satisfied	total	satisfied	not satisfied	Programme	% satisfied	total	satisfied	not satisfied	Programme	% satisfied	total	satisfied	not satisfied
RCMP CGC	85%	54	46	8	Calgary VOM	29%	7	2	5	Ottawa referred	42%	12	5	7
Virginia 4-site CGC	93%	15	14	1	Ottawa VOM	69%	16	11	5	Winnipeg referred	48%	67	32	35
Indianapolis CGC	93%	52	48	4	Orange VOM	70%	20	14	6	Langley referred	60%	42	25	17
Bethlehem violent CGC	94%	17	16	1	Winnipeg VOM	74%	96	71	25	Albuquerque nonreferred	71%	28	20	8
Minnesota 12-site CGC	95%	159	151	8	Santa Babara VOM	76%	21	16	5	Oakland referred	74%	19	14	5
Bethlehem property CGC	98%	50	49	1	England 2-site VOM	79%	16	13	3	Minneapolis nonreferred	77%	71	55	16
Ipswich FGC	100%	50	50	0	Langley VOM	83%	37	31	6	Minneapolis referred	80%	40	32	8
Logan FGC	100%	53	53	0	Albuquerque VOM	85%	41	35	6	Albuquerque referred	83%	36	30	6
					Oakland VOM	85%	36	31	5	Bethlehem viol. referred	85%	13	11	2
					Minneapolis VOM	85%	59	50	9	Bethlehem prop. referred	85%	20	17	3
					Austin VOM	92%	46	42	4	Bethlehem viol. nonreferred	88%	16	14	2
					Santa Clara VOM	95%	39	37	2	Oakland nonreferred	100%	12	12	0
					Los Angeles VOM	97%	138	134	4	Bethlehem prop. nonreferred	100%	30	30	0
Weighted	95,0%	450	427	23	Weighted	85,0%	572	486	86	Weighted	73,0%	406	297	109
Unweighted	94,8%				Unweighted	78,4%				Unweighted	76,2%			

Table 7.4. Offender fairness

Fully restorative practices

Programme	% fair	total	fair	not fair
RCMP CGC	77%	54	42	12
RISE p.property CGC	86%	64	55	9
Bethlehem violent CGC	88%	17	15	2
RISE violent CGC	89%	35	31	4
RISE retail CGC	94%	47	44	3
RISE Drink Driving CGC	95%	376	358	18
Minnesota 12-site CGC	98%	159	156	3
Logan FGC	100%	53	53	0
Ipswich FGC	100%	50	50	0
Bethlehem property CGC	100%	50	50	0
Virginia 4-site CGC	100%	15	15	0
Weighted	94,4%	920	868	52
Unweighted	93,3%			

Mostly restorative practices

Programme	% fair	total	fair	not fair
Orange VOM	52%	20	10	10
Calgary VOM	57%	7	4	3
Ottawa VOM	69%	16	11	5
Santa Babara VOM	76%	21	16	5
Sonoma VOM	80%	13	10	3
Langley VOM	81%	37	30	7
Albuquerque VOM	82%	41	34	7
Winnipeg VOM	83%	96	80	16
England 2-site VOM	89%	16	14	2
Minneapolis VOM	90%	59	53	6
Austin VOM	91%	46	42	4
Oakland VOM	94%	36	34	2
Los Angeles VOM	98%	138	135	3
Weighted	86,7%	546	473	73
Unweighted	80,1%			

Non-restorative practices

Programme	% fair	total	fair	not fair
Winnipeg referred	47%	67	31	36
Ottawa referred	47%	12	6	6
Langley referred	69%	42	29	13
Albuquerque nonreferred	71%	28	20	8
Oakland referred	74%	19	14	5
Minneapolis nonreferred	77%	71	55	16
Bethlehem prop. referred	80%	20	16	4
RISE reatil nonreferred	81%	41	33	8
RISE Drink Driving nonreferred	81%	349	282	67
Minneapolis referred	81%	40	32	8
Bethlehem viol. nonreferred	81%	16	13	3
Bethlehem viol. referred	85%	13	11	2
RISE violent nonreferred	85%	33	28	5
Albuquerque referred	86%	36	31	5
RISE p.property nonreferred	92%	72	66	6
Bethlehem prop. nonreferred	97%	30	29	1
Oakland nonreferred	100%	12	12	0
Weighted	78,6%	901	708	193
Unweighted	78,4%			

Statistical test

Kruskal–Wallis one-way analysis of variance, chi-square @ $p < .05$, two-tailed (groupings). Because dichotomous variables follow a binomial distribution, the assumption of equal subgroup variances (homoscedasticity) for the normal analysis of variance tests would be violated. Kruskal-Wallis is a distribution-free test of whether several independent samples come from the same population and requires only that the underlying variable have a continuous distribution with at least an ordinal level of measurement. The Kruskal-Wallis test replaces the actual values of the data by ranks, producing a statistic that is distributed approximately as chi-square, thereby providing a nonparametric alternative to one-way analysis of variance (ANOVA) (SPSS 1994; Winkler and Hays 1975: 802–4).

Results

Victim perceptions

Figure 7.4 shows the results of the victim satisfaction ratings by category of practice. Means across categories were computed with and without sample size weightings. The differences between categories are dramatic and statistically significant as shown in Table 7.6 (chi-square = 23.1, $p < .001$ unweighted samples; chi-square-964, $p < .001$ weighted samples). Nine of the top ten ranked programmes are conferencing programmes and nine of bottom ten ranked samples are the non-restorative comparison groups.

Three community group conferencing (CGC) programmes reported 100 percent victim satisfaction (Wagga Wagga, Bethlehem violent offences and Virginia 4 site). Satisfaction among RISE's violent and personal property victims was much lower than other conferencing samples. Among the mediation samples, the L.A. VOM programme reported unusually high victim satisfaction, and four programmes were much lower than other mediation samples (England, Orange, Langley and Alberquerque). The four top-ranked non-restorative comparison samples were all from the Bethlehem project.

The comparison of means demonstrates the order of victim satisfaction predicted by the Restorative Practices Typology: 91 per cent for fully restorative practices (conferencing), 82 per cent for mostly restorative practices (victim–offender mediation), and 56 per cent for the non-restorative (traditional justice system) comparison samples. This order is consistent whether averages are measured as weighted or unweighted. The first null hypothesis of no differences between victim satisfaction by

Table 7.5. Programme participant samples

Fully restorative programmes (FGC and CGC)

Community group conferencing programmes
  Wagga Wagga, AUS (Moore and Forsythe (1995))
    Juvenile offenders (30) and their victims (6)
  Bethlehem, USA (McCold and Wachtel (1995))
    Juvenile property offenders (50) and their victims (40)
    Juvenile violent offenders (17) and their victims (12)
  RISE Canberra, AUS
    Adult drunk driving offenders (376) (Sherman *et al.* (1998, 1999))*
    Juvenile property offenders (64) and their victims (40)
    Juvenile retail offenders (47)
    Juvenile and young adult violent offenders (35) and their victims (26)
  Minnesota, USA (12 sites) (Fercello and Umbreit (1998))
    Juvenile property offenders (61) and their victims (56)
  Royal Canadian Mounted Police (Chattergee (1998))
    Juvenile property offenders (54) and their victims (62)
  Indianapolis Police (USA) (McGarell *et al.* (2000))
    Juvenile offenders under 15 years of age (52) and their victims (50)
  Virginia, USA (4 sites) (McCold 1999)
    Juvenile offenders (15) and their victims (8)

Family group conferencing programmes
  Queensland, AUS (3 sites) (Hayes Prinzler (1998))
    Juvenile offenders (113) and their victims (90)
      Palm Island – numbers estimated from total.
      Ipswich – numbers estimated from total.
      Logan – numbers estimated from total.

Mostly restorative programmes (VOM and VORP)
  England, UK (2 sites) (Umbreit Roberts (1996))
    Juvenile offenders (16) and their victims (19)
  Canada (4 sites) (Umbreit *et al.* (1995), Umbreit (1996)
      Calgary – young burglary offenders (7) and their victims (7)
      Langley – juvenile offenders (37) and their victims (38)
      Ottawa – adult offenders (16) and their victims (41)
      Winnipeg – adult violent offenders (96) and their victims (88)
  US (4 sites) (Umbreit and Coates (1993)
      Albuquerque – juvenile property offenders (41) and their victims (40)
      Austin – juvenile property offenders (46) and their victims (38)
      Minneapolis – juveniles property offenders (59) and their victims (80)
      Oakland – juvenile property offenders (36) and their victims (42)
  California, USA (6 sites) (Evje and Cusmann (2000))
      Los Angeles – offenders (138) and their victims (133)
      Mendocino – offenders (38) and their victims (44)
      Orange – offenders (20) and their victims (27)
      Santa Barbara – offenders (21) and their victims (21)

Santa Clara – offenders (39) and their victims (39)
Sonoma – offenders (13) and their victims (9)

Non-restorative justice programmes
9 Northeastern States, USA (Schulman and Bucuvalas (1999))
Public, proportional representative sample (4,015)
Crime victims whose offenders were caught – derived from the larger sample (483)

Nonreferred cases (matched)
Bethlehem, USA (CGC)
Juvenile property offenders (30) and their victims (20)
Juvenile violent offenders (16) and their victims (14)
Albuquerque, USA (VOM)
Juvenile property offenders (28) and their victims (25)
Minneapolis, USA (VOM)
Juvenile property offenders (71) and their victims (72)
Oakland, USA (VORP)
Juvenile property offenders (12) and their victims (10)
RISE, AUS
Adult drunk drivers (349)
Juvenile retail theft offenders (41)
Juvenile property offenders (72) and their victims (62)
Young violent offenders (33) and their victims (27)
Langley, CAN (VOM)
Property offenders (42) and their victims (37)
Ottawa, CAN (VOM)
Adult violent offenders (42) and their victims (37)
Winnipeg, CAN (VOM)
Adult violent offenders (42) and their victims (37)

Referred cases (nonparticipants)
Bethlehem, USA (CGC)
Juvenile property offenders (20) and their victims (12)
Juvenile violent offenders (13) and their victims (18)
Albuquerque, USA (VOM)
Juvenile property offenders (36) and their victims (33)
Minneapolis, USA (VOM)
Juvenile property offenders (40) and their victims (51)
Oakland, USA (VORP)
Juvenile property offenders (19) and their victims (19)

*Victim satisfaction and offender fairness for RISE excluding subjects assigned to the conference group who did not actually participate in a conference was provided by Sherman and Strang, November 13, 2000

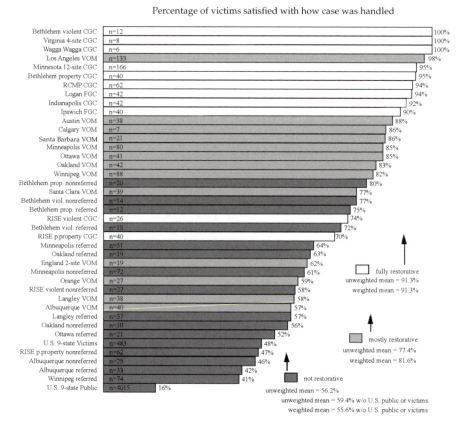

Figure 7.4. Percentage of victim satisfaction by program and category

category is rejected. The second null hypothesis of ordinal relationships different than predicted is also rejected for victim satisfaction.

There were 35 programme samples which reported both victim satisfaction and fairness. Programmes reporting a high proportion of victim satisfaction also tended to have a high proportion of victims rate the process as fair ($r = .815$, $p < .001$). As shown in Figure 7.5, eight of the top ten programmes ranked by victim fairness are fully restorative and eight of the bottom ten programmes are non-restorative. Once again, RISE's victims of violent juvenile crime were less likely to rate the process as fair (77 per cent) than the average of fully restorative programmes (96 per cent). Los Angeles was the only mediation sample to report 100 per cent

Table 7.6. Kruskal-Wallis one-way ANOVA – victim satisfaction by category of practice

	Proportion of victims satisfied									
	Unweighted					Weighted				
Programme category	Mean Rank	Cases	Chi-square	DF	Signifi-cance	Mean rank	Cases	Chi-square	DF	Signifi-cance
Not restorative	10,8	16	23,1	2	0,0000	329,6	535	960,6	2	0,0000
Mostly restorative	21,6	13	Corrected for ties			896,0	613	Corrected for ties		
Fully restorative	32,7	10				1221,8	444			
Total		39	23,1	2	0,0000		1592	963,5	2	0,0000

victim fairness, and Calgary's VOM programme (43 per cent) was much lower than the average for mostly restorative programmes (85 per cent). Again, the four highest ranked non-restorative programmes were all Bethlehem control groups.

Differences between the three categories of practice were statistically significant as shown in Table 7.2 (chi-square = 14.8, $p < .001$ unweighted samples, chi-square-713, $p < .001$ weighted samples) and in the order predicted by the Restorative Practices Typology. Thus, with regard to victim's sense of fairness, the first null hypothesis of no differences is rejected and the second null hypothesis of different ordering is rejected.

Offender perceptions

Figure 7.6 presents the results showing the proportion of offenders who reported being satisfied with the way their case was handled for 34 programme samples. The pattern among offenders is not as dramatic as it was for victims, but a similar pattern emerges. The non-restorative pro-gramme offender samples have greater variation in satisfaction ranking than among the victim samples. Two non-restorative samples reported 100 per cent offender satisfaction (Bethlehem property non-referred, and Oakland non-referred). Overall, 73 per cent of offenders rated the non-restorative programmes as satisfying.

Among the mostly restorative programmes, Los Angeles (97 per cent) and Santa Clara (95 per cent) reported higher offender satisfaction than

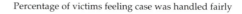

Percentage of victims feeling case was handled fairly

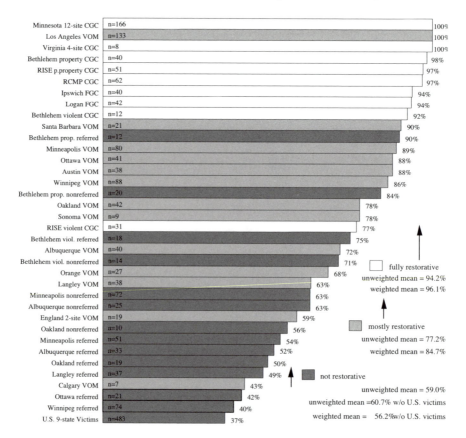

Figure 7.5. Percentage of victim fairness by program and category

other mediation samples. The Calgary VOM had the lowest proportion of offenders (29 per cent) report satisfaction with the way the case was handled. Overall, mostly restorative programmes reported an average of 85 per cent offender satisfaction. Among the fully restorative programmes, the Royal Canadian Mounted Police study was the only conferencing programme to report offender satisfaction below 90 per cent (85 per cent). Both FGC programmes reported 100 per cent offender satisfaction. Over all, fully restorative programmes reported an average of 95 per cent offender satisfaction.

Differences in offender fairness rankings between categories of practice were statistically greater than the differences within categories as shown

Table 7.7. Kruskal-Wallis one-way analysis of variance – victim fairness by category of practice

	Proportion of victims rating process as fair									
	Unweighted					Weighted				
Programme category	Mean rank	Cases	Chi-square	DF	Signifi-cance	Mean rank	Cases	Chi-square	DF	Signifi-cance
Not	11,4	14	14,8	2	0,0006	337,3	457	705,4	2	0,0000
Mostly	18,4	13	Corrected for ties			770,8	583	Corrected for ties		
Fully	28,9	8				1085,9	401			
Total		35	14,8	2	0,0006		1441	713,2	2	0,0000

in Table 7.8 (chi-square = 9.9, $p < .001$ unweighted samples, chi-square-522, $p < .001$ weighted samples). Among offenders' sense of satisfaction with the way their case was handled, the first null hypothesis of no differences is rejected and the second null hypothesis of different ordering is also rejected.

The proportion of offenders reporting satisfaction is highly related to the proportion of offenders who report they were treated fairly ($r = .898$, $df = 33$, $p < .001$). Figure 7.7 shows the proportion of offenders reporting that their case was handled fairly by programme and category of practice. The averages across categories were higher for fully restorative programmes (94 per cent) than for mostly restorative programmes (87 per cent) and both were higher than in the non-restorative category (79 per cent).

Four of the top five programmes ranked by offender fairness (100 per cent) were fully restorative programmes. Conferencing programmes tend to be rated as more fair among property offenders (>90 per cent) than among violent offenders (88–89 per cent). Results from the Royal Canadian Mounted Police were unusual among the fully restorative programmes, with only 77 per cent of offenders reporting they were treated fairly. Overall, 94 per cent of offenders rated fully restorative programmes as fair.

Only three of the 13 mediation programmes report offender ratings of fairness above 90 percent. Four mostly restorative programmes (Santa Barbara, Ottawa, Calgary and Orange) had lower rating than the average of non-restorative programmes. Again, the only mediation programme to report offender fairness above 95 per cent was Los Angeles. The non-restorative programmes demonstrate greater variation than other

Percentage of offenders satisfied with how case was handled

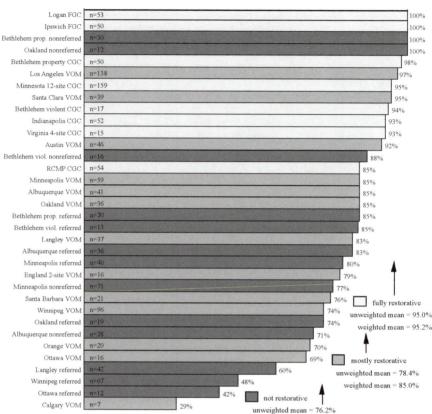

Figure 7.6. Percentage of offender satisfaction by program and category

categories with an overall average of 79 per cent of offenders reporting being treated fairly.

The differences between fully, mostly, and non-restorative categories were statistically greater than the differences within categories as shown in Table 7.9 (chi-square = 8.4, $p < .05$ unweighted samples, chi-square-425, $p < .001$ weighted samples). Therefore, the null hypothesis of no group differences on ratings on offender fairness is rejected. The null hypothesis of different ordering is also rejected.

The overall results of victim and offender sense of satisfaction and fairness are shown in Figure 7.8. Fully restorative programmes are rated as more satisfying and fair for both victims and offenders than other

Table 7.8. Kruskal–Wallis one-way analysis of variance – offender satisfaction by category of practice

| | Proportion of offenders satisfied | | | | | | | | | |
| | Unweighted | | | | | Weighted | | | | |
Programme category	Mean rank	Cases	Chi-square	DF	Signifi-cance	Mean rank	Cases	Chi-square	DF	Signifi-cance
Not	14,2	13	9,8	2	0,0074	411,4	406	518,1	2	0,0000
Mostly	14,9	13	Corrected for ties			668,5	572	Corrected for ties		
Fully	27,1	8				1046,5	450			
Total		34	9,9	2	0,0073		1428	522,0	2	0,0000

categories of practice. Overall, offenders rated non-restorative pro-grammes as more fair and satisfying than did crime victims. The average proportion of victims and offenders reporting satisfaction and fairness are consistent across samples of the fully and mostly restorative categories. However, among the non-restorative samples, victims were less likely than offenders to feel satisfied and treated fairly (56 per cent for victims, 73 per cent and 79 per cent for offenders).

Restorative justice seeks to provide crime victims with a satisfying experience of justice, so satisfaction seems a more sensible measure of victim response than fairness. Likewise, offenders who feel they are treated fairly are likely to be satisfied with the process, so fairness seems a better measure of offender response. While any combination of these measures should produce similar results, Figure 7.9 presents placement of programme samples jointly by victim satisfaction and offender fairness. There is a strong positive relationship between offender fairness and victim satisfaction ($r = .482$, $df = 35$, $p < .01$).

Ideally, restorative programmes produce balanced outcomes for both victims and offenders which we call 'programme parity'. Programme parity is shown as a diagonal line in Figure 9 with a ± 15 per cent zone highlighted on either side of it. From the restorative perspective, there is something to be said for programmes which are equally fair to offenders and satisfying to victims even if they are less than ideal in satisfaction or fairness. Programmes which fall outside this 15 per cent parity zone may be said to be overly offender focused (lower right) or overly victim focused (upper left).

Seven of the nine fully restorative programmes are within the zone of parity (victim offender differences <15 per cent). The RCMP CGC

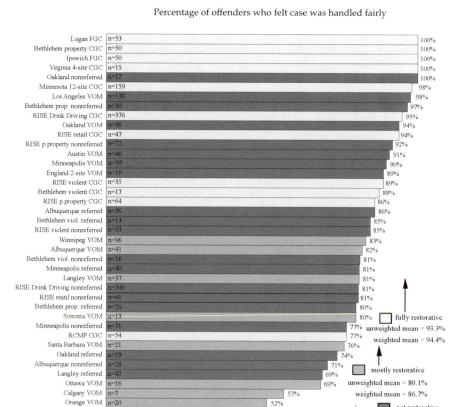

Figure 7.7. Percentage of offender fairness by program and category

programme was a bit too victim focused (17 per cent) and the RISE personal property CGCs were overly offender focused (16 per cent). Among the fully restorative programmes, only the Virginia 4 – site programme received a perfect restorative rating. Eight of the twelve mostly restorative programmes are within the zone of parity, with Ottawa VOM (16 per cent) and Calgary VOM (29 per cent) too victim focused and Langley (23 per cent), Alberquerque (25 per cent) and the England VOM (27 per cent) programmes overly offender focused. The Los Angeles VOM gets nearly perfect restorative ratings and, although neither victims nor offenders rated the Orange VOM highly, at least it achieved parity.

Table 7.9. Kruskal–Wallis one-way analysis of variance – offender fairness by category of practice

	Proportion of offenders rating process as fair									
	Unweighted					Weighted				
Programme category	Mean Rank	Cases	Chi-square	DF	Signifi-cance	Mean rank	Cases	Chi-square	DF	Signifi-cance
Not	17,4	17	8,4	2	0,0148	616,0	616	387,0	2	0,0000
Mostly	18,2	13	Corrected for ties			1181,0	546	Corrected for ties		
Fully	30,0	11				1410,2	1205			
Total		41	8,4	2	0,0146		2367	390,4	2	0,0000

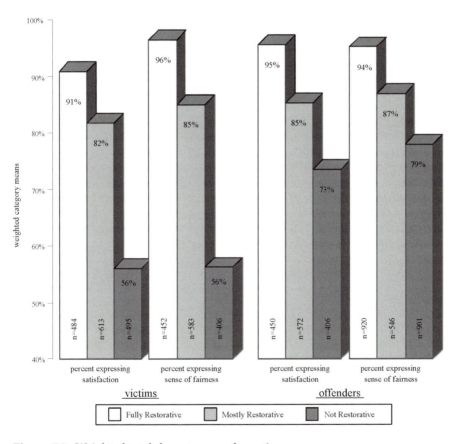

Figure 7.8. Weighted totals by category of practice

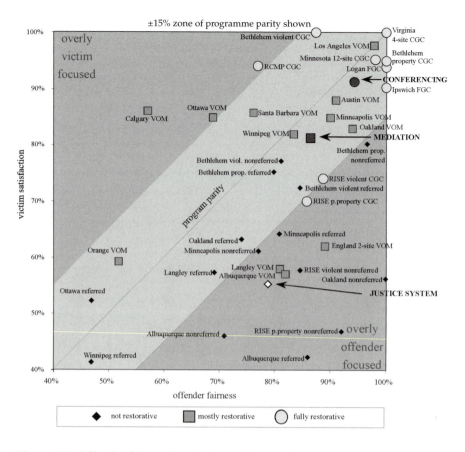

Figure 7.9. Offender fairness by victim satisfaction by program (with weighted category averages)

All but one of the fifteen non-restorative samples were on the offender focused side of the line of parity, and eight were beyond the zone of parity. Only the Ottawa comparison sample was above the line of parity, but neither victims nor offenders were very pleased with their treatment. Once again the four highest ranked non-restorative samples were from the Bethlehem control groups.

The weighted averages of programme categories demonstrate that both restorative categories are relatively balanced between victims and offenders, with mediation 5 per cent below and conferencing 3 per cent below parity. The mean of programme means for non-restorative samples (23 per cent) demonstrates the overly offender focused approach and the current court practice is well outside the zone of parity.

Discussion

On average, victims and their offenders rate as more satisfying and fair those programmes which include their communities of care (conferences) than those programmes which exclude their communities of care (victim–offender mediation). On average, victims and their offenders rate as more satisfying and fair those programmes which include victims (victim–offender mediation) than those programmes which exclude victims (traditional justice). The results provide a limited and partial validation test of the Restorative Practices Typology and our restorative justice theory. A fuller test of the Restorative Practices Typology would compare victims', offenders' and their supporters' perceptions from a wider variety of programme types in every section of the typology and a wider variety of non-restorative programmes. Such a variety of similar measures is not currently available so that a more complete validation of the full Restorative Practices Typology is beyond the scope of this chapter. Nonetheless, the unequivocal nature of the results provides an important partial validation of the theoretical construct and is sufficient to propose it as a working model.

These conclusions remain open to continuing validation testing as evaluation studies, which are currently proliferating, report on fully, mostly and partly restorative and non-restorative practices. Cross-programme comparisons are only possible with similarly measured questions. Some studies only report satisfaction as a scale average (i.e. 3.44 on a 4-point scale) so that such results are not comparable with forced choice satisfied or not-satisfied scales. Further, there is a danger that comparisons between very satisfied and satisfied or dissatisfied and very dissatisfied measure more about how willing respondents are to score extreme values than it does about their perceptions of the process. Efforts should continue to refine research measures, but this should not preclude asking the most direct and simple questions of participants. There is a stronger argument to be made for standardization than sophistication at this point in theory development. The simple measures presented here sufficiently distinguished programme performance for cross-comparison purposes.

The secondary research methodology used in this paper can only play a limited role in validity testing, but it is a useful first step. Similar analyses are possible to test a variety of programme assumptions. For example, if police are less effective facilitators than volunteers or professional social workers, then comparing the results of similar programmes by type of facilitator should reveal the truth of this assertion. If spending a long period of time preparing participants before bringing them together is necessary for an effective restorative process, then programmes that do this should, on average, outperform programmes which do not. Many other assumptions about best practices can be put to this simple empirical test.

The Restorative Practices Typology, by definition, creates a research dilemma. Restorative justice is about meeting the needs of the direct stakeholders, yet only fully restorative programmes involve all three sets of affected parties. A full measurement of 'restorativeness' would include the satisfaction and fairness experienced by victim, offender and their communities of care in relationship to each category of practice. But, for instance, offenders are largely unaware of services being offered to their victims and family members of victims and offenders do not participate in most processes. So research cannot possibly measure programme effects on all the direct stakeholders for most of the categories.

One also needs to recognize the threat of the ecological fallacy, that is, what is true for relationships between variables measured in the aggregate is not necessarily true at the individual level of analysis. Because programmes in one category of practice produce higher results on the average than programmes in other categories, it does not necessarily follow that it will also be true for an individual set of stakeholders. Aggregate relationships need to be tested at the individual level of analysis, for particular victims, offenders, and members of their communities of care. More complete validation of the full theory and corresponding restorative hypotheses will be a complex undertaking. Beyond measurement comparability, there is an additional research difficulty of distinguishing the interactive effects between the transformation, collaboration, empowerment, and involvement dimensions in the proposed theory.

Conclusions

The Restorative Practices Typology is consistent with the empirical evidence and passes this initial test of theory validation. The results demonstrate that victim satisfaction, offender sense of fairness, and the parity of outcomes between the two are better, on average, for conferences than for victim–offender mediation and that both conferencing and victim–offender mediation are better than the non-restorative justice system.

Comparisons of any new approach, such as restorative justice, must be measured against existing practice. While this may seem obvious, there is a tendency to compare new programmes to perfection and criticize them when they fail to meet that impossible standard (e.g., Young 2000).

Further, the fact that outcomes are better for fully restorative approaches should not be perceived as a denigration of mostly restorative or partly restorative practices. They have their place in the restorative justice tent (Bazemore and Walgrave 1999; McCold 2000) when they are the most restorative practice that can be accomplished under a given set of circumstances. However, the Restorative Practices Typology and the partial validation presented in this paper does raise the question of why one would limit a restorative intervention to less than full involvement of all the direct stakeholders whenever that is possible, consistent with Walgrave's subsidarity principle (Walgrave 1999: 141–2).

Another implication of this chapter's findings is that the bar of good restorative practice standards has been raised by the advent of conferencing. The 95 per cent-and-above levels of satisfaction and fairness reported by participants in conferencing programmes have created a problem for evaluation. At these levels, statistical distinctions becomes meaningless because a few unusual cases, which have nothing to do with programme characteristics, can account for the differences in outcomes.

The final implication of the Restorative Practices Typology for restorative justice programmes is obvious. One should always try to involve victims, offenders and their communities of care in responses to crime. New restorative programme design should begin by trying to serve as many of the direct stakeholders as possible. Furthermore, fully restorative practices should begin to replace existing partly or mostly restorative practices. Those restorative practices which include all direct stakeholders, such as conferences and circles, should constitute the bull's-eye on the restorative justice target.

References

Babbie, E. (1995) *The Practice of Social Research* (7th edn). NY: Wadsworth Publishing.

Bazemore, G., and Walgrave, L. (1999) 'Restorative Juvenile Justice: In Search of Fundamentals and an Outline for Systemic Reform' in G. Bazemore and L. Walgrave (eds) *Restorative Juvenile Justice: Repairing the Harm of Youth Crime.* Monsey, NY: Criminal Justice Press.

Black, H. (1990) *Black's Law Dictionary* (6th edn). St. Paul, MN: West Publishing.

Braithwaite, J. (1999) 'Restorative Justice is Republican Justice' in G. Bazemore and L. Walgrave (eds) *Restorative Juvenile Justice: Repairing the Harm of Youth Crime.* Monsey, NY: Criminal Justice Press.

Braithwaite, J., and Strang, H. (2000) 'Restorative Justice In Civil Society' in H. Strang and J. Braitwaite (eds). *Restorative Justice in Civil Society.* New York: Cambridge University Press.

Chatterjee, J. (1999) 'A Report on the Evaluation of RCMP Restorative Justice Initiative: Community Justice Forum as Seen by Participants', Research and Evaluation Branch, Community Contract and Aboriginal Policing Services, Royal Canadian Mounted Police, Ottawa, March.

Christie, N. (1977) 'Conflicts as Property', *British Journal of Criminology*, 17(1): 1–15.

Claassen, R. (1995) 'Restorative Justice Principles and Evaluation Continuums'. Paper presented at National Center for Peacemaking and Conflict Resolution, Fresno Pacific College, May.

Declaration of Leuven on the Advisability of Promoting the Restorative Approach to Juvenile Crime (1998) in G. Bazemore and L. Walgrave (eds) *Restorative Juvenile Justice: Repairing the Harm of Youth Crime*. Monsey, NY: Criminal Justice Press.

Evje, A. and Cusman, R. (2000) 'A Summary of the Evaluations of Six California Victim Offender Reconciliation Programs'. Report to the California Legislature, The Judicial Council of California, Administrative Office of the Courts, Center for Families, Children and the Courts, May.

Fatic, A. (1995) *Punishment and Restorative Crime-Handling: A Social Theory of Trust*. Aldershot, UK: Avebury Ashgate Publishing.

Fercello, C. and Umbreit, M. (1998) 'Client Evaluation of Family Group Conferencing' in '12 Sites in 1st Judicial District of Minnesota'. Center Restorative Justice and Mediation, School of Social Work, University of Minnesota.

Hayes, H. and Prinzler, T. (1998) 'Making Amends: Final Evaluation of the Queensland Community Conferencing Pilot'. Center for Crime Police and Public Safety, Griffith University, Brisbane, AUS.

Marshall, T. (1996) 'The Evolution of Restorative Justice in Britain', *European Journal on Criminal Policy and Research*, 4: 21–43.

McCold, P. (1996) 'Restorative Justice and the Role of Community', in B. Galaway and J. Hudson (eds). *Restorative Justice: International Perspectives*, Monsey, NY: Criminal Justice Press, 85–101.

McCold, P. (1998a) 'Restorative Justice: Variations on a Theme' in L. Walgrave (ed.). *Restorative Justice for Juveniles: Potentialities, Risks and Problems for Research*. Belgium: Leuven University Press.

McCold, P. (1998b) 'Restorative Justice Handbook'. UN Alliance of NGOs on Criminal Justice and Crime Prevention (New York), Working Party on Restorative Justice. Corrections Compendium. American Correctional Association 23(12): 1–4, 20–28.

McCold, P. (1999) 'Virginia Conferencing Project: Evaluation Results'. Community Service Foundation, Pipersville, PA.

McCold, P. (1999) 'Police-facilitated restorative conferencing: What the data show! Paper presented to the International Conference on Restorative Justice for Juveniles, International Network for Research on Restorative Justice for Juveniles, Fort Lauderdale, Florida, November 7–9, 1998 [NCJRS #177563].

McCold, P. (2000) 'Toward a Mid-range Theory of Restorative Criminal Justice: A Reply to the Maximalist Model', *Contemporary Justice Review*, 3(4): 357–414.

McCold, P., and Wachtel, B. (1998) 'Restorative Policing Experiment: The Bethlehem Pennsylvania Police Family Group Conferencing Project'. (NCJRS #177564 and #177565), US Department of Justice, National Institute of Justice. Washington DC: National Criminal Justice Reference Service.

McGarrell, E., Olivares, K., Crawford, K. and Kroovand, N. (2000) 'Returning to the Community: The Indianapolis Juvenile Restorative Justice Experiment'. Hudson Institute Crime Control Policy Center, Indianapolis, IN.

Moore, D. B. and Forsythe, L. (1995) 'A New Approach to Juvenile Justice: An Evaluation of Family Conferencing in Wagga Wagga. A Report to the Criminology Research Council'. Wagga Wagga, NSW Australia: Centre for Rural Social Research, Charles Sturt University–Riverina.

Moore, D. B. (1996) 'Criminal Action – Official Reaction: Affect Theory, Criminology, and Criminal Justice' in D. Nathanson (ed). *Knowing Feeling*. New York, NY: W.W. Norton.

Nathanson, D. (1992) *Shame and Pride: Affect, Sex, and the Birth of the Self*. New York, NY: W.W. Norton.

Nathanson, D. (1998) 'From Empathy to Community'. Paper presented at Conferencing A New Response To Wrongdoing , Minneapolis, MN, August 6–8. Available at www.realjustice.org

Nelsen, J. (1996) *Positive Discipline*. New York: Ballantine Books.

Schulman, R. and Bucuvalas, Inc. (1999) 'What Do We Want (and What Are We Getting) From the Criminal Justice System? Comparing the General Public's Expectations and Perceptions with Crime Victims' Experiences'. The Council of State Governments/Eastern Regional Conference, New York, NY.

Sherman, L., Strang, H., Barnes, G., Braithwaite, J., Inkpen, N. and The, M. M. (1998) 'Experiments in Restorative Policing. A Progress Report on the Canberra Reintegrative Shaming Experiments (RISE) to the National Police Research Unit'. Canberra ACT: Australian National University.

Sherman, L., Strang, H., Barnes, G., Braithwaite, J., Inkpen, N. and The, M. M. (1999) 'Experiments in Restorative Policing. A Progress Report on the Canberra Reintegrative Shaming Experiments (RISE) to the National Police Research Unit'. Canberra ACT: Australian National University, July. Available at www.aic.gov.au/rjustice/rise/progress/1999.html

SPSS. (1994) *SPSS 6.1 Syntax Reference Guide*. Chicago, IL: SPSS, Inc.

Tompkins, S. (1995) 'The Varieties of Shame and its Magnification' in E. V. Demos (ed.). *Exploring Affect: The Selected Writings of Silvan S. Tompkins*. New York: Cambridge University Press.

Umbreit, M. S. (1994) *Victim Meets Offender: The Impact of Restorative Justice and Mediation*. Monsey, New York: Willow Tree Press.

Umbreit, M. S. (1996) 'Restorative Justice Through Mediation: The Impact of Programs in Four Canadian Provinces' in B. Galaway and J. Hudson (eds). *Restorative Justice: International Perspectives*. Monsey, NY: Criminal Justice Press.

Umbreit, M. S. and Coates, R. (1993) 'Cross-Site Analysis of Victim–Offender Mediation in Four States.' *Crime and Delinquency*, 39(4): 565–585.

Umbreit, M., Coates, R., Kalanj, B., Lipkin, R. and Petros, G. (1995) 'Mediation of Criminal Conflict: An Assessment of Programs in Four Canadian Provinces'.

Executive Summary Report. St. Paul, MN: The Center for Restorative Justice and Mediation, University of Minnesota.

Umbreit, M. and Roberts, A. (1996) 'Mediation of Criminal Conflict in England: An Assessment of Services in Coventry and Leeds'. Center for Restorative Justice and Mediation, School of Social Work, University of Minnesota.

Wachtel, T. (2000a) 'Defining Community: Who Should Participate in a Conference?' *Forum*, Newsletter Issue 9. Bethlehem, PA: Real Justice.

Wachtel, T. (2000b) 'Restorative Justice in Everyday Life: Beyond the Formal Ritual' in G. Burford and J. Hudson (eds) *Restorative Justice in Child Welfare.* Monsey, NY: Criminal Justice Press.

Wachtel, T. and McCold, P. (2000) 'Restorative Justice in Everyday Life' in J. Braithwaite and H. Strang (eds). *Restorative Justice in Civil Society.* New York, NY: Cambridge University Press.

Walgrave, L. (1999) 'Community Service as a Cornerstone of a Systemic Restorative Response to Juvenile Justice' in G. Bazemore and L. Walgrave (eds). *Restorative Juvenile Justice: Repairing the Harm of Youth Crime.* Monsey, NY: Criminal Justice Press.

Weitekamp, E. G. M. (1999) 'The History of Restorative Justice' in G. Bazemore and L. Walgrave (eds). *Restorative Juvenile Justice: Repairing the Harm of Youth Crime.* Monsey, NY: Criminal Justice Press.

Winkler, R. and Hays, W. (1975) *Statistics: Probability, Inference and Decision* (2nd edn). New York: Holt, Rinehart and Winston.

Young, R. (2001) 'Just Cops Doing Shameful Business? Police-Led Restorative Justice and the Lessons of Research'. Centre for Criminological Research, University of Oxford.

Zehr, H. (1990) *Changing Lenses: A New Focus for Crime and Justice.* Scottsdale, PA: Herald Press.

Chapter 8

Restorative justice and the future of diversion and informal social control

Gordon Bazemore and Colleen McLeod

Introduction

In mainstream juvenile justice policy debates, restorative justice proponents often suffer from a problem of 'disconnect'. Essentially, advocates have promoted restorative justice on the basis of its potential for providing a more satisfying experience for individual victims, offenders and their supporters, a principle-based appeal also consistent with demonstrated empirical outcomes associated with restorative justice conferencing programmes (Umbreit 1999; Van Ness and Schiff 2001). But while many policymakers and juvenile justice administrators are now interested in restorative justice – if only because of its trendiness – many also struggle to figure out whether, and how, restorative justice 'fits' within the larger juvenile justice agenda. Though restorative justice advocates may smugly conclude that this is simply because these practitioners have the wrong agenda, administrators also legitimately want to know how the feelings of individual victims and offenders relate to the achievement of broader, often mandated, objectives of their agencies. And no matter how narrowly conceptualized some of these system objectives may seem to be (Griffiths and Corrado 1999), some are also linked to more universal public concerns with community safety, sanctioning and censure of crime, fairness and justice – and to public expectations that juvenile justice agencies and systems demonstrate effectiveness in addressing these concerns.

Some have suggested that restorative justice does indeed have implications for addressing these community-level expectations – and that a normative theory of restorative justice should make it possible to articulate distinctive restorative approaches to achieving sanctioning, rehabilitation and public safety outcomes (Braithwaite and Roche 2001; Bazemore and Walgrave 1999). However, for the most part, there has been a lack of apparent resonance between restorative justice discourse and juvenile justice policy, and between such discourse and broader collective needs. One such universal need is to strengthen community capacity for informal social control in the response to youth crime (Braithwaite 1989, 1994; Pranis and Bazemore 2000). Therefore, making connections between restorative principles and informal social control at the policy level would require a restorative 'model' or guiding philosophy of intervention in the arena of juvenile justice generally referred to as diversion.

Because juvenile diversion programmes have become the primary location for restorative justice practice in many jurisdictions, it is somewhat ironic that diversion *policy* remains for the most part unaddressed in restorative justice literature (for exceptions see Braithwaite 1994; Walgrave and Bazemore 1999). Restorative justice advocates are of course not opposed to the idea of diversion, especially when cases are actually being removed from a more adversarial process, and few would have objections to filling up the diversion 'space' with more open and inclusive decision-making approaches that attempt to repair the harm of youth crime.[1] However, given the absence of a holistic vision in current policy and practice, expanding restorative justice as a diversion option also holds significant risks, such as the concern that practical application will be limited almost exclusively to the informal front-end of juvenile justice systems where restorative practice will compete for low-level delinquency cases with a variety of marginal and/or dubious programmes (Schiff and Bazemore 2001). We are therefore in agreement with those who wish to avoid such a future by expanding the application of restorative intervention for use with serious and chronic offenders (Corrado, this volume; Umbreit, this volume).

Yet, it is important that restorative justice advocates do not abandon the diversion context. With this in mind, the first objective of this chapter is to apply the normative theory of restorative justice (i.e. restorative principles) to the development of a new policy of juvenile justice informalism that could displace diversion, as we know it. Achieving this objective will also require better theories of intervention. Unfortunately, normative theories of restorative justice are not often linked to relevant etiological theories of crime – in this case, especially those that address the community/crime relationship (Skogan 1990; Braithwaite 1989) and those that address concerns with the potential harm of criminal justice intervention when disconnected from community needs and resources (Rose and Clear 1998). Hence, a second objective is to encourage the development of intervention theory linking restorative practice to enhancements in informal *social control* (Hunter 1985) and *social support* (Cullen 1994) processes within communities. Such theory should also guide policy related to diversion, which could in turn connect principled, front-end restorative justice practice to these processes, and to a distinctive strategy for nurturing and shaping informal community responses to youth crime. In addition, theory informed by restorative principles should provide the basis for a critical analysis of the new juvenile justice system expansionism in the past decade, and of the more general professionalization of socialization and social control functions in the response to youth crime and trouble (McKnight 1995; Bazemore 1999).

What would a restorative approach to diversion look like? What would an analysis informed by restorative justice principles teach us about the relationship between the policy and practice of informal justice and issues of social control, and what insight might be provided to guard against the traps and failures of informalism in previous movements (Abel 1982). To develop these arguments, we briefly examine the lessons of three decade-long juvenile diversion experience in the US as a case study in how incomplete policy frameworks actually contributed to a strengthening of formal social control (Cohen 1985; Polk 1984) and a weakening of informal control processes rather than achieving their original goal of minimizing youth involvement with formal juvenile justice agencies.

Modern diversion: the US experience

While the US juvenile court was effectively insulated from critical scrutiny in its first fifty years of operation (Platt 1977), by the middle of the 1960s a new critique of the court as harmful and stigmatizing had brought together a wide range of child advocates, defence attorneys, parents, academics and other concerned citizens who had begun to scrutinize the court from the perspective of due process and children's rights, and demanded juvenile justice reform. A growing widespread disillusionment with the court's ability to provide either effective treatment or protective care and custody was based on an examination of often harsh conditions of confinement under which thousands of young people around the country were held for indefinite periods of time for 'status offences' such as truancy, running away from home and vague charges of being ungovernable. These conditions could scarcely be viewed as consistent with the 'best interests' rationale for court intervention, and could only be seen as punitive and potentially harmful (Schwartz 1989; Miller 1991). By the early 1970s, diversion had emerged as a core component of a comprehensive national policy and programmatic response based on this critical view of the court that included due process, deinstitutionalization and decriminalization as additional components (Empey 1982). Together, these three components of the policy reform 'package' seemed to be aimed directly at protecting young people from the damage assumed to result from juvenile court intervention.

Diversion as policy and programme

The modern history of the diversion experience in the US is now well known to international students of juvenile justice, and has been replicated to some degree in much of the Western world (Walgrave and Bazemore 1999). The majority of scholars have generally viewed diversion as a failed policy (e.g., Polk 1987; Lemert 1981). However, competing inter-pretations contributed to a growing academic debate in the 1980s in which the relative success or failure of diversion became a topic of some dispute (Polk 1987). On the one hand, critics of diversion viewed it as a failure because diversion programmes were utilized for young people who would never have been referred to the formal juvenile justice system. On the other hand, those who viewed diversion as a success argued that diversion programmes provided important services to youth at risk and reduced the likelihood of recidivism. These different interpretations are primarily a function of different standards of success, and resulted from viewing the problem through two distinctive 'policy lenses' (Ingram and Schneider 1991) that ultimately guided implementation of diversion policy and practice in the U.S., and also framed retrospective analyses of diversion based on distinctive visions of informal justice and social control.

The libertarian lens

Rooted in a critique of the court, diversion as a *policy* was originally promoted as part of a general effort to emphasize the limits of the formal juvenile justice system to address the needs of young people and communities facing problems of youth crime (Polk 1984), and the need to discourage use of the juvenile court for non-serious offences and troublesome youth behaviours that could best be handled by community institutions and social services (Lemert 1971). Informed in part by the rise in popularity of the labelling perspective in the 1960s (Becker 1963; Lemert

1971), the assumption behind a policy to remove large numbers of youth from eligibility for formal juvenile justice intervention was because the response to an individual exhibiting behaviour viewed as delinquent might ironically do more harm than good. Through the *libertarian lens*, such harm would result from a stigmatizing effect on processed youth and from a kind of self-fulfilling prophecy that would take the form of 'secondary deviance' (Lemert 1971), in which additional delinquency could occur as the actor internalizes a deviant self-concept.[2] Diversion policy therefore became widely understood to encompass all efforts to avoid or minimize formal contact with the court. As the 1967 President's Commission on Crime, Law Enforcement, and Administration of Justice (hereinafter President's Crime Commission, or PCC) saw it, the formal court process:

> ... should be used only as a last resort. In place of the formal system, dispositional alternatives should be developed for dealing with juveniles, including agencies to provide and coordinate services and procedures to achieve necessary control without unnecessary stigma (p. 8).

Initial policy statements appeared to say little about reducing troublesome and delinquent behaviour as a primary diversion goal, yet a core assumption underlying the libertarian response was that many problems of youth trouble and offending would 'self-correct' if stigmatizing intervention could be avoided. Given these assumptions, the solution or strategy was as Schur (1973) put it, to 'leave the kids alone whenever possible,' *and* to promote 'judicious nonintervention' (Lemert 1971) through educational and other efforts aimed at expanding community tolerance limits (Schur 1973). The best empirical evidence – which indicates that the vast majority of first offenders do not repeat regardless of whether any intervention occurs (Elliott 1994) – suggests that the self-correction hypothesis had validity, and most US communities could arguably have benefited from an expansion of tolerance. However, such 'solutions' to what was viewed as a growing problem of unsupervised minor offenders and 'youth at risk' seemed to amount to the policy equivalent of neglect. Depicting the problem as simply the need to 'close the door' of the juvenile court to many of the very problems of youth crime and trouble of concern to families and communities must, in retrospect, have been unsatisfying to citizens and policymakers that had grown accustomed to an expansion of professional services as young people at the crest of the baby-boom generation were becoming adolescents. The problem with this policy of non-intervention as the primary response to youth crime and trouble was its message to citizens – and the policy-makers who aimed to represent their interests – to 'get used to it'. Such a response, which also became viewed as part of a one-dimensional 'rights-based' agenda (Glendon 1991), showed indifference to the problems of communities and families struggling to find solutions to problems presented by youth at risk, and created even more distrust and eventual opposition to juvenile justice intervention that built support for the new focus on punishment, determinacy and transfer policies (Feld 1999).

Regarding policy goals and outcomes, critics of diversion had by the mid-1970s become more vocal in their insistence that diversion was *not* reducing the likelihood of stigmatization by the court (e.g., Klein 1976). However, the problem of most concern, widening the net – or the expansion of the population of young people who were becoming involved in juvenile justice intervention – was viewed by many as a rather vague and generally irrelevant issue. For the public, the question of primary importance was: what could be done to meet the needs of young people who seemed to lack supervision and/or present risk factors that require some response. And the lack of answers to such questions, and the apparent absence of an alternative strategy for responding to youth crime and trouble, reflected the limits of the non-interventionist libertarian perspective, and ultimately contributed to a growing emphasis on diversion as a *programme* vs. diversion as a *process*.

The interventionist lens

Despite the recommendations of the PCC and other relatively clear statements of intent (Lemert 1971; Schur 1973), there was increasing dis-agreement about the exact meaning of the term diversion, and diversion policy by the mid-1970s seemed to be focused on multiple, and at times incompatible objectives, with practice referring to:

> policies as diverse as doing nothing to programs indistinguishable from existing juvenile justice practices … the simple act of deflecting juveniles away from the juvenile justice system (or) … the develop-ment of alternative strategies or programs for dealing with juveniles outside the range of the formal processing mechanisms of the juvenile court … (Jensen and Rojek 1998: 439).

With the rapid demise of the libertarian approach, and a short-lived experimentation with a youth development strategy focused on insti-tutional reform and advocacy in school and work (Polk and Kobrin 1972), interventionists took advantage of a perceived need to 'do something' (see Finkenhauer and Gavin 1999). For a growing number of practitioners and policymakers, juvenile justice policy could not simply neglect the apparent needs of diverted young people for services and supports (Binder 1998), regardless of whether they were referred to programmes as an alternative to formal processing, nor could administrators ignore the expectations of communities that such services be provided. The core assumption behind the interventionist view of diversion as a *programme* was that many young people had needs and exhibited risks that demanded services and intervention, and these youths were likely to move toward criminal careers unless their problems could be ameliorated through early intervention in the form of effective treatment. The focus was no longer on whether diversion was hitting the appropriate target population to be removed from formal system processing; rather, the new standard of success became reducing recidivism and whether programmes were effective in identifying and addressing perceived needs and risks of young people (Whitehead and Lab 1998). Because such needs and risks seemed almost unlimited, the development of more diversion programmes and referral of youth to these programmes became a sign of success in its own right.

While libertarians had sought to limit the size and reach of the juvenile justice system, interventionists seemed intent on expanding it through the development of popular new programmes. Polk (1987) describes this transformation in diversion policy ironically as, 'less meant more' – what began as an attempt to decrease formal system intervention resulted in more programmes and more assessment to diagnose the problems that resulted in referrals to them. At the policy level, more was better as the interventionists committed government agencies to a service agenda that was clearly viewed by many youth advocates as helpful (Binder and Geis 1984; Binder 1998), despite the fact that by intervening with youth who would not have been processed in the formal court system, diversion failed to function as an alternative to that system.[3] Hence, despite Federal policy statements encouraging the focus on the process of removing young people from court (PCC), jurisdictions appear to have expanded the number of programmes available. In essence, federal funding for diversion appears to have been used to extend the juvenile justice system rather than to remove youth from it (Polk 1987).

The answer to the question of how net-widening actually occurred goes to the heart of several key problems with the interventionist perspective. First, the view of diversion as a programme, and the more-is-better perspective, seemed to define no limits on the need for intervention, and such programmes became increasingly popular for reasons less related to the resonance of the critique of the juvenile court than to more pragmatic concerns. As Whitehead and Lab (1998) suggest, a key factor in the experience of new programmes, and therefore net-widening, was simply the widespread availability of federal funding for diversion programmes in the 1970s and 1980s, as well as the perceived linkage to reduction in workload.[4] In addition, once funded, some programmes no doubt experienced difficulty getting the number of referrals originally anticipated, and to avoid losing funds and possibly jobs, some diversion programme directors no doubt began seeking referrals elsewhere. In this way, diversion funding created clear incentives for programmes to 'find' other troubled youth, and in doing so, widened the net as a matter of agency 'self-aggrandizement' (Rojek 1982).

Finally, the most significant and far-reaching problem with the interventionist approach – and the one that ultimately contributed most to net-widening and system expansion – was the message sent to community groups and institutions. Despite good intentions to help young people at risk in the community, programme directors needing clients no doubt solicited referrals from schools, police, parents, community members and neighbourhood groups and institutions that might otherwise have continued to respond to conflict and youth trouble and deviance informally. As these groups now recognized other 'expert' options for getting rid of the youth problem, diversion programmes, and the many prevention and intervention programmes that soon became virtually indistinguishable from them, usurped the community's role and responsibility and expanded the reach of the formal system, ultimately with destructive consequences:

> When agents of the state become the key problem solvers, they might be filling a void in community; but just as in interpersonal relationships, so in community functioning, once a function is being performed by one party it becomes unnecessary for another to take it on … In localities where formal social control systems become the main regulating mechanism, informal control systems may atrophy like dormant muscles, and citizens may come to see the formal system as existing to mediate all conflicts (Clear and Karp 1999: 38).

In addition, as Moore and O'Connell (1994) observe, when government programmes undercut the community's role in socializing young people and responding to crime and disorder, the impact may be systemically criminogenic because these programmes 'perpetuate the illusion that the state, rather than civil society, is ultimately responsible for social order'. Moreover, assuming that citizens learn responses to youth crime in part by *participating* in such responses, the professionalization of social control and social services may, 'deprive people of opportunities to practice skills of apology and forgiveness, of reconciliation, restitution, and reparation ... (and has) deprived civil society of opportunities to learn important political and social skills.' (Moore 1994: 7).

As McKnight (1995) argues, when the role of the justice system is not defined in concert with the community's role, justice and social service programmes are likely to overextend their reach and contribute to the isolation, rather than reintegration, of people in trouble. One reason is that despite their unique professional orientation, most juvenile justice and social-service systems have in common a deficit focus emphasizing identification of needs and risks and the provision of services intended to correct presumed pathologies and dysfunctions that ultimately lead people 'out of community and into dependency' and away from those that 'support people in community life.' (McKnight 1995: 20).[5] Ultimately, interventionists uncritically placed their faith in government programmes to take over responsibilities that they were never capable of handling, while creating a demand for new services and programmes, and a view of them as *prima facie* benevolent, rather than potentially harmful both to young people and community life. However, neither they nor their libertarian critics who emphasized the harmful potential, gave any attention to the community and institutional role in the socialization of young people, focusing instead on regulating the amount of government intervention to be provided.

This absence of a vision of the community role in the response to youth crime was therefore a major factor in the expansion of juvenile justice on the front-end of the system that was to follow in the decade of the 1990s. While service programmes based on deficit or 'medical model' assumptions have come to dominate the youth policy landscape and seem to know no limits to their growth and regeneration in new forms (Finkenhauer and Gavin 1999), the reality is that young people grow up in communities – not treatment programmes. Ultimately, it is families, extended families, teachers, neighbours, ministers and others who provide both support and guidance in the socialization process. Today, the over-extension of juvenile justice programmes has produced communities ultimately deficient in informal youth socialization resources and increasingly reliant on institutions of formal social control (Polk 2001).

Diversion today and the new expansionism: the rise of 'interventionism plus'

Diversion *programmes* are now institutionalized as a common fixture of the juvenile justice landscape in most US jurisdictions – many of which have legislation or policy authorizing continuing funds for what has become a wide range of programmes. Diversion programmes have become so tightly linked to juvenile court intake procedures in most urban jurisdictions that their value and effectiveness is seldom questioned. In fact, most policymakers assume that the absence of such programmes would overwhelm dockets and increase workloads beyond current capacity, even though it remains impossible to establish that diversion as a policy ever actually resulted in a decline in formal court processing or instituted a workable process for removing youth in trouble from these systems and reconnecting them to their communities (Whitehead and Lab 1998).

In addition, juvenile justice policy appears in the 1990s to have entered a new era that has pushed interventionism to a new and qualitatively different level. A new expansionist juvenile justice premised on a view of youth crime through a policy lens that we may refer to as *interventionism plus* is best characterized by two primary components. First, in the decade of the 1990s, there has been an almost complete abandonment of the initial trend toward 'limiting' the policies of 70s and 80s – diversion, de-institutionalization, due process and decriminalization. In an apparent response to new 'get tough' legislative initiatives that removed court jurisdiction over more serious crimes and mandated transfer of increasing numbers of young people to adult courts (Feld 1999), the 1990s have seen many states stretch the boundaries that limit the reach of their juvenile justice system on the lower end of the youth misbehaviour spectrum (Butts and Mears 2001). Policymakers now appear to be oblivious to the lessons of the diversion experience, and raise few questions about the capacity of social service and criminal justice agencies to respond effectively to a wide array of youth problems once viewed as the primary responsibility of families and communities. Juvenile courts in many parts of the US are now taking back jurisdiction – generally relinquished during the decades of the 1970s and 1980s over youth behaviour such as truancy, runaway and a range of status offences such as smoking – often by establishing new courts or other quasi-formal programmes to address these behaviours.

Secondly, 'zero tolerance' appears to have become a new mantra with unquestioned moral authority and logic that seems to magically justify all manner of due process violations, new and old forms of confinement, forced treatment and punishment, and outright exclusion of young people who cause trouble for authorities in a variety of educational, criminal justice, social service and other contexts. Because youth in the 1990s can enter the system in far easier ways than in the past few decades, many problem-solving and conflict-resolution practices that would traditionally have been employed in various informal contexts (e.g. schools) seem now to be bypassed, providing a fast-track into the juvenile justice system with one result being a significant increase in residential placements for youth charged with misdemeanours and first offenders in some large states (Fader *et al.* 2001). Reinforcing zero-tolerance as a response to young people cutting across a range of system and professional ideologies has been the emergence of new, stronger collaborations between once 'loosely coupled' components of criminal justice systems with generally incompatible agendas. The new smooth and surprisingly seamless coordination between law enforcement and social services (e.g. welfare, prevention and treatment agencies) to implement new forms of front-end intervention such as, for example, centralized assessment centres (Wilson 2000) may signal a merger in some cases between prosecution/enforcement and public health sectors that McKnight has referred to as the 'new medical establishment' (1995). What appears to have emerged is a deficit-focused, clinical model of intervention focused on the risks and needs of young people as a softer legitimization for expanded formal control with fewer procedural safeguards buttressed by the political power of crime control ideology (see Cohen 1985). By pursuit of the common goal of more effective identification and processing of youth-at-risk, collaboratives in support of new expansionist polices combine 'soft side' counselling, remedial education, and substance abuse programmes with more aggressive and coercive law enforcement and expanded prosecution and suppression components (i.e. gang units). Completely lost is the now seemingly anachronistic concern of original diversion advocates with the criminogenic, stigmatizing influence of bringing together large groups of troubled youth in a way that must surely reinforce a deviant identity (Bazemore 1985). Even more in the background in the face of such centralized mobilization of multidisciplinary experts is support for a reinvigorated community response, as citizens and community groups may be led to question the need for any non-professional role.

Beyond libertarian and interventionist perspectives: informal social control, social support and restorative justice

How then might restorative justice policies regarding diversion and informal responses to youth crime and trouble differ from those of libertarians and interventionists, and what contribution can they make in the new, more difficult, climate of expansionism? How would one interpret the history of diversion applying the principles and normative theory of restorative justice and how, if at all, would such an interpretation differ from the perspective of libertarian and interventionists on the success or failure of diversion?

The restorative justice 'lens': principles for a new informalism

Although restorative justice advocates share some of the concerns with proponents of each viewpoint, the restorative vision and intervention agenda appears to challenge and rise above long-standing strands of debate in criminal and juvenile justice informed by the three dominant policy perspectives. For us, restorative justice is best understood as a way of thinking about crime and other troublesome behaviour that emphasizes the harm of such behaviour to the victim, offender and community and therefore regards 'justice' as something more than punishing or treating those found guilty of lawbreaking; crime is important precisely because of the harm it causes, and therefore, 'creates obligations to make things right.' Moreover, restorative justice potentially includes all responses to crime that attempt to do justice by repairing the harm, or 'healing the wounds', caused by crime (Bazemore and Walgrave 1999). Ultimately, the normative theory of restorative justice is best defined by the following core principles (Van Ness and Strong 1997).

(1) The principle of repair: Justice requires that we work to heal victims, offenders and communities that have been injured by crime.

(2) The principle of stakeholder participation: Victims, offenders and communities should have the opportunity for active involvement in the justice process as early and as fully as possible.

(3) The principle of transformation in community and government roles and relationships: We must rethink the relative roles and respon- sibilities of the government and the community; in promoting justice, government is responsible for preserving order and the community is responsible for establishing peace.

Through the restorative justice policy lens, crime is viewed as a collective problem of weak relationships within communities, made weaker still when crime occurs. Given this, the criteria for judging the success of an intervention outcome is the extent to which harm is repaired (principle (1)), the extent to which key stakeholders are actively engaged in decision-making about such repair (principle (2)), and the extent to which communities increase their capacity to respond to crime and conflict working with the criminal justice system in a supporting, rather than directive role (principle (3)). Such reparative processes and outcomes seem to offer a broader framework that replaces punishment and treatment as the primary currencies of intervention and provides a new metric for gauging the success of such intervention, and juvenile justice reform itself. Here, relationship-building has become for many an overarching goal of restorative justice linked at the micro level to larger community building objectives (Pranis and Bazemore 2000). Despite these differences and disconnects between the agenda of restorative justice and those of more dominant intervention protocols, restorative justice is generally compatible with most other criminal justice objectives – public safety, sanctioning, offender rehabilitation and victim service (Bazemore and Walgrave 1999). Similarly, it is also possible to find some common ground with libertarians, interventionists and even crime control advocates who have now become part of the new expansionist coalition on the issue of diversion and informal social control.

Neither 'soft on crime', nor supportive of expanded punishment (Van Ness and Strong 1997; Zehr 1990), most restorative justice proponents stand with advocates of rehabilitation and treatment (interventionists) in affirming the need to actively respond to a range of problems that may be related to offending and at-risk behaviour with a variety of evidence-based interventions aimed at asset-building and reintegration (Bazemore 1998). However, restorative justice advocates also insist that the complex problems of youth crime and deviant behaviour are bigger than the risks and needs of the offender and therefore cannot be resolved by services and surveillance in the absence of effective engagement of neighbourhoods and socializing institutions where young people spend most of their time (Bazemore et al. 2000). Here, restorative justice advocates will ultimately stand with libertarians on many issues related to limiting the growth and power of the formal system because they too question the value of such intervention and are especially critical of the recent expansionism in juvenile justice (Christie 1977; Bazemore 1999). As proponents of a harm-focused paradigm, restorative justice advocates are concerned that programmes and policies aimed at helping stakeholders do not actually create additional problems for them, but rather provide space for community-driven processes to emerge and prosper in order to cultivate community responsibility for establishing peace.

With regard to interpretations of the diversion experience, net-widening is only part of the story, and not necessarily the most important part of it. The goal is to offer a cogent explanation for the failure of diversion to accomplish its original objectives of reducing the harm of court intervention. Proponents of restorative justice acknowledge that youth crime and behavioural problems do not go away simply by ignoring them, and would share with interventionists (including crime control advocates) the concern that a non-response to problems of youth crime is neither respectful to communities, nor politically feasible. However, both interventionist and libertarian perspectives promote simplistic views that ignore the community as a stakeholder capable of playing a fundamental role in the response to youth crime. Following Black (1976), we suggest that the expansion of formal law, and more generally of criminal justice systems, is in part a result of a decline in the role and functioning of community informal social control. In addition, changes in the extent and nature of criminal justice expansion may themselves weaken informal controls as part of a reciprocal impact (Rose and Clear 1998). That is, 'state controls, which typically are directed at individual behavior, have important secondary effects on family and neighborhood structure [that] impede the neighborhood's capacity for informal control [and thereby] exacerbate the very problems that lead to crime in the first place.' (Rose and Clear 1998: 469). Yet, with the rare exception of some writers who give primary emphasis to the role of public 'socializing' institutions such as schools and the workplace in the prevention and reduction of youth crime (e.g., Polk and Kobrin 1972; Polk 1984), neither libertarian nor inter-ventionists provide any analysis of the problem, or solution beyond simply expanding or restricting juvenile justice intervention. From this perspective, diversion may be truly viewed as a case study in how efforts to centralize, professionalize and expand juvenile justice, social services and even prevention, sent, and continue to send, messages to com-munities to 'leave crime to the experts.' In doing so, justice policymakers not only widened system nets, but also weakened *community nets* ultimately leaving communities helpless and hapless.

The restorative vision cannot therefore be simply characterized as anti-intervention, nor reduced to a 'hands-off' approach. More consistent with a communitarian approach (Etzioni 1996; Braithwaite 1994), restorative community justice seeks rather to promote a community 'hands on' agenda, and to do so in part through government action that casts justice agencies and professionals in a significantly different role. In contrast to the interventionist or expansionist view, intervention is not a job that should be left to government alone, and the restorative lens therefore seeks to bring into focus strengths in offenders, victims and communities that can be mobilized to rebuild or strengthen relationships. Finally, restorative intervention must avoid sending messages that young people who have harmed others will be 'diverted' from responsibility and accountability (Maloney 1998), focusing instead on new forms of accountability based on the obligation to repair harm to victims and victimized communities (Bazemore and Umbreit 1995).

In summary, both libertarian and interventionist analyses neglect to consider the diversion experience in the light of broader historical changes in community social control and changes in the role and responsibility assumed by criminal justice and professional service systems in the response to youth crime and trouble (e.g. Cohen 1985). Moreover, neither perspective gives adequate attention to the role and potential influence of informal social control, nor its place in a coherent youth policy or a responsive criminal justice agenda informed by a broader theoretical perspective on communities and crime (Braithwaite 1989; Bursik and Grasmick 1993). Such an agenda would be sensitive to the relationship between criminal justice and communities in the context of the harm of intervention (Rose and Clear 1998), and to research on the resiliency of offenders, victims and communities which documents conventional commitments and positive relationships even in the most high-risk environments (Maher 1991; Fishman 1990).

Restorative justice theory and policy: building social capital through strengthening informal social control and support

How might the normative theory of restorative justice, and restorative practice, connect with the larger concern about use of informal processes such as diversion and general policy regarding informal justice? How in addition might restorative principles be linked to broader etiological theory pertinent to communities and crime and what theory of intervention might connect restorative practices to community level outcomes?

Restorative justice theories-in-use have important implications for guiding programmatic responses to individual crimes, offenders and victims (Bazemore 2000) (see Table 8.1). However, many of us forget about some of the more macro, societal and community-level implications of theoretical perspectives derived from restorative justice principles and related literatures. For example, while the theory of reintegrative shaming is frequently discussed in social–psychological terms applicable to the explanation of the impact of family group conferencing (Braithwaite and Mugford 1994; Morris and Maxwell 2001), the broader societal and community implications for a sociological theory of crime are clearly summarized in the following statement: 'low crime societies are societies in which citizens do not mind their own business.' (Braithwaite 1989).

This core proposition of reintegrative shaming theory needs to be further developed, specified, and tested at middle-range, neighbourhood, and institutional levels. Thus far however, strong initial empirical support is provided from research in Chicago neighbourhoods that finds a strong

Table 8.1. Emerging restorative justice theories of intervention

Exchange theory		Accepting responsibility Making things right Repair … fixing what's broken Restoring balance 'Earned redemption'
Interpersonal dialogue		Empowering and giving 'voice' to victims and other stakeholders Gaining information and reassurance Apology and acknowledgement of harm and wrongdoing Human connection Expression of feelings/emotions – process over outcome
Reintegrative shaming	Individual level	Denounce the behaviour, not the offender Strong disapproval of act and norm affirmation, with expression of support for offenders and victims by family and others who matter to them Avoid stigmatizing 'shaming' – voice of victim is sufficient to induce feelings of shame in offender Community members committed to reintegration of offender and victim
	Community/ collective level	Low-crime communities are those where people don't mind their own business Community members set limits on behaviour and provide informal social control without exclusion
Community healing/ capacity building		Collective responsibility for crime and repair/healing Inclusion and connection important in their own right The resolution and healing lies in the group Sanctioning, rehabilitation, community safety interventions seamless and integrated – blurred distinctions between quality of life, community needs, criminal justice and social justice Emphasis on private and parochial controls and mutual support vs. professionals and justice system – 'community as driver'

and robust association between involvement of neighbourhood adults in discipline and norm affirmation activity with other peoples' children and youth crime (Sampson *et al.* 1997). That study's emphasis on 'collective efficacy' as the organizing concept, underlying informal social control as a factor in reducing youth crime, not only expands social disorganization theory (e.g., Bursik and Grasmick 1993), but also provides an important link to intervention that should be especially pertinent to restorative justice practitioners (Bazemore 2000).

A second macro-level insight pertinent to the diversion experience and to informal social control is Christie's well-known conceptualization of crime as 'stolen conflict' (1977). Though essentially a normative, rather than an etiological statement, this 'theft' or gradual inheritance of community conflict and crime by the state is, as suggested earlier, linked causally, by some new theorists of social disorganization, directly to the disempowerment of informal, community-level social controls (Rose and Clear 1998; Clear *et al.* 2001). As illustration, the harm of state intervention in the specific form of the incarceration of large numbers of young men operates as a predictor of high crime rates in a community and weakens community control mechanisms (Rose and Clear 1998). We believe that the lessons of the diversion experience and other research attentive to the potential harm of criminal justice intervention (e.g. Finkenhauer and Gavin 1999) suggest that the negative impact of formal criminal justice intervention can be generalized beyond the impact of incarceration to include a range of practices, including diversion (Polk 1987). Thus, expanding juvenile justice programmes may weaken neighbourhood cultural and structural supports for regulating behaviour and displace more naturalistic sources of control and support for young people such as those that once played a significant role in urban African–American communities (Wilson 1987), and may still play such a role in indigenous communities (Griffiths and Hamilton 1996).

To generalize beyond these unique cases, the concept of social capital provides a useful frame of reference for connecting neighbourhood efficacy in the response to youth crime and a theory of social control. Social capital refers to the set of social skills and resources needed to bring about and maintain positive community life (Putnam 2000; Coleman 1988); it constitutes the norms and networks that people in a community rely on to solve their own problems, rather than looking to outside support (Rose and Clear 1998). For Rose and Clear (1998), social capital is important to the informal control of youth crime as, 'it is the essence of social control ... the very force collectives draw upon to enforce order ... what enables groups to enforce norms...' (p. 454). Social capital is a vital organizing concept used to account for a variety of quality-of-life indicators in communities.

We suggest that social capital in response to youth crime and juvenile justice intervention will take two forms – informal social control and social support. These forms are best understood by considering the various types of social control that become resources in the response to youth crime and secondly, the resources that consist of informal community-based forms of social support. Both provide vital linking concepts that can indeed connect informal, community-driven responses to youth crime to restorative practices, and both to theory-driven collective outcomes.

Social control

Sociologist Albert Hunter (1985) has differentiated three general types of social control. Public controls are those imposed by the state and generally implemented through the various agencies of the criminal justice system. Private controls are informal constraints imposed by families and extended families, and have historically been a primary concern of juvenile court intervention (Whitehead and Lab 1998). However, this concern was typically operationalized as a deficit-focus that tended to blame families for the problems of young people in trouble while providing little in the way of intervention to shore up private controls (and little in the way of social support for these families). Therefore, as public controls have come to play a more dominant role and as juvenile and criminal justice agencies have assumed greater responsibility, both private social controls, and the third type of social control, parochial controls – those exercised by community institutions and groups (Hunter 1985) – have become substantially weaker, often with distressing consequences. Using parent–teacher associations (PTAs) as an example of parochial control, Rose and Clear (1998) note that these various forms of social control are interdependent and mutually reinforcing. The PTA is more likely to exert positive impact on children's behaviour and learning when parents know and interact with each other – when parents do not attend PTA, 'this organization ceases to exist as a mechanism of parochial control': moreover, without both forms of informal control, public controls are extremely limited:

> … public controls can operate in the neighborhood without regard for private and parochial controls, although often not as well. For instance, the police can do their jobs regardless of the state of the local PTA. Further, police can make the streets safe so residents can attend the local PTA meeting. They cannot, however, make residents want to attend that meeting. Only well-functioning private controls can manage that (Rose and Clear 1998).

When present in communities, this informal parochial, or 'village-level', control has been empirically associated with low rates of youth crime (Sampson *et al.* 1997) and when dormant or weak, may be viewed as a net loss in an essential form of neighbourhood social capital that some proponents of restorative justice ultimately wish to see replenished. The concern is that increased state intervention shifts the control of resources from the local to the public, which creates a dependency upon the state; this over-reliance on formal controls may hinder the ability of certain (already weak) communities to foster other forms of control, and as a result, these communities experience more disorganization (Rose and Clear 1998). When neighbours call the police to deal with problems of excessive noise, they have 'summoned public controls to shore up private and parochial controls' and families, schools and neighbourhood groups who refer their problem young people for professional help to diversion programmes may in fact have 'replaced parochial control with public control' (Rose and Clear 1998: 446). If restorative justice advocates wish to change this pattern – and contribute to Braithwaite's goal of ensuring that citizens do not choose to 'mind their own business' in addressing youth crime and trouble – they may seek to fill the void in parochial and private controls with restorative decision-making processes that provide the space and the tools necessary for adults to intervene firmly, and respectfully, in the lives of young people in trouble (Braithwaite 1994; Pranis and Bazemore 2000).

Specifically, restorative conferencing models (Bazemore and Umbreit 2001) are potentially well-placed to summon the private controls of families and extended families in the broader context of parochial control aimed at reinforcing behavioural and disciplinary norms. To the extent that such processes also continue to increase the skills and willingness of neighbourhood adults to informally censure destructive and harmful behaviour by young people, and reinforce other families in doing the same, they will have expanded and strengthened what may be conceptualized as a kind of 'public safety social capital'.

Social support

A theory and practice informed by restorative justice can never be only about social control. Restorative justice theory and practice is also strongly grounded in a new/old idea in criminology and criminal justice – 'social support' (Cullen 1994). Cullen and his colleagues (1999) have recently observed that the 'provision of affective and/or instrumental (or material) resources ... [through] intimate or confiding relationships ... [or] as a property of (cultural or structural) macro-level social units', is a critical but neglected causal factor 'inversely associated with crime in a variety of empirical studies' (p.190). Social support is therefore a potentially preventative and rehabilitative factor that seems to be fundamentally associated with one or more social relationships between the providers and recipients of such support. We may view the quality and strength of such support as directly related to the connections young people develop – through kinship, friendship and instrumental affiliations – to individuals and social groups, and to the overall quality of the nurturing and socialization process. Both are dependent upon the strength of care and concern, linked for young people to the sustained affective commitment of one or more caring adults (Werner 1986). Though most critical in the early childhood years, research on adolescents and young adults also consistently affirms the importance of the 'bond' to conventional institutions and supportive adults, both in preventing crime and in increasing the likelihood that young offenders will make the transition from criminal to conventional lifestyles (Hirschi 1969; Elliott 1994).

Social support is associated with societies that invest heavily in generous income enhancements for citizens, and in educational opportunities (Cullen 1994). Though most commentators have used the concept of social support to advocate for expanded social services and treatment programmes (Cullen *et al.* 1999), it is within informal community networks that social support has its most robust influence on young people. At the micro, informal level, where reintegration and integration actually occur, personal relationships with 'natural helpers' (Annie E. Casey Foundation 2001) – McKnight (1995) refers to them as 'community guides' – often act as bridge and buffer between the offender and the community, smoothing the way for the development of additional connections between the offender, law-abiding citizens and legitimate institutions. These informal opportunity networks become part of the human capital for young offenders, and all young people who need to gain access to institutional roles (e.g., in work, education and community groups). Such roles provide them with a legitimate identity and a 'bond' to the conventional community (Polk and Kobrin 1972; Bazemore *et al.* 2000), thus increasing the likelihood that they will make the transition from delinquent and deviant careers to conventional lifestyles (Hirschi 1969; Sampson and Laub 1993; Elliott 1994). As the number and strength of such relationships increases, and as these relationships provide additional access to legitimate roles for more youth at risk, they in turn build social capital for social support at the neighbourhood level.

Restorative practices seem particularly well suited to strengthen what could be labelled 'private social support' by, for example, engaging families in family group conferencing or family support groups. Such practices also strengthen 'parochial social support' by, for example, engaging community members in reparative boards and in community service projects in which they work together with young people on initiatives that meet local needs and may also help to reconnect victims and offenders with their natural communities of care, or to mobilize new sources of support in a kind of naturalistic ceremony of reintegration (Braithwaite and Mugford 1994; Bazemore 2000). To the extent that restorative interventions actually do build new relationships between young people and law-abiding adults (or strengthen old ones), they can indeed contribute to the reservoir of social capital needed to guide and nurture young people and reintegrate those in trouble. In summary, restorative practices may be useful tools in an effort to rebuild the community social capital needed to respond to youth crime and trouble. Using restorative programmes in this way, however, will require thinking strategically about where restorative practice and policy might fit within the current system of juvenile justice informalism as structured through diversion processes and programmes.

Restorative justice practice in the informal context: reframing diversion

Diversion is likely to remain a major, if not primary location for restorative practice. On the positive side, those pursuing restorative practices have already changed the content and goals of diversion intervention by focusing on repairing the harm of crime and the obligation of the offender to the victim and the community. They are also doing much to meet the needs of victims of less serious crimes – never before a primary consideration for most diversion programmes – and to send a different message to victims and the community about core expectations and objectives for informal processes (Umbreit 1999; Bazemore 2000). On the negative side however, changing the practice of diversion – and even doing away with the use of the term diversion (Maloney 1998) – will not by itself solve the primary problem of cooptation of restorative justice programmes as part of the new interventionism-plus juvenile justice agenda. In a future scenario that would be predicted by libertarian critics of the diversion experience and of the emerging restorative justice movement (Polk 1987; Feld 1999), restorative programmes at the diversion level may provide yet another avenue for the system to process cases, while simultaneously bringing more youth under the umbrella of juvenile justice control.

One response from the restorative side to critics who assert that restorative practices will widen the net (Feld 1999; Levrant *et al.* 1999) is that there is nothing to suggest that restorative justice programmes will be any more invasive than other diversion programmes – and for various reasons will quite possibly be less so (Bazemore and Walgrave 1999). Because we believe a positive future for restorative justice is tightly linked to the 'less so' scenario, the 'no worse' argument seems unsatisfactory except to deflect premature criticisms and put things in perspective. One solution to the problem of net-widening would be for restorative programmes to simply refuse to accept diversion cases, focusing instead on post-dispositional referrals; yet abandoning the diversion to the myriad range of other often dubious and even demonstrably harmful programmes (e.g., Finkenhauer and Gavin 1999) that clearly widen the net, while failing to offer any of the benefits for the victim, offender and community of restorative intervention, seems not to address the issue of greatest concern to those who are unhappy with the expansionist agenda itself.

To address this concern, restorative programmes in the diversion context need a more meaningful standard of success than simply avoiding net-widening. Such a standard may be one that turns the problem of net-widening on its head by asking whether and to what extent programmes build community capacity for informal support and control, or strengthen 'community nets' (Braithwaite 1994). Following Christie (1977), programmes in the diversion space should at a minimum avoid 'stealing the conflict from its community of origin'. Diversion programmes under the expansionist or interventionist umbrella may therefore be seen as simply another 'thief of conflict' when they are viewed not as alternatives to court or other formal processes, but as a dumping ground for problems once addressed informally in private and parochial contexts. In stealing the conflict from families, neighbours and schools, restorative programmes would not strengthen community nets, and like any other diversion programme would be vulnerable to weakening them while providing yet another path of entry into the formal system.

Restorative diversion programmes could easily fit into the expansionist agenda, or alternatively shift the focus of informal responses to community-building as a primary outcome. For example, a programme that conducts family group conferences may find itself receiving the vast majority of its referrals from juvenile court intake for low-level school-related incidents. It may simply accept these referrals gladly, arguing that the benefits compared to the experience of court likely outweigh the problem associated with siphoning conflict out of the school as its community of origin and relieving educators and students from their responsibility for responding to this conflict. The dilemma for the programme is to determine the probability that it indeed provided an alternative to court – not an easy decision in a climate of zero-tolerance policies in schools in many of the states that allow suspension or expulsion for minor rule violations and conflicts once addressed at the classroom or schoolyard level. In the context of the new expansionism, programme professionals must decided whether they wish to be complicit in a process designed to extend diversion programmes to the lowest level of community responsibility while maintaining decision-making control in the hands of courts and prosecutors and making few if any changes in how more serious cases are processed.

Another similar family group programme may also choose to accept a limited number of such court-referred school conflict cases. However, the rationale behind this decision might be to both build a relationship with the school and collaborate with and educate the court, but in addition for the programme to pursue a different strategy based on a distinctive understanding with the school administration. This strategy would devote a portion of staff time to an assignment working directly with school personnel to establish conferencing programmes in the classroom with teachers and school staff as facilitators and develop a whole-school alternative disciplinary procedure to eventually displace zero tolerance policies. The primary objective of this approach is to keep the resolution of conflict in the school and assist staff and students in developing and enhancing skills in restorative decision-making at all levels; one ultimate goal is to reduce the number of suspensions and expulsions – and the referrals to court that often accompany these – while creating a safer and more peaceful school environment.

In the former case, the programme, regardless of its possible help to victim and offender, has basically become a kind of 'safety valve' for relieving schools, families, neighbours, local police and other community groups from their responsibility for resolving crime, conflict and related problems once addressed at the neighbourhood level, rather than as a real alternative to non-inclusive, adversarial decision-making. In sucking conflict from its community of origin via the juvenile justice system, the programme has not simply widened the net of formal control, but also arguably contributed to the deskilling of the school as a potentially safe and peaceful community. In the latter case, the programme has helped build social capital in the form of capacity for community resolution of conflict in a way that does not widen the net and empowers students and school personnel as citizens with a stake in how conflict is managed in their community. While these are subtle differences, they are highly significant in terms of long-term focus and impact of informal restorative practices. These differences also seem to provide an important test of complicity in the expansionist system as contrasted with the values associated with restorative principle (3): empowering the community, while using government/professional resources to facilitate conflict resolution and build community capacity.

Concluding remarks: the future

The problem of disconnect in restorative justice has been identified as a result of a failure to focus on larger community-level outcomes that currently influence juvenile justice agendas. In this chapter we have argued that diversion policy and practice could be positively influenced by an analysis informed by restorative principles applied beyond the constraints of individual cases. One such agenda is the need to support informal social control and support the development of a restorative justice approach to 'doing,' and analysing, informal responses to youth crime.

Connecting with mainstream juvenile justice policy should not of course be the primary objective of restorative justice. Indeed, the objective of a restorative justice approach should be to challenge and transform such policy while providing systemic alternatives to it. Specifically, diversion as we know it should not simply be influenced by restorative practices; it should *become* restorative justice (though the latter should not be limited to the informal context) (Bazemore and Walgrave 1999). We have argued that the history of diversion in the US provides a case study in the inadequacy of libertarian and interventionist policy visions. Diversion programmes not only widened the juvenile justice net, but more importantly, like other forms of expansion in public social control (Rose and Clear 1998), also weakened informal, community-based control and supportive responses to problems in the socialization of young people. These responses are generally those that restorative justice practice should seek to build upon and enhance.

The restorative justice lens should focus on diversion as a process and programme that is neither inherently evil (the libertarian view) nor inherently good (the interventionist view), but rather flawed in its failure to engage community. A restorative theory of intervention should therefore point diversion policy and practice in new directions. Building on the insights of research and theory on the role of community in crime generation based on social disorganization and harm perspectives (Braithwaite 1989; Bursik and Grasmik 1993), social capital theory and research (Putnam 2000; Coleman 1988), and the normative theory of 'republican justice' (Braithwaite and Pettit 1990; Braithwaite and Parker 1999), we have suggested an outline for a new theory of informal social control and social support that should have practical utility in the transformation of what has been a very weak, and often harmful, version of informalism in juvenile justice (Polk 1987; Cohen 1985). In moving towards a more collective, community-building vision, it is at least possible that the restorative justice framework may be capable of avoiding the individualizing tendencies of both treatment and punishment paradigms and may, as Sampson and Wilson (1995) suggest, provide 'a community-level perspective ... [that] lead[s] away from a simple "kinds of people" analysis to a focus on social characteristics of collectivities that foster violence (and crime).' (p. 54).

In an alternative, more optimistic possible future scenario for informal justice, it will be principles, not programmes and system-driven policy that must guide development. Informed by the community and restorative justice paradigms (Van Ness and Strong 1997; Clear and Karp 1999), such principles could guide the development of a more affirmative strategy for community social control that may increase the likelihood that informal restorative decision-making processes will strengthen rather than weaken the community response to youth crime. In the absence of such a vision, theory and strategic approach, restorative justice practices, like all other diversion programmes, are vulnerable to being swallowed up in the new expansionist juvenile justice agenda. Ironically, these restorative justice practices may all too easily 'fit in' in a collaborative expansionist policy environment where, as Cohen (1985) suggests, everyone seems to be 'delivering the same message' regardless of the practical realities of justice systems that, despite rhetoric to the contrary, have been disconnected from the communities they serve for decades.

Based on this potential, we suggest a general five-part solution to guide development of an implementation strategy. First, restorative justice advocates need to be unequivocal in their challenge to the punishment/control/harm paradigm under which there appear to be no limits to pain administered by the state (Christie 1981). While new forms of accountability that reinforce offender responsibility, redemption and citizenship while allowing vindication and new options for victims (Toews-Shenk and Zehr 2001) can be negotiated depending on the specific needs of communities and victims, restorative justice must keep repair and relationship building as its primary objectives in the response to youth crime. Second, though restorative justice should seek to fill up the diversion space with new forms of community-building and conflict resolution, the restorative agenda experiences an insurmountable loss in potency if pigeonholed in the diversion policy and programme context, and should rather be adapted for use throughout systems and communities in response to all crimes. Third, the goal must be to demonstrate real change in the nature of social control so that government assumes a supportive role in facilitating informal community-driven processes. Fourth, informalism alone, especially the romantic kind that some restorative justice advocates seem to promote, is insufficient (Abel 1982). Therefore, restorative justice implementation must be tied to an equal emphasis on a strong social welfare state (Braithwaite 2000), albeit one in which there has been significant transformation in the professional role and criminal justice agency mandate, both in terms of support for informalism, and also in the nature of the formal justice process itself. Finally, efforts to use restorative justice processes to transform the community response to youth crime and trouble are insufficient without an institutional reform approach using youth development principles to guide organizational and inter-organizational change in socializing institutions such as school and work. The latter must focus on the development of new roles for young people to contribute to the common good and enhance a sense of belonging and citizenship for youth while also working toward transformation of both learning and disciplinary structures within these communities of socialization (Polk and Kobrin 1972; Polk 1984), using the inclusive participatory principles of restorative justice in the school environment (Riestenberg 1996).

There are of course good reasons for scepticism, and we are especially aware of the dangers of abstract appeals to community Walgrave, this volume). As Cohen (1985) suggests:

'community' is a 'magic word' that 'lacks any negative connotations' (p. 117) and 'rolls off the tongues of correctional administrators … as easily as … radical community activists' (p. 36)… Almost anything can appear under the heading of 'community' and almost anything can be justified if this prefix is used (p. 116).

Although restorative justice in the US appears to be generating a surprising and qualitatively different amount of citizen involvement in justice processes, a formidable barrier to meaningful community participation for most formal justice systems is the pejorative view of 'citizens as clients' (McKnight 1995) and the tendency of some professionals to dismiss the possibility of community as partner, much less a driving force, in the response to youth crime (Pranis 1997). Whereas the empirical evidence drawn from the experience of community policing in some jurisdictions also creates significant doubts about this willingness and capacity of citizens and community groups to come forward (e.g., Rosenbaum, Lurgio and Davis 1998), what we have learned from the restorative justice experience thus far seems to challenge the commonly accepted wisdom of an apathetic public (Hudson *et al.* 1996; McCold and

Wachtel 1998; Umbreit 1999). Citizen involvement in Vermont's reparative probation programme has sustained state-wide volunteer boards for almost a decade (Perry and Gorcyzyk 1997; Karp and Bazemore 2001), and hundreds of citizens have participated in neighbourhood youth panels or accountability boards, as well as family group community conferencing, victim–offender mediation, and peacemaking circles (Bazemore 1997).

Nonetheless, our European friends will likely remain sceptical about the prospect of enhancing the community role in the response to youth crime, and about the wisdom of such strategies, especially in countries like the US where, by European standards, 'community' is really nowhere in evidence (Kerner and Weitekamp, this volume). Aspirations for an engaged community in this context may indeed seem like appeals to magic, or at least be dismissed as Utopian thinking. However, we remind our colleagues of Lode Walgrave's observation that there is 'nothing so practical as a good utopia'. And, we may even turn for guidance to the most seemingly pessimistic critics such as Stanley Cohen himself, who has stated his 'preference to be pragmatic about short-term possibilities, but Utopian about constructing long-term alternatives.' (1985: 116). With this in mind, we acknowledge that all restorative justice advocates are in one sense Utopians. Hence, rather than dismiss the community ideal outright, we encourage debate concerning the utility of our visions for ultimately using restorative justice to enrich the quality of life in communities, while also repairing harm to individual victims and offenders.

Notes

1. Indeed, with the right vision and attention to community level justice outcomes, an informal process such as restorative conferencing that engages citizens in non-adversarial decision making could form the basis for building and expanding a parallel, informal justice track that could seek to maximize displacement of formal processing (Braithwaite 1999; Van Ness 2001) – even to the point of making the concept of diversion itself an anachronism. Generally, diversion has not fit comfortably within the discourse of restorative justice (Walgrave and Bazemore 1999).
2. Applying these ideas to the juvenile court, diversion advocates argued that regardless of intent, court intervention often creates a 'spoiled identity' for young people (Schur 1973). Once the young person begins to accept the view of himself as a delinquent and confronts the changes in the response of others to him/her, including restrictions in options to pursue success in legitimate institutions such as school and work, choice of friends or peer group might also be further limited (Polk and Kobrin 1972; Bazemore 1985). An increasing association with deviant peers might then provide a context for learning new

delinquency, as well as for further change in self-concept, and also damage the public image of the stigmatized individual resulting in additional exclusionary responses on the part of legitimate society.

3. Because diversion as a process meant that the court and juvenile justice system would relinquish a great deal of its jurisdiction and control (PCC 1967; Lemert 1971), what has come to be known as 'pure diversion' literally meant that police or other juvenile professionals would be encouraged not to take young people to court – by releasing them outright or returning them to their homes, schools or community-based agencies (Klein 1976).

4. Because of its appeal to a growing perception in the early 1970s of the limited resources available to the court to manage the sheer volume of cases being processed through the system, the workload argument is one that seems especially important in convincing judges and other court decision-makers to support the diversion concept. Some states have legislation authorizing funds for diversion programmes (Roberts 1998), and many jurisdictions have developed a wide range of community treatment alternatives to which offenders may be referred through an informal process generally involving an admission of responsibility for the offence in exchange for avoiding a formal court hearing and an official record of delinquency. In much of the US, the term 'diversion' has become almost synonymous with these programmes.

5. With a few exceptions – such as programmes focused primarily on restitution or community service and youth employment (Schneider 1986) – most diversion programmes included a core common element, counselling (Whitehead and Lab 1999). Most ultimately came to define their mission as providing or referring youth to therapeutic and/or remedial interventions which were in actual practice consistent with the traditional individual treatment mission of the court (Polk 1984). The primary competing philosophy, youth development, leaned heavily towards advocacy at both the individual and institutional level (e.g., school reform). Promoted for a brief period of time by the national Office of Youth Development in the Bureau of Health and Human Services, it focused on encouraging development of new positive roles for all youth aimed at helping them to gain skills and experience to become resources to their communities (Polk and Kobrin 1972; Pearl and Reissman 1966; Pearl et al. 1978; Bird et al. 1978; Pitman and Fleming 1991).

References

Abel, R. L. (1982) 'Introduction' in R. Abel, *The Politics of Informal Justice: Comparative Studies, 2. Studies on Law and Social Control*. New York: Academic Press.

Annie E. Casey Foundation (2001) *Walking Our Talk in the Neighborhood: Partnerships Between Professionals and Natural Helpers*. Baltimore, MD: Annie E. Casey Foundation.

Bazemore, G. (1985) 'Delinquent Reform and the Labeling Perspective', *Criminal Justice and Behavior*, 12(2): 131–69.

Bazemore, G. (1997) 'The "Community" in Community Justice: Issues, Themes and Questions for the New Neighborhood Sanctioning Models', *The Justice System Journal*, 19(2): 193–228.

Bazemore, G. (1998) 'Restorative Justice and Earned Redemption: Communities, Victims and Offender Reintegration', *American Behavioral Scientist*, 41(6): 768–813.

Bazemore, G. (1999) 'The Fork in the Road to Juvenile Court Reform', *The Annals of the American Academy of Political and Social Science*, 564(7): 81–108.

Bazemore, G. (2000) 'Community Justice and a Vision of Collective Efficacy: The Case of Restorative Conferencing' in *Criminal Justice 2000* (vol. 3). Washington, DC: National Institute of Justice, US Department of Justice

Bazemore, G., Nissen, L. and Dooley, M. (2000) 'Mobilizing Social Support and Building Relationships: Broadening Correctional and Rehabilitative Agendas', *Corrections Management Quarterly*, 4(4): 10–21.

Bazemore, G. and Umbreit, M. (1995) 'Rethinking the Sanctioning Function in Juvenile Court: Retributive or Restorative Responses to Youth Crime.' *Crime and Delinquency*, 41(3): 296–316.

Bazemore, G. and Umbreit, M. (2001) 'A Comparison of Four Restorative Conferencing Models.' *Juvenile Justice Bulletin*, Office of Juvenile Justice and Delinquency Prevention. Office of Justice Programs. US Department of Justice.

Bazemore, G. and Walgrave, L. (1999). *Restorative Juvenile Justice: Repairing the Harm of Youth Crime*. Monsey, NY: Criminal Justice Press.

Becker, H. S. (1963). *Outsiders: Studies in the Sociology of Deviance*. New York, NY: Free Press.

Binder, A. (1998). 'Juvenile Diversion' in A. Binder (ed.) *Juvenile Justice, Policies, Programs, and Services*. Chicago, IL: Nelson-Hall.

Binder and Geis (1984) '*Ad Populum* Argumentation in Criminology: Juvenile Diversion as Rhetoric'. *Crime and Delinquency* 30(2): 309–33.

Bird, T., Beville, S. L., Carlson, O. and Johnson, G. (1978) *A Design for Youth Development Policy*. (Monograph) Washington, DC: US Department of Health, Education, and Welfare.

Black, D. (1976) *The Behavior of Law*. New York: Academic Press.

Braithwaite, J. (1989) *Crime, Shame, and Reintegration*. New York: Cambridge University Press.

Braithwaite, J. (1994) 'Thinking Harder About Democratizing Social Control' in C. Alder and J. Wundersitz (eds) *Family Group Conferencing in Juvenile Justice: The Ways Forward of Misplaced Optimism?* Canberra, AUS: Australian Institute of Criminology.

Braithwaite, J. (1999) 'Restorative Justice: Assessing Optimistic and Pessimistic Accounts' in *Crime and Justice: An Annual Review of Research*, 25, University of Chicago.

Braithwaite, J. (2000) 'The New Regulatory State and the Transformation of Criminology,' *British Journal of Criminology*, 40: 222–38.

Braithwaite, J. and Mugford, S. (1994). 'Conditions of Successful Reintegration Ceremonies: Dealing with Juvenile Offenders', *British Journal of Criminology*, 34(2): 139–71.

Braithwaite, J. and Parker, C. (1999) 'Restorative Justice is Republican Justice' in G. Bazemore and L. Walgrave (eds) *Restorative Juvenile Justice: Repairing the Harm of Youth Crime*. Monsey, NY: Criminal Justice Press.

Braithwaite, J. and Pettit, P. (1990) *Not Just Desert. A Republican Theory of Criminal Justice*. Oxford: Oxford University Press.

Braithwaite, J. and Roche, D. (2001) 'Responsibility and Restorative Justice' in G. Bazemore and M. Schiff (eds) *Restorative Community Justice: Repairing Harm and Transforming Communities*. Cincinnati, OH: Anderson.

Bursik, R. J., Jr., and Grasmick, H. G. (1993) *Neighborhoods and Crime: The Dimensions of Effective Community Control*. New York: Lexington.

Butts, J. and Mears, D. (2001) 'Reviving Juvenile Justice in a Get-Tough Era', *Youth and Society*, 33(2): 169–98.

Christie, N. (1977) 'Conflict as Property.' *British Journal of Criminology*, 17(1): 1–15.

Christie, N. (1981) *Limits to Pain*. Oxford, UK: Martin Robertson.

Clear, T. and Karp, D. (1999) *The Community Justice Ideal: Preventing Crime and Achieving Justice*. Boulder, CO: Westview Press.

Clear, T., Rose, D. and Ryder, J. (2001) 'Incarceration and the Community: The Problem of Removing and Returning Offenders', *Crime and Delinquency*, 47(3): 335–51.

Cohen, S. (1985) *Visions of Social Control: Crime, Punishment, and Classification*. New York: Polity Press.

Coleman, J. (1988) 'Social Capital in the Creation of Human Capital,' *American Journal of Sociology* (Supplement) 94: S95–S120.

Corrado, R. This volume.

Cullen, F. T. (1994) 'Social Support as an Organizing Concept for Criminology', Presidential Address to the Academy of Criminal Justice Sciences, *Justice Quarterly*, 11: 527–59.

Cullen, F. T., Wright, J. P. and Chamlin, M. B. (1999) 'Social Support and Social Reform: A Progressive Crime Control Agenda'. *Crime and Delinquency*, 45: 188–207.

Elliott, D. (1994) 'Serious Violent Offenders: Onset, Developmental Course, and Termination', 1993 Presidential Address. *The American Society of Criminology. Criminology*, 32(1).

Empey, L. T. (1982) *American Delinquency: Its Meaning and Construction*. Homewood, IL: Dorsey Press.

Etzioni, A. (1996) 'The Responsive Community: A Communitarian Perspective', *American Sociological Review*, 61(1): 1–12.

Fader, J., Harris, P., Jones, P. and Poulin, M. (2001) 'Factors Involved in Decisions On Commitment to Delinquency Programs for First-Time Juvenile Offenders', *Justice Quarterly*, 18(2): 323–41.

Feld, B. (1999) 'Rehabilitation, Retribution and Restorative Justice: Alternative Conceptions of Juvenile Justice,' in G. Bazemore and L. Walgrave (eds), *Restorative Juvenile Justice: Repairing the Harm of Youth Crime*, Monsey, NY: Criminal Justice Press.

Finckenhauer, J. and Gavin, P. (1999) *Scared Straight: The Panacea Phenomenon Revisited*. Prospect Heights, IL: Waveland Press.

Fishman, L. (1990) *Women at the Wall*. Albany, NY: SUNY Press.

Friel, C. M. (2000) 'Introduction to Volume 2: A Century of Changing Boundaries', Introduction in Volume 2, Boundary Changes in Criminal Justice Organization: Criminal Justice 2000. Washington, DC. National Institute of Justice, US Department of Justice.

Glendon, M. (1991) 'Does the U.S. Need Good Samaritan Laws?' *The Responsive Community*, 1: 9–15.

Griffiths, C. and Corrado, R. (1999) 'Implementing Restorative Youth Justice: A Case Study in Community Justice and the Dynamics of Reform' in G. Bazemore and L. Walgrave (eds) *Restorative Juvenile Justice: Repairing the Harm Caused by Youth Crime*. New York: Criminal Justice Press.

Griffiths, C. T. and Hamilton, R. (1996) 'Spiritual Renewal, Community Revitalization and Healing. Experience in Traditional Aboriginal Justice in Canada', *International Journal of Comparative and Applied Criminal Justice*, 20(1): 285–310.

Hirschi, T. (1969) *Causes of Delinquency*. Berkeley, CA: University of California Press.

Hudson, J., Galaway, B., Morris, A., and Maxwell, G. (1996) 'Introduction' in J. Hudson, B. Galaway, A. Morris and G. Maxwell (eds) *Family Group Conferences: Perspectives on Policy and Practice*. Monsey, NY: Criminal Justice Press.

Hunter, A. J. (1985) 'Private, Parochial and Public Social Orders: The Problem of Crime and Incivility in Urban Communities' in G. D. Suttles and M. N. Zald (eds) *The Challenge of Social Control: Citizenship and Institution Building in Modern Society*. Norwood, NJ: Aldex Publishing.

Ingram, H. and Schneider, A. (1991) 'The Social Construction of Target Populations', *Administration and Society*, 23(3): 353–351.

Jensen, G. F. and Rojek, D. G. (1998). *Delinquency and Youth Crime*. Prospects Heights, IL: Waveland Press, Inc.

Karp, D. and Bazemore, G. (2001) 'Restorative Justice Volunteers Tell Their Story: A Summary Account of the Citizen Justice', unpublished monograph, Balanced and Restorative Justice Project, Community Justice Institute, Florida Atlantic University, Ft. Lauderdale, FL.

Kerner, H. J. and Weitekamp, E. This volume.

Klein, M. S. (1976). 'Issues in Police Diversion of Juvenile Offenders' in R. M. Carter and M. W. Klein (eds) *Back on the Street: The Diversion of Juvenile Offenders*. Englewood Cliffs, NJ: Prentice Hall.

Lemert, E. M. (1971). *Instead of Court: Diversion in Juvenile Justice*. Rockville MD: National Institute of Mental Health.

Lemert, E. M. (1981). 'Diversion in Juvenile Justice: What Hath Been Wrought?', *Journal of Research in Crime and Delinquency*, 18: 34–46.

Levrant, S., Cullen, F., Fulton, B., and Wozniak, J. (1999). 'Reconsidering Restorative Justice: The Corruption of Benevolence Revisited?', *Crime and Delinquency*, 45(1): 3–27.

Maher, L. (1991) 'Punishment and Welfare: Crack Cocaine and the Regulation of Mothering' in C. Feinman (ed.) *The Criminalization of a Woman's Body*. New York: Haworth.

Maloney, D. (1998) 'The Challenge of Restorative Community Justice'. Address at the Annual Meeting of the Juvenile Justice Coalition, Washington, DC, February.

McCold, P. and Wachtel, B. (1998) *Restorative Policing Experiment: The Bethlehem Pennsylvania Police Family Group Conferencing Project.* Pipersville, PA: Community Service Foundation.

McKnight, J. (1995) *The Careless Society: Community and Its Counterfeits.* New York: Basic Books.

Miller (1991) *Last One Over the Wall.* Columbus, OH: Ohio State University.

Moore, D.B. (1994) 'Illegal Action – Official Reaction'. Unpublished paper. Canberra, ACT: Australian Institute of Criminology.

Moore, D. and O'Connell, T. (1994) 'Family Conferencing in Wagga-Wagga: A Communitarian Model of Justice' in C. Adler and J. Wundersitz (eds) *Family Group Conferencing and Juvenile Justice the Way Forward or Misplaced Optimism?* Canberra, Australia: Australia Institute of Criminology.

Morris, A. and Maxwell, G. (2001) 'Restorative Conferencing' in G. Bazemore and M. Schiff (eds) *Restorative Community Justice: Repairing Harm and Transforming Communities.* Cincinnati, OH: Anderson.

Pearl, A. and Reissman, F. (1966) *New Careers for the Poor.* New York: The Free Press.

Pearl, A., Grant, D. and Wenck, E. (eds) (1978) *The Value of Youth.* Davis, CA: Dialogue Books.

Perry, J. G. and Gorcyzk, J. F. (1997) 'Restructuring Corrections: Using Market Research in Vermont', *Corrections Management Quarterly*, 1(3): 2–35.

Pitman, K. and Fleming, W. (1991) 'A New Vision: Promoting Youth Development'. Testimony before the US House Select Committee on Children, Youth, and Families. 30 September. Washington, DC: Academy for Educational Development.

Platt, A. (1977). *The Child Savers: The Invention of Delinquency.* Chicago, IL: University of Chicago Press.

Polk, K. (1984). 'Juvenile Diversion: A Look at the Record', *Crime and Delinquency* 30, 648–59.

Polk, K. (1987) 'When Less Means More: An Analysis of Destructuring in Criminal Justice', *Crime and Delinquency*, 33, 358–78.

Polk, K. (2001) 'Positive Youth Development, Restorative Justice, and the Crisis of Abandoned Youth' in *Restorative and Community Justice: Repairing Harm and Transforming Communities.* Cincinnati, OH: Anderson.

Polk, K. and Kobrin, S. (1972) *Delinquency Prevention Through Youth Development.* Washington, DC: Office of Youth Development.

Pranis, K. (1997) 'From Vision to Action: Church and Society', *Presbyterian Church Journal of Just Thoughts*, 87(4): 32–42.

Pranis, K. and Bazemore, G. (2000) 'Engaging Community in the Response to Youth Crime: A Restorative Justice Approach'. Monograph, prepared for the Office of Juvenile Justice and Delinquency Prevention, Balanced and Restorative Justice Project, US Department of Justice, Washington, DC.

President's Commission on Crime and Law Enforcement (1967). Task Force Report: Juvenile Delinquency and Youth Crime. Washington, DC: GPO.

Putnam, R. (2000) *Bowling Alone: The Collapse and Revival of American Community*. New York: Simon and Shuster.

Riestenberg, N. (1996) *Restorative Measures in the Schools*. Roseville, MN: Minnesota Department of Children, Families and Learning.

Roberts, A, (1998) *Juvenile Justice: Policies, Programs and Services*. Chicago, IL: Nelson-Hall.

Rojek, D. G. (1982) 'Juvenile Diversion: A Study of Community Cooptation' in D. G. Rojek and G. F. Jensen (eds) *Reading in Juvenile Delinquency*. Lexington MA, DC Heath: 316–321.

Rose, D. and Clear, T. (1998) 'Incarceration, Social Capital and Crime: Implications for Social Disorganization Theory', *Criminology*, 36(3): 471–479.

Rosenbaum, D., Lurgio, and Davis, R. (1998) *The Prevention of Crime: Social and Situational Strategies*, West/Wadsworth Contemporary Issues in Crime and Justice Series, New York: International Thomson Publishing Company.

Sampson, R. J. and Laub, J. H. (1993) *Crime in the Making: Pathways and Turning Points Through Life*. Cambridge, MA: Harvard University Press.

Sampson, R., Rodenbush, S., and Earls, F. (1997) 'Neighborhoods and Violent Crime: A Multi-Level Study of Collective Efficacy', *Science Magazine*, 277 (August).

Sampson, R. J. and Wilson, J. (1995) 'Toward a Theory of Race' in J. Hagan and R. D. Peterson (eds) *Crime and Urban Inequality*. Stanford, CA: Stanford University Press.

Schiff, M. and Bazemore, G. (2001) 'Exploring and Shaping the Future' in G. Bazemore and M. Schiff (eds) *Restorative Community Justice: Repairing Harm and Transforming Communities*. Cincinnati, OH: Anderson.

Schneider, A. (1986) 'Restitution and Recidivism Rates of Juvenile Offenders: Results From Four Experimental Studies,' *Criminology*, 24(3): 533–552.

Schur, E. M. (1973) *Radical Nonintervention: Rethinking the Delinquency Problem*. Englewood Cliffs, NJ: Prentice Hall.

Schwartz, M. (1989) *(In)Justice for Juveniles*. Lexington MA: Lexington Books.

Skogan, W. (1990) *Disorder and Decline: Crime and the Spiral of Decay in American Neighborhood*. New York: Free Press.

Toews-Shenk, B. and Zehr, H. (2001) 'Restorative Justice and Substance Abuse: The Path Ahead', *Youth and Society*, 33(2): 314–28.

Umbreit, M. (1999) 'Avoiding the Marginalization and McDonaldization of Victim Offender Mediation: A Case Study in Moving Toward the Mainstream' in G. Bazemore and L. Walgrave (eds) *Restorative Juvenile Justice: Repairing the Harm of Youth Crime*. Monsey, NY: Criminal Justice Press.

Umbreit, M. This volume.

Van Ness, D. (2001) 'Toward a Systemic Model of Restorative Justice', presentation to Restorative Justice Advanced Trainers' Conference, Community Justice Institute, Florida Atlantic University, Ft. Lauderdale, FL.

Van Ness, D. and Schiff, M. (2001) 'Satisfaction Guaranteed? The Meaning of Satisfaction in Restorative Justice' in G. Bazemore and M. Schiff (eds) *Restorative Community Justice: Repairing Harm and Transforming Communities*. Cincinnati, OH: Anderson.

Van Ness, D. and Strong, K. (1997) *Restoring Justice.* Cincinnati, OH: Anderson.

Walgrave, L. and Bazemore, G. (1999) 'Reflections on the Future of Restorative Justice for Juveniles' in G. Bazemore and L. Walgrave (eds) *Restorative Juvenile Justice: Repairing the Harm of Youth Crime.* Monsey, NY: Criminal Justice Press.

Werner, E. (1986) 'Resilient Offspring of Alcoholics: A Longitudinal Study from Birth to 18', *Journal of Studies on Alcoholics,* 47, 34–40.

Whitehead, J. T. and Lab, S. P. (1998). *Juvenile Justice: An Introduction.* Cincinnati, OH: Anderson.

Wilson, W. J. (1987) *The Truly Disadvantaged: The Inner City, the Underclass, and Public Policy.* Chicago: University of Chicago Press.

Wilson, J. (2000) 'Benefits and Challenges of Community Assessment Centers'. Bulletin, Office of Juvenile Justice and Delinquency, US Department of Justice, Washington, DC.

Zehr, H. (1990) *Changing Lenses: A New Focus for Crime and Justice.* Scottsdale, PA: Herald Press.

Chapter 9

Restorative conferencing for juveniles in the United States: prevalence, process, and practice[1]

Mara Schiff and Gordon Bazemore

Restorative justice practices have increasingly gained prominence as viable justice-system strategies throughout the last few decades. Various programmes, practices and systemic initiatives have arisen in the United States (Umbreit 2001; McCold and Wachtel 1998; Bazemore and Schiff 2002), Europe (Walgrave 1999; Weitekamp 1999; Young and Hoyle 2002; Miers 2001), Australia (Daly 2001; Sherman *et al.* 2000), New Zealand (Morris and Maxwell 2001), and Canada (Stuart 2001; Bonta *et al.* 1998). These have ranged from small, *ad hoc* initiatives in local communities (e.g., in many US states), to system-wide initiatives intended to alter the manner in which young people are processed through the juvenile justice system (e.g. in Australia and New Zealand). There have, however, been few systematic attempts to capture the prevalence of such initiatives in a single country and to examine the degree to which practice is operating consistent with, and informed by, restorative values and principles (Bazemore and Schiff 2002).

Such community-based, informal decision-making alternatives to court and other adversarial processes for dealing with youthful offending have proliferated across the United States since the late 1980s and early 1990s (Bazemore 2000). Described in this paper as *restorative conferencing* programmes,[2] these alternatives encompass a variety of decision-making processes and administrative models that have arisen in response to concerns about the effectiveness of traditional youth sanctioning approaches focused on incapacitation, punishment and individual treatment or pre-ventative responses administered by traditional diversion programmes, probation and community corrections (Bazemore and Umbreit 2001). In contrast, restorative conferencing approaches generally stress a variety of goals including: repairing harm to victims and communities, direct offender accountability to those harmed by the crime, victim and offender healing, relationship building, offender reintegration and community ownership and participation (Bazemore and Griffiths 1997; Clear and Karp 1999; Braithwaite 1989; Schiff 1998; Umbreit 1999; Pranis 2001).

Despite this growing interest in restorative community justice in general (Bazemore and Schiff 2001) and restorative conferencing in particular, very little is known about how, where and to what degree these decision-making models are operating within the United States (Schiff 1998; Kurki 2000). Research in this field remains very much in its infancy, and there are considerable gaps in our ability to answer some basic descriptive questions about restorative conferencing. The variety of models and intervention strategies that have been designated under the broad heading of 'conferencing' (Bazemore and Umbreit 2001) have inspired a number of questions about how such programmes work. For example, there is little knowledge about programme demographics, organizational location and structure, how conferencing programmes interact with the traditional justice system and the degree to which restorative values and principles are consistently incorporated into restorative conferencing schemes.

The purpose of this chapter is to present information from a national study recently completed and designed to answer some of the basic questions about restorative conferencing in the United States. The data presented here are based on (1) a national search of conferencing pro-grammes currently operating in the US conducted during October 1999 through June 2000 and, (2) a national survey disseminated in August 2000 focused on the nature of the conferencing process within and across different programme models and to assess, in a general way, the 'restorativeness' of each programme based on specific criteria (e.g., repairing harm, stakeholder involvement and government community relationships).

This chapter does not examine programme effectiveness, nor does it attempt to offer a definitive classification of all known programme models and adaptations. Moreover, it does not attempt to define restorativeness; but rather relies on programme self-identification to be considered restorative. While we cannot claim to provide an exhaustive count of all conferencing programmes currently operating, these findings do however provide a basic, 'snapshot' summary which can assist in making general estimations of the extent to which, and how, conferencing/dialogue programmes are operating nation-wide. Perhaps most importantly, this information gives a baseline from which to track the expansion or depletion of conferencing programmes in the United States and the manner in which programme practices are remaining consistent or changing over time.

Methodology in brief[3]

This research uses a very broad definition of a restorative conference that includes *any* encounter in which those affected by a specific offence or harmful behaviour come together in a face-to-face dialogue to discuss first, the impact of the act and second, to determine how the harm it has caused can be repaired. This encounter typically follows a finding of guilt and/or an admission of responsibility by offenders choosing to participate. In the conferencing process and subsequent reparative actions, stakeholders generally seek a resolution that meets the mutual needs of victim, offender and community *as well as* constructs obligations or sanctions designed to repair the harm to the greatest extent possible (Bazemore 2000).

A number of data sources and data collection methodologies were utilized to locate restorative youth conferencing/dialogue programmes around the United States. This data collection effort was exploratory in nature, using existing databases whenever possible and snowball sampling and other informal techniques for identifying programmes.

First, an extensive Internet search of restorative justice programmes was conducted, focusing specifically on those including a restorative conferencing/dialogue component. This included a comprehensive search through several Internet search engines of all known websites (e.g., RealJustice,[4] Victim-Offender Mediation Association), as well as keywords applicable to this study (e.g., 'restorative', 'mediation', 'conferencing'). Although limited to those programmes maintaining their own website or referred to in another's, this information provided the basis for developing a national database of current programmes and contact information.

Second, juvenile justice specialists, state court administrators and other knowledgeable persons (e.g., Balanced and Restorative Justice Co-ordinators, restorative justice programme directors) in each state were identified and contacted by telephone and/or e-mail and asked to identify restorative justice conferencing/dialogue programmes in their jurisdiction. These respondents in each state and Washington, DC were identified through several sources, including: (1) a previous Balanced and

Restorative Justice Project (BARJ) study on restorative justice policy implementation (O'Brien 1998);[5] (2) the National Center for Juvenile Justice's (NCJJ) list of Juvenile Justice Specialists; and, (3) State Court Administrators identified through their national organization, the National Association of State Court Administrators.

In addition to the above strategies, a comprehensive national survey was disseminated in August, 2000 to all known and potential restorative conferencing programmes. As the goal was to capture as many programmes as possible and, in particular, those smaller and lesser-known programmes that were unlikely to appear on other national lists (e.g., programmes begun by persons trained in conferencing by RealJustice, the country's largest conferencing training organization, who may or may not have initiated programmes and who were not yet on any other national mailing list), we oversampled persons and programmes trained in conferencing or who might have had any connection with a conferencing programme. We disseminated 2475 surveys; our subsequent research later approximated 773 actual programmes operating throughout the United States (Schiff et al. 2001).

Upon completion of the data collection, 218 programmes responded to our survey, from which 181 valid responses were derived.[6] Based on previous work, we categorized these responses into five primary, generic conferencing categories that represent the majority of programme models currently operating in the United States (Bazemore and Umbreit 2001; Bazemore and Griffiths 1997; Bazemore 2000; Umbreit 2001). Our four basic models included: victim–offender mediation and dialogue (VOM/D); family group conferencing (FGC); sentencing and peacemaking circles (circles); neighbourhood boards and panels (boards); and multiple-method programmes. These represented the majority of responses to the survey as well as the best of our knowledge about what is currently occurring nation-wide.

From our research identifying approximately 773 conferencing programmes operating across the country (Schiff et al. 2001), this suggested a final response rate of 23 per cent among known youth conferencing programmes when considering individual survey responses; this increases to 29 per cent (226 programmes) when considering the individual programmes represented by these responses (i.e., a large number of neighbourhood boards are represented as a single programme in the survey because one director oversees all these individual boards). As the purpose of this research was purely exploratory and descriptive, we are satisfied that we have an adequate number of survey responses to make some very general assumptions about the conferencing process; however, we do not suggest nor advocate that the findings presented here be considered representative of the general population of conferencing programmes currently operating in the United States.

Findings

Macro-level prevalence data

Findings indicate that juvenile restorative conferencing programmes are quite widespread, especially when compared with the relative paucity of programmes other than victim–offender mediation as recently as ten, or even five years ago (Umbreit and Greenwood 1997). The study also revealed differential use of conferencing across states and across counties within states, a preference for different models in some states, and much greater use of some models than others around the country, and within specific states.

Conferencing programmes in the United States[7]
Figure 9.1 indicates that 94 per cent (N = 48) of states currently have some form of conferencing/dialogue programme in place. While this suggests that conferencing/dialogue programmes are generally well-represented across the country, it is important to note that states vary considerably in the number and variety of programmes currently in operation, as well as in the numbers of persons actually served by these programmes; moreover, not all areas within a state are necessarily represented, or well represented, by such programmes. Some states may have a variety of programmes in several jurisdictions, while others – including some densely populated states – may have one or two small projects operating in a single locality only.

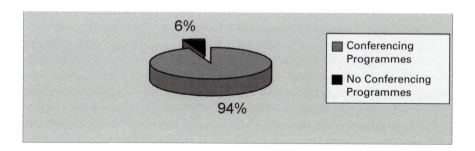

Figure 9.1. Percentage of states reporting restorative conferencing programmes as of January 2001, *n* = 51*

Most programmes are primarily designed to serve their own county residents. Seventy-four percent of US counties include under 50,000 people, hence examining the proportion of counties in each state served by restorative conferencing/dialogue programmes gives a better general sense of the proportion of state residents who might potentially be served by such a programme.[8] While almost all states can claim at least one restorative programme, most counties do not have conferencing programmes. California, Massachusetts, Delaware, Alaska and Vermont lead the way with 50 per cent or more counties reporting restorative conferencing/dialogue programmes; among these, Vermont and Alaska have the greatest number of counties with restorative conferencing programmes, with 86 per cent and 70 per cent, respectively. In California, 50 per cent of counties are served and Minnesota, despite having by far the most diverse range of programmes available, actually serves less than half of its population (36 per cent). In more than half of the states ($N = 30$), only 15 per cent or fewer counties claim restorative conferencing/dialogue programmes. Data indicate only 13.5 per cent of all counties nationally report having restorative conferencing programmes, a more conservative picture than is initially apparent when states are used as the unit of analysis (data not shown).

Individual programme model prevalence
If, in general, conferencing can be said to be relatively widespread throughout the states, it is not the case that all models are equally common in each state. Figure 9.2 indicates that victim–offender dialogue is the most common model, followed by boards. As the oldest type of conferencing programme operating in the United States, it is not surprising that VOM/D programmes are more widely represented than other, more recent restorative interventions, as they account for over one-half of all programmes included in this count ($N = 393$; 51.1%). The second most prevalent type of restorative programme, boards, represent slightly under one-third of programmes identified to date ($N = 227$; 29.3%).

Boards may occur in a variety of forms and take on several different names, including Neighborhood Accountability Boards (NABs) such as those in San Jose, California and various cities in Arizona, the Community Accountability Boards (CABS) in Denver, Community Restorative Panels in Vermont (which account for virtually all of that state's restorative decision-making programmes – the adult equivalent of these panels are well-known as Reparative Boards e.g., Karp and Walther 2001), and diversion panels known by various names – for example, the Youth Aid Panels in Pennsylvania. Finally, the generally newer family group and community conferencing programmes represent 12 per cent ($N = 93$) of

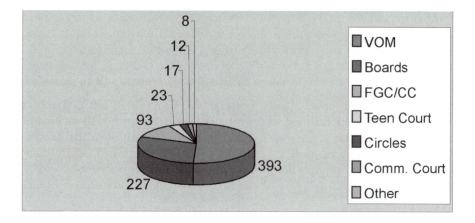

Figure 9.2. Number and type of restorative conferencing programmes in the US as of January 2001, $n = 733$

restorative conferencing programmes nationally, and teen courts, circles, community courts and 'other' comprise the remaining 8 per cent of programmes.[9]

State preferences and diversity in use
To better understand how particular programmes are distributed among leading restorative conferencing/dialogue states, Figure 9.3 examines the distribution of programmes by state. Arizona and Pennsylvania predominantly use boards, while Minnesota and Colorado have among the most diverse range of programmes, including conferencing, VOM/D, boards and circles. Texas, Ohio and Colorado have a large concentration of VOM/D programmes. Interestingly, despite its geographic distance from most US states using restorative conferencing approaches, Alaska appears to be one of the more eclectic states in terms of restorative justice, boasting a variety of programmes including victim–offender dialogue, circles, traditional family group and community conferences and community courts. These programmes are few in number, however, and generally spread across an expansive geographic region. Figure 9.3 shows considerable disparity in programme distribution within and between states, suggesting that local jurisdictions may have independently determined their own implementation strategies, and programmes have arisen somewhat organically within states. That is, there does not seem to be any single or simple strategy that characterizes state implementation patterns; rather, programme composition may be random or may reflect needs,

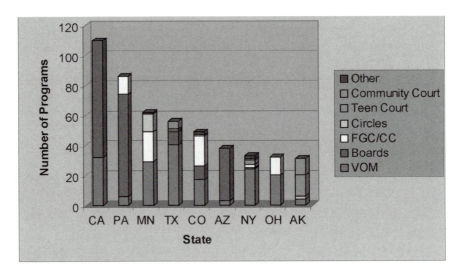

Figure 9.3. Variety of restorative conferencing programmes by state among nine leading states as of January 2001

stage of development, knowledge of, and/or resource availability within each individual state. Detailed data confirming this hypothesis is not available from this research.

Multiple models and hybridization

It is important to note that although most agencies or organizations focus on one conferencing model, some practice multiple techniques and there appears to be a growing tendency for single programmes to offer several types of conferencing interventions. That is, as programmes gain knowledge of and training in other programme models, they may be inclined to offer multiple alternatives within one organization, depending, ideally, upon the needs and wishes of victims and offenders. Individual programmes may primarily emphasize VOM, for example, but occasionally offer peacemaking circles or family group conferencing. Although the precise degree to which this occurs is uncertain, some preliminary information suggests a possible trend. To identify the extent of this trend, we examined the results from our sample of 181 programmes responding to the previously-mentioned national survey (representing about 23 per cent of the number of programmes we approximate exist nation-wide). This indicated that 67 per cent of programmes responding to the survey reported using used one conferencing practice only, while 30 per cent reported employing multiple practices (the remaining 3 per cent did not respond to the question).

While this sample cannot be generalized to represent *all* restorative conferencing programmes, these figures suggest that using multiple practices may be likely to continue as organizations develop internal competence as well as more integrated inter-programme networks of communication. In addition, as restorative conferencing expertise develops, it may be that practical distinctions between the models blur, creating a 'hybridization' of programme types and modes of service delivery. For example, a board or panel programme may change its format from the traditional model of panelists who deliberate with little or no input from victim and offender, to one in which participants sit in a circle and a facilitator seeks input from victim, offender, community members, family and supporters (Bazemore 1997). In so doing, such a programme would begin to function more like a family group conference than a traditional board (for example, the Director of a NAB in Santa Cruz, CA reports that she has always used a family group conferencing model despite inheriting the name 'neighborhood board' (Bazemore and Schiff 2002).

Intermediate-level conferencing process data

Of particular interest to this study was the extent to which models varied on some key structural and processual characteristics. There is virtually no data currently available on how such programmes 'do what they do', or accomplish the day-to-day tasks of conferencing, and how this might vary across model types. To this end, this research, based on the national survey mentioned earlier, asked questions about funding sources, organizational locations, referral sources and charges, point of intervention, size of conference and number of participants. In addition, we asked about the importance of some key restorative values and principles to assess the extent to which programmes considered this a critical part of their mission. In sum, the survey was designed to help better understand the nature, structure and tasks of various conferencing processes and programmes.

Funding

Almost 80 per cent of programmes responding to our survey reported that they maintained a separate budget for their programme aside from the regular agency budget. Among the 133 valid responses to this question (excluding those with no separate budget or who did not report valid responses), just over 8 per cent of programmes operate on budgets of under $5,000 and 17 per cent have funding of $15,000 or less. About 36 per cent are funded at between $35,000 and $100,000, and 20 per cent operate on over $100,000 per year. FGC programmes are most likely to operate with lower funding levels while VOM, and the few circle programmes who responded to this survey, tended to run on higher budgets. When examined in conjunction with staffing patterns (see below), these funding levels suggest that programmes operate with a small percentage of full-time-equivalent (FTE) staff with the bulk of the conferencing work done primarily by volunteers.

Staffing

Most programmes operate with less than one full-time paid or volunteer administrator dedicated to the programme. The average number of volunteer administrators is 0.21 and the average number of paid administrators is 0.91 among programmes responding to this question. The total average number of volunteer staff for any programme is 26; the average number of paid staff is about 3.5. Almost 36 per cent of the programmes reported have no paid mediators/facilitators. The average number of paid mediators/facilitators was just under two and the highest number in any programme was 26. The majority of programmes (51 per cent) operate with ten or fewer volunteer mediators/facilitators; 76 per cent have 25 or fewer such staff. Two board programmes reported having as many as 350 and 450 such volunteers.

Overall, this suggests that restorative conferencing programmes are primarily maintained through the efforts of volunteers with less than one full-time paid administrator responsible for overseeing the work of a large number of volunteers. All programmes report fewer paid staff than volunteers, implying that the actual work of conferencing is accomplished through the heavy use of community volunteers.

Referral source

Among all restorative conferencing programmes responding to the survey, probation was the most common referral source. The least common referrals were from community-oriented sources, e.g., schools, community groups and victim advocates, suggesting that in this group of programmes, the formal system is most likely to contact the programme. FGC programmes were more likely to accept referrals from law enforcement than from any other referral source and, correspondingly, were the most likely *practice type* to accept law enforcement referrals (i.e., were more likely than VOM, circles or boards to accept such referrals). FGC programmes were also least likely to accept judicial referrals. This is not surprising given that the FGC model most commonly practised in the US derives from the Australian Wagga-Wagga approach where law enforcement officers may initiate and facilitate conferences before court referral. When compared to other programmes types, FGC programmes were also most likely to report accepting referrals from prosecutors and schools, while circles and multiple practice programmes reported taking referrals from judges more often than other programmes. Boards/panels, VOM/D and multiple-practice programmes were most likely to take case referrals from probation. This is especially predictable for board/panel programmes, which are often housed in probation or correction departments. Though not as predictable for VOM/D, it is not surprising given that 90.1 per cent of VOM programmes report taking cases pre-court and probation is often the agency that handles pre-court diversion in many jurisdictions.

Charge types

In order to determine the types of cases conferencing programmes deal with, we asked programmes to tell us how many cases they took with each of a variety of charges during the last year. Overall, the charge *least likely to be excluded* from restorative conferencing programmes responding to the survey was minor assault, followed by property damage and personal theft charges. Those *most likely to be excluded* from the conferencing process are those involving serious drug charges, domestic violence and minor drug charges. Anecdotal evidence suggests the possibility that conferencing programmes may feel ill-equipped to handle the potentially complicated ancillary issues that may accompany such cases (e.g., Bazemore and Schiff 2002). When examining which programmes are more likely to accept particular charges than others, circle programmes were more likely than other practices to accept more severe charges, such as serious assault, serious drugs and domestic violence; multiple practice programmes were considerably more likely than other practices to accept referrals for breaking and entering. Other charges reported by survey respondents included alcohol, arson, auto theft, behavioural problems, disorderly conduct, harassment, forgery, trespass, weapons, truancy and runaway, among other charges.

Processing referral point in process

When examining the processing point at which cases are accepted for conferencing, Table 9.1 shows that 85.2 per cent of survey respondents report that they take cases prior to court referral. In other words, less than 15 per cent of programmes limit themselves to post-adjudicatory or post-dispositional cases. On average, 45.2 per cent of all programmes responding to the survey take referrals after adjudication and 51.2 per cent after sentence (note that these are not mutually exclusive categories and programmes may report accepting cases at several points in the process). Respondents report that, on average, 62 per cent of their conferences occur during pre-court diversion, while on average about 13 per cent are

Table 9.1. Per cent of total programmes that report accepting programmes at several points in the case process

Point in process when when referrals taken	Programme type					
	VOM	Multiple practice	Circle	FGC	Board/ panel	Total (N)
Pre-court	90.1	81.8	60.0	81.6	76.9	85.2 (144)
After adjudication	53.3	54.5	40.0	28.9	23.1	45.2 (76)
After sentence	55.4	63.6	60.0	36.8	38.5	51.2 (87)

accepted after adjudication and about 23 per cent occur after sentencing (data not shown). When comparing across programme types, VOM is the most likely practice to conference cases prior to court intervention and least likely to accept referrals later in the process; multiple-practice programmes are most likely to take cases after adjudication as well as after sentencing. Of particular interest is that FGC and board programmes are *considerably less likely* to take cases following adjudication or sentence than are VOM, multiple-practice or circle programmes.

Number of people present at the conference
With the increasingly apparent tendency for programme models to include participants beyond just the victim and the offender (Umbreit 1999, 2001; Bazemore and Umbreit 2001), we were interested in examining how many people, on average, participated in different types of conferences. Table 9.2 shows that programmes report, on average, about seven people typically participate in a conference; the largest number of participants reported by any programmes was 22 (not shown).

When asked how many of these are volunteer facilitators or part of a co-ordinating committee, programmes reported that the average was 1.77. When examining the average number of people present by type of programme, the data suggest that for VOM programmes this number is 5.43, for multiple practice the number increases to 6.86, for circles the average is 11.8, for FGC programmes the number is 9.54 and for boards/panels, 9.23. The relatively high number of participants for VOM suggests that this is no longer primarily a dyadic process reserved for victims, offenders and the mediator, but rather that there is increasing involvement of additional parties, such as family members. When asked the average number of staff that are generally present, programmes reported 1.26; 93 per cent of programmes report that there are two or fewer staff-persons present at the conference (not shown).

Table 9.2. Average number of people present at the conference

VOM	5.43
Multiple practice	6.86
Board/panel	9.23
FGC	9.54
Circle	11.83
Total average	7.1

'Restorativeness' of the models

There is considerable evidence that the best programmatic intentions do not always result in implementation of those intentions in everyday practice (Pressman and Wildavsky 1973; Clemons and McBeth 2001). In this study, we were interested in exploring the degree to which actual practice in restorative conferencing reflects the mission, values and intention of the programmes specifically and of restorative justice generally. There is little available literature that examines this question in practical, empirical terms, and none for programmes within the United States. Of particular importance to this study, and to subsequent research, policy and practice in restorative justice, was to better understand the relationship between the vision and the practices of restorative conferencing programmes. For our purposes, two components were central to that understanding: first, to what extent do survey respondents identify dimensions of restorative justice principles as primary to their mission and, second, to what extent do such programmes feel they are able to implement those principles in actual practice. In other words, we were interested in the relationship between programmatic goals 'on paper' or in theory, and the degree to which programmes feel they are able to achieve such goals in their everyday practice.

For purposes of this study, our primary definition of restorativeness is derived from the three key principles of restorative justice identified by Van Ness and Strong (1997). These principles include: repairing the harm, engaging and involving key stakeholders, and developing and maintaining government/community partnerships (Bazemore and Schiff 2002). Other characteristics have been identified by both the theoretical (Braithwaite 1989; Van Ness and Schiff 2001; Bazemore and Griffiths 1997; Bazemore 1997) and empirical literature (Umbreit 2001; Maxwell and Morris 1993; Morris and Maxwell 2001; Sherman, Strang and Woods 2000; McCold and Wachtel 1998) as important to understanding restorativeness either as components of the key principles cited above or as independent variables important in their own right; this paper reports on responses to those characteristics most closely associated with the three key principles described by Van Ness and Strong (1997). The following shows how survey respondents view the importance of certain key programme goals, and how well they believe they are meeting those goals in practice. As the numbers in many of these cells are regrettably low, the results must be viewed with caution and perhaps some scepticism. It is best to consider this data as preliminary and as only a very basic indication of what programmes are actually both intending and accomplishing.

Repairing harm

Perhaps the most important indicator of restorativeness is the extent to which the conference focuses on repairing the harm caused by the offence (Zehr 1990). Reparation plays a central role in the mission of most programmes and is arguably the central characteristic that characterizes a programme as restorative. As expected, Table 9.3 shows that the vast majority of programmes (97 per cent) responded that repairing harm was either 'very important' or 'extremely important' to their programme's vision, and over 90 per cent those report that they are either meeting or exceeding those goals in actual practice. Programmes that report repairing harm to be 'extremely important' are most likely to also report that they are exceeding their goals; however, among programmes that say they are not meeting their goals, over three-quarters also say that the goal is extremely important.

Key stakeholder involvement

Victim role

Victim participation
According to Van Ness and Strong (1997), the second key principle of restorative justice focuses on the extent to which key stakeholders other than the offender are involved in restorative deliberation and agreement processes. This is, to a large degree, what differentiates restorative conferencing from traditional intervention strategies. Table 9.4 shows that the vast majority of programmes responding to the survey consider victim participation to be either very important or extremely important (97.6 per cent). Although this is not surprising, it is worth noting that while the majority of programmes indicate that they are either meeting or exceeding their goals in this area, 13.2 per cent acknowledge that they are not

Table 9.3. The importance of repairing harm by actual achievement of goals

	Not meeting goals		Meeting goals		Exceeding goals		Total	
Not at all important	—		1	0.8%	—		1	0.6%
Not very important	—		—		—		—	
Somewhat important	—		4	3.1%	—		4	2.4%
Very important	3	23.1%	28	21.5%	1	4.8%	32	19.5%
Extremely important	10	76.9%	97	74.6%	20	95.2%	127	77.4%
Total	13	100%	130	100%	21	100%	164	100%
Percentage of total responding	7.2%		79.3%		12.8%		100%	

Table 9.4. The importance of victim participation by actual achievement of goals

	Not meeting goals		Meeting goals		Exceeding goals		Total	
Not very important	—		1	0.8%	—		1	0.6%
Somewhat important	1	4.5%	2	1.6%	—		3	1.8%
Very important	3	13.6%	11	8.5%	1	6.3%	15	9.0%
Extremely important	18	81.8%	115	89.1%	15	93.8%	148	88.6%
Total	22	100%	129	100%	16	100%	167	100%
Percentage of total responding	13.2%		77.2%		9.5%		100%	

meeting this goal, a bit higher than the percentage of programmes reporting that they are not meeting their goal of repairing harm. Other research suggests this figure may be low (Bazemore and Schiff 2002). Programmes that say this goal is extremely important are the most likely to report that they are exceeding their goals.

Victim satisfaction

Another dimension often considered both theoretically and practically important to restorative programmes is victim (and offender) satisfaction with the process (Umbreit 2001; Van Ness and Schiff 2001). Table 9.5 indicates that when asked how important this was to their programme's mission and how well they thought they were meeting this goal, the majority of conferencing programmes responded that it was very or

Table 9.5. The importance of victim satisfaction by actual achievement of goals

	Not meeting goals		Meeting goals		Exceeding goals		Total	
Not very important	—		1	0.8%	—		1	0.6%
Somewhat important	—		11	9.2%	1	3.2%	12	7.2%
Very important	8	47.1%	27	22.7%	3	9.7%	38	22.8%
Extremely important	9	52.9%	80	67.2%	27	87.1%	116	69.5%
Total	17	100%	119	100%	31	100%	167	100%
Percentage of total responding	10.2%		71.3%		18.6%			

extremely important, and the vast majority felt they were meeting their goals in this area (89.9 per cent). Less than 8 per cent felt this was somewhat or not very important and those who felt victim satisfaction was extremely important were most likely to be exceeding their goals in this area.

Offender role

Offender reintegration

There are a number of other offender-related characteristics that differentiate restorative processes from traditional justice decision-making. A significant concern is the degree to which programmes consider offender reintegration to be important, and there was some variation among programme responses. Table 9.6 suggests that the majority of programmes considered offender reintegration either very important or extremely important (87.9 per cent), and 12 per cent considered this not at all, not very or somewhat important. However, compared to other victim and offender-related variables, a relatively high proportion of programmes (N = 29, 18.4 per cent), felt they were not achieving their goals in this area, while 9.5 per cent felt they were exceeding them.

Offender accountability

All programmes that responded to this question felt that holding offenders accountable was either very important or extremely important. The vast majority of programme felt they were meeting or exceeding their goals in this area (see Table 9.7).

Table 9.6. The importance of offender reintegration by actual achievement of goals

	Not meeting goals		Meeting goals		Exceeding goals		Total	
Not at all important	—		1	0.9%	—		1	0.6%
Not very important	1	3.4%	—		1	6.7%	2	1.3%
Somewhat important	4	13.8%	12	10.5%	—		16	10.1%
Very important	14	48.3%	41	36%	1	1.8%	56	35.4%
Extremely important	10	34.5%	60	52.6%	13	86.7%	83	52.5%
Total	29	100%	114	100%	15	100%	158	100%
Percentage of total responding	18.4%		74.7%		9.5%		100%	

Table 9.7. The importance of holding offenders accountable by achievement of goals

	Not meeting goals		Meeting goals		Exceeding goals		Total	
Very important	1	12.5%	36	27.3%	—		37	22.7%
Extremely important	7	87.5%	96	72.7%	23	100%	126	77.3%
Total	8	100%	132	100%	23	100%	163	100%
Percentage of total responding	4.9%		81%		14.1%		100%	

Community role

Community involvement

Another key stakeholder not traditionally involved in justice decision-making is the community. While community can have many different interpretations (Crawford and Clear 2001; Clear and Karp 1999), in this case we refer to the geographic community in which the event occurred. Almost one-third (31.8 per cent) of programmes report that community involvement is 'not at all', 'not very' or 'somewhat' important. This may reflect the large proportion of survey respondents from VOM programmes which often do not consider community involvement in the conferencing process to be part of their programmatic model or intention. In Table 9.8, forty programmes, or just over 25 per cent, report that they are

Table 9.8. The importance of community involvement by actual achievement of goals

	Not meeting goals		Meeting goals		Exceeding goals		Total	
Not at all important	1	2.5%	3	2.7%	—		4	2.5%
Not very important	1	2.5%	7	6.2%	—		8	5.1%
Somewhat important	17	42.5%	21	18.6%	—		38	24.2%
Very important	12	30%	39	34.5%	1	25%	52	33.1%
Extremely important	9	22.5%	43	38.1%	3	75%	55	35%
Total	40	100%	113	100%	4	100%	157	100%
Percentage of total responding		25.5%		72%		2.5%		100%

Table 9.9. The importance of building local community capacity to respond to crime by actual achievement of goals

	Not meeting goals		Meeting goals		Exceeding goals		Total	
Not at all important	1	1.6%	2	2.4%	—		3	2.0%
Not very important	3	4.8%	1	1.2%	—		4	2.6%
Somewhat important	11	17.5%	20	24.4%	—		31	20.4%
Very important	24	38.1%	35	42.7%	—		59	38.8%
Extremely important	24	38.1%	24	29.3%	7	100%	55	36.2%
Total	63	100%	82	100%	7	100%	152	100%
Percentage of total responding		41.4%		53.9%		4.6%		100%

not meeting their goals in this area, which is high compared to the number of programmes that admit not meeting their goals with either victims or offenders. In addition, only four programmes say they are exceeding their goals in this area, which is lower than reported on other key stakeholder dimensions.

Importance of building local community capacity to respond to crime
Some restorative conferencing theorists believe it is important that conferencing build local community capacity to respond to crime (e.g., Clear and Karp 1999). Recent literature on the role of social capital (Putnam

2000) and collective efficacy (Sampson, Roedenbush and Earls 1997) with respect to criminal justice initiatives led us to be curious about the extent to which programmes themselves perceived this as part of their vision and how well they felt they were achieving these goals. As indicated in Table 9.9, about one-fourth of programmes felt this was not at all, not very or somewhat important; the remaining 75 per cent expressed that building community capacity was very or extremely important to their pro- gramme's mission or vision. However, over 40 per cent felt they were not achieving their goals in this area, the highest percentage for any restorativeness question on the survey. While at first glance it might seem that this is a reflection of the large percentage of VOM programmes included in the survey, as VOM does not include community members in their conferencing approach, VOM programmes do often use community members as volunteer mediators, which would be an important contributor to building local community capacity. As such, this may be a reflection of the ambiguity of this factor's importance to the theory and practice of conferencing programmes. There does not appear to be much consistency about whether programmes believe this is, or should be, important to their mission and what to do to carry it out.

Summary and discussion

In sum, it is clear that restorative conferencing for young offenders has become increasingly popular as a viable response to youthful offending. While the data presented here are preliminary, they suggest several important general findings:

- almost every state is experimenting with restorative conferencing processes, and the vast majority of states (94 per cent) offer at least one programme;

- the current study identified 773 programmes nationwide, although programmes are most prevalent in a few key states (e.g., California, Pennsylvania, Minnesota, Texas, Colorado, Arizona, New York, Ohio, Alaska);

- a variety of models are represented nationally, although VOM and community boards are clearly dominant;

- when examining programme distribution at the county level, it is apparent that most communities are not well served by restorative conferencing programmes;

- there appears to be a trend towards integrating multiple practices within one organization;

- states using conferencing are both regionally and politically diverse, suggesting that there is no tendency for restorative programmes to proliferate or cluster in a particular geographic region or within a particular political environment.

Though some may continue to view conferencing as something of a marginal or 'trendy' innovation, our conservative estimate of 773 programmes nation-wide, and the finding that all but three states have a least one programme, may indicate a more firm commitment to restorative justice decision-making practices in the United States than has been previously documented. However, though there is generally growing familiarity with conferencing and substantial experimentation with multiple models, there is no evidence regarding the extent to which jurisdictions seek to make conferencing a real alternative for most, or even specific categories, of offences by young people even in the most active states. Nor does conferencing appear to be widely available locally as an option for all but a minority of juvenile cases. Not surprisingly, most programmes utilize the more longstanding VOM/D model. The next most frequently used model, community boards, may be a holdover from a pre-restorative justice era, though there are numerous examples of other approaches.

Current anecdotal evidence suggests that, in some states, conferencing programmes may operate as small, *ad hoc* initiatives in community-based organizations which do not seem to have strong formal relationships to the justice system (e.g., Alabama, Iowa, Montana). In contrast, it appears that some states have strategies designed to encourage experimentation with various conferencing models by providing funding and training and technical assistance (e.g., Pennsylvania, Minnesota, Colorado). In so doing, these states have encouraged the creation of both formal and informal associations of conferencing programmes – both regionally and state-wide (e.g., The Colorado Forum on Restorative and Community Justice, The Minnesota Restorative Services Coalition).

The data presented here find that programmes typically have relatively small budgets and make extensive use of volunteer staff. They tend to get most referrals from probation and law enforcement and to take case referrals prior to formal court intervention. They generally handle relatively low level cases such as minor assault. On average, seven people are typically present at a conference, with even the traditionally dyadic VOM model generally having over five people present. This may suggest some movement towards a 'blurring' of programmatic distinctions that have, in the past, characterized different programme models. This is also supported by recent literature (e.g., Umbreit 2001).

Finally, the data tentatively suggest that there is at least awareness of, if not commitment to, restorative justice principles and practices among juvenile justice professionals. While the numbers presented here are perhaps too small to draw definitive conclusions, they do indicate that programmes are conscious of and are, at least in theory, making an effort to integrate key restorative principles into their day-to-day work. The data presented here suggest that nearly all programmes responding to the survey felt that repairing harm was an important goal and the vast majority felt they were meeting or exceeding their goals in this area. The persons present at a conference, ranging from about 5.5 to almost 12, and averaging about seven peoples per conference, clearly suggests the relatively consistent inclusion of additional stakeholders in the process. In addition, the vast majority of programmes feel that victim and offender participation are very important or extremely important and that they are, for the most part, meeting their goals. While slightly fewer programmes indicate the importance of community involvement, it remains true that almost 70 per cent of programmes still report that this is very or extremely important although they appear to have somewhat more trouble meeting goals in this area.

As most conferencing programmes are housed in private agencies but funded by government, this creates an opportunity for governments to empower communities to initiate and manage processes specific to their own localities. While this data says nothing about the extent to which this is actually occurring, it does suggest an opportunity to consciously and conscientiously choose such a relationship. Most referrals clearly come from government sources (i.e., probation, judges, law enforcement) suggesting some form of partnership between governmental justice agencies and private, community-based organizations. However, many programmes (especially family group and community conferencing) are housed in police and/or probation agencies, suggesting that the work has not been turned over to local non-governmental organizations. This is, though, tempered by the fact that many such agencies use community volunteers to perform the work in, as volunteer facilitators or board members.

Building local community capacity to respond to crime seems to be an ambiguous aspect of restorative conferencing programmes, as there is more variation in perceptions of the importance of this dimension as well as in programme capacity to meet it. Programmes were most likely to acknowledge their inability to meet goals in this area, which may reflect uncertainty regarding the relevance of this to their own programme and whether, and to what extent, this should be included in programme mission. A competing explanation is that this is an especially difficult dimension to identify and measure, and hence programmes are unsure about how to recognize this when it is occurring and, subsequently, how to measure the degree of its presence. At the same time, given that there are few models for how to achieve this goal, programmes may be unsure how to develop and maintain this capacity as they must, to a large extent, learn as they go.

Limitations of the research

This exploratory research provides previously unavailable macro-level information about the numbers, types and distribution of restorative conferencing programmes in the US. By identifying where such programmes locate, target populations and service provision strategies, it becomes increasingly possible to characterize the breadth and scope of restorative conferencing programmes nation-wide.

There are however, several limitations of this research. For example, there is the likelihood that our exploratory sampling approach has resulted in underestimating the actual number of programmes in use. However, the problem of respondents self-identifying their programme as an example of restorative conferencing, with little opportunity to confirm the degree of consistency with restorative principles, leaves room for mischaracterization and inappropriate counting of programmes. It is important to bear such limitations in mind, as this study has important implications for informing and directing future research, and for better understanding the broader context within which wise policy and practice decisions should be made. The fact that there are now many programmes calling themselves restorative suggests a need to examine programmes against some criteria for 'restorativeness' both in programme vision and in reality.

Secondly, the 'snowball' approach, though necessary at this exploratory stage, is likely biased toward more established and well-marketed programmes, and will therefore probably undercount newer and less well established programmes. More generally, in the context of an emerging and ever-changing movement, restorative programmes as a rule are likely to be low-profile. Hence, while it is possible to over-count in instances where a programme identified at one time (e.g. during our national survey) may later terminate its services, it is more likely that under-counting is a greater problem in this inventory.

Third, the data presented here are limited by the need to 'lump' many different types of programmes together under single, generic headings. While there are clearly some basic model prototypes, there are also many departures created to suit local jurisdictional needs. The extent of these variations, the purposes they serve and their effectiveness are critical questions for understanding the nature of restorative innovations. Furthermore, it would be helpful to understand the extent to which existing conferencing programmes tend to follow standard practice guidelines or adapt to suit individual jurisdictional and stakeholder needs. That is, while conferencing practices should be community-driven and reflect the character of their native communities, many newly initiated programmes are modelled directly after programmes in other com-munities and locals. This certainly does not indicate a problem as pro-grammes *should* learn from one another, although it does suggest that new conferencing/dialogue developments are, at least initially, less likely to be organic products of the community and more likely to reflect practices and procedures initiated elsewhere. The degree to which it is possible to understand the evolution of restorative conferencing practices may make it easier to identify what practices are best suited for what types of environments.

Finally, our survey response rate was somewhat lower than we had hoped for and, as a result, numbers in some of the individual reporting categories are quite small. As such, it is difficult to make broad generali-zations about restorative conferencing from this group and we must qualify that these findings may not be representative of *all* restorative conferencing programmes nationwide. Also, as mentioned earlier, several of the survey respondents from board programmes oversee a number of boards across their regions. Consequently, while the number of board programmes responding to the survey is quite low, it may in fact represent far more boards that could be accounted for here. It is possible that this is true for more programmes than we were able to identify and hence the number of programmes represented by these data may be greater than we realize, which would 'throw off' the percentages reported in particular categories.

Conclusion

These data offer valuable insight into the 'real world' of restorative conferencing for youth. This is the only information of its kind available about conferencing programmes in the United States that directly reports what programme directors from a variety of conferencing models say about their practices. Until now there has been little more than anecdotal evidence from individual programmes or programme models that uncovers the day-to-day practical world of restorative conferencing. This data offers an early picture of 'what's going on out there' beyond the limited margins of individual programme or practice. Subsequent research should continue to focus on designing methodologies that reflect the non-traditional nature of restorative intervention and the relationship of practice to theoretical principles. Moreover, data on the nature, scope and prevalence of restorative conferencing should be regularly updated. In particular, attention should be paid to individual programmes and the manner in which they translate conceptual constructs into daily practice.

In the end, the value of this research is in its important contribution to understanding the nature, scope and day-to-day work of restorative conferencing programmes. To the degree that restorative conferencing represents the next generation of justice intervention for youthful offenders, victims and communities, this work provides critical early information about how such work is accomplished, how theories of intervention coincide with practice, and how research can best capture some of the crucial intricacies and nuances of restorative justice intervention.

Notes

1. This research was generously supported by grants from the National Institute of Justice (1999-CJ-IX-0060) and the Robert Wood Johnson Foundation. The opinions and conclusions reported herein, however, reflect those of the authors only and should not be considered to reflect those of the funding agencies.
2. Although the term 'conferencing' has historically been limited to descriptions of one or another form of 'family group conferencing' (McCold 2000; Maxwell and Morris 1993), more recent terminology has sought to characterize a more generic decision-making process that emphasizes theoretical and philosophical differences between restorative and non-restorative decision-making and minimizes rather minor practical and administrative variations (Braithwaite and Parker 1999; Braithwaite 1999; Morris and Maxwell 2001; Bazemore 2000).
3. The methodological details of this study are published elsewhere, so they are not extensively presented here. For more detailed information on methodology and data collection, see Schiff, Bazemore and Erbe 2001 and Schiff and Bazemore 2002.
4. RealJustice is known as the country's largest training organization in what is known as the Wagga-Wagga model of family group conferencing. The authors thank them for their extreme generosity in providing us information on their trainees in order to help facilitate this research.
5. The Balanced and Restorative Justice Project (BARJ) is funded by the Office of Juvenile Justice and Delinquency Prevention. In addition, data are drawn from

an ongoing multi-year, multi-site national project research study currently being conducted under the auspices of the National Institute of Justice (grant # 1999-CX-IJ-0060) and the Robert Wood Johnson Foundation. The descriptive findings of this study are part of a more comprehensive study of restorative justice conferencing in the US that includes: (1) a national survey to provide additional analysis of conferencing model components and variations in administrative structure and practice; (2) selected in-depth key informant interviews with programme administrators in several states characterized by more extensive use of one or more models focused on process, performance outcomes, and system interaction issues; (3) an in-depth, ethnographic mini-case studies in two states.

6. Some surveys representing one conferencing model, boards, were completed by a single programme director who was responsible for several actual boards, i.e., one programme director may oversee up to 15 individual neighbourhood boards. We later learned that the 14 responses from directors of board/panel programmes in fact represented 59 separate boards. These are counted as one programme in the survey, which may result in undercalculating the actual number and representativeness of board programmes.

7. Although the four basic programme models described earlier are the predominant forms of conferencing available in the United States, there are a few others that were included in this study because they self-identified as being a restorative decision-making programme. While subsequent research in this study would exclude such programmes, they are included here as this is a broadly representative, though not exclusive, examination of programmes self-reporting as restorative conferencing programmes.

8. Includes Washington, DC. While counties vary in population from a low of 140 to a high of over nine million, the average county consists of about 25–50,000 individuals. It is the case, however, that neighbourhood board programmes may serve multiple neighbourhoods and thereby have more widespread impact. Some programmes may only serve a particular neighbourhood, town or city, while others may be are open to referrals countywide.

9. The 12 teen courts and 17 community courts self-identified and/or were identified by informants as including restorative conferencing components and, given our basic criteria, we included these in our general prevalence count. Subsequent survey data did not include these programme models as we could not verify that these were indeed consistent with our general definition.

References

Bazemore, G. (1997) 'The Community in Community Justice: Issues, Themes and Questions for the New Neighborhood Sanctioning Models', *The Justice System Journal*, 19(2): 193–228.

Bazemore, G. (2000) *Community Justice and a Vision of Collective Efficacy: The Case of Restorative Conferencing*. Washington, DC: US Department of Justice.

Bazemore, G. and Griffiths, C. (1997) 'Conferences, Circles, Boards, and

Mediations: The "New Wave" of Community Justice Decisionmaking', *Federal Probation,* 61(2).

Bazemore, G. and Schiff, M. (2002) *Emerging Grounded Theory in Restorative Justice Decision-making: A Qualitative Case Study of Juvenile Justice Conferencing Programs.* Final Report to the National Institute of Justice and the Robert Wood Johnson Foundation. Unpublished manuscript.

Bazemore, G. and Umbreit, M. (2001) 'A Comparison of Four Restorative Conferencing Models.' *Juvenile Justice Bulletin,* February. Washington, DC: Office of Juvenile Justice and Delinquency Prevention.

Bonta, J., Rooney, J. and Wallace-Capretta, S. (1998) *Restorative Justice: An Evaluation of the Restorative Resolutions Project.* Solicitor General Canada (October 1998).

Braithwaite, J. (1989) *Crime, Shame, and Reintegration.* New York: Cambridge University Press.

Clear, T. and Karp, D. (1999) *The Community Justice Ideal.* Boulder, Colorado: Westview Press.

Clemons, R. S. and McBeth, M. K. (2001) *Public Policy Praxis.* New Jersey: Prentice-Hall.

Crawford, A. and Clear, T. (2001) 'Community Justice: Transforming Communities Through Restorative Justice?' in G. Bazemore and M. Schiff (eds) *Restorative Community Justice: Repairing Harm and Transforming Communities.* Cincinnati, OH: Anderson.

Daly, K. (2001) 'Restorative Justice in Australia and New Zealand: Variations, Research Findings, and Prospects' in A. Morris and G. Maxwell (eds) *Restoring Justice for Juveniles: Conferencing, Mediation and Circles* ch 4. Oxford: Hart Publishing.

Kurki, L. (2000) 'Restorative and Community Justice in the United States' in M. Tonry (ed.) *Crime and Justice: A Review of Research.* Chicago: University of Chicago Press.

Maxwell, G. and Morris, A. (1993) *Family Participation, Cultural Diversity and Victim Involvement in Youth Justice: A New Zealand Experiment,* Wellington, New Zealand: Victoria University.

McCold, P. and Watchel, B. (1998) *Restorative Policing Experiment: The Bethlehem, Pennsylvania, Police Family Group Conferencing Project.* Pipersville, PA: Community Service Foundation.

Miers, D. (2001) *An International Review of Restorative Justice.* Crime Reduction Research Series Paper 10. London: Home Office.

Morris, A. and Maxwell, G. (2001) 'Restorative Conferencing' in G. Bazemore and M. Schiff (eds) *Restorative Community Justice: Repairing Harm and Transforming Communities.* Cincinnati, OH: Anderson.

Pranis, K. (2001) 'Restorative Justice, Social Justice, and the Empowerment of Marginalized Populations' in G. Bazemore and M. Schiff (eds) *Restorative Community Justice: Repairing Harm and Transforming Communities.* Cincinnati, OH: Anderson.

Pressman, J. and Wildavsky, A. (1973) *Implementation.* Berkeley: University of California Press.

Putnam, R. (2000) Bowling Alone: The Collapse and Revival of American Community. New York, NY: Simon and Shuster.

Sampson, R., Raudenbush, S. and Earls, F. (1997) 'Neighborhoods and Violent Crime: A Multi-Level Study of Collective Efficacy', *Science*, (August): 277.

Schiff, M. F. (1998) 'Restorative Justice Interventions for Juvenile Offenders: A Research Agenda for the Next Decade', *Western Criminology Review*, 1(1) available: at http://wcr.sonoma.edu/vlnl/schiff.html

Schiff, M. and Bazemore, G. (2001) 'Dangers and Opportunities of Restorative Justice: A Response to Critics' in G. Bazemore and M. Schiff (eds) *Restorative Community Justice: Repairing Harm and Transforming Communities*. Cincinnati, OH: Anderson.

Schiff, M. and Bazemore, G. (2002) *Understanding and Evaluating Community Youth Sanctioning Models*. Final report prepared for the National Institute of Justice. Washington, DC: Department of Justice.

Schiff, M., Bazemore, G. and Erbe, C. (2001) 'Understanding Restorative Justice: A Study of Youth Conferencing Models in the United States'. Updated paper presented at the Annual Meeting of the American Society of Criminology. San Francisco, CA: November.

Sherman, L., Strang, H., and Woods, D. J. (2000) *Recidivism Patterns in the Canberra Reintegrative Shaming Experiments*. Canberra: Australian National University.

Stuart, B. (2001) 'Guiding Principles for Designing Peacemaking Circles' in G. Bazemore and M. Schiff (eds) *Restorative Community Justice: Repairing Harm and Transforming Communities*. Cincinnati, OH: Anderson.

Umbreit, M. (1999) 'Avoiding the Marginalization and McDonaldization of Victim–Offender Mediation: A Case Study in Moving Toward the Mainstream' in G. Bazemore and L. Walgrave (eds) *Restoring Juvenile Justice: Repairing the Harm of Youth Crime*. Monsey, NY: Criminal Justice Press.

Umbreit, M. (2001) *The Handbook of Victim–Offender Mediation*. San Francisco, CA: Jossey-Bass.

Van Ness, D. and Schiff, M. (2001) 'Satisfaction Guarenteed? The Meaning of Satisfaction in Restorative Justice' in G. Bazemore and M. Schiff (eds) *Restorative and Community Justice: Repairing Harm and Transforming Communities*. Cincinnati, OH: Anderson.

Van Ness, D. and Strong, K. (1997). *Restoring Justice*. Cincinnati, OH: Anderson.

Walgrave, L. (1999) 'Community Service as a Cornerstone' in G. Bazemore and L. Walgrave (eds) *Restorative Juvenile Justice: Repairing the Harm of Youth Crime*. Monsey, NY: Criminal Justice Press.

Weitekamp, E. (1999) 'The History of Restorative Justice' in G. Bazemore and L. Walgrave (eds) *Restorative Juvenile Justice: Repairing the Harm of Youth Crime*. Monsey, NY: Criminal Justice Press.

Young, R. and Hoyle, C. (2002) 'New, Improved Police Led Restorative Justice? Action-Research and the Thames Valley Police Initiative' in A. von Hirsch, A. Bottoms, J. Roberts, K. Roach and M. Schiff (eds) *Restorative Justice and Criminal Justice: Competing or Reconcilable Paradigms*. Oxford, England: Hart Publishing.

Zehr, H. (1990) *Changing Lenses: A New Focus for Crime and Justice*. Scottsdale, PA: Herald Press.

Chapter 10

Restorative justice for children: in need of procedural safeguards and standards

Christian Eliaerts and Els Dumortier

At the beginning of the twenty-first century, the restorative justice (RJ) movement is still a rising movement. Its concept attracts more and more practitioners and academics, as well as politicians (Van Ness 1999b). Moreover, it is clear that this growing interest in restorative justice is not limited to just one country or continent. On the contrary, at the latest United Nations Congress on the Prevention of Crime and the Treatment of Offenders, held in Vienna from 10 to 17 April 2000, several practitioners, academics and politicians from all continents were gathered to discuss RJ practices and its implementation. RJ seems to have become, especially for juveniles, an important approach for responding to their crimes. However, this evolution towards a possible large-scale implementation of RJ as the (basic) model of response to juvenile crime also evokes some necessary concerns. After all, as some RJ pioneers have already noticed, the acknowledged informality and the lack of rules in RJ might easily lead to practices which fail to respect some fundamental basic human rights, or to non-RJ practices masquerading as RJ (Braithwaite 2000: 2). Such practices, especially when implemented on a large scale, might impose a real threat to the credibility of the whole RJ movement (Walgrave and Bazemore 1999: 371). Consequently, the question arises whether the call for informality within the RJ movement should not be tempered by the need for clear standards and procedural safeguards, especially with respect to juveniles. In this chapter, in the first part, we discuss five reasons why RJ is, in our opinion, in need of procedural safeguards and standards. In the second part we try to analyse some safeguards and standards that could guide RJ.

Why restorative justice for children needs procedural safeguards

Many RJ advocates present informality as one of the corner-stones of the RJ paradigm (Zehr 1990; Braithwaite 2000). Informality is favoured in order to promote understanding and hence an easy participation of 'all parties with a stake in a particular offence' in order to 'deal with the aftermath of the offence and its implications for the future' (Marshall 1996). If not, it is feared, legal formalism and rule setting would hinder the participation, healing and empowering character of the RJ processes (McCold 1999: 27).

Formalism as a protection for individual citizens

Nevertheless, this claim for informality poses some serious problems. First of all, a lack of written rules inevitably leads to obscurity. As a consequence, RJ can be and is already being implemented in a variety of ways, sometimes even within quite small areas. Although this situation might be acceptable during an experimental phase, it becomes quite difficult to defend on a permanent basis, unless, of course, uniformity in procedures, practices and rights ceases to be valued as a goal of the justice system and of society at large. However, this situation could easily turn RJ into some kind of middle-aged *droit coutumier* (local custom) (Gilissen and Magits 1989), where every district knew its own RJ rules, principles and organization and, as a consequence, lead to disparity and uncertainty for offender(s) and victim(s). History has shown on numerous occasions that vagueness in procedures and rights easily invokes arbitrariness and injustice. In the seventeenth and eighteenth centuries, great efforts were made in several western countries to implement Universal Declarations and Bills of Rights in order to protect people from unnecessary, disproportionate or inhuman actions on the part of the authorities or that of other citizens. Although procedures and formalism can discourage participation of offenders, victims and the community in dealing with crime, it also, at the same time, protects citizens against unwanted interventions in their lives.

The juvenile protection experience

During the twentieth century, most western countries abolished several principles of penal law in order to implement a new and promising juvenile protection model (Muncie 1999: 257; Feld 1999: 20; Platt 1977; Christiaens 1999); the reaction of the criminal justice system will no longer be in relation to the seriousness of the offence, but to the welfare of the young delinquent. Moreover, the child will not be subject to a formal, penal procedure they hardly understand, but to an informal procedure in which the judge will act as some kind of father figure. The optimism surrounding this new progressive juvenile law was so great that the law was voted for unanimously in the Belgian Parliament in 1965. Nevertheless, the child protection movement was soon heavily attacked.

Two main reasons can be distinguished. First of all, the *lack of legal rights* and formality poses some serious problems. By seeking to meet the needs of each individual child, traditional concepts of criminal justice are overturned (Muncie 1999: 257–259; Feld 1999; Christiaens 1999). To make the easy participation of the juvenile possible, the open court is abandoned during the preliminary stages; instead, an informal procedure is implemented with a specialized juvenile judge. The right to legal assistance is abandoned in the preliminary stages of the procedure, as it might hamper a good, informal contact between the judge and the juvenile. The adversarial roots of formal legal procedure are also abandoned; whether a crime has been committed or not, and whether a juvenile is guilty or not, is not really at stake, but only how the juvenile can be helped. Following the same kind of reasoning, victims are also encouraged to take a back seat 'in the best interests of the child'. Moreover, a lack of proportionality helped to contribute to the demise of the rehabilitation paradigm (Van Ness 1999a: 274); measures aimed at assuring the future welfare of youths rather than punishing them for their past offences came to dominate (Feld 1999: 19). As a consequence, judges imposed indeterminate and disproportionate sentences that would potentially continue for the duration of their minority (Feld 1999: 19). Finally, even the principle of legality fades away, for juveniles can be in need of help even when they have not committed a crime, and powers to intervene have been established, according to which, instead of legality, the discretion of the juvenile justice professionals involved becomes one of the guiding principles within juvenile justice practice.

Secondly, in practice, the *aim of protection* seems not to have been attained either. In many western countries, the number of custodial sentences is rising (Newburn 1997: 641). Furthermore, state homes and institutions for juveniles display a remarkable resemblance to adult prisons (Platt 1977: 146). In the seventies, research began to reveal that much of the target group of the juvenile justice system is composed of ethnic minorities and juveniles from lower classes, and that the juvenile justice's social-control function in respect of these, and even a discriminating role in society is hard to deny (Feld 1999: 18; Muncie 1999; Newburn 1997). Measures designed to protect society are often viewed by this group as a pandering to middle-class or white values which are very different from the values that apply to their own lives, and paternalistic assessments and *adult-centric* attitudes run counter to many juveniles' views and opinions, weakening their position. A lack of legal rights and assistance intensifies this weak position of the juvenile vis-à-vis the juvenile judge and all the other adult experts in juvenile justice. Furthermore, stating in books that minors must no longer be punished, but rather protected, does not mean that, in practice, those within the juvenile justice system will never feel a need to punish young offenders. Similarly, stating that within the RJ paradigm the only aim is to repair damage (the stated goal), and not to punish, does not mean that in practice no minor will be punished (real goal). In fact, throughout the evolution of the juvenile justice system, we have seen the application of different models which have led in practice to conflicting goals and interpretations of the measures (see Christiaens 1999), where goals can change at different stages of the procedure and where those who participate in the procedure may defend different (possibly conflicting) views on the goals and the characteristics of the measures applied.

The evolution towards youths as subjects of rights

Following these critics, in the United States, the Supreme Court observes that 'there may be grounds for concern that the child receives the worst of both worlds; he gets neither protections [due process] accorded to adults, nor the solicitous care and regenerative treatment postulated for children' (*Kent v. United States*, 383 US 555 1966). Several decisions of the European Court of Human Rights also obliged, and still oblige, European states to reformulate some fundamental penal principles towards young offenders. The need for procedural guarantees and legal rights for young offenders was also accentuated by the International Convention on Children's Rights, signed by almost all countries. It seems that at the beginning of the twenty-first century, as contrasted with the beginning of the twentieth, young offenders have become more respected as real subjects of rights instead of mere objects, in general as well as within juvenile justice legislation and practice.

However, even today, we cannot say that children and young people have the same rights as adults when they are accused of having committed an offence; for instance, in Belgium the principle of proportionality and the principle of legality remain unsatisfied. In other words, the evolution towards more respect for children's rights has not yet reached its final goal. Therefore, the question arises whether the implementation of a 'new', informal restorative model, with no clear rules, nor rights, will not hamper this fragile evolution (see also Freeman 1997: 5).

The failures of the protection paradigm should remind RJ practitioners of the importance of fundamental human rights and procedural guarantees for juveniles. On the other hand, the implementation of these fundamental human rights, and procedural guarantees, should not paralyse the restorative justice philosophy either – a too strict 'just desert' (Von Hirsch 1993) interpretation might easily invoke a 'get tough on youngsters approach', where any space for restorative justice is constricted.

The need for a judicial instrument

If RJ wants to be taken seriously by the traditional justice system and the public, a judicial translation of its aims and procedures becomes necessary. After all, to fit RJ in the existing legal system and legal traditions of a state, it must be seen to be practical to do so. Without rules, rights and standards, the judicial system (and the public) will have nothing to go on. On the one hand, this causes major possibilities for adaptation, such that RJ would be used and abused as the judicial system pleases. On the other hand, a lack of clarity on RJ rules can create a refusal on the part of the system to actually send cases to RJ processes. It might also imply a two-level system, where only minor cases are seen as amenable for RJ processes and serious cases are still handled by the traditional system on the basis of repressive penal principles. After all, even within juvenile justice practice, traditional principles of punitive justice towards offenders were never seriously undermined by the welfare model. 'The two systems [penal and welfare] have in effect become vertically integrated and an additional population of customer–clients has been identified in order to ensure that they both have plenty of work to do' (Thorpe *et al.* 1980: 22–3; referred by Muncie 1999: 260).

Where is the difference?

Finally, regulation is needed to clarify the differences between RJ, the penal model and the protective model. For the moment, we distinguish five elements. First of all, within RJ, the juvenile is held responsible for his delinquent behaviour. He is not going to be rehabilitated, but he is going to be confronted with his criminal behaviour and be required to repair the harm caused by his offence. Secondly, the minor should be considered as a full member of the RJ process. As a consequence, there should be a certain space for his story, his views and his background (youth) culture. In contrast to the rehabilitative approach, purely paternalistic and/or middle-class assessments should be avoided, otherwise, RJ might be viewed as pandering to middle-class values (see Bell 2000: 15). Special vigilance is also needed in order to avoid purely *adult-centric* attitudes. Because, 'even now with the focus there is on children, it is on children seen through the prism of an adult lens' (Freeman 1997: 2). Moreover, youths in trouble, especially those from disadvantaged backgrounds, are particularly vulnerable to imposition by adult authorities (Feld 1999). Thirdly, to make sure the minor will be protected against illegal or disproportionate responses from the state or the community, procedural guarantees and human rights should, in contrast to the protection model, be implemented, respected and evaluated. Even without official criminal proceedings (diversion), the principles of justice, equality and protection of the offender (from forced confessions, unreasonable demands by the victim, etc.) must be guaranteed (Dünkel 1996: 59). Next, and as contrasted with both the penal and protection models, the victim should also be approached as a full stakeholder in the process. Hence, his or her background culture should also be taken into consideration and his or her procedural guarantees and human rights be established. Finally, and again as contrasted with both (retributive) penal and protection models, the reaction to the offence should aim primarily at repairing, in a constructive and reasonable way, the harm caused to the victim.

Content of some basic procedural safeguards and standards within RJ[1]

National and international debates on the need for procedural safeguards within RJ have already started and have led to certain statements. Therefore we would like to analyse within this second part, and of course within the limits of this contribution, five bottlenecks which seem, in our opinion, still in need of further regulation: (1) the principle of pro-portionality, (2) the principle of voluntary participation, (3) the right to (legal) assistance, (4) the outcome of the RJ process and its influence on the criminal justice system and (5) the presumption of innocence. In addition, we would also like to discuss some problems surrounding the debate on standards for RJ – a practice might be respectful of fundamental pro-cedural guarantees and human rights of those involved, but this does not make the practice a restorative one.

As sources for our research, we have used some internationally known RJ documents (such as the Declaration of Leuven and the Restorative Justice Handbook). Secondly, we have taken into account some articles from RJ advocates as well as RJ critics, who have analysed certain procedural and human rights problems within RJ. Finally, we have also looked at certain sources from intergovernmental bodies, such as the United Nations and the European Union. In this regard, we have specifically taken into account the UN Preliminary Draft Elements of a Declaration of Basic Principles on the Use of Restorative Justice Programmes in Criminal Matters (annexed to the ECOSOC Resolution 2000/30-E/CN. 15/2000/7) and the Recommendation on Mediation in Penal Matters (No. R (99) 19) adopted by the Committee of Ministers of the Council of Europe (15 September 1999).

The principle of proportionality

Proportionality remains a difficult burden within RJ discussions. Some RJ advocates are in favour of letting the offender, the victim and the community decide themselves what kind of sanction and proportionality they find appropriate (McCold 1999; Van Garsse 1999). However, coercion, pressure and fear of being pursued or punished severely might encourage young offenders to restore more than they think is just. Therefore, we must then ask whether there should not be guidance available that would leave freedom to negotiate, but that would also avoid unwarranted disparity (Van Ness 1999a: 274–5). Moreover, the restorative proportionality based on the seriousness of the harm caused to the victim and society proposed by some RJ advocates (Declaration of Leuven 1997: no. 72) might imply severe restorative actions on the part of the minor. For example, a minor who writes his signature on a wall might cause more material damage than another young offender who intentionally breaks someone else's nose. When the restorative actions are only related to the degree of material damage, less serious offences with a high degree of material damage would become more difficult to restore than serious offences with a low degree of material damage.

This need for proportionality does not imply, in our opinion, the use of strict retributive proportionality. Instead, we think the creation of a retributive minimum and a retributive maximum could offer the retributive limits within which victims and offenders can agree on forms of reparation. Moreover, these retributive limits could also act as a 'default setting' in cases where no informal resolution proved possible (Cavadino and Dignan 1997: 248) and the case is sent to the criminal justice system. The UN Draft Declaration (2000, issue no. 7) and the European Recommendation on Mediation in Penal Matters (1999, issue no. 31) seem to go in the same direction when they state that 'agreements should contain only reasonable and proportionate obligations'. The European Committee explains further in its explanatory memorandum that there should be 'correspondance between the burden on the offender and the seriousness of the offence'. However, it continues with the quite vague terminology of 'within rather wide limits' (p. 24). To clarify this vagueness, it would probably be appropriate for states to create and legalize these limits. Such a situation, however, would imply the creation and implementation of a new juvenile justice system, based on some kind of juvenile penal code.

A legally based, but not strict, retributive proportionality might also prevent mediation from leading to more severe reactions on young people's offences than is the case in the traditional juvenile justice system. After all, especially when minor first offences are involved which cause substantial damage, the use of restorative proportionality easily leads to more severe measures. Minors are often not in a position to repay the damage without some financial help from their family. Hence, when their family refuses to help or when the victim requires that the minor effects the restoration himself, often the minor has got no other choice than to work to pay back the debts. In some countries, such as Belgium, restitution funds have been created to pay a certain amount of money towards the victim for each hour the minor works for the community. Such a situation, however, obliges some minor offenders to work many hours for the community in order to repair the damage and complete the mediation successfully. Sometimes, a restorative measure that is in proportion to the seriousness of the harm can result in quite a severe measure for a young offender, even more severe than a sanction taken by the traditional juvenile justice system. Hence, Braithwaite's proposition that any outcome of a RJ process might not transgress the maximum foreseen in the conventional justice system looks very appealing (Braithwaite 2000: 6; Dünkel 1996: 58).

In addition, some Belgian restitution funds use a rather questionable way by paying youngsters for their community service. This means that the older you are, the more you earn per hour. As a consequence, however, this also implies that older minors have to work less than younger minors to restore the same damage. From a pedagogical point of view, this situation is quite difficult to defend, because the older you are, the more responsibility you can and should bear. Therefore a principle of proportionality that takes into account the seriousness of the offence and the age of the offender appears to be more just.

The use of proportionality might also temper the net-widening effect many projects are dealing with, especially when they are working at the level of the public prosecutor. Net-widening occurs when the public prosecutor's office is seen to select cases that would have been dismissed under the older system. Both in Belgium and elsewhere, the mediation procedure appears to have given rise to such net-widening. This need not be seen as a negative outcome in all respects, if only because more victims can be taken care of. Net-widening does impose a problem, however, if it occurs in a predominantly repressive way. For example, first offenders who have committed a small offence might be obliged from now on to work many hours in order to repair the damage and avoid any further judicial procedure. The introduction of the mediation procedure can also be expected to lower the age of criminal responsibility. Mediation centres will then induce a situation whereby children under the age of criminal responsibility are considered responsible for their acts and can consequently be punished by working to pay back damage repair costs (Falck 1991). Therefore, the kind of offences and minors who are amenable for RJ processes at the level of public prosecutor administration should be made explicit by means of (legal) guidelines; following the European Recommendation (1999, issue no. 7) and the UN Draft Declaration (2000, issue no. 11) there 'should be guidelines, with legislative authority when necessary, defining and governing the use of mediation in penal matters. Such guidelines should in particular address the conditions for the referral of cases to restorative justice programmes'.

The public prosecutor is in a position where he can easily abuse the system of mediation. Were the public prosecutor only to dismiss mediation cases whereby the young offender has effectively been working a number of hours to repay the victim, mediation would become very hard to distinguish from an imposed community service. In such a case, the Public Prosecutor's Office could be seen to be turning victim–offender mediation into an instrument to issue a hidden form of community service (Dumortier, Eliaerts and Vanderhaegen 1998). To protect young people against exaggerated hidden community services at the level of public prosecutor administration, a clear legal maximum might be appropriate at public prosecutor's level. On the juvenile judge's level, where the procedural guarantees are (or should be) better guaranteed, this maximum may be much higher.

The principle of voluntary participation

In RJ literature, and in European and UN documents, the voluntary acceptance and the voluntary commitment of the offender and the victim are stressed. RJ must be a opportunity for offender and victim, not an obligation. Indeed, if parties participated in a RJ procedure because they are obliged to, the restorative philosophy and goals of mediation would be betrayed (McCold 1999; Stassart 1999: 7; Van Garsse 1999: 123). However, it is hard to pretend that, in practice, a minor has a free choice and is in no way obliged to participate, when his unwillingness to co-operate can be sanctioned by prosecution before the juvenile court and/or a harsher punishment from the juvenile judge (Trépanier 1993); after all, the minor knows that the Public Prosecutor or the juvenile judge will eventually evaluate the result of mediation. To state that minors participate in this kind of victim–offender mediation on a voluntary basis therefore seems to represent a good example of 'mystified language' (Van De Kerckhove 1977). Following this discourse, in which mediation is described as extra-judicial, not obligatory, on offer, voluntarily accepted, etc., in practice no legal rights are organized either. This situation seems to resemble the heavily criticized (also by RJ advocates) treatment model, where youngsters were not punished either, at least not following the treatment discourse, and therefore did not need a lot of procedural guarantees either (Dumortier 2000).

We wonder if the terminology 'informed consent' (as used at certain points within the European Recommendation) instead of 'voluntary' is not more desirable. Indeed, before giving their consent to participate in a RJ process, the young offender as well as the victim 'should be fully informed of their rights, the nature of the process and the possible consequences of their decision' (European Recommendation, 1999, issue no. 10; UN Draft Declaration, 2000 issue no. 12, b). Thereby it must be made clear, as is foreseen in the European Recommendation (1999, issue no. 2) and the UN Draft Declaration (2000, issue no. 7) that the 'parties may withdraw their consent at any time'. Moreover, 'neither the victim nor the offender should be induced by unfair means to accept mediation' (European Recommendation, 1999, issue no. 11), nor any other RJ process. Especially when minors are involved, vigilance is needed to avoid coercion on the part of the public prosecutor, the mediators, or the minor's parents on the young offender. Therefore, before agreeing to participate, the need for legal advice becomes crucial. Besides, informed consent on the part of the juvenile, as well as on that of the victim, could also be formalized by signing a document wherein all relevant information on RJ procedures and rights is incorporated.

Right to legal assistance

Taking into account the necessity of consent and the right to be fully informed before giving this consent, legal assistance becomes almost unavoidable. In order to enable a practice where legal assistance or advice can be given, the minds of certain lawyers need to mature to the idea that mediation presents a valid alternative for conflict resolution in which the parties try to arrange the damage themselves. This system of mediation ought not to be transformed into a practice whereby the victim and the offender's lawyer get involved into a process of mediation. The role of the lawyer in this system therefore is mainly to ensure that the minor's elementary rights are safeguarded; he enables a minor to avoid consenting to co-operation in the mediation process on the basis of coercion from the criminal justice system or from the mediation centre, when that minor considers himself innocent. Minors should not accept unreasonable damage claims out of ignorance, either. Besides, it must be mentioned that arranging damage repair is a difficult problem, which triggers a number of questions in which legal advice might be very relevant (Dumortier, Eliaerts and Vanderhaegen 1998: 362).

Therefore and following both the European Recommendation (1999, issue no. 8) and the UN Draft Declaration (2000, issue no. 12) 'the parties should have the right to legal assistance'. However, such a large formulation might suggest that lawyers are allowed to play the principal role during the mediation. Such a situation would inevitably lead to a 'rejuridication' (Groenhuijsen 2000: 446) of the conflict. Hence the proposed solution by the UN Draft Declaration might be, for the moment, more suitable: 'the parties should have the right to legal advice before and after the restorative process' (see also Van Ness 1999). Nonetheless, two remarks should be made when minors are involved in a RJ process. First of all, the question arises whether this assistance of a lawyer before and after the process should be obligatory or, on the contrary, a right that can be waived by the minor. If the right to assistance can be waived, then youngsters will have to be well informed. Within Belgian juvenile justice practice, youngsters often waive this right, because they wrongly think their parents will have to pay a lawyer's bill. They also assume that a lawyer will hamper their chances of a quick and good settlement of the case by the juvenile judge. In the US, too, many juveniles are not represented, for it is said that they have waived their right to council (Feld 1999: 22). Secondly, the question arises whether a lawyer, or at least a confidante, should not be present also during the RJ process. After all, minors can be put under enormous pressure by their parents and extended family, by the victim, by a police officer, by a judicial actor, etc. As contrasted with adults, minors might be more in need of assistance during the process than we assume. Therefore, scientific research and evaluations should closely observe if and when minors are in need of assistance during the RJ process. Independent evaluation interviews with minors who have participated in a RJ process could also clarify their feelings and needs for assistance.

Finally, to prevent lawyers from stealing the conflict again and formalizing RJ processes too much, education is needed. From such education, lawyers should on the one hand acquire specialization in juvenile law and problems closely linked to it and, on the other hand, they could also use special training in RJ and its underlying principles (Van Ness 1999a: 269).

Influence of RJ outcome on subsequent criminal justice proceedings

Following the UN Draft Declaration (2000, issue no. 11b) and the European Recommendation (1999, issue no. 5), guidelines and standards should address 'the handling of cases following a restorative process'. Such guidelines are essential to avoid discretion on part of the judicial actors and to bring clarity to the young offenders, as well as to the victim(s) (Dünkel 1996).

Level of the public prosecutor

The question of what should happen with a successful RJ process at the level of the public prosecutor is closely linked to the kind of cases the public prosecutor can choose for the RJ process. As mentioned before, both in Belgium and abroad, the mediation procedure appears to have given rise to a net-widening effect. In other words, the public prosecutor's office seems to select cases that would have been dismissed under the older system. In such a situation, it appears advisable that a successful RJ agreement should stop all further possible proceedings.

If, however, clear criteria for selection of the cases are implemented and public prosecutors are obliged to select only cases amenable for further judicial proceedings, then it might be necessary, in the interests of community, to leave the possibility of further actions open. However, to avoid discretion on the part of the public prosecutor, perhaps guidelines could state what kind of successful RJ outcomes can never be prosecuted further. These criteria could be that the damage has been restored and that the minor has been sufficiently confronted with the consequences of his behaviour. To find out whether the minor has been confronted *sufficiently*, reference could be made to the retributive minimum stipulated in some kind of juvenile penal code (see the principle of proportionality). Besides, discharges based on mediated agreements should have the same status as judicial decisions and should preclude prosecution in respect of the same facts (*ne bis in idem*; see European Recommendation 1999, issue nr. 17).

When the RJ process turns out to be unsuccessful, the opposite question arises, i.e. should the public prosecutor always institute proceedings? Again, the answer is linked to the kind of cases the public prosecutor selects for these RJ processes. If the public prosecutor only selects minor cases that normally would have been dismissed, then the public prosecutor should be very careful about prosecution. Indeed, a prosecution of these cases would lead to the unpleasant conclusion that minor offenders who normally would have been totally left alone are now facing a real trial on the basis of an unsuccessful RJ process.

If, on the contrary, the public prosecutor selects cases that normally would have been prosecuted, then it does appear important to leave the possibility to prosecute open. However, the first question to be addressed concerns the definition of 'unsuccessful mediation'. Is the mediation process a downright failure when one out of many conditions has not been fulfilled? One might argue that the process has far from failed when the offender has convincingly complied with most conditions and proves to have learned something. Is it fair, in such cases, that he can still face additional punishment?[2] There are reasonable grounds, therefore, to argue that, in this scenario, the public prosecutor's office better examines the expediency of prosecution in each particular case where the RJ process failed.

Level of the juvenile judge
At the level of the juvenile judge, restorative processes should be available as well. Indeed, following the UN Draft Declaration (2000, issue no. 6) and the European Recommendation (1999, issue no. 4) 'restorative programmes should be (generally) available at all stages of the criminal justice process'. Otherwise, RJ will probably not be capable of becoming a basic approach for reacting to juvenile delinquency. After all, if RJ is only possible at the level of the public prosecutor, a two-level system might easily develop, whereby only minor offences are sent to RJ processes and the serious offences continue to be punished (harshly) by the traditional justice system. Therefore, if RJ also wants to deal with the serious cases, RJ processes should be available for cases already prosecuted by the public prosecutor. Of course, such a way of working has nothing to do with diversion, because the young offender and the victim know they will face a judge at the end of the road. Nevertheless, this scenario still incorporates certain advantages. First of all, net-widening will probably occur less than at the level of the public prosecutor, because the public prosecutor normally only prosecutes the more serious cases. Secondly, victim and offender are given the opportunity to influence the judge's decision. Thirdly, the evaluation of the RJ outcome by an independent, impartial judge can be seen as a procedural guarantee for the offender and the victim, as well as for society. After all, a judge must take the interests of all involved parties into consideration. Besides, if one of the parties does not accept the evaluation of the judge, appeal is always possible. Therefore, judges should always give reasons for why they refuse to take a successful RJ outcome into consideration or why they impose a sanction on top of the restorative efforts already taken by the young offender.

The question arises whether guidelines should not clarify when the judge can refuse successful RJ outcomes or when he can impose extra punishments. Indeed, vigilance is needed to avoid double punishment of youngsters. On the one hand, young offenders will have to fulfil restorative efforts during the RJ process towards the victim. On the other hand, the juvenile judge can still impose sanctions or punishments in order to restore the damage caused to society. Such practices could reinforce the punishment climate vis-à-vis minors. In this respect, sufficient guarantees need to be built in to ensure that 'the interests of the victim' do not legitimate, in practice, a double punishment of youngsters. A (legal) 'default setting' with a retributive minimum and maximum could limit discretion in the RJ process (see above), as well as in the traditional juvenile-justice procedure following.

Whenever a RJ process is not successful, the question arises if, and how, this should influence the traditional justice procedure. The European Recommendation remains remarkably silent on this question. In contrast, the UN Draft Declaration (2000, issue no. 15) clearly states that 'a lack of agreement may not be used as justification for a more severe sentence in subsequent criminal justice proceedings'. Nevertheless, we wonder if judges will not punish more harshly those young offenders who were not willing to fulfil any restorative effort. Even though the UN Draft Declaration (2000, issue no. 13) claims that 'discussions in restorative processes should be confidential and should not be disclosed subsequently, except with the agreement of the parties', we wonder if judges will not find out, in an informal way, how the young offender actually performed. Within the Belgian experiment on family group conferences, for example, the attendance of a social worker from the social youth services might be implemented. However, these social workers are often in close (informal) contact with the juvenile judge. And how to prevent victims from using information they received during these confidential sessions? Shall we punish victims who reveal confidential information?

Besides, is it fair that information on the RJ process is not communicated to the judge in cases where the offender does co-operate entirely, but is being confronted with the victim's unwillingness to do the same? What course to take when the offender totally refuses to co-operate, knowing that a RJ process is demanded by a victim in need of answers? Information about the restorative proceedings and its influence on subsequent judicial decisions can become quite important for both victim and young offender.

Presumption of innocence

The European Recommendation (1999, issue no. 14), as well as the UN Draft Declaration (2000, issue no. 8) state that 'participation should not be used as evidence of admission of guilt in subsequent legal proceedings'. This statement is made in respect for the presumption of innocence. Nevertheless, following the European Recommendation, 'the basic facts of a case should normally be acknowledged by both parties as a basis for mediation' (1999, issue no. 14). But is it actually possible to acknowledge criminal facts without admitting guilt? Are juvenile judges not going to interpret participation as an admission of guilt? Moreover, within the European recommendation, as well as in the UN Draft, the RJ Handbook and RJ literature in general, reference is always made to the offender instead of the accused (Groenhuijsen 2000). Even the name 'victim–offender mediation' explicitly refers to the victim and the offender, not the accused. Therefore, we wonder if it would not be more logical to state that offenders who participate waive their right to be presumed innocent (of course only for the facts they acknowledge). Again, good, legal advice is indispensable before minors waive this right.

Besides, if the minor admits a crime, should this act entail the acceptance of all damages the victim claims to have suffered? Or, on the contrary, should only the damage accepted by young offenders be amenable for an immediate mediation? This latter option might imply a decision from a (civil) judge on the damage in dispute.

Basic standards for good practice

As already mentioned, to prevent RJ practices from being implemented in a bad or non-restorative way, there seems to be no other solution than creating standards. Within RJ literature there is already a bulk of material that tries to clarify what can and what cannot be called restorative, but not, however, unanimously. Moreover, within RJ literature, standards are often vague, intention-based and/or morally charged. For example, following McCold, 'the primary goal of restorative justice is to repair the injuries that were created by the crime by addressing the needs of the victim (for healing), offender (for responsibility) and the communities (for empowerment)' (McCold 1999: 3). Although McCold further explains what specific kind of needs he (together with other RJ advocates) thinks the three stakeholders have or should have, the question still arises how we can scientifically evaluate whether these needs are actually met. Moreover, the question arises whether it is actually possible and ethically just to describe what kind of needs the stakeholders (should) have. Is a family group conference in which the victim merely wants the stolen money back, without any healing aspects, not a restorative practice? And are the offences committed by a young offender always 'wrong', as apparently McCold assumes (1999: 8)? In certain communities, homosexuality is seen as an offence, as an 'injury to (heterosexual) people and relationships'. Should homosexual youngsters who live in those communities, if they are sent to a family group conference for their 'crime', admit that they were 'wrong'? What, in fact, is the definition of being 'wrong'? After all, what is 'wrong' for certain people might be quite 'right' for others. In other words, if restorative justice envisions informal enforcement of 'community norms', then who defines the 'community' and the 'norms'?

Following Bazemore and Walgrave, restorative justice is 'every action that is primarily oriented towards doing justice by repairing the harm that has been caused by a crime' (Bazemore and Walgrave 1999: 48). Even court-imposed 'sanctions should be included within the restorative justice definition, so long as their primary intent is to reinforce an obligation to make amends to the victim and the victimized community' (Bazemore and Walgrave 1999: 48). However, such an intention-based definition creates various bottlenecks. Is the imprisonment of a young offender by a judge with the intent to symbolically repair the harm caused to society and the victim actually a restorative action? Is the only difference between a punishment and a restorative action the intent with which it has been administered (Bazemore and Walgrave 1999: 47)? Such reasoning, however, implies that within current (Belgian) juvenile justice institutions, minors are never punished either, for every action is taken, at least following the protection paradigm discourse, with the intent to help the young offenders and not to punish. Moreover, how can we scientifically evaluate if a measure has been imposed with the primary intent to repair the harm? Besides, stating that the intention of the measure is to repair the harm does not mean that the involved minor will not feel punished, or that judicial actors will never feel the need to punish young offenders (see above). Therefore, it might be more appropriate to elaborate objective RJ standards and specific guidelines (Dünkel 1996: 49) of good practice, instead of vague RJ intentions, needs and/or goals. For example: who must be contacted first within a RJ process: the victim or the offender? Who must contact them: a RJ representative or a judicial one? What is the make-up of a panel in family group conferences like? When can young offenders make an appeal to restitution funds? How should RJ representatives report to judicial representatives? Should they use standard forms or should they individualize each report?

These practice guidelines should best be reinforced by the authorities to prevent every project having its own guidelines, its own (restorative) justice. Nevertheless too rigid an implementation of centralized guidelines could hamper local traditions of handling crimes. Therefore, 'good' RJ practices might also imply respect for the local community's culture, the victim's lifestyle and background culture, as well as the offender's lifestyle and background (youth) culture. At least, the use of standards would offer a more objective touchstone to evaluate daily practices in regard to the prevailing satisfaction research (Schiff 1999: 330; Umbreit 1996; Stassart 1999). After all, satisfied people do not always turn the practice into a restorative justice one.

Conclusion: in search of procedural safeguards and standards

To prevent the RJ movement from generating the same evils as the child protection movement, we think a human rights approach, together with real RJ codes of good practice (not just intents, aims or needs), might offer an instrument towards good and real RJ practice, respectful of fundamental human rights. On the one hand, this will offer us a more objective and clear instrument to fulfil independent scientific research. On the other hand, a judicial RJ instrument is in the interest of the minor, as well as the victim. Indeed, more clarity on rights and obligations within RJ processes would exist towards offender and victim. However, before creating such a judicial translation, the legal position of both offender and victim should be thoroughly analysed and discussed.

Nevertheless, (even) a regulation of RJ will not lead from definition towards 'good' implementation. Proclaiming rights and standards is not the same as observing them (Van Ness 1999: 265). Differences between law in books and law in action (or RJ in books and RJ in action) will inevitably occur. Neither welfare, nor penal justice, nor restorative justice, will ever be present in pure form. In particular, the youth justice model contains elements of different models, thus ensuring that a complex, ambiguous and confused mélange of policies and practices exists at any one time (see Muncie 1999: 301). Therefore, besides a regulation of RJ, education and training of those involved in both the judicial and restorative functions (such as mediators) remains a necessity (Van Ness 1999: 270). After all, people, not books, will have to implement RJ. Sufficient financial means, workable structures, well formed staff, and also a judicial RJ instrument that functions as some kind of common anchorage, all seem, in our opinion, indispensable factors towards real and just RJ practices.

Notes

1. Within the scope of our research we try to analyse, among other things, the legal position of minors involved in RJ processes. As a consequence, the rest of our contribution is especially focused on this topic. This, however, does not mean that the victim's procedural safeguards and human rights are always respected within RJ and that no problems occur. Neither do we interpret these problems as being less important.
2. In the case of adult offenders, the probation officers propose always to prosecute, so as to discourage the offender and his lawyer's speculations considering the possibility of dismissal (speculations which induce non-co-operation in the mediation process).

References

Bazemore, G. and Walgrave, L. (1999) *Restorative Juvenile Justice: Repairing the Harm of Youth Crime.* Monsey/NY: Criminal Justice Press.

Bell, C. (2000) 'A Web of Confusion: The Search for a Theoretical Principle Underpinning the New Juvenile Justice System', *Youth Justice Matters*, June 2000: 12–15.

Braithwaite, J. (2000) 'Standards for Restorative Justice. Address to UN Congress on the Prevention of Crime', paper presented to the 10th UN Congress on the Prevention of Crime and the Treatment of Offenders, 13th of April 2000, Vienna, Austria, available at www.restorativejustice.org

Cavadino, M. and Dignan, J. (1997) 'Reparation, Retribution and Rights', *International Review of Victimology*, 4: 233–253.

Christiaens, J. (1999) 'The Juvenile Delinquent and his Welfare Sanction', *European Journal of Crime, Criminal Law and Criminal Justice*, (1): 5–21.

Declaration of Leuven (1997) On the Advisability of Promoting the Restorative Approach to Juvenile Crime in G. Bazemore and L. Walgrave (eds) *Restorative Juvenile Justice: Repairing the Harm of Youth Crime.* Monsey/NY: Criminal Justice Press.

Dumortier, E. (2000) 'Neglecting Due Process for Minors: A Possible Dark Side of the Restorative Justice Implementation?', paper presented to the 10th UN Congress on the Prevention of Crime and the Treatment of Offenders, 13th of April 2000, Vienna, Austria, available at www.restorativejustice.org

Dumortier, E., Eliaerts, C. and Vanderhaegen, R. (1998) 'Critical Assessment of Community Service and Mediation for Juvenile Offenders in Brussels. A discussion of the project BAS!' in L. Walgrave (ed.) *Restorative Justice for Juveniles. Potentialities, Risks and Problems.* Leuven: Leuven University Press.

Dünkel, F. (1996) 'Täter-Opfer-Ausgleich. German Experiences with Mediation in a European Perspective', *European Journal on Criminal Policy and Research*, (4): 44–66.

European Recommendation on Mediation in Penal Matters (No R (99) 19), adopted by the Committee of Ministers of the Council of Europe, 15 September 1999.

Falck, S. (1991) 'Community Mediation Centers on the Right Track or Side-Tracked?' in A. Snare (ed.) *Youth, Crime and Justice, Scandinavian Studies in Criminology* (vol. 12). Oslo: Norwegian University Press.

Feld, B. (1999) 'Rehabilitation, Retribution and Restorative Justice: Alternative Conceptions of Juvenile Justice' in G. Bazemore and L. Walgrave (eds) *Restorative Juvenile Justice: Repairing the Harm of Youth Crime.* Monsey/NY: Criminal Justice Press.

Freeman, M. (1997) *The Moral Status of Children. Essays on the Rights of the Child.* The Hague/Cambridge/Dordrecht; Martinus Nijhoff Publishers/Kluwer Law International.

Gilissen, J. and Magits, M. (1989) *Historische Inleiding Tot het Recht (Historical Introduction to Law).* Antwerpen: Kluwer.

Groenhuijsen, M. S. (2000) 'Mediation in het Strafrecht. Bemiddeling en Conflictoplossing in vele Gedaanten', *Delikt en Delinkwent*, (5): 441–448.

Marshall, T. (1996) 'The Evolution of Restorative Justice in Britain', *European Journal on Criminal Policy and Research*, (4): 21–43.

McCold, P. (1999) 'Toward a Holistic Vision of Restorative Juvenile Justice: A Reply to Walgrave', paper presented to the 3rd International Conference on Restorative Justice for Juveniles. International Network for Research on Restorative Justice for Juveniles, Belgium, October 24–27.

Muncie, J. (1999) *Youth and Crime. A Critical Introduction.* London: Sage.

Newburn, T. (1997) 'Youth, Crime and Justice' in M. Maguire, R. Morgan and R. Reiner (eds) *The Oxford Handbook of Criminology.* Oxford: Clarendon Press.

Platt, A. (1977) *The Child Savers.* Chicago/London: The University of Chicago Press, 240 p.

Restorative Justice Handbook, statement submitted by the Alliance of Non-governmental Organizations in Crime Prevention and Criminal Justice, 10th UN Congress on the Prevention of Crime and the Treatment of Offenders, 10–17 April 2000, Vienna, Austria.

Schiff, M. (1999) 'The Impact of Restorative Interventions on Juvenile Offenders' in G. Bazemore and L. Walgrave (eds) *Restorative Juvenile Justice: Repairing the Harm of Youth Crime.* Monsey/NY: Criminal Justice Press.

Stassart, E. (1999) *Wetenschappelijke Ondersteuning bij de Implementatie en Ontwikkeling van het Provinciaal Vereffeningsfonds (Scientific Support for the Implementation and Development of the Provincial Restitution Fund).* Leuven: Katholieke Universiteit Leuven.

Trepanier, J. (1993) 'La Justice Réparatrice et les Philosophies de l'Intervention Pénale sur les Jeunes', paper presented at the 9th Journées Internationales de Criminologie Juvénile, Vaucresson, June 1993.

Umbreit, M. (1996) 'Restorative Justice Through Mediation: The Impact of Programs in Four Canadian Provinces' in B. Galaway and J. Hudson (eds) *Restorative Justice: International Perspectives.* Amsterdam: Kugler.

UN Preliminary Draft Elements of a Declaration of Basic Principles on the Use of Restorative Justice Programmes in Criminal Matters, annexed to the ECOSOC Resolution 2000/30-E/CN. 15/2000/7.

Van de Kerckhove, M. (1977) 'Des Mesures Répressives aux Mesures de Sûreté et de Protection', *Revue de Droit Pénal*, 245–79.

Van Garsse, L. (1999) 'Herstelrechtelijk Jeugdsanctierecht? Bedenkingen Vanuit de Bemiddelingspraktijk (Restorative Youth Sanction Model? Remarks from the Mediation Practice)' in G. Decock and P. Vansteenkiste (eds) *Herstel of Sanctie (Restitution or Sanction)?* Gent: Mys and Breesch.

Van Ness, D. (1999a) 'Legal Issues of Restorative Justice' in G. Bazemore and L. Walgrave (eds) *Restorative Juvenile Justice: Repairing the Harm of Youth Crime.* Monsey/NY: Criminal Justice Press.

Van Ness, D. (1999b) 'A Restorative Future for Juvenile Justice', paper presented to the 3rd International Conference on Restorative Justice for Juveniles, Leuven, October 1999.

Von Hirsch, A. (1993) *Censure and Sanctions.* Oxford: Clarendon Press.

Walgrave, L. (ed.) (1998) *Restorative Justice for Juveniles. Potentialities, Risks and Problems.* Leuven: Leuven University Press.

Walgrave, L. and Bazemore, G. (1999) 'Reflections on the Future of Restorative Justice for Juveniles' in G. Bazemore and L. Walgrave (eds) *Restorative Juvenile Justice: Repairing the Harm of Youth Crime.* Monsey/NY: Criminal Justice Press.

Zehr, H. (1990) *Changing Lenses: A New Focus for Crime and Justice.* Scottdale, PA: Herald Press.

From the 'sword' to dialogue: towards a 'dialectic' basis for penal mediation

Grazia Mannozzi

The idea of justice reflected in its allegoric personification[1]

Traditional iconography represents Justice as a female figure, at times blindfolded, holding scales in her left hand and a sword in her right (Schild 1988) (see Figure 11.1). Although the allegoric personification of Justice is often also associated with other elements (the sceptre, the lictor's fasces, cornucopias, later with the orb and angels' wings) these never become constant symbols as do the scales and the sword (Kissel 1984: 104; Jacob 1994).

Justice is primarily referred to as a 'woman' (Zdekauer 1909: 7). In this context, it should be pointed out that while it was not from art that the idea came to endow Justice with a female persona, it was art that crystallized it by drawing on mythology. From antiquity until today, Justice, as 'goddess' or 'virtue' (whether as an imperial or cardinal virtue), has always been female in traditional iconography: from Roman coins (see Figure 11.2) to miniatures, from bas-reliefs (Kissel 1984: 35) to sculptures, from frescos to carvings. According to a recent interpretation of Roman and Christian iconography, the portrayal of Justice as a female may refer back to an idea of justice as *mediation* between divine, absolute and inexorable law, and the fallible conduct of man on Earth (Edgerton 1980: 32) (see Figure 11.3).

One may ask why the representation of blindfolded Justice with her scales and sword became a 'perfect allegory' (Robert 1994), maintaining its

Figure 11.1. Drawing based on 'Justitia thront über König und Bettler' (1566) by Justinus Gobber, cf. Kissel 1984, 110

Figure 11.2. Drawing based on Roman coins: (A) 'Justice' (Age of Tiberius); (B) 'Equity' (Age of Vespasian); (C) 'Equity' (Age of Marcus Aurelius), cf. Jacob 1994, 220

Figure 11.3. Drawing based on 'Stanza della Segnatura in Vaticano' (1508–1511) by Raphael, cf. Kissel 1984, 37

characteristics over the centuries despite evolution in the idea of justice, and especially despite radical changes in trial paradigms and punishment.

Possibly, the single elements of the allegory connote ideological constants, which have not been influenced by the cultural, political or ideological inputs that significantly conditioned the models of justice dominating each historical epoch. We thus need to briefly examine the meaning of each component of this 'perfect allegory' to establish how relevant they may be to the idea of justice we have inherited from the twentieth century.

Let us begin with what is historically the most recent element introduced: the blindfold. There are no uncertainties over its interpretation. Appearing only at the end of the fifteenth century (von Möeller 1905: 108), the blindfold symbolizes, in the opinion of all scholars, the indifference the judge should show towards the appearance of those who appear in court – in a word, the judges' impartiality regarding the social and economic conditions of those on whom they pass judgement.

Figure 11.4 Drawing based on 'Die Gerechtigkeit mit Kranich' (1495) by Albrecht Dürer, cf. Kissel 1984, 43

The scales (Figure 11.4) are a figurative element recalling the Aristotelian doctrine of justice – based on the dichotomy between *distributive* justice and *commutative* justice – and, more generally, on the concept of equity. The scales – both weighing and moderating – are also a metaphor for the idea of proportion which, since the tradition embodied in the Old Testament, has been the inspiring principle behind the *ius dicere* (administration of justice) as well as the criterion by which to decide how punishment is to be applied (*Letter to the Romans*, 13, 10).

Lastly, the sword constitutes the most controversial element in the allegoric representation. This is because of its many iconographic variants. Indeed, while it is almost without exception held in the right hand, it is at times wielded menacingly and at others lowered, and has many different symbolic allusions.

To begin with, one may observe how the sword, from ancient times on, has borne ritual and mytho-logical significance and is a con-stant presence in sagas and myths. In law, the sword – apart from indicating the weapon which the executioner traditionally carried or used in corporal punishment – is one of the symbols of the Law itself. Together with the sceptre, the sword symbolizes the power of *ius dicere*. Additionally, as the exclusive emblem of the power of *ius dicere*, it tends to reinforce the prohibition of recourse to private law enforcement (as in vendettas or feuds). Thus, from this point of view, the sword is also a symbol of the duty to observe the peace as established by public authority.

In essence, this figurative element – which appeared in the twelfth century and has been interpreted solely as the symbol of 'public enforcement against private vengeance' (Jacob 1994: 225) – has been accorded a significance which, while reflecting the tradition, is in some respects excessively reductive.

In addition to the interpretation of the sword as a symbol of power – which may also derive its legitimacy from Justinian's *Institutiones* (*Corpus iuris civilis*, II, 2) – an alternative can be proposed, according to which the sword may represent the instrument with which '*trancher les litiges*' (to cut disputes).

The sword, in other words, would refer to the idea that it cuts the Gordian knot, as we know from history, of those controversies which are not amenable to judicial resolution.

While this hypothesis is difficult to prove, it remains a suggestive interpretation, as it is not without plausibility. It introduces the main theme of this chapter on the meaning and value of penal mediation, by posing a crucial question: are some controversies really intractable, so that the knot of conflict can only be severed, or is every dispute amenable to settlement, if only one can find the correct way to mediate it?

The problem, more generally, is ultimately whether mediation can represent the successful attempt to overcome the authoritarian model of conflict resolution which, intrinsically and structurally, is always violent, because the type of justice which 'gives each to his own' ('*suum cuique tribuere*') (Ulpiano, *Digesta*, 1,10,1; Giustiniano, *Institutiones*, 1,1,3) must of necessity resort to the sword to drastically end each dispute, at the expense of cutting every link between the contending parties at the same time.

To answer this question we must examine the juridical–philosophical meaning of mediation.

The limits of current definitions of mediation

Mediation, as a form of intervention in the context of restorative justice, has not yet received a true definition in the Italian legal system. The only law relating to mediation – and this purely in a civil law context – is Article 1754 Civil Code, which indicates the mediator as 'the person who brings together two or more parties to complete a transaction, who is not tied to any of the parties by any other relationship.'

In the absence of a legal definition, one is forced to make use of doctrinal concepts of victim–offender mediation. Nevertheless, at least in the Italian legal system, none of the definitions proposed truly reflects the complexity of mediation, in that they mainly address its procedural aspects.

Mediation continues to be seen in its limited role as mere interposition between any number of parties in dispute. Hence its definition is akin to that of the mediator: the 'third' and therefore 'neutral' party whose role is to settle a conflict originating in a crime or that has expressed itself through a crime, by re-establishing a relationship between the offender and the victim.

In France, a definition has been proposed which seems to fit the final definition of 'juridical product' quite well: mediation is described as 'a mostly formal process through which a neutral third party attempts, by exchanges between the parties, to get them to express their own point of view and to seek, with his/her help, a solution to the conflict between them' (Bonafé-Schmitt 1992).

This concept – among the most quoted in the specific literature of this field – has attracted almost unanimous agreement. Yet, even in this case, the terms are only descriptively indicating the procedural aspects of mediation. In effect, current definitions only describe what is *happening* through mediation, but not what mediation really *is*.

In search of the foundations of mediation

Premise: dialectic, knowledge and mediation

What is really necessary is a theoretical and political framework for mediation, otherwise we are destined sooner or later to reduce mediation to a further, simplistic means with which to resolve conflicts.

We believe that the theoretical framework of reference is essentially philosophical in nature and relates back to a concept termed 'dialectic' which has played a fundamental role in European historical and juridical traditions.

It is unnecessary to trace back the history of the idea of dialectic which, beginning with Aristotle through to Hegel, has become an integral part of our cultural heritage, before acknowledging that a philosophical framework of a dialectical type is of fundamental importance not only as an interpretative key for mediation, but also, more generally, as an epistemological paradigm for the whole of the juridical system.

Dialectic, in its original meaning, is the practice of dialogue, or structured discussion, which brings us to the discovery of reality and to knowledge of the natural disposition of things. Under Hegel, dialectic took on its well-known triadic logical–conceptual structure, divided into the enunciation of the thesis, the antithesis and the *synthesis*, which represents the final acquisition of knowledge. For Hegel, at the end of the dialectic process lay knowledge of things, that is, where reality and thought coincide.

Contemporary philosophy, and here we are referring mainly to Sartre, seems to have abandoned the dialectical method in the speculative sense and to assume that the subject and reality can in no way be related to one another. Such a difference would exist between the actuality of 'being' against the 'nothing' in the knowing subject that 'between them no interaction can occur, thus creating a dualism that is so radical that these opposites can no longer compete with one another' (Ost and van de Kerchove 1995: 67). In the 'negative' philosophies of the twentieth century, dialectic has appeared as a spent category of thought, with neither an independent place nor any important epistemological role.

The dialectical concept and especially its *method*, however, cannot be considered definitively liquidated by Nihilist philosophies. In the mid-1950s Merleau-Ponty formulated a concept of dialectic which improved both on the Hegelian paradigm, and the organization of so-called 'negative' thought. Starting from the incompatibility between the two positions briefly described above (or rather, from the perfect opposition of the two), Merleau-Ponty, after announcing that the problem of the equivalence between the two terms could not be solved and decrying some of their fallacies, introduces the model of 'good dialectic', to which he attributes a fundamental role in knowledge of reality.

We shall now seek to define the contents of this concept by clarifying the concept of 'knowledge'.

The modern approach to the problem of knowledge is mainly based on the concept of relation. Knowledge always implies that a relation exists between A and B – where A and B indicate two subjects, or rather, a subject and an object. Even the interpretation of a written text, whether of a literary or juridical nature, can be considered a dialectical process.

According to Merleau-Ponty, the dialectical process of knowledge goes beyond the rigid duality between 'being' and 'the world' and is founded on the multiplicity of the relations which tie together both 'being' and 'the world'. He applies the concepts of 'implication', 'participation' and 'interworld', under the assumption that each 'relation' between A and B necessarily involves a plurality of relationships, which are expressed as a variety of positions. Each of these relations leads to another by virtue of its own movement. Thus, we have mutual reversal and generation at the same time.

The thought that expresses these concepts cannot be insulated from these transformations: thought in itself is somehow involved in change and is forced step by step to go through the process; therefore, it does not skim over the surface as if it had not been involved. Hence, there is no dialectic that does not also carry with it the thinking subject (Ost and van de Kerchove 1995: 68).

The first firm assumption that we can make at this stage is that *knowledge does not have a static character*, but a *dynamic* one. Moreover, it always involves interaction between the knowing subject and the object to be known.

This means, to use Merleau-Ponty's words, that 'dialectical thought affirms that each term (A and B) can be itself only when it moves towards the opposite term, it becomes what it is through movement' (Merleau-Ponty 1964: 124).

It is worthwhile pointing out how the distinctive exchange between two terms, A and B, already brings the idea of mediation to the foreground, because – as Merleu-Ponty again observes – 'each term is its own mediation, a quickening existence ... which produces the other' (Merleau-Ponty 1964: 124).

But let us proceed by degrees. The process of knowledge, of which we have until now appreciated only the diachronic character, needs a spatial dimension to become active. This 'territory' cannot only be the *object* to be known, with the complete exclusion of the knowing *subject*, nor only that of the latter, since acquiring knowledge is not just an internal process. The territory in which the dynamic process of knowledge occurs is in reality the 'space' which exists between these two realities – the *knowing subject* and the *object* – also termed appropriately as the space of the *'entre-deux'* ('between-two') (Ost and van de Kerchove 1995: 42 ff.). In reality it is a 'non-place' – whose 'extremes and centre are entwined together ... internal and external, inside and outside penetrate each other' (Ost and van de Kerchove 1995: 45), a place where knowledge becomes 'communicative experience'.

Hence, in Merleau-Ponty's dialectic 'each term (A and B) is subjected to the test of passage through the *entre-deux*' – which, we add, is an *inter-subjective* space that is both neutral and 'communicative' – becoming, through the other, what it itself is called upon to become (Ost and van de Kerchove 1995: 69).

'Good dialectic' is therefore experience in action, an incessant rite of passage. Yet, we observe, is this not the meaning of mediation? – something which never grasps absolute and final truth, unlike what takes place in the Hegelian paradigm. The new dialectic is, in contrast, 'without synthesis', where no acquisition becomes definitive because 'being and thought cross and clamber over each other without blending into a consolatory identity' (Ost and van de Kerchove 1995: 70). The lack of synthesis means that dialectic 'is a constantly reintroduced thought, which rejects both the pure negative and the pretence of finally reaching a new positive' (Ost and van de Kerchove 1995: 70).

To conclude, one may speak of a 'hyperdialectic', to be understood as an opening without synthesis and without a single direction, moving towards plurality and the complex relationships of existence.

Within this reconstruction of modern 'dialectics', we can indicate a second fixed point: between 'knowledge' and 'mediation' where a reciprocal relationship exists. Mediation is a form of knowledge which allows relations between two different poles to be redefined (typically between different subjects). Vice-versa, it cannot be disputed that knowledge is a form of mediation – an example is interpretation, which is typically mediation between the written word and the reader (Betti 1955: 70 ff.).

The very bi-univocal nature of the relationship between knowledge and mediation, while giving us a measure of the 'complexity' of the epistemological problem of understanding, also indicates the potential shown by the communicative space between subjects.

Given these premises regarding dialectic, knowledge and interpretation, we can now proceed to prove and verify whether one can transfer the results attained by Merleau-Ponty in the field of dialectics to that field of mediation we are most interested: between the offender and the victim of a crime.

Mediation as a dialectical process

The above considerations allow the following general definition of mediation to be proposed: mediation is a dialectical process of knowledge activation (where the term 'dialectical' means that knowledge occurs dynamically, within the communicative space between subjects).

This definition gives prominence to at least three essential aspects of mediation:

Mediation is a form of knowledge based on communication

Some preliminary considerations of the 'communicative' nature of mediation is called for here. Mediation is not a complete novelty in our juridical tradition: it emerges in a gloss by Accursius to the *Digesta* in which the mediator (*proxeneta*) is defined as '*qui inquirit voluntates aliorum vel ad munera, vel ad contractus, vel ad amicitias feciendas, vel similia*' (one who seeks the will of others with respect to services, agreements, the establishment of friendship, or similar) (Accursius, *Glossa, ad Digest.*, L, 14). We have here an enlightened insight into mediation. Over time, however, the economic or 'bartering' attributes of mediation began to predominate, leaving its other meanings in the shadows. Thus the 'communicative' aspects of mediation were left in the background, unless we count as exceptions some fleeting indirect references and approaches due to the weight of the civil law tradition (Vidari 1893: 549).

The communicative–relational component plays a fundamental role in penal mediation (Castelli 1996). Unlike penal sanctions, which normally involve a variety of restrictions on personal freedom such as privation of personal liberty, reductions to personal possessions, restrictions on freedom of movement and injunctions – all apportioned according to a set scale – mediation makes use of only one instrument, at least in its initial stages: *language*. Consequently, 'if there is no relationship with others except through the spoken word, if in an even wider sense, no relationship other than language exists with the world, if, according to this essential meaning, each word is *addressed*, then an understanding of *dialogue* and *entretenir* become philosophically fundamental' (Ost and van de Kerchove 1995: 46).

Victim–offender mediation is therefore a *relational process*, in which, initially through the exchange of the written and addressed word, then by indemnifying conduct, social communication is re-established between the perpetrator and the victim of a crime.

The correctness of this approach – according to which the 'exchanged' word constitutes the essence of mediation – is confirmed by sociological theories which view society as 'a network of co-operation through communication' (Habermas 1981: II, 223).

Habermas has had this to say on the subject:

That which bonds socialised individuals to each other and ensures the integration of society is a network of communicative gestures which appear valid only in the light of cultural traditions – not of mechanisms of the system extraneous to the intuitive understanding of the participants. The universe of life which is derived from common cultural traditions, coincides in its extension with society; and it is this universe that concentrates all social events under the floodlight of joint attempts at interpretation, giving everything that happens in society the transparency of something one can always discuss even if everything is (still) not clearly understood (Habermas 1981: II, 223).

As a corollary to this point, one can conclude that civil society does not only need norms stiffened by punishments, but also – and this argument is particularly cogent for 'complex' modern societies – an ethic of communication which can provide legitimacy for, and confirm the validity of, norms.

In his essay, Dahrendorf argues that the validity of norms does not rest only on punishment or power, but also on the 'consensus of those concerned, consensus which is attained through rational debate and by the force of plausible arguments' (Dahrendorf 1991: 67; Paliero 1992: 849).

Moreover, 'consensus' and 'conflict' represent two opposites which express the whole social dynamic in all its complexity. 'Each system presents an open bright face which is associative, organising, functional and a hidden dark virtual face, which is its negative' (Morin 1977: 119). These two faces are in constant tension: the task of mediation is, then, to recognize the conflict and to attempt to re-establish communication between those individuals that are opposed to each other by antagonisms that are created within the social system (Ost and van de Kerchove 1995: 83).

Mediation is carried out on 'neutral' ground
This is the space *inter-subjects* where it becomes possible to redefine the relationship between subjects that are opposing each other. This aspect will be dealt with again further on, when the active role of the mediator will be discussed.

In its phenomenology, mediation is an activity which is at the same time free and regulated
Just as the interpretation of the juridical norm invokes respect for the letter of the law and the need to adjust laws according to social needs, so mediation must be able to move in a space which is neither so small as to suffocate any dialectical movement, nor so wide as to allow excessive movement. Mediation must occur within the framework of rules that on the one hand allow communicative multi-directionality, while on the other impeding anarchic application.

To sum up, mediation would be the intellectual path from A to B, or the emergence of what Hegel called the *'Sein-für-Anderes'* (self for others), allowing these two poles, distinct but connected, to enter into a resonant relationship. At this stage, a point of clarification must be made: one must not think that the term path evokes a 'third way', a compromise or the 'middle ground'. In fact, the path is the (dialectical) movement that leads to knowledge, but which also abhors compromise and does not necessarily occupy the middle ground between A and B.

In penal mediation, the two distinct but connected poles are obviously represented by the *perpetrator* of the crime and the *victim*. We are dealing with two *distinct* poles created by virtue of the conflict originating in the offence. However, at the same time they are connected by that crime which has cut off their channel of communication, because from a logical standpoint, they are also 'reunited' as a pair of 'opposites'.

The role of the mediator

If mediation is – according to our proposed definition – a dialectical process of knowledge activation, one must ask what must be the role of the mediator, the principal agent necessary for mediation to take place.

We know that the primary objective of victim–offender mediation is the resolution of a conflict originating in (or exacerbated by) a crime, and the re-building of the social bond between perpetrator and victim (Peachey 1989: 14). We also know that it is just such an objective which sets mediation apart from the instruments of indemnifying justice, i.e. redress for damage or compensation, which are usually considered part of traditional penal law.

Therefore, what needs to evolve in a dialectical sense and by means of dialectic is the social communication which has been blocked, 'freezing' a reality that may take on the connotation of 'conflict' or 'dispute' (Ceretti 1998: 39). In other words, a dialectical movement is required which leads to 'knowledge' and which, in the particular case of penal mediation, brings the offender to an understanding of the motives, feelings, and the need for compensation for the victim. Likewise, the victim must gain awareness of the personal, family and social condition of the offender, not to mention the reasons behind the crime. This reciprocal understanding of each other should trigger a process of the offender taking responsibility, which will lead them, if the mediation is successful, to regret their actions and express the desire to make amends for the damage caused to the victim.

Mediation, by promoting the meeting of offender and victim and encouraging mutual understanding, does not stop at inhibiting the exacerbation of the conflict, but also attempts to 're-compose' the dispute, re-establish social communication, and at least indirectly strengthen the sense of collective security. Despite the traditional belief that only punishment for crimes can control the social alarm factor, either increasing or decreasing the sense of collective security, it is plausible that mediation can also provide a significant contribution in this direction. Only if the victim comes to consider the offender as a person do they cease to harbour blind hatred towards a faceless evil, personified more by the *role* of the delinquent than by the real *person* behind it (Buniva 1998: 236). On a social level, a changed attitude on the part of the victim towards the offender could positively influence 'community' expectations regarding the future conduct of the minor, which normally are negative. In this manner, the validity of the well-known 'self-fulfilling prophecy' (Watzlawick, Beavin, and Jackson 1971: 88) – criminological theory about the criminal future of an offender, formulated by the supporters of the 'labelling approach' – may be proved wrong.

Mediation, precisely because it is based on the communicative management of conflict, can thus act as a factor for social stabilization and an instrument promoting social consensus (Friedman 1978: 221).

As far as the explanatory role the mediator are concerned, it must be emphasized that the mediator is a neutral third party, who cannot and must not apportion blame nor impose or suggest – unlike in arbitration – their own solutions.

From the above premises, the activity of the mediator should be directed to satisfying two objectives:

Rebuilding between the parties the communicative 'inter-subjective' space

What is lacking in conflict is the common space defined in terms of the dialectic of knowledge as the *'entre-deux'* space, where the meeting of the needs of each of the two parties can be held. In the traditional penal trial, the victim is distanced from the offender, the bond between the two subjects is broken forever in order to protect the offender from the threat of private vengeance, a legacy from archaic clan justice. At least in Italy, this is even more true in juvenile trials, where to enhance the (re)educational efforts toward the minor, the victim cannot claim damages (see Art. 10 Act 448/1988).

The mediator should instead be able to 'work his/her way into the crux of the controversy so as to "triangulate" it, creating the space needed to re-establish communication from one to the other' (Ost and van de Kerchove 1995: 50). From this specific viewpoint, it is immaterial for the mediator if the 'intervention will lead to conciliation or to a sentence, to a pardon or to conviction, since … the parties have been induced to find a way out of the impasse their stubbornness had led them to. The dual relationship risked being blocked … by their irremovable opposition. The accepted inter-position by a third party recreates a space which brings transpositions back into play' (Buniva 1998: 236).

Helping the victim and the offender find a common language that can lead to the conflict being overcome

The conflict originating with the crime is experienced emotionally by the victim and the offender in a diametrically opposite manner. The victim often harbours feelings of anger – if not hatred or vengeance – towards the offender and generally has lost faith in the institutions called upon for protection (or which should have provided protection). In contrast, the offender, if not totally devoid of sentiment, may be indifferent or disdainful towards the victim. At the same time they may feel rebellious against 'the rules' and the system which intends to punish them. In regard to the same 'event' – the crime – offender and victim have greatly varying interpretations. In time these become more deep-seated and transform the conflict into a dispute, a social condition in which the other party is no longer seen as an 'adversary' but as the 'enemy'.

The penal system does not normally deal with these side-effects of crime; yet they are the very building blocks of restorative justice. Likewise, mediation neglects one-way interventions – i.e. rehabilitative efforts directed only at the offender or mere deterrence strategy – which are typical features of traditional penal justice.

The task of the mediator is to lead the victim and the author to a shared interpretation of the crime, especially with reference to the 'human factor', thus mitigating the conflicting nature of the relationship. This can take place particularly through a 'return to the event/crime, the development of their respective positions and the understanding of a third position which is what emerges in mediation' (Buniva 1998: 236). Mediation can be considered to have ended when the parties have come up with a *new interpretation* of the event.

From this point of view, philosophical studies on *interpretation* as an epistemological category provide us with an interesting key of interpretation, which we believe would be useful to describe briefly.

These studies start with an assumption according to which there can be no *existence* without *interpretation* to the extent that each existence could be defined as 'an interpreting existence' (Betti 1955: 83). One infers that there can be infinite interpretations of the external world, since it would be unthinkable to insist on the correctness of only one viewpoint.

The expression of these interpretations is the task of language – consisting of words or other forms of expression (for example, gestures or art). Language has what can be defined as a 'representative' or 'semantic' function (Betti 1955: 65). Understanding can therefore be seen as a psychological phenomenon with a triadic structure: there is an *object*, a *sign* (the word) and an *interpreter* (the knowing subject).

If we consider that the foundation of civil society lies in 'the fundamental need to be recognised' (Betti 1955: 63), for the other consociate 'men come to understand each other ... by mutually setting in motion the same link in the chain of one's representations or concepts and ... by touching the same chord of one's spiritual instrument ... in such a manner that in the listener or reader ideas are created which correspond to those expressed by the author' (Betti 1955: 64).

In mediation the key problem is to find a common *sign*, allowing the victim and the offender to construct an interpretation of the crime which does not make them adversaries of one other. Such an interpretation constitutes a vital premise for the offender to resolve to offer redress for the damage done. Moreover, it provides a justification for the victim not to oppose any form of indemnification, which would otherwise consign the wrongdoer to the isolation of a negative criminal role.

Hence, the mediator would seek to encourage a 're-reading' of the offence, allowing both the victim and the offender to constructively confront one another through a linguistic sign which does not exacerbate or perpetuate the conflict.

It may be interesting to note that, in regard to the relationship between mediation and interpretation, the philosophical school of thought which goes by the name of 'behaviourism' explicitly re-connects semiotic processes with processes which involve mediation (intervention of a third party), where the third party is represented by the sign (the representing form).

In the light of this interpretative key, we would assign a double role in mediation to the 'third party': the 'third party' is the *sign,* that is, the word. But the 'third party' is also the *subject,* that is, the mediator, who looks for that sign and tries to activate it. In fact, the mediator carries out, as we have seen, a guiding role towards the objective of the dialectical evolution of offender/victim conflict, which principally takes place through language.

Intermediate result

At this stage, we can suggest a more analytical definition of penal mediation, which also covers the specific aspects connected with the role of mediator and the reverberating effects which mediation has on the community of reference: mediation is a dialectical process of knowledge activation between offender and victim (which may also act as a factor for social stability), in which the mediator is called upon to rebuild the communicative space between the subjects and find a common 'sign' helping to overcome the conflict.

The concept we have proposed brings together all the previously presented interpretations of mediation: the philosophical interpretation, which emphasizes the dialectical aspects of mediation; the sociological interpretation, which highlights its possible supplementary usefulness as a factor promoting social stability; and the psychological interpretation, which expresses its communicative role between subjects.

Mediation and the law: from the 'complex society' to the 'law of complexity'

Although we have made no direct reference to it until now, the foundation for the 'new dialectic' by Merleau-Ponty is the fact that the epoch in which we live, labelled as *post-modern,* is an 'era of complexity', in which all cultural, economic and social events, given the proximity of the global village, are closely interrelated. Contemporary democratic societies are characterized by a plurality of political, religious, philosophical and moral doctrines, which may even be mutually incompatible, yet still be based on reasonable premises (Rawls 1994: 58).

In this social panorama of 'high complexity', many values coexist together with 'reasonable' doctrines which may be mutually incompatible in terms of how they orient their adherents (one has only to think of the controversy over issues relating to bio-ethics or abortion). Such a reality may entail going beyond the application of 'fixed' rules and norms to seek open solutions to attract a 'quota' of consensus from many different sources.

In essence, this is the theory proposed by Rawls, who holds that guaranteeing a 'stable and well ordered' society means creating 'overlapping consensus', this being a consensus which is 'neutral' with respect to any single *Weltanschauungen*. In other words, 'where irreconcilable positions exist, the possibility ... of overcoming the impasse is given by the creation of spaces for intersection or overlap founding a public basis for the justification of fundamental institutions' (Ceretti 1998: 33).

This means substituting the binary logic leading to the exclusion of one of the two sides to a dispute – *this* or *that* – with 'ternary' logic allowing us to formulate 'a mobile and multiple relation, the very image of complexity' (Ost and van de Kerchove 1995: 7).

From this point of view we can, for a start, say that mediation appears capable of gathering to itself that 'overlapping consensus' theorized by Rawls. Indeed, mediation constitutes a 'liberal' kernel within the judicial system, which side-steps ethical or metaphysical concepts of justice. It does not avail itself of the 'power' expressed through the application of punishment. It does not advocate one-way solutions, it attaches no stigma, but is more simply based on reasonableness. The handing of conflicts back to society and the pursuit of solutions both compensating the victim and inducing the offender to become more responsible, make mediation a 'political' model of justice, capable of obtaining consensus which is neutral in terms of the single *Weltanschauungen* making up society (Rawls 1994: 30). The change of paradigm made necessary by the events characterizing a 'complex society' in turn influences those philosophical and juridical doctrines which make society their object.

We can now go back to the problem of the dialectical essence of mediation, where it becomes possible to describe in greater detail how the above-mentioned change in paradigm has contributed to revealing the inadequacy of the Hegelian dialectical model. For in this model, 'reality' and 'thought' end up becoming identical, thus constituting a 'limited' philosophical horizon, a simplifying solution for a problematic reality.

If our era is to be complex one, then dialectic must also adopt a model of complexity, becoming a method that is sceptical of synthesis as bestowing definitive knowledge, instead privileging 'space' and the 'path' as leading to a greater understanding of reality.

The consequences of this philosophical revolution on a juridical level are worthy of note, particularly if we consider that 'each epoch carries with it a specific theory of law' (Rawls 1994: 3).

The first important consequence could be defined as the *crisis of Kelsen's paradigm*.

If ours is indeed the age of complexity, this suggests the inadequacy of Hans Kelsen's juridical theory, which endeavoured to isolate 'law' as pure form. It seems increasingly difficult to single out a *Grundnorm*, which can self-legitimize itself and also shield itself from the incessant creation and self-modification to which all law is subjected. Ironically, the principal impetus towards this change derives from the base of Kelsen's pyramid, the 'base' which he believed depended wholly on its apex.

We are of course referring to teachings which are derived as much from 'consensus-based' theories as from 'conflict-based' models of law, and particularly to the importance of channelling social consensus with regard to the choices of primary criminalization (Paliero 1992: 851). Sociological research leads us to believe that in our ever more complex penal systems, it is no longer feasible to take a 'single factor' approach to the problem of criminalization, based exclusively on 'consensus' or on 'conflict'.

In this field too, 'multi-factor' approaches are beginning to emerge, in which *consensus* and *conflict* coexist and play different roles according to the area being protected. This does not necessarily imply that one should completely embrace the so-called 'evolutionary model' which holds that 'in a diachronic perspective, all incriminating options evolve from conflict based models to consensus based ones' (Hopkins 1975: 614). What is really necessary is a change in perspective, to grasp what we could define as the 'fourth dimension' of juridical systems in complex societies: the dialectical dimension.

The hypothesis lying at the base of this reconstruction takes its starting point from the deficiencies in Kelsen's paradigm, in which a perfect dichotomy exists between 'law' and 'non-law'. Instead, a dialectical approach is proposed to tackle the problem of the creation and validity of juridical norms. As Carson seems to have discerned, 'in respect of penal legislation as a whole an adequate analysis demands to be conducted relative to each given point in chronological space and calls for a conceptual scheme which allows each single incriminating norm to be placed in continuous movement between the extreme poles of consensus and conflict' (Carson 1974: 78).

Once again, the concept of *entre-deux* comes to our aid: in this case it indicates the neutral space between *consensus* and *conflict,* in which the options associated with criminalization challenge each other. In turn, this dimension gives us a measure of the complexity of the social systems that law is called upon to regulate. The second consequence is that, in such a scenario, mediation tends to become the cornerstone of the 'law of complexity'.

Whenever law is recognized as having the historical function of settling disputes (*rectius* of mediation of social conflicts), how can one claim that law should fulfil this task by rejecting mediation in advance? Mediation should become part of the system not so much as an instrument of crime policy or as an alternative to punishment, or even as a device of depenalization, but as an autonomous state response to social conflict. Indeed, it does not represent 'a simple "alternative to justice", but a deeper phenomenon which not only expresses the healing of relations between the state and civil society in regard to conflict management, but also an evolution of our society towards greater plurality of models of social regulation' (Bonafé-Schmitt 1997: 48). It is no coincidence that those 'legal systems characterised by a high degree of complexity of conflicts and social relationships (for example, France and the USA) have more greatly developed research into ways of improving the system of behavioural regulation based on the exercise of judicial power' (Bouchard 1992: 192).

This tendency towards a more widespread use of mediating and compensatory instruments, which seeks to mend the fragmentation of the conflict and its estrangement from the rest of the community, can perhaps be seen in the increased recourse to models for the solution of conflicts that lie outside the judicial system. Here, at least in the Italian juridical context, we are making reference both to arbitration, which constitutes a contractual mode of defining disputes, and to 'the judicial attempt to conciliate' which acts as a filter for judgement (both are devices to 'deflate' the Italian judicial system, which is so clogged with cases as to be near collapse).

To sum up, mediation represents an indispensable instrument for the management of conflicts arising in modern societies which are highly complex systems. By *system* we mean a 'set of objects and relations between objects and their attributes, in which *objects* are components or parts of the system, *attributes* the qualities of these objects and *relations* that "keep the system together"' (Watzlawick, Beavin and Jackson 1971: 110). The centrality of mediation comes from its role in *settling* the conflict, which may also have a significant indirect impact on the stability of the

241

social system. In this regard, it is worthwhile pointing out that a system can be considered 'stable in respect of a number of its variables if these tend to stay within set limits' (Watzlawick et al. 1971: 119). From this standpoint, crime amounts to a blow to the stability of the system, because criminal actions go beyond the limits of what is permissible. Sometimes crime creates a relationship between the criminal and the victim which the behavioural experts call 'homeostatic', meaning that no change can occur *from within* the relationship itself.

This is a condition that traditional penal law is not equipped to deal with. From the point of view of penal law, the relationship between the offender and the victim is not so important: what counts when a crime is committed is finding an offender to punish. The crime remains a substantially incomprehensible act, no one is interested in why it was committed or what events led to it. Although the motive does count, it is vital only in evidence. In addition, the very 'motives leading to delinquency' have marginal importance, given that they are considered only when determining the severity of the punishment to be meted out.

If from the standpoint of penal law, a crime is 'incomprehensible', this occurs because the field of observation of penal law is not large enough to include the context from which the crime sprang. In this respect, mediation provides more wide-ranging and sophisticated instruments. In fact, mediation can widen the field of investigation to cover the origins of the crime, the effects that the crime may have on other individuals, the reactions of others to the criminal behaviour and the context in which all this occurs. In other words, 'the focus of interest shifts from the artificially isolated element [the offender] to the relationships between each part of the wider system [the relationship between offender and victim]' (Watzlawick et al. 1971: 15).

Such a relationship is characterized by a type of irreversibility where the offender and the victim are somehow caught up in an 'endless game', as if they were prisoners of the respective antagonistic roles which penal law has cast them into. Mediation intervenes dynamically in this relationship both by reconstructing the crime and by formalizing the trial rules which govern the application of penal law.

The mediator works directly on the relationship between offender and victim. As an outsider, he is able to stimulate what the relational micro-system created by the crime is not otherwise capable of producing for itself: changing its own rules (Watzlavick et al. 1971: 224). By revisiting the crime, the process of bringing the offender to recognize their responsibilities can commence and the type of compensation to be given to the victim established. Only in this manner can the damage to the social order have more than a symbolic chance of settlement.

Does justice still need the sword?

The observations made regarding mediation as a dialectic model for the solution of conflicts, and as the cornerstone for that 'law of complexity' which characterizes post-modern societies, invites us to reflect again briefly on the meaning of that allegory of justice, evoked at the beginning of this paper.

What elements of the allegorical representation of justice can, in the final analysis, be preserved? And what should be opportunely abandoned or substituted? A symbolic constant should indeed be the representation of justice in the feminine gender, if one agrees with Edgerton's suggestive interpretation that this feature calls to mind the idea of mediation. If the Law is to be a 'structure for peace' (Cotta 1992: 379) it is unthinkable for it to ignore mediation, which is, intrinsically, as recently affirmed by Umbreit, a 'pathway towards peace' (Umbreit 1995).

The scales, as an emblem of the principle of proportion, would also continue to be an indispensable element, given that the amount and/or the means of reparation – whether achieved through mediation or 'imposed' by the law – require proportionality with the damage inflicted by the crime in all its aspects, and hence be comprehensive of the victim's mental suffering.

Finally, one should consider whether Justice still needs the sword – in other words, if a new paradigm of justice can be envisioned that does not make recourse to the sword to 'punish' or 'sever'.

In this sense, the vision of Beccafumi could be considered prophetic (*La Giustizia*, painting attributed to Domenico Beccafumi 15th–16th centuries – Lille, Museum of Fine Art) when, at the end of the fifteenth century, he restored the olive branch to Justice, and depicted at her feet in chains both Negligence and 'excessive Severity', the latter holding a blunted sword (see Figure 11.5). A vision of Justice as an instrument of peace is also exemplified in a fresco by Ambrogio Lorenzetti, one of the masterpieces of fourteenth century Italian art: 'The Allegory of Good Government', in which, next to Justice seated on her throne we also see the representation of Peace. Can we imagine Justice 'without a sword', that is, a Justice without the sole aim of punishing offenders, but as an instrument for social peace, reached through dialogue? In such an approach, mediation appears to be the key element. In the interpretation proposed above, mediation emerges primarily in its communicative–relational aspects (Burnside and Backer 1994: 53). At least initially, mediation seeks both to create a channel of communication between the victim and the offender and to bring out the real needs of the victim (attention, safety, compensation). In this manner, mediation can act as a catalyst for a process of social pacification within the community.

Figure 11.5. Drawing based on 'La Justice', attributed to Domenico Beccafumi (1486–1551), cf. Jacob 1994, 224

We should overcome that concept of jurisprudence which for decades has 'denied (or rather disavowed) the human value of law' presenting law 'as merely the external form of an act of will to which it simply accords the threat of punishment' (Cotta 1992: 379). By recourse to mediation we can re-endow the law with the faculty of representing a structure for peace. Indeed, the Law should be *per se* a '*structure for peace*, both for its explicit typological character which contrasts conflict … and for its intention to substitute conflict and imposition of power, [they both] always possible given the human condition, with dialogue, which is the discourse of reason' (Cotta 1992: 381).

Notes

1. For his invaluable assistance in providing the historical background for this section, I would like to thank Prof. Dario Mantovani (Professor of Roman Law at the University of Pavia, Italy).

References

Betti, E. (1955) *Teoria Generale della Interpretazione*, Milano.
Bonafé-Schmitt, J. P. (1997) 'Lavori di Utilità Sociale: La Nozione di Riparazione' in *Mediazione/Riparazione. Un'Alternativa Possibile nella Giustizia Minorile*, Proceedings of the training course held in Turin, June-November, 1996, Torino.
Bonafé-Schmitt, J. P. (1992) *La Médiation: Une Justice Douce*, Paris.
Bouchard, M. (1992) 'Mediazione: Dalla Repressione alla Rielaborazione del Conflitto' in *Dei Delitti e delle Pene*.
Buniva, F. (1998) 'L'Esperienza di Mediazione Penale nell'Area Torinese' in L. Picotti (eds) *La Mediazione nel Sistema Penale Minorile*, Padova.
Burnside, J. and Backer, N. (1994) *Relational Justice: Repairing the Breach*, Winchester.
Carson, W. G. (1974) 'The Sociology of Crime and the Emergence of Criminal Laws' in Rock-McIntosch (eds) *Deviance and Social Control*, London.
Castelli, S. (1996) *La Mediazione. Teorie e Tecniche*, Milano.
Ceretti, A. (1998) 'Mediazione: Una Ricognizione Filosofica' in L. Picotti (eds) *La Mediazione nel Sistema Penale Minorile*, Padova.
Cotta, S. (1992) 'Il Diritto: Struttura di Pace', in *Iustitia*.
Dahrendorf, R. (1991) *Legge e ordine*, Milano.
Edgerton, S. Y. (1980) 'Icons of Justice' in *Past and Present*.
Friedman, L. M. (1978) *Il Sistema Giuridico nella Prospettiva delle Scienze Sociali*, Bologna.
Habermas, J. (1981) *Theorie des Kommunikativen Handelns* (vol. II), Frankfurt.
Hopkins, A. (1975) 'The Sociology of Criminal Law' in *Social Problems*.
Jacob, R. (1994) *Images de la Justice. Essai sur l'Iconographie Judiciaire du Moyen Age à l'Âge Classique*, Paris.
Kissel, O. R. (1984) *Die Darstellung der Iustitia*, München.
Merleau-Ponty, M. (1964) 'Interrogation et Dialectique' in *Le Visible et l'Invisible*, Paris.
Morin, E. (1977) *La Méthode: La Nature de la Nature*, Paris.
Ost, F. and van de Kerchove, M. (1995) *Il Diritto ovvero i Paradossi del Gioco*, Milano.
Paliero, C. E. (1992) 'Consenso Sociale e Diritto Penale', in *Riv. it. dir. proc. pen.*
Peachey, D. (1989) 'The Kitchner Experiment' in M. and B. Wright-Galaway (eds) *Mediation and Criminal Justice*, London.
Rawls, J. (1994) *Liberalismo Politico*, Milano.
Robert, C. N. (1994) *Une Allégorie Parfaite. La Justice, Vertu, Courtisane et Bourreau*, Geneva.
Schild, W. (1988) 'Bemerkungen zur Ikonologie des Jüngsten Gerichts' in L. Carlen

(eds) *Forschungen zur Rechtsarchäologie und Rechtlichen Volkskunde* (vol. 10), Zürich.

Umbreit, M. (1995) *Mediating Interpersonal Conflicts. A Pathway to Peace*, St. Paul.

Vidari, E. (1893) *Corso di Diritto Commerciale*, Milano.

von Möeller, E. (1905) 'Die Augenbinde der Justitia' in *Zeitschrift für Christliche Kunst*.

Watzlawick, P., Beavin, J. H. and Jackson, D. D. (1971) *Pragmatica della Comunicazione Umana. Studio dei Modelli Interattivi, delle Patologie e dei Paradossi* (1967), Roma.

Zdekauer, L. (1909) *L'Idea di Giustizia e la sua Immagine nelle Arti Figurative*, Macerata.

Chapter 12

Punishment, guilt, and spirit in restorative justice: an essay in legal and religious anthropology

Robert E. Mackay

Introduction – two stories

The virgin suicide

Roberto Calasso tells a story about a drought in ancient Thebes (Calasso 1994: 163–166). Food is running out, and the king sits facing a file of people giving out what food was stored, to the notables first, and then to the poor. Eventually, an orphan girl called Charila comes before him. The king pulls off his sandal and throws it in her face. Presumably she is expected to chew the leather. She goes away. Many remain hungry.

A plague follows and the famine does not abate. The king consults the Pythian oracle. He is told 'Appease Charila, the virgin suicide.' People do not know what this means. Was Charila a forgotten mythical figure? Was the statement some form of riddle? Then one of the priestesses of Thebes remembered who Charila was. She had been about to join their order, 'the rustling ones', 'the Brides of the Wind'. She was found in the woods, dead, swinging in the wind, hanging from a tree branch. She is given a loving burial. But this is not enough. The priestesses advise the king to re-enact the original scene. This time everyone who comes before the king is fed. Then an effigy of Charila is brought before him. Once again he flings a sandal at her. The effigy is then taken away to be buried with the remains of the girl.

At a Japanese railway station in the era of Meiji

Lafcadio Hearn relates that one day he saw a remarkable encounter at the railway station in Kumamoto where a man was being escorted under police guard (Hearn 1994: 144–146). The prisoner, who had confessed to the murder of a police officer, was met at the station by a crowd, including the police officer's widow and her son. The meeting had been staged. A police officer summoned the pair and addressed the very young boy held in his mother's arms:

> 'This is the man who killed your father four years ago. You had not yet been born; you were in your mother's womb. That you have no father to love you is the doing of this man. Look at him' – here the officer, putting a hand to the prisoner's chin, sternly forced him to lift his eyes – 'look well at him, little boy! Do not be afraid. It is painful, but it is your duty. Look at him!' (Hearn 1994: 145)

The boy stared at the prisoner. The prisoner dashed himself to his knees despite the chains, and begged for forgiveness:

> 'Pardon! Pardon! Pardon me, little one! That I did – not for hate was it done; but in mad fear only, in my desire to escape. Very, very wicked have I been; great unspeakable wrong have I done you! But now for my sin I go to die. I wish to die; I am glad to die! Therefore, O little one, be pitiful! forgive me!' (Hearn 1994: 145).

Then the whole crowd, including the police officer, began to sob.

These two tales are very striking, and illustrate the grounds of some important reflections on the legal and religious anthropology of restorative justice. In this chapter I wish to argue that anthropology (including historical studies of religion) provides us with a number of important insights which are challenging for proponents of restorative justice. In particular, the findings of anthropology from different eras and places suggest that 'restorative' practices and attitudes can co-exist with strong currents of punitiveness and violence, and often incorporate strong religious elements relating to sacrifice, and appeasement of the dead and of the spirit world. These findings lead us to consider the implications of grafting dispute resolution practices associated with traditional and ancient cultures onto the legal systems of the contemporary nation state.

My thesis is simple. We cannot simply speak of restorative justice replacing retributive justice, unless we bind into our theory an understanding of the powerful dynamics represented by punishment, guilt and spirit.

My approach draws on three ethnographic studies and studies of ancient Greek religion and penology.[1] I also draw upon Nietzsche's reflections on punishment and guilt in *The Genealogy of Morals* and upon Rouland's work on legal anthropology. This approach is inevitably both eclectic and far from comprehensive. It lays itself open to the charges of over-generalization and conflation of different concepts and practices. However, the gathering of material from different times and places suggests common themes. Provided that we are alert both to the difference in the practices and concepts of modernity to those of the societies that are the subjects of the studies I have used, as well as to the similarities – but by no means identity – between those other societies, we will see that there is a weight of human knowledge and experience which has a bearing upon our attempts to create restorative systems of justice.

The genealogy of punishment revisited

It is widely held that criminal justice is descended from social responses to the breach of taboos (Mauss 1968; Mauss 1974; Durkheim 1984). Crime originated in a breach of the sacred, offence against the gods or spirits. Offences against other people could usually be compensated for materially, but often sacrifice and shaming played a part in the settlement of harm insofar as a taboo was broken. When kings arrogated to themselves divine status or at least descent, they assumed the rights associated with the gods. Those who entered their personal space trod on holy ground. Those who broke the peace committed a sacred crime. The humble common-law offence of breach of the peace derives from the extension of this peace to the area of the whole kingdom.

What is less often noticed is that early forms of punishment, particularly outlawry and capital execution, drew upon the practices of the hunt, of war and of sacrifice. Indeed, some animal sacrifices involved substitution of human beings, either as propitiation or as scapegoats. Capital execution is the sacrifice of the culprit. Even after modern states have abolished capital execution, the sacred thinking is sustained. In the United Kingdom we still have the life sentence as mandatory for murder. This sentence was conceived explicitly as a diversion from capital punishment. Even a recent research publication in the UK persevered in referring to murder as a 'capital' offence (Brett *et al.* 1995). So abolition of a practice does not abolish the subtle links to the sacred thinking behind it.

Nietzsche in his second essay on '"Guilt", "Bad Conscience" and Related Matters' in *The Genealogy of Morals* (Nietzsche 1990) reminds us of the gory practices of early (medieval) systems of justice. He makes the important point that the motivation to punish in contemporary societies is complex, difficult to account for. However, the practices of punishment are to be distinguished from the motives: 'I presuppose here that the procedure itself antedates its use for the purposes of punishment and that the latter [the expectations attending on the execution of such procedures] has only been projected into the procedure, which had existed all along, though in a different framework.' (Nietzsche 1990: 212).

But before there were criminal justice systems, there were systems of composition, of regulated feuding, and even before that divine punishments and private vengeance. We say 'before', as if history describes an evolutionary curve. But is this the case? It is clear that the modern state, for all its universal and rationalist aspirations to manage the contingencies of social life, does not replace 'private justice' in all cases. Indeed the restorative justice movement itself, while extolling the forward looking nature and the humaneness of its ethos, in fact makes a virtue of evoking the values of a more 'ancient' way of dealing with 'wrongdoing'. Rouland contends that vengeance is not a savage instinct, but an elaborate system of exchange, while punishment does not derive from vengeance. '[P]unishment and vengeance coexist in all societies, traditional or modern.' (Rouland 1994: 273). If Rouland is correct, the 'mayhem' or unfettered violence which is in his view wrongly associated with the vindicatory system, but which is associated with sacrifice and punishment, must derive from something else.

Malinowski's account of punishment among the Trobriand Islanders suggested that the principles of punishment were vague, methods of retribution fitful, governed by chance rather than by any fixed institutions. Methods of punishment were a by-product of non-legal institutions and customs: sorcery, magic, ritual suicide, the power of the chiefs, the supernatural consequences of breaching taboos, and personal vindictiveness. Crime itself was vaguely defined: an outburst of passion, breach of taboo, indulgence in too high ambition or wealth not sanctioned by tradition, conflict with a chief. Most definite prohibitions were elastic because there was an elaborate system of evasion (Malinowski 1961: 98–99). Similarly, among the Nuer, some infractions of taboo can be warded off by sacrifice (Evans-Pritchard 1956).

There is both divergence and convergence in the ancient ways. There is both composition and punishment. Thus some forms of punishment are seen as composition. For the injury inflicted, the victim may enjoy the pleasure of inflicting pain in return. As Nietzsche says: 'There is no feast without cruelty, as man's entire history attests. Punishment, too, has its festive elements.' (1990: 198). Saunders (1991) suggests that vengeance beyond the level of compensation, the 'extra', that in which the victim takes pleasure, is to restore *time* or honour. We recall the description by Foucault of the execution by *amende honorable* in his shocking rhetorical prologue to *Discipline and Punish* (Foucault 1997). In English, the terms 'having' or 'taking satisfaction' have the related meanings of taking vengeance, fighting a duel, sexual 'conquest' and rape. Evil is repaid with evil. (See also Nietzsche 1990: 196.)

The development of penal sanctions does not in any way lessen the violence of vengeance. However, the victim is displaced as the protagonist by the state. If, as Nietzsche suggests, punitive practices derive from the pleasures of inflicting pain upon a defenceless victim in war, they provide the victor with the choice of whether or not to ritualize the infliction of pain. In contrast, the state will normally resort to ritual, unless the offender is caught in hot pursuit, in which case it may be dispensed with. The obvious source of ritual is sacrifice. Although taken out of context, Evans-Pritchard's observation about the sacrificial practices of the Nuer is of extreme relevance: 'Sacrificial slaughter thus stands at the very centre of the idea of killing, and sacrificial flesh at the very centre of the idea of feasting.' (Evans-Pritchard 1956: 296).

Burkert develops this idea further (Burkert 1983). Ritual is concerned with preserving social structures. Sacrifice brings to mind the sacredness of life by juxtaposition with death. Substitution of an animal at the last moment in a ritual was common enough. However, Burkert suggests that there comes a point where civilization demands more:

> With the progressive growth of consciousness, civilisation came to demand absolute seriousness – one could no longer *pretend* to kill men. For this reason the death penalty became the strongest expression of governmental power, and, as has often been shown, the criminal's execution at a public festival corresponded to a sacrificial ritual. In ancient times, the death penalty was not so much aimed at profane murderers as at those who entered an 'untouchable' sacred precinct, went into a house of the mysteries unconsecrated, or laid a branch upon the wrong altar. The tabu almost became an excuse to find a victim for releasing the sacred impulses of aggression. (Burkert 1983: 45)

He also states that in the ancient world, hunting, sacrifice and war were interchangeable (Burkert 1983: 46). One wonders whether in the modern world the use of such terms as 'war on crime', 'man hunt', 'making a (terrible) example' and 'frying', or the practices of the public parade of Chinese convicts prior to execution, or the private viewings of American executions, do not reveal similar but unacknowledged motives and connections.

If punishment is associated with sacrifice, what is crime? Crime is an overlooking. In the story of Charila, Calasso tells us that the goal for the Delphic theologians was not mindless devotion but knowledge.

> To expiate a crime didn't mean to do something that was the opposite of that crime but to repeat the same crime with slight variations in order to immerse oneself in guilt and bring it to consciousness. The crime lay not so much in doing certain things but in having done them without realizing what one was doing. The crime lay in not having realized that Charila had disapppeared. (Calasso 1994: 165).

If crime manifests a lack of self-knowledge, as Nietzsche wrote, punishment served at best to increase it:

> There can be no doubt that we must look for the real effect of punishment in a sharpening of man's wits, and extension of his memory, a determination to proceed henceforth more prudently, suspiciously, secretly, a realization that the individual is simply too weak to accomplish certain things; in brief, an increase of self-knowldedge. What punishment is able to achieve, both for man and beast, is increase of fear, circumspection, control over insticts. Thus man is *tamed* by punishment, but by no means *improved*; rather the opposite. (Nietzsche 1990: 216).

Like Evans-Pritchard's interpretation of divine punishments among the Nuer, Nietzsche accounts for the experience of punishment not as training or treatment, but as that of a sickness. Sickness brought about by a 'spirit of the air' does not induce resentment so much as a sense of guilt (Evans-Pritchard 1956: 51). In the world of the Toba-Batak of Northern Sumatra, where an offender escaped human punishment he was at the mercy of the gods (Vergouwen 1964), just as he was in the heroic age of Greece (Saunders 1991).

Can we account for punishment? The discourse of punishment goes round and round. Did not Foucault once refer to the idle chatter of criminologists? It had already travelled (at least?) one full circuit by the time of Thucydides in 427 BC when the Athenians debated what to do with their rebellious allies, the Mytilenians. Diodotus urged moderation in terms which are striking in their familiarity:

> Cities and individuals are alike, all are by nature disposed to do wrong, and there is no law that will prevent it, as is shown by the fact

that men have tried every kind of punishment, constantly adding to the list, in the attempt to gain greater security from criminals. It is likely that in earlier times the punishments even for the greatest crimes were not as severe as they are now, but the laws were still broken, and in the course of time the death penalty became generally introduced. Yet even with this, the laws are still broken. Either, therefore, we must discover some fear more potent than the fear of death, or we must admit that here certainly we have not got an adequate deterrent. So long as poverty forces men to be bold, so long as the insolence and pride of wealth nourish their ambitions, and in the other accidents of life they are continually dominated by some incurable master passion or other, so long will their impulses drive them into danger. (Thudydides 1977: 220).

Herein we see the antecedents of sociological, psychological and even genetic explanations of criminal behaviour as well as an exposition of the paradox of punishment – that no matter how terrifying the punishments we can devise, they will never deter all potential law breakers.

Beyond the punishments that are meted out by humans, those who avoid detection may not escape the attention of God, gods, spirits or ghosts. The dead may exact vengeance. Almost universally God or the gods are recognized as having the power to punish (Evans-Pritchard 1956; Saunders 1991; Vergouwen 1964).

The examination of the historical associations of punishment with the sacred and with war should alert us to the need to consider the reform of our penal system with more caution. The Furies were given an honoured place in Athens after their ways were superseded by the courts in the Oresteian story. Punishment is associated both with attempting to raise consciousness and the inspiration of fear. Burkert suggests that all orders and forms of authority in human society are founded on institutionalized violence (Burkert 1983: 1). Restorative justice is strongly associated with the aim of reducing the role of punishment, and sometimes fudging the question of whether sanctions such as compensation are punishment. Restorative justice worries about its relationship with punishment. The debate between those who support deferred prosecution (with the threat of punishment) in mediation and reparation, and those who support the waiver model (once colourfully described by a prosecutor, a part-time soldier, as the 'fire-and-forget' model) attests this uneasiness. However, can restorative justice alone bear the psychological and spiritual pressures created by infraction and harm which are so powerfully expressed in ancient practices and early modern codes of punishment?

The meaning of guilt

In modern English, guilt has two connotations: one juridical, the other psychological. The juridical meaning is that a guilty person has been proven to have committed, or has admitted to having committed, an offence with *mens rea*. Act and intention are found proven together. The other psychological meaning has more to do with a feeling, akin to a private sense of badness for a wrong action, of pollution. Both must be distinguished from the sense of shaming, which is a public and associated with loss of face. Both meanings are associated with a sense of responsibility. Sometimes the psychological sense of guilt is touched by a sense of unreality, of being tricked into a wrong position. Stocker (1990) writes of the sense of 'dirty hands' one experiences when one takes a course of action which, even if unavoidable and exonerable, leaves one with a sense of pollution.

It is this latter sense of guilt which most resembles pre-modern conceptions. Calasso with characteristic verve captures this sense:

> For the Homeric heroes there was no guilty party, only guilt, immense guilt. That was the miasma that impregnated blood, dust and tears. With an intuition the moderns jettisoned and have never recovered, the heroes did not distinguish between the evil of the mind and the evil of the deed, murder and death. Guilt for them is like a boulder blocking the road: it is palpable, it looms. Perhaps the guilty party is as much a sufferer as the victim. In confronting guilt, all we can do is make a ruthless computation of the forces involved. And when considering the guilty party, there will always be an element of uncertainty. We can never establish how far he is really guilty, because the guilty party is part and parcel of the guilt and obeys its mechanisms. Until eventually he is crushed by it perhaps, perhaps abandoned, perhaps freed, while the guilt rolls on to threaten others, to create new stories, new victims. (Calasso 1994: 94–95).

Malinowski provides a striking example of what can happen when guilt of this nature becomes public, overtaking the individual. He describes how a husband-to-be accused a young man of having sexual relations with his future bride. There was nothing special about this type of sexual freedom, not even that the young man and the girl were related and that they had broken the incest taboo. This type of thing happened all the time, provided it remained discreet. However, once the issue became public, and nobody could ignore the matter, the shame and the force of the taboo were overwhelming. The young man climbed a high tree, condemned the behaviour of the jealous bridegroom, laid upon him the guilt of his own death, and threw himself to the ground in expiation of his own guilt at breaching the incest taboo (Malinowski 1961: 80–85). The jealous bridegroom was therefore subject to curse, and to the threat of vengeance by the dead man's kin.

So the guilt rolls on. How do ancient and traditional systems deal with this? The key to this is anxiety. In sacrifice one faces up to the connections between life and death, sexual reproduction and aggression. In affirming the continuity of life, one also faces annihilation (Burkert 1983: 38). Sacrifice shares with ritual and drama the capacity to deal with anxiety head on by recreating it, and disposing of the negative forces at work through catharsis. Some guilt can be expiated. Sacrifice can be made to reduce the risk of retaliation by the spirits (Evans-Pritchard 1956). It reinforces social continuity (Burkert 1983). The purpose of sacrifice is to restore harmony in and through the heightening of awareness of aggression and sexuality in the ritual. Then reparation must be made for the dead animal or human in the sacrifice: 'The shock felt in the act of killing is answered later by consolidation; guilt is followed by reparation, destruction by reconstruction…' (Burkert 1983: 38). But does the feeling of guilt really equate with responsibility? If to be guilty is to be a victim of fate, or of 'some incurable master passion', can we hold someone responsible for their actions? According to Nietzsche the Greek solution to this problem involved the gods:

> 'How can such a thing [criminal behaviour] happen to people like us, nobly bred, happy, virtuous, well educated?' For many centuries noble Greeks would ask themselves this question whenever one of their number had defiled himself by one of those incomprehensible crimes. 'Well, he must have been deluded by a god,' they would finally say, shaking their heads. This was a typically Greek solution. It was the office of the Gods to justify up to a certain point, the ill ways of man, to serve as 'sources' of evil. In those days they were not agents of punishment but, what is nobler, repositories of guilt. (Nietzsche 1990: 228).

Guilt attached not to intention but to action itself. Nietzsche refers to the origin of the German word for guilt – *schuld* in the verb *schulden* – to be indebted (Nietzsche 1990: 194). It is the wrong act, the harm done, that attracted the punishment or the requirement for compensation. Bad intention made the matter worse, but mistakes were still a source of guilt. Liability is strict. Among the Nuer, if a person was sick, and could not account for it, it would be necessary to discover what taboo had been broken, even accidentally. Guilt can therefore be associated with pollution, and pollution is contagious. The guilty person may not associate with others in particular ways, or else the persons with whom he is in contact may also bring down divine punishment upon themselves. However, the spirits can be appeased by the intention of the wrongdoer to fulfil an obligation.

This sense of liability can be seen in an account of a stabbing among the Nuer. Evans-Pritchard recounts a complex set of exchanges between two friendly villages after a boy from one village wounded a boy from the other. The offender's spear is sent over and subjected to magical treatment to reduce the victim's pain and inflammation. A goat is sent over as a signal that if the victim dies, full compensation will be made to avoid a feud, and as a contribution to a sacrifice to avoid death. A Leopard Skin Chief (with mediatory functions) from another village prophesies that the boy will not die and reinforces the story that the wounding was an accident (Evans-Pritchard 1956: 111). Despite the fact that this is an accidental occurrence, the offender has attracted the full weight of the Nuer reparative system upon his shoulders.

The modern notion of responsibility is very different to that found in ancient times and traditional societies. Nietzsche suggested that punishment was not meted out because an offender could have behaved otherwise, and therefore deserved it, but because people were enraged by the offender's behaviour. The offender, on being punished 'no more felt a moral pang than if some terrible unforeseen disaster had occurred, if a rock had fallen and crushed him' (Nietzsche 1990: 215). Punishment, so far from developing a sense of guilt in the contemporary sense of pangs of conscience or remorse, in fact retards it (1990: 214). He further observes, and this has strong intuitive resonance: 'True remorse is rarest among prisoners and convicts: prisons and penitentiaries are not the breeding grounds of this gnawer' (1990: 214).

Expiation, purification and compensation are three ways whereby guilt can be extinguished. However, the bloodfeud does not extinguish guilt, indeed, it perpetuates it when it becomes vendetta. As Burkert relates of Achilles' feelings about the death of Patroclus, death is mastered when the mourner becomes a killer (Burkert 1983: 53), a sentiment eerily reflected in Kadare's novel *Broken April* about the bloodfeud in twentieth-century Albania (Kadare 1990). The only safe way for a community to deal with capital execution and to avoid vendetta, and thus end the cycle of guilt, is for it to institute courts. One can kill a killer, but not a court (Saunders 1991: 71). However, it is important to notice that in the case of Orestes, although the hero was purified from the spiritual implications of his involvement in matricide and feuding, it was for the newly constituted court to decide his fate (Aeschylus 1977).

What these reflections underscore is that in traditional and ancient societies which have practised restorative measures, the whole way in which guilt is experienced, measured and responded to is very different to the way in which it is dealt with in modern societies. Responsibility for offences reaches much further than the need to make amends to a victim, or to rectify a ritual offence. An offence can unleash dangerous spiritual currents and consequences for the offender. The notion of moral responsibility is very different. Traditional societies do not have a separation of the moral and the spiritual. By spiritual is not meant some idealization of the moral, but practical beliefs in the existence of spirits, gods and ghosts, together with the power of magic, the role of taboo and of totemic animals. All of these entities have a direct impact on the doings of humankind, and it is in the context of their perceived agency that human systems of dealing with offence can be said to have emerged.

The domain of spirit

In ancient and traditional societies the domain of the spirit cannot be avoided. All of human behaviour is attended with taboo. Animals are imbued with spirit. The divine is palpable. This has immediate implications for offences against humans. If a person is killed, their ghost lives on, and can exert influence. Among the Toba-Batak of Northern Sumatra, even if a person is only hurt or stunned, their *tondi* or attendant spirit may leave them. It is of the utmost importance that the spiritual consequence of any physical harm is dealt with effectually. Only the perpetrator of the offence can bring the *tondi* back to their human host. A person who has been deserted by their *tondi* may be prey to an evil spirit. In the case of the dead, among the Nuer it is essential that a ghost's capacity to wreak vengeance is contained.

The process of settling a dispute arising from insult and injury was closely recorded by Vergouwen (1964). This process combined elements of healing the practical as well as the spiritual breach. It involved different degrees of humiliation or abasement. A ceremonial meal is offered by the offender and his family to the victim as a recognition of guilt. It was also intended to strengthen the victim's *tondi*. It is accompanied by financial recompense, known as the 'stone of the meal'. Certain ritual prescriptions associated with purification and of a magical nature are followed in the course of the meal. The offering of the meal was itself a punishment (1964: 92–95; 356–357). However, meals were also associated with worship of the

ancestors, and therefore with the promotion of harmony and the expression of respect. Vergouwen records a Toba-Batak saying: 'What has
been agreed over meat and rice is absolutely settled' (1964: 92).

Despite such positive methods, Vergouwen also records that there were
outlawries and summary executions. A murderer could be killed and
eaten, at least before the Dutch took over. However, he could be ransomed
from the 'slaughter-pole' if his relatives swore to pay full compensation.
He also related a practice of ritual killing of a youth by pouring boiling
lead into his mouth. As a *bagu* his remains could then be deployed in
conflicts to harm one's enemies (Vergouwen 1964: 100), and could attack a
person who had lost his *tondi*. Conflict can thus be conducted through
each of the spiritual, human and the material dimensions.

We have seen already how the gods, or God, can institute punishment.
Ancient and traditional societies relied on this facility. Indeed they
invoked it together with other spiritual powers such as sorcery to deter
potential offenders and to terrify actual offenders into confession
(Malinowski 1961). Even in medieval times the ordeal was used to invoke
divine intervention.[2] In Anglo-Saxon laws, an accused person would be
cleared of charges by the oath-helping of his peers. The binding of the
offender into an acceptance of divine retribution through the taking of
special oaths was much practised by the Toba-Batak and was woven into
their system of conflict resolution. Such oaths were constructed using
formulas from sympathetic magic such as the much feared 'two stones'
oath:

A large stone, a small stone,
the resting place of the *sitapi-tapi* bird.
The great die, the insignificant die,
And no one is left to stoke the fire. (Vergouwen 1964: 403).

Oaths are taken on the oath-stone in the central market place. The stone is
the dwelling place of the spirits of the ancestors who are invoked by
the playing of the community *gondang*. Great supernatural powers are
released by playing the *gondang*. Homage is paid to the stone (Vergouwen
1964: 404). Once an oath is taken there is no further recourse to legal
measures.

Keeping at bay the influence of the dead is a major preoccupation of
ancient and traditional societies. Not only did a killer have to fear the
rancour of the victim's kin, he had to face the spirit of his victim, to say
nothing of the wrath of God, whether or not he escaped detection by a
witch doctor. Among the Nuer the most dangerous period for the killer
was before the mortuary rites of the victim were completed. In fact, a dead

person with any type of grievance, whether or not they have uttered a curse, can be a source of *cier* – vengeance – to the living. It is only when a person has undergone the mortuary rites that he becomes a ghost. Ghosts can have a positive role in settling bloodfeuds. However, they also haunt their relatives for not pursuing compensation for their deaths. *Cier* can only be averted by sacrifice to God and amends to the ghost. It is important too in minor offences to recognize that this lays the offender open to God's punishment (Evans-Pritchard 1956).

This gives rise to a view that to confess is the safest and best thing for an offender to do. This is a way to avert punishment from God and vengeance by the dead. Much value is placed on bringing out all causes of resentment and grievance and dealing with them, particularly during certain sacrifices (Evans-Pritchard 1956: 193). Among the Trobriand Islanders, if an offender knew that a sorcerer was at work, it could well induce a confession and the payment of compensation (Malinowski 1961: 86). Among the Toba-Batak the proper course of action for someone who has offended another is to offer a meal, which is the act of confession (Vergouwen 1964: 93).

Among the Nuer, any form of infraction creates a state of spiritual danger that must be averted. The rituals and sacrificial requirements for dealing with homicide are very extensive. The involvement of priests and Leopard Skin Chiefs emphasizes for us the spiritual dimension of these processes. The feasting associated with mortuary rites and the settling and prevention of feuds is a by-product of the sacrifices of animals to God, and is associated with the payment of compensation of cattle. Cattle themselves are sacred property, not least because cattle are thought to possess souls. Furthermore, a dead man will need a wife who will give him children, and thus preserve his lineage: his brother will act on his behalf, cohabiting with the wife (Evans-Pritchard 1956: 296).

In ancient Greece, the gods were present too in sacrifice. Burkert relates that at the end of the Choes Festival the priestess is given to Dionysus as a bride. The god is revived in the sexual act. He adds:

We recognise here too the enduring elements of those prehistoric restitution meals. Just as the animal's bones – more importantly its skull – had been deposited at a specific site – or, rather, raised and consecrated – so here the mask, the equivalent of the skull, was set up after the sacred wine had been consumed: the deity was present. In this way, the ritual attempted to document the restoration of order after its violation, the continuance of life through death. (Burkert 1983: 237).

Here, and elsewhere, we see a strong interweaving of the spiritual, the human and the material dimensions. This sense was so strong in ancient Greece that Plato in *The Laws* could not omit reference to the role of the murdered victim's spirit in his practical proposals for a constitution and legal system for *Magnesia* (Plato 1960: 254–255). The wrath of the victim, according to the teaching of venerable and primitive myth, which is not to be despised, will cause him to disturb the offender, entering the offender's thoughts. The offender must avoid this by going into exile for a year. He also makes reference to vengeance beyond the grave, in reincarnation, for egregious murders:

> … a truth firmly believed by many who have learned it from the lips of those who occupy themselves with these matters at the Mysteries, that vengeance is taken on such crimes beyond the grave, and when the sinner has returned to our world once more, he must infallibly pay Nature's penalty – must be done by as he did – and must end the life he is now living by the like violence at another's hands. (Plato 1960: 260).

A killer in *Magnesia* is polluted and may not enter temples or the market or any other public place. If near relatives do not pursue the accused by proclaiming excommunication, they themselves will be polluted, subject to evil omen and the wrath of heaven (Plato 1960: 260–261).

Plato recognized that in the creation of his ideal state it was necessary to give credence and place to ancient beliefs. This is despite the status of *The Laws* as one of the most sophisticated practical models of a legal and political constitution ever constructed, drawing upon psychological insights into moral responsibility as a foundation for penology.

Discussion

In this tour of different eras and societies we have seen that all the institutions which we associate with reparation are enveloped with very different practices and concepts to those of modernity. Rouland argues that when considering the legal institutions of other societies we must pay attention to their systems. We must come to terms with their inherent composition. He suggests that although mediation is a feature of both modern and acephalous societies, we cannot assume that each possesses the same form of dispute settlement. Instead we must analyse the role of mediation in relation to other ways of settling disputes (Rouland 1994: 162).

What emerges from these accounts is a number of variant positions in relation to punishment, guilt and spirit in the handling of dispute.

If human punishment derives from sacrifice, the substitution of human for animal, the animal having already substituted for the human, and if these in turn are associated with the hunt, and with mortuary rites, this reveals a very different context to that in which we are developing restorative justice in the contemporary world. For human punishment of this type is bound up with the notion of compensation. Compensation is accomplished through pleasure in violence, after other sources of compensation or expiation have been deemed insufficient. But even these lesser forms of compensation which do not demand the blood of the offender, demand the blood of a sacrificial animal. Blood always comes into the matter. Compensation, however variable in its forms, is the norm. How different it is in modernity. Although some states still exact the death penalty and mutilation, most societies derive their punishment systems from the prison – the ascetic tradition of self-punishment, imposed and therefore as ineffective as corporal punishment. However, where the death penalty is maintained, it is not clear that an atavistic motivation for compensation as pleasure is not in play. What, therefore, are we attempting to achieve in the resuscitation of compensatory practices? Perhaps we must turn the question on its head, and ask whether, despite a distaste for imprisonment, it has not saved many lives.

What its proponents require to do is to provide an account of restorative justice that recognizes and gives place to the feelings of rancour and anger of the community and the victim of crime, as well as the need for imposing social order. In the examples we have studied, the requirements of rancour, anger and social order may take precedence over the requirement for material composition. However, as the second introductory example from Japan makes clear, reconciliation of a certain type took place in the face of an overwhelming requirement to punish.[3] How far should restorative practices, or a restorative system of justice, incorporate features that were previously manifested by sacrifice, ritual and feasts?

If we turn to guilt we see there two problems to be faced. These have to do with the nature of guilt itself and the relative weight placed on the facts of the matter and the need for reconciliation.

On the first point, the traditional notion of guilt was more fuzzy than that found in modern systems of law. The sense of guilt as misfortune may, however, reflect more accurately the experience of many young offenders trapped in cultures of drug-taking, or responding to adverse social conditions of actual or relative deprivation. Here the notions of a rational actor having chosen a wicked path who must receive his just deserts, or alternatively made subject to a cognitive rehabilitation programme which will help him recognize his responsibility so that he will not do it again (i.e. become such a rational actor in the face of actual or relative deprivation) fail to convince. Guilt as misfortune requires a different approach. How far does restorative justice, as it is currently practised, provide offenders the opportunity to reverse the conditions of their guilt – their misfortune? In fact, does not the story of Charila who was placed at risk by the harshness of the king, make us reflect that it is perhaps the young offender who is left 'swinging in the wind', when we have overlooked the causes of his behaviour and forgotten him in custody? The rationalist accounts of both the retributive and the rehabilitative models, I suspect, simply do not make sense to many a young offender, by which I mean, are not felt to be true, or even understood.

However, guilt as misfortune is not the whole story in the traditional account. That it is unfortunate does not imply absence of liability, rather the reverse. It is the strict liability for actions in traditional societies which marks them as different from modern societies. Absence of malice will, as the example of the Nuer stabbing incident shows, influence the way in which the community comes to a view about accepting compensation rather than engaging in a feud, but the whole process of sacrifice and expiation had to be fulfilled to settle the case. In modern societies, at least in theory, the intention of the offender is a necessary condition for imposing the label of criminality, except in certain offences imposing strict liability. Accidental death does not incur criminal sanction, nor sometimes any real sanction at all. Contrast the Nuer example, for instance, with a case in the UK of causing death by careless driving. In such a case, the severity of the penalty is determined by the culpability of the action and not by its outcome. The civil aspect of the case is dealt with by insurance. A modern offender could therefore walk away from the slaying with a fine and an increased insurance premium. Indeed a corporate offender in a negligence case may fare even better.

On the second point, as can be seen from the example of Toba-Batak mediators, emphasis is placed not so much on the facts of the matter, which may be disputed and, as likely as not, unascertainable, but on how to restore peace. As Vergouwen noticed, the settlements imposed by mediators always contained a rule for future conduct. Settlements of this type contained binds for both the victim and the offender, imposing reciprocities. Civil law and criminal law are interwoven. Mediators also function as arbitrators and judges. Chiefs rely in their judgements on a feeling for the concrete, the importance of the individual case in the milieu in which it occurred, and this means that they do not operate on the basis of case law (Vergouwen 1964: 417–418). This discretionary approach is the heart of this traditional system of justice, whereas in modern systems of law, including those where restorative justice is beginning to be established, it is on the fringe. Discretion is tolerated in the gaps permitted by legal principle and precedent.

Finally, we need to reflect on the place of spirit in criminal justice. In modern societies, except those implementing *sharia* law, the legal systems are explicitly secular. The use of the term 'spiritual' in a secular context reflects a notion of idealism rather than any sense of the operation of spirits, gods or God. It is not even the case that traditions of society can bind our behaviour, our sense of morality or right and wrong. Where notions of the spirit come into play is in the championing of spiritual values such as forgiveness derived from, *inter alia,* Judaeo-Christian theologies. Even under traditional *sharia* conditions, the law of God cannot legally be imposed on unbelievers. In the contemporary Judaeo-Christian context, ideas of forgiveness and the operation of the Spirit, Wisdom or God does not supplant the secular system of law. Church and State are separate. Thus in contemporary society spirit cannot suffuse the operating principles of secular institutions in the way that it does permeate the life and institutions of traditional societies.

Since the antecedents of restorative justice, the roots from which it is so self-consciously drawn, are inextricably bound up with religious systems involving God or gods, spirits, ghosts and witchcraft, can we in good conscience borrow mediatory practices without their spiritual framework, and simultaneously claim that this will suffice for the requirements of a modern criminal justice system? The debate about legal acculturation cannot be avoided. When sentencing circles and conferencing are adapted either for continued use by traditional or by modern societies, what degree of recognition is given to the spiritual elements of the original processes? To what extent can methods inspired by practices in traditional societies truly resonate with traditional processes of community dispute settlement managed by elders who function both as mediators and as sacrificial priests?

Perhaps we must finally recognize that mediation in modern societies is indeed a child of religion. For example, early mediators in Scotland, *amicales compositores,* were usually churchmen. The ancient Scottish system of *assythment* (settlement) of bloodfeud (abolished 1978) drew heavily on Christian notions of forgiveness and reconciliation (Mackay 1992: 242–255). Rituals at the church underscored agreements (Brown 1986). Even here, however, the ritual is not completely sanitized. The offender is forced to kneel, to hand over a sword to the victim's kin. The victim's family's sense of honour, and possible loss of face in not pursuing the feud, is assuaged by the ritual humiliation of the offender. The offender is relieved of the feud by the *letter of slainis*, which explicitly requires all branches of the victim's kin to grant forgiveness and to forswear further prosecution. Material compensation is required (Brown 1986).

Burkert expressed concern about the breakdown of the ritual tradition in modernity, and contemplated in its wake the emergence of manifestations of wild and destructive social violence in the midst of seemingly rational social orders. He saw the ideal of a new non-violent man as a protest of hope over the tradition of violence and anxiety. He argued that

> '... our knowledge of the traditions that proved themselves in the past and thus survived in the various experiments of human development should not be lost as we proceed, by trial and error, toward an uncertain future.' (Burkert 1983: 297).

Conclusion

J.L. Mackie made an important observation about the development of law and dispute resolution on which it is fruitful to meditate: 'Devices for compromise and adjustment of conflicts between individuals have grown up, largely automatically but with some help from deliberate invention, over many thousands of years, and have been widely accepted into moral thinking and into various legal systems.' (Mackie 1982: 283).

We find that we need to revive a sense of connection with our own roots. What we need to recognize is that where restorative practices were operative in the past or in traditional societies, these included elements that are redolent of a sterner and bloodier worldview. These elements had clear psychological foundation in the need to deal with powerful emotions of horror, revulsion, grief, anger and resignation. We may not like these traditional approaches, but we cannot dispense with the need to find compensatory mechanisms that take these emotions seriously.

Notes

1. The ethnographic studies are Evans-Pritchard's work on Nuer religion, Malinowski's study on crime in the Trobriand Islands, Vergouwen's study of *adat* customary law in Northern Sumatra. The Greek studies comprise Burkert's work on sacrifice, Calasso's study of myth, and Saunder's study of penology. Plato's *The Laws* is also indispensable. These are referenced fully when cited.
2. An example from contemporary Indonesia was reported in The Guardian newspaper on 27.10.98: 'Suspects accused in a wave of murders linked with the

occult in Eastern Java have survived a trial by ordeal. The twelve had to dress in white shrouds and recite Islamic prayers at a mosque in Panti on Sunday. Priests said that if they had been guilty, the suspects would have died on the spot. More than 150 people have died – some of them Muslim clerics accused of sorcery – in the attacks which locals believe are tied to black magic.'

3. This example is quite hard for supporters of restorative justice to deal with. Japan is often cited as a strong example of a society concerned with reconciliation and composition and less concern for retribution (Braithwaite 1989; Haley and Neugebauer 1992). However, this picture is only a partial account of Japanese penal culture. The temple on the site of the Kotsukappara execution ground in Tokyo states that it comforts the souls of around 200,000 souls said to have been executed there during the previous 300 years until 1887, an average of two beheadings a day (Seidensticker 1991: 16–17). Capital punishment has continued from the Meiji era until the present day.

References

Aeschylus (1977) *The Oresteia* (tr. R. Fagles). Harmondsworth: Penguin.

Braithwaite, J. (1989) *Crime, Shame and Reintegration*. Cambridge, UK: Cambridge University Press.

Brett, C., Schluter, M. and Wright, M. (1995) *Relational Prison Audits*. The Relationships Foundation, Scottish Prison Service Occasional Paper No 2.

Brown, K. M. (1986) *Bloodfeud in Scotland 1573–1625*. Edinburgh: John Donald.

Burkert, W. (1983) *Homo Necans* (tr. P. King). Berkeley: University of California Press.

Calasso, R. (1994) *The Marriage of Cadmus and Harmony* (tr. T. Parks). London: Vintage.

Durkheim, E. (1984) *The Division of Labour in Society* (tr. W.D. Halls). London: Macmillan.

Evans-Pritchard, E. E. (1956) *Nuer Religion*. Oxford: Clarendon Press.

Foucault, M. (1997) *Discipline and Punish*. Harmondsworth: Penguin.

Haley, J. O. and Neugebauer, A. M. (1992) 'Victim–Offender Mediation: Japanese and American Comparisons' in H. Messmer and H.-U. Otto (eds) (1992) *Restorative Justice on Trial*. Dordrecht: Kluwer.

Hearn, L. (1994) *Writings from Japan*. Harmondsworth: Penguin.

Kadare, I. (1990) *Broken April*. London: Harvill.

Mackay, R. E. (1992) 'The Resuscitation of Assythment? – Reparation and the Scottish Criminal Law', *Juridical Review*, 3.

Mackie, J. L. (1982) 'Cooperation, Competition and Moral Philosophy' in A. M. Colman (ed.) *Cooperation and Competition in Animals and Humans*. New York: Van Norstrand Reinhold.

Malinowski, B. (1961) *Crime and Custom in Savage Society*. London: RKP.

Mauss, M. (1968) 'Systemes Religieux et Juridiques de quelques Populations Archaiques', *Oeuvres 1*. Paris: Les Editions de Minuit.

Mauss, M. (1974) 'La Religion et les Origines du Droit Penal d'apres un Livre Recent', *Oeuvres 2*. Paris: Les Editions de Minuit.

Nietzsche, F. (1990) *The Birth of Tragedy* and *The Genealogy of Morals* (tr. F. Golffing). New York: Doubleday.

Plato (1960) *The Laws* (tr. A. E. Taylor). London: Dent Dutton, Everyman.

Rouland. N. (1994) *Legal Anthropology* (tr. P. G. Planel). London: The Athlone Press.

Saunders, T. J. (1991) *Plato's Penal Code*. Oxford: Clarendon Press.

Seidensticker, W. G. (1991) *Low City, High City – Tokyo from Edo to the Earthquake (1867–1923)*. Cambridge, MA: Harvard University Press.

Stocker, M. (1990) *Plural and Conflicting Values*. Oxford: Clarendon Press.

Thudydides (1977) *The History of the Peloponnesian War* (tr. R. Warner). Harmondsworth: Penguin.

Vergouwen, J. C. (1964) *The Social Organization and Customary Law of the Toba-Batak of Northern Sumatra* (tr. J. Scott-Kimble). The Hague: Martinus Nijhoff.

Chapter 13

The role of shame, guilt, and remorse in restorative justice processes for young people

Gabrielle Maxwell and Allison Morris

Introduction

Shame is a response by an individual – to feel shame. It is also a method of sanctioning others – to shame someone. This distinction is of fundamental importance since the consequences of attempts by others to shame, may, in fact, result in a range of different emotions in the person they are trying to shame and these may or may not include shame. Also, feeling shame may occur independently of any shaming by others.

There is now a considerable amount of literature on shame, and its role in both everyday life and in the criminal justice system is much debated. Within the criminal justice system, for example, Braithwaite's (1989) landmark book *Crime, Shame and Reintegration* argues that shame used or experienced in a particular way can prevent reoffending but used or experienced in other ways can increase the chances of reoffending.

The first half of this chapter briefly reviews some examples of linguistic deconstructions of shame, guilt and remorse before turning to a brief review of some of the empirical literature on these emotions. In doing this, we have deliberately selected the work which we see as most relevant to criminal justice events. As we will see, much of this debate turns on understanding the variety of feelings, including guilt and remorse, that can be seen to come under the broad heading of shame and on the context in which shame occurs and is managed. In the second part of the chapter, we focus on the role of shame in the criminal justice process by examining Braithwaite's theoretical analysis of shame and shaming and then the research findings on the role of shame, guilt and remorse in family group conferences in New Zealand. Finally, some conclusions are drawn about the importance of shame and the way in which it must be handled if negative consequences are to be avoided.

Considering shame, guilt and remorse

Linguistic analyses of shame, guilt and remorse

Many authors have tried to unwrap shame, guilt and remorse through a process of intellectual analysis. For example, Sabini and Silver (1997: 1), in the introduction to their paper, write that their purpose was to analytically pry apart guilt and shame using 'linguistic intuitions and common experience' as well as data from a series of empirical studies. In fact, however, they rejected the conclusions of the empirical studies they reviewed and instead concluded on the basis of their 'intuitions and experience' that 'shame is a fundamentally aesthetic response to our judgements of our character' and is effective in preventing 'many of us doing things the world is better off without our doing' (1977: 12). This rejection of data in favour of intuition and common experience is at odds with usual scientific conventions.

Thomas (1999: 133) describes remorse as 'part of an ethic of care for that which we value'. As such, he views the expression of remorse as a demonstration of respect for victims and their loss and as acknowledgement of their rights: an acknowledgement which they could expect indicated a preparedness on the part of offenders to refrain from further offending. Similarly, Taylor (2000) sees remorse as inherently linked with the acceptance of responsibility for harm, unlike shame and guilt which are, in her view, often linked to negative self-image as much as to regret for harm done. Borgeaud and Cox (1999: 135) report that some have called remorse 'the most dreadful human sentiment', because of the inability of 'undoing' the acts that have given rise to it.

Such speculative analyses are problematic. It is difficult to know how to evaluate their accuracy. The same words are given somewhat different meanings by different authors. And none of these authors offer empirical evidence to substantiate their claims.

Empirical research on shame, guilt and remorse

The following brief review of the empirical research on shame, guilt and remorse deals with key studies chronologically. A series of studies around the 1940s and '50s focused on the two themes of cultural differences and individual differences. After a period of neglect, the same two themes were revisited in the 1980s and '90s when researchers built on and extended the earlier work.

Shame, guilt and national character

A critical analysis of shame and guilt as national characteristics was central to Benedict's (1946) classic work *The Chrysanthemum and the Sword*. In this book, she suggested that a fundamental difference between the American and Japanese national character lay in the extent to which the Japanese felt shame in failing to meet the demands of others, typically through 'loss of face', while Americans responded with guilt to the failure to meet internalized standards of behaviour. Riesman *et al.* (1950) built on this work. They suggested that people varied in the extent to which they were 'tradition directed', 'inner directed' or 'other directed' and that emotions were felt differently when rules were breached depending on these three different orientations. 'Tradition directed' people who breached norms and values derived from ancestral traditions were likely to experience shame. By contrast, 'inner directed' people responded with guilt when they breached norms and values that were internalized and 'other directed' people responded with anxiety when they faced peer dis- approval of their behaviour. Guilt, shame and anxiety were thus seen as three alternative emotional responses to breaches of the social order depending upon whether the individuals had learnt to depend on traditional values, internalized personal standards or peer group approval in evaluating the acceptability of their behaviour. Although the evidence produced to support these theories has been criticized as insufficient to validate these distinctions (Creighton 1990), the hypotheses about cultural difference in the expression and experience of emotions remain current topics, which we return to later.

Shame in individual development

Erikson published in 1950 his important theoretical book on ego develop- ment. He was primarily concerned with the stages of development of the individual. He saw critical childhood dilemmas as, for example, being those of 'trust versus mistrust', 'autonomy versus shame and doubt', 'initiative versus guilt', 'industry versus authority' and so on at various points in childhood development. Thus, for Erikson, shame was opposed to autonomy and was differentiated from guilt, which, at a later develop- mental stage, was opposed to initiative. Guilt, therefore, superseded shame in the developmental hierarchy, but both shame and guilt were reactions defining developmental maladaptation as opposed to the adaptive modes of autonomy and initiative. Erikson's analysis was very influential among developmental psychologists but his theory is inherently difficult to test. It has, nevertheless, contributed to the theoretical frameworks that have underpinned the further research on individual differences discussed in the next section.

Synthesizing the influence of culture and individual differences

Psychologists writing on the use of emotional sanctions, such as shame and ridicule, have suggested that their effectiveness depends on the individual's readiness to feel shame, loss of face or guilt and on the association between such feelings and the sense of self-esteem (Inkeles and Levinson 1969). This analysis incorporated the ideas of both Riesman and Erikson and suggested that the individual's propensity to respond with different emotions to the same circumstances depends on their upbringing, whether in terms of culture or developmental activity. Inkeles and Levinson (1969) also supported Benedict's contention and pointed to evidence from cross-cultural analyses of different propensities to respond with either shame or guilt. They cited work by Dick (1952) that suggested that, under pressure, Russians were likely to respond with aggression-guilt. On the other hand, the loss of face in China was seen by La Barre (1946, cited in Inkeles and Levinson 1969: 472) 'as so central as a sanction … that the sense of sin is nearly absent'. As a result of this analysis, Inkeles and Levinson (1969: 472–472) suggested that 'social systems that emphasize guilt, shame or ridicule as sanctions will require for effective functioning that their members show, as a characterological trait, relatively high readiness to suffer loss of self esteem or feelings of shame and guilt'. This synthesis of earlier work influenced research of the '80s and '90s.

Distinguishing shame and guilt

Tomkins (1987) added yet another component to conceptualizations of the impact of emotions on individuals with his development of 'affect theory' which detailed evidence of the way emotions in adults are shaped by socialization. He viewed shame as standing for a family of emotions, which includes embarrassment, contempt, ridicule, humiliation and feeling put down. The nature of these emotions are defined and experienced somewhat differently by different people depending on their past history as well as on their temperament.

Thus it is perhaps not surprising that empirical studies have not always been able to distinguish shame and guilt. Tangney (1991) demonstrated a substantial correlation between proneness to shame and proneness to guilt. She also linked these to empathic responsiveness and contended that those who are more empathic to others are less prone to shame but are more prone to guilt. However, Harris has reported contrary findings.

Harris (1999a, 1999b) carried out a study designed to measure separately the shame, guilt and embarrassment felt by offenders who had recently experienced a community group conference. However, factor analysis of the self-report scales used in his study indicated that shame and guilt could not be separated; items measuring both concepts emerged on the same statistical factor, which Harris refers to as shame/guilt. Embarrassment in the sense of concern about one's public image was also unable to be differentiated from shame/guilt, although embarrassment in the sense of self-consciousness and social awkwardness was. He concluded that the absence of an empirical distinction in the eyes of offenders suggested that identifying the difference between the two emotions is not a critical issue – people may not experience shame and guilt differently. Harris's findings also did not support a distinction between a concern for others' opinions (or loss of face) and one's own judgement of having done something wrong (ethical identity). Zandbergen (1996, cited in Harris, 1999b) also demonstrated that offenders in an experimental project often reported feeling both shame and guilt and that the two responses could not be readily disentangled.

The consequences of shame
As well as considering the complexity of the subjective experience, several writers have focused on the consequences of shame. Nathanson (1997) suggested that, whatever form subjective experiences take, when shame (or one of its related emotions) is triggered the individual will engage in one of four patterns: withdrawal, attack self, avoidance, or attack other. Responses related to withdrawal include the normal reactions of shyness, hiding oneself, lowering one's eyes. At the pathological end, Nathanson placed reactions of depression, prolonged silence and withdrawal from the company of others. He suggested that attacking self includes such reactions as self-blame, which can be part of an apology and a loss of self-esteem. At the extreme end, it involves masochistic acceptance of brutal treatment from others. Avoidance involves engaging in other activities that distract from pain and humiliation. It can result in people seeking relationships with others who do not trigger feelings of low self-worth. It can be particularly problematic if alcohol or drugs are used excessively as ways of numbing painful emotion. Attacking others can also vary in the extent to which its consequences are antisocial: negative thoughts and even remarks can be relatively harmless if the recipient remains unaware of them but the direct expression of emotional and physical abuse and

aggression is potentially exceedingly harmful. It is Nathanson's (1997: 352) view that:

> Wherever we see fights we must look for shame... The sado-masochistic interchange is always and only about shame... Those who are brought up in homes or neighbourhoods that give but little solace for the pain of shame will move steadily towards the more pathological range of its expression. Although behaviour can be launched for a wide range of reasons, when we see a disturbed child or adult act in the ways described by the compass of shame, we must try to explain the resultant psychopathology in terms of what we know about affect itself and the specific pathways for shame. The range of shame far exceeds anything ever dreamed in our earlier systems of psychology.

Nathanson is not alone in such views. Lewis (1971) suggested that shame has negative psychological consequences. He argued that the consequences of shame are often an inability to feel empathy, depression, powerlessness, anger and hostility to others. Olthof (2000) concluded, in a review of recent psychological literature, that inducing shame and or guilt in an offender could lead to a desire to avoid being in such a situation again, but that it was potentially risky in that it could evoke further negative, anti-social and hostile behaviour. Miller (1996: 151) called shame the 'bedrock of much psychopathology'. Vagg (1998: 250) suggested that shame could produce feelings of 'humiliation, rage and desire for revenge rather than feelings of guilt and remorse' and labelling theorists (for example Lemert 1971) similarly argued that labelling or stigmatizing an offender increases the likelihood of subsequent deviant behaviour. They introduced terms like 'secondary deviance' and 'deviance amplification' to capture this.

Such negative views of shame are confirmed by the empirical research of Tangney and her associates (1991, 1992 and 1996). The 1991 article is entitled 'Moral affect: The good, the bad and the ugly' where empathy is seen as good, guilt as bad and shame as ugly in the extent to which they are linked to altruism. Shame proneness has been related by Tangney and her associates to a lack of empathy (1991); to maladaptive responses such as anger, including malevolent intentions; direct, indirect and displaced aggression; self directed hostility and negative long term consequences (1992); and to anger, aggression, suspiciousness, resentment, irritability, a tendency to blame others for negative events and indirect expressions of hostility (1996).

Cultural importance of shame for Maori

Metge (1986) examined the concept of *whakamaa* amongst traditional Maori through a series of in-depth interviews with people from a variety of different tribal groups. She also drew from her observations during a lifetime of anthropological research among Maori. She saw *whakamaa* as a response which cannot easily be defined in English. It can refer to the deep sense of shame accompanying wrongdoing, is akin to an illness and has serious consequences for psychological functioning. It also encompasses a wide variety of feelings from shyness, through embarrassment, uncertainty, inadequacy, fear, hurt, to depression and shame, feelings which are not necessarily associated with wrongdoing.

Whakamaa is demonstrated in a variety of ways, the most notable of which is a physical switching off where the body becomes completely still, the eyes and head are lowered and all responses are shut down. Other behavioural patterns include: turning one's body away or hiding one's face; restlessness (usually in response to milder forms of the emotion); flight from the situation (a more extreme response); or boisterousness which can be displayed by getting drunk, swearing, babbling or hyperactivity. Anger was not mentioned as part of *whakamaa* but Metge believes that this is because, in most cases, it is suppressed. She commented that, if a person is pushed too far into *whakamaa* violence could result.

She identified a variety of causes of *whakamaa*. The most central is a loss of *mana*. *Mana* has two main meanings: the most common refers to power and authority of a respected figure but it is also used to refer to self-esteem, self-respect and identity. *Whakamaa* is inevitably associated with a loss of *mana* in one or both of these senses and is greater when *mana* is high to begin with. The proximate causes may be: perception of lower status because of youth, poverty, lesser ability or being unable to meet obligations; uncertainty or confusion about what to do or how to behave; perception of wrongdoing being put down or criticized, especially when fault or wrongdoing is accepted; or on being singled out. *Whakamaa* can also be felt on behalf of others who are associated with the self (for example, by members of one's family). All these causes are likely to be present in encounters between young people, their families and the criminal justice system.

Metge's analysis of the consequences of *whakamaa* echoes some of the themes that emerged from the empirical research on shame reviewed earlier. If the sense of *whakamaa* is not extreme, it can help children to learn what they should or should not do and be a spur to achievement. However, in more extreme cases, *whakamaa* undermines a person's sense of self-worth, their *mana*, and it affects their relationship with the group as a whole. It is viewed as being both spiritual and psychological. It is seen as an illness but it is not purely individual as one's associates are also involved and affected by it. In extreme cases, withdrawal is so marked that it results in a psychiatric diagnosis. Because of the centrality of relationships in the generation of *whakamaa* and in the nature of the response to it, the individual alone cannot overcome the more serious forms of it. *Mana* can only be restored with the help of others.

Metge expressed concern over the way in which *whakamaa* is responded to by others and devoted several chapters to discussing how it can be best dealt with. In particular, she suggested that reintegration into the social fabric depends on: first, the cause and intensity of *whakamaa* being properly diagnosed; second, the discernment and kindliness of others in treating it appropriately; and third, the availability of escape routes. She gave a number of examples of the way others release the sense of *whakamaa*; by speaking for the shamed person, by sitting beside them, by reaching out and touching them, and by pulling them back into the social group. The offenders themselves could often make these actions possible by accepting criticism and displaying contrition, often non-verbally rather than verbally. Prevention of *whakamaa* is best achieved, she suggested, by 'cultivating the caring love of others' (Metge 1986: 123) and avoidance of excessive praise or blame. She states in conclusion:

> *Whakamaa* has serious negative consequences and functions and some positive ones. No one is immune from attack but in general those with less mana are most vulnerable. Properly handled, the negative aspects of *whakamaa* can be minimised and even turned to good account. Mishandled, *whakamaa* can be exceedingly damaging to the *whakamaa* person and the social fabric, especially when it becomes ingrained and chronic. Denied outlet or healing, it can erupt in violence.

Summarizing so far

The linguistic analyses reviewed in this chapter do not, in general, accord with empirical data. On the other hand, the empirical data appear to match the commonly held wisdom of traditional Maori about the 'sickness' of *whakamaa*. Certainly, the understandings of shame and its associated emotions offered by Tangney, Nathanson, Metge and others all agree in pointing to the potential power and danger of shame and the need to manage it carefully if negative consequences are to be avoided.

The implication of these analyses for criminological theories of the consequences of shaming sanctions is to suggest, first, that such sanctions – to the extent that they induce feelings of shame or guilt – are likely to reduce self-esteem; and, second, shame or guilt may or may not result depending on the personality of the person who is being sanctioned. Although the psychology of shame is still much debated, the common theme in these various analyses is that shame and its associated emotions are felt variably depending on both the social and cultural context and the individual's personality. Against this backdrop we now turn to theory and research about the role of shame in the criminal justice system and in family group conferences as an example of restorative justice processes.

Shame and restorative justice processes

Braithwaite on crime, shame and reintegration

In the previous sections, we examined analyses of shame, guilt and remorse from both a non-empirical and an empirical perspective. In the remainder of this chapter, we examine analyses of the role of shame in response to crime, also from a non-empirical and an empirical perspective. Braithwaite (1989) set up a model of crime control. In this section, we try to convey the gist of Braithwaite's views on shame, guilt, remorse and reintegrative shaming, although it is difficult to summarize a book and numerous articles in a paragraph or two. There seem to us five key areas.

First, Braithwaite saw shame and guilt as intimately entwined. He said that 'guilt is only made possible by cultural processes of shaming', that 'to induce guilt and to induce shame are inextricably part of the same social process' and that 'the consciences that cause us guilt are ... formed by shaming' (1989: 57). He added here also that, from the offender's perspective, 'guilt and shame may be indistinguishable'. This view is supported by the work of Harris (1999a, 1999b) and Tangney and her associates (1991, 1992, 1996) to which we have already referred.

Second, Braithwaite defined shaming as 'all social processes of expressing disapproval which have the intention or effect of invoking remorse in the person being shamed and/or condemnation of others who become aware of the shaming' (1989: 100). What is important for Braithwaite then is that it is 'disapproval' which is the mechanism for invoking 'remorse'. Disapproval (shaming), in Braithwaite's usage, can take a variety of forms: a frown, gossip or formal acts by the state, and he describes apology by the recipient as 'the most powerful form of shaming' (1999: 5). This is different from what is conventionally or popularly thought of shaming. It appears that Braithwaite saw the expression of disapproval as both signifying the intention of the person disapproving and its effect on the recipient (offender). This contrasts with our suggestion that these two aspects, the intention of the disapprover and the effect on the recipient, are different and that it is effect that is crucial. We come back to this point later.

Third, Braithwaite suggested that the shame which matters most was not 'the shame of remote judge or police officer but the shame of the people they most care about' (1993: 37). This is consistent with the view advanced by Metge (1986). This takes us indirectly to the fourth area.

The distinction Braithwaite made between 'stigmatic shaming' and 'reintegrative shaming' is crucial. Braithwaite is firmly opposed to stigmatic shaming and sees it as counter-productive. As already noted, there is a substantial body of research that shows that shame can have negative consequences for self-esteem. Reintegrative shaming, on the other hand, is seen as likely to be effective in controlling crime (1989: 4). Reintegrative shaming means that the offence rather than the offender is condemned and the offender is reintegrated with (included) rather than rejected by society (excluded). This is said to be achieved through certain steps:

- disapproving of the offence;

- sustaining a relationship of respect for the offender and not labelling the offender as bad or evil;

- not allowing the offending to be viewed as the offender's main characteristic; and

- re-accepting the offender through 'words or gestures of forgiveness' (1989: 100).

Braithwaite and Mugford (1994) elaborated 14 conditions for successful reintegrative shaming. These included 'uncoupling' the offence and the offender so that the offence can be viewed as 'bad' (and denounced) but not the offender; facilitators who identify with all participants as well as the public interest; the empowerment of victims, offenders and families through control of the process; the encouragement of empathy and generosity; rituals of inclusion and reintegration; avoidance of power imbalances; completion of agreed outcomes; and further 'ceremonies' if reintegration fails.

Fifth, Braithwaite saw communitarian societies as able to deliver both 'more potent shaming ... and shaming which is more reintegrative' (1989: 87). Communitarian societies are societies characterized by a 'densely enmeshed interdependency', 'mutual obligation and trust' and 'group loyalty' (1989: 86). This analysis could be seen as applying to the shame-oriented societies described by Benedict (1946) and Riesman et al. (1950) and to Maori society as described by Metge (1986).

Implementing shame and remorse

Stigmatic shaming

Historically, many of the rituals of the criminal and penal systems served to signify the separation and segregation of defendants: for example, the placing of defendants in public stocks or the wearing of distinctive clothing by prisoners. Some rituals continue to signify this: for example, the isolation of the offender in the courtroom vis-à-vis the other players. Without doubt, however, stigmatic shaming has had a troubling revival, particularly in the United States (Massaro 1991; Garvey 1998; Karp 1998). For example, there have recently been examples of convicted child molesters being required as a condition of their probation to place in a newspaper an advert proclaiming their status along with their photograph and of offenders being required to wear signs, which again alert us to their status. Lee (1998) provided another example of stigmatic shaming from England: police cautioning in the 1990s, at least in some areas. Stigmatic shaming was achieved by such strategies as manipulating the spatial arrangements in the room in which the caution was to occur so that the child would be in front of and close to the police officers while the parents were placed behind the child so that the child could not see them, or by dressing down the child and highlighting his or her status as an offender. These examples, of course, have no place in restorative justice processes.

Reintegrative shaming

There are currently at least three versions of conferencing which are based on 'reintegrative shaming': diversionary conferencing in Canberra, the model of conferencing promoted by Real Justice in parts of the United States and elsewhere, and restorative conferencing in the Thames Valley police authority. Police officers have been quite involved in these forms of conferences as facilitators and, partly as a result of this, conferences may be held in police facilities. Sometimes, facilitators follow scripts aimed at eliciting certain key responses from offenders, although there has been some debate about the appropriateness or usefulness of this. All three versions have been (and are continuing to be) evaluated (Sherman *et al.* 1998; McCold and Wachtel 1998; Young and Goold 1999) and a range of positive findings have emerged, especially in any comparisons between conferencing and courts.[1]

However, some concerns have also been raised. For example, Walgrave and Aertsen (1996) question the value of shaming by official representatives of the community such as by police officers. As noted earlier, reintegrative shaming demands that the offender should respect the shamer or at least should acknowledge the legitimacy of the shamer's authority. There is some doubt that this exists vis-à-vis the police among those young people most likely to be part of a conference (Anderson *et al.* 1994; Aye Maung 1995).

Also, Young and Goold (1999), in their evaluation of restorative conferencing in the Thames Valley police, found a number of similarities between restorative conferencing and stigmatic shaming: in particular, the dominance of the police officers in the conferences and their apparent stress on deterring the child from future criminal behaviour. Thus, at that point in their evaluation, Young and Goold described the shift from 'degrading cautioning ceremonies to reintegrating shaming sessions' to be 'incomplete' (1999: 137). More generally, Loader (1996) highlighted the police's ambivalence to young people. This too must affect their ability to shame reintegratively.

This leads us to an important point. It has to be the individual being disapproved of/shamed and not the disapprover/shamer who will determine whether or not the disapproval/shaming is actually reintegrative: the disapprover/shamer cannot determine its effect on the offender. Despite our good intentions, therefore, the disapproval/shaming which we intend to be reintegrative might be taken by the offender to be stigmatic. The benchmark for actions must be their impact, not their intent.

The role of shame in conferencing

Retzinger and Scheff (1996), on the basis of observing nine community conferences in Australia and discussions with certain Australian criminologists, sought to clarify the emotional process involved in conferencing. To paraphrase their views: awareness and negotiation of shame dynamics are presented as the key to effective conferences. The core sequence for them is the expression of genuine shame and remorse by the offender followed by the victim taking at least a first step towards forgiving the offender. This sequence is seen as regenerating repair and restoration of the bond between victim and offender that was severed by the offender's crime and is the key to reconciliation, victims' satisfaction and decreasing recidivism. However, they also recognized the danger that a poorly-managed conference could increase the offender's shame without necessarily resulting in any effective apology from him or her or in movement by the victim towards the acceptance and forgiveness that can reduce the potentially negative consequences of shame for the offender. Indeed, they saw the victim's moral indignation itself as being comprised of both anger and shame; the hidden shame component was seen as arising because being offended against was itself potentially humiliating. Thus, unresolved moral indignation may lead to further negative consequences for the victim as well as the offender. Their conclusions were that conferences must be managed in ways that ensure an early response before negative feelings become established and amplified, that avoid intentional shaming, that use skilful questioning to elicit the hurt of the victim rather than allowing a focus on moral indignation, and that use silence to encourage the offender to reflect on what has happened and express their remorse. These issues are picked up again in the next section on conferencing in New Zealand.

Conferencing in New Zealand

Family group conferences in New Zealand are not scripted and the format they take is very much in the hands of the participants who are also consulted about the venue for and timing of the meeting. Participants are guided by a facilitator (the youth justice coordinator) but sometimes this role will be handed over, too, if it is culturally appropriate to do so. We have observed many family group conferences, and these are frequently very emotional experiences; indeed, the expression of emotion is expected and accepted. One of the primary aims of family group conferences is to give offenders a sense of the consequences of their actions and an understanding of how victims feel. This is done not by a process which emphasizes disapproval (shaming), but by a process which emphasizes the effects of the crime on the victim.

We would not wish to convey the impression that this always happens or that participants are always satisfied with the way the process is handled or with the agreements reached. But we have commonly observed victims express their hurt and anger and we have commonly observed offenders express their sorrow and regret. We have also observed many examples of inclusion, re-acceptance, even reconciliation: hugs and handshakes between offenders and victims, invitation from victims to offenders and their families to join them for a meal, offers of jobs or accommodation by victims to offenders and so on. It is important also to note here that the emotional tone of a conference is not static. Hence victims who are initially angry may end up comforting the offender or the offender's family; and victims who are grief-stricken may receive some comfort from seeing the offender's remorse.

It is likely that, on occasion, as a result of these experiences, young offenders (and their families) do feel shame. And it is also quite likely that, on occasion, disapproval of both the offence and the offender is expressed. However, there is certainly nothing in the processes or practices of family group conferences in New Zealand which is explicitly geared towards expressing disapproval in order to invoke shame or remorse in the offender. On the other hand, there is a hope or expectation that the offender will accept responsibility for his or her offending and its consequences, that this will result in a better understanding on the offender's part, and that this will result in the offender showing remorse. The emphasis then is not so much on the specific intent of the disapprover/ shamer, but on the effects on the offender.

Remorse and reintegration

In 1990–91, we (Maxwell and Morris 1993) carried out research on the New Zealand youth justice system that included interviewing a sample of young offenders and their parents who had been involved in a family group conference. Some six years later we examined the reconvictions of these young offenders and reinterviewed as many of these young offenders (and/or their parents) as possible (Maxwell and Morris 1999). A proportion of young offenders – over a quarter – were not reconvicted at all over this period, and a similar proportion were persistently reconvicted. A number of different types of statistical analysis were carried out to discover what distinguished those persistently reconvicted from those not reconvicted.

Young offenders and their parents were specifically asked a number of questions about the family group conference they participated in and what had happened in the years after the conference. A number of important findings emerged:

- not being made to feel a bad person or a bad parent (not feeling shamed) was significantly related to not being reconvicted;

- the young person feeling remorse[2] or the parents feeling that their son or daughter was sorry for what they had done was significantly related to not being reconvicted; and

- feeling good about oneself and that life had gone well was also significantly related to not being reconvicted – these young people had jobs and positive relationships with a partner.

There were also connections among these three sets of variables. For example, among the most important variables in the discriminant analyses to explain reconviction were 'feeling shamed at the conference', 'not being remorseful', not getting a job or training after the conference, and not having close friends.

Collectively, these findings provide some support for Braithwaite's notion of reintegrative shaming: he stressed the importance of invoking remorse and rejected stigmatic shaming. However, the research does not show that disapproval (shaming) was necessarily the mechanism which invoked the remorse. Another way of interpreting these data is that empathy or understanding the effects of offending on victims was the trigger. If this interpretation is right, the practice and policy implications would be very different from a continuing emphasis on shaming (disapproval).

Conclusion

The analysis in the first part of this chapter of the theory and research on shame and related emotions such as guilt and embarrassment leads to the conclusion that these are not clearly distinguishable from one other. There is little consistency in the labels used by different people in different circumstances. Rather, as Tomkins (1987) suggested, shame stands for a family of emotions in much the same way as Metge (1986) indicated that the Maori word *whakamaa* encompasses a variety of emotions. However, as the work by Tangey and others suggested, there are sometimes detectable differences between emotions such as guilt and shame, but these vary according to the individual and according to the context. The work of Benedict (1946), Riesman and others (1950) agreed with that of later authors (Tomkins 1987; Nathanson 1997) who suggested that culture could be one of the contexts that lead to differences in the ways feelings are experienced. The consequences of experiencing shame and related emotions also vary. Nathanson (1997) pointed to withdrawal, attacking self, avoidance and attacking others as possible responses, and this analysis is remarkably similar to the outcomes identified by Tangney and her associates (Tangney 1991; Tangney *et al.* 1992, 1996) and to many of the responses to *whakamaa* described by Metge (1996).

Much of the literature reviewed in the first part has implications for the management of restorative conferencing. Metge (1986) pointed to the importance of the responses of others to feelings of shame if severe adverse consequences for the individual, the members of their group and/or others are to be avoided. Braithwaite and Mugford (1994) and Retzinger and Scheff (1996) suggested that, in the context of restorative conferences, it is important that there is support for those who feel shamed, to encourage apologies and to enable some movement towards forgiveness and acceptance back into the social group if outcomes are to be re-integrative and constructive.

Encouraging offenders to feel remorse about the harm they have caused and to apologize for what they have done are critical restorative values. What we have questioned is Braithwaite's choice of the words 'shame' or 'shaming' to describe the mechanisms used for invoking remorse. This may be just a semantic quibble, but we do not think so. It is the use of these words (and the ideas they arouse) which is at the root of some of the difficulties observed in translating the theory of re-integrative shaming into practice (the research on restorative conferencing within the Thames Valley police referred to earlier points to this).

In our research on re-offending (Maxwell and Morris 1999) we have pointed to the constructive potential of remorse and the destructive potential of stigmatic shaming. We also suggested that it may be empathy which triggers remorse, not shaming (disapproval) and so the emphasis for implementing restorative justice may need to be not on processes of shaming (disapproval) but on processes which focus on the consequences of offending for others (for families and communities as well as for victims) and on repairing the harm. The challenge is to get behind the rhetoric to understand what is going to produce constructive outcomes for young people.

Notes

1. To date, the evaluation of conferencing by the Thames Valley police is less positive but this is ongoing action research and practice is likely to have changed since the interim evaluations.
2. This construct was made up of the young person remembering the conference, completing the tasks agreed to, feeling sorry for what s/he had done and feeling that s/he had made good the damage done.

References

Anderson, S., Kinsey, R., Loader, I. and Smith, C. (1994) *Cautionary Tales: Young People,Crime and Policing in Edinburgh*. Aldershot: Avebury.

Aye Maung, N. (1995) *Young People, Victimisation and the Police: Summary Findings*. Home Office Research Study No. 140, London: HMSO.

Benedict, R. (1946) *The Chrysanthemum and the Sword: Patterns of Japanese Culture*. Boston: Houghton Mifflin.

Borgeaud, M. and Cox, C. (1999) 'The Most Dreadful Sentiment': A Sociological Commentary. Chapter 11 in M. Cox (ed.) *Remorse and Reparation*. London: Jessica Kingsley Publishers.

Braithwaite, J. (1989) *Crime, Shame and Reintegration*. Cambridge: Cambridge University Press.

Braithwaite, J. (1993) 'Shame and Modernity', *British Journal of Criminology*, 33: 1–18.

Braithwaite, J. (1997) 'Conferencing and Plurality': Reply to Blagg, *British Journal of Criminology*, 37: 502–06.

Braithwaite, J. (1999) Restorative Justice: Assessing 'Optimistic and Pessimistic

Accounts'. *Crime and Justice: A Review of Research* (vol. 25). Chicago: University of Chicago.

Braithwaite, J. and Mugford, S. (1994) 'Conditions of Successful Reintegration Ceremonies: Dealing with Juvenile Offenders', *British Journal of Criminology*, 34(2): 139–71.

Creighton, M. R. (1990) Revisiting Shame and Guilt Cultures: A forty-year pilgrimage. 18(3); Elhos; *Journal of the Society for Psychology Anthropology.*

Erikson, E. H. (1950) *Childhood and Society*. New York, Norton.

Garvey, S. (1998) 'Can Shaming Punishments Educate?, *The University of Chicago Law Review*, 65: 733–94.

Harris, N. (1999a) Can State or Civil Institutions Shame? Conference Paper presented at Restorative Justice and Civil Society, 16–18 February, Canberra.

Harris, N. (1999b) 'Shaming and Shame: An Empirical Analysis'. Unpublished PhD Thesis. Australian National University: Canberra.

Inkeles, A. and Levinson, D.J. (1969) 'National Character: The Study of the Modal Personality and Sociocultural Systems' in G. Lindzey and E. Aronson (eds) *The Handbook of Social Psychology (2nd edn)*. Cambridge, MA: Addison Wesley.

Karp, D. (1998) 'The Judicial and Judicious Use of Shame Penalties', *Crime and Delinquency*, 44(2), 277–94.

Lee, M. (1998) *Youth, Crime and Police Work*. Houndsmill: Macmillan.

Lemert, E. (1971) *Instead of Court: Diversion in Juvenile Justice*. Washington: US Government Printing Office.

Lewis, H. B. (1971) *Shame and Guilt in Neurosis*. New York: International Universities Press.

Loader, I. (1996) *Youth, Policing and Democracy*. Houndsmill: Macmillan.

Massaro, T. (1991) 'Shame, Culture and American Criminal Law', *Michigan Law Review*, 89: 1880–944.

Maxwell, G. M. and Morris, A. (1993) *Families, Victims and Culture: Youth Justice in New Zealand*. Wellington: Social Policy Agency and Institute of Criminology, Victoria University of Wellington.

Maxwell, G. M. and Morris, A. (1999) *Understanding Reoffending*. Wellington: Institute of Criminology, Victoria University of Wellington.

McCold, P. and Wachtel, B. (1998) *Restorative Policing Experiment*. Pipersville: Community Service Foundation.

Metge, J. (1986) *In and Out of Touch: Whakamaa in Cross Cultural Context*. Wellington: Victoria University Press.

Miller, S. (1996) *Shame in Context*. Hillsdale: Analytic Press.

Nathanson, D. L. (1997) 'Affect Theory and the Compass of Shame' in M. R. Lansky and A. P. Morrison (eds) *The Widening Scope of Shame*. Hillsdale: The Analytic Press.

Olthof, T. (2000) 'Shame, Guilt, Antisocial Behaviour and Juvenile Justice: A Psychological Perspective'. Paper presented at a Symposium 'Punishing Children', Utrecht, 8–9 June, 2000.

Retzinger, S. M. and Scheff, T. J. (1996) 'Strategy for Community Conferences: Emotions and Social Bonds' in J. Hudson and B. Galaway (eds) *Restorative Justice: International Perspectives.* Monsey: Criminal Justice Press.

Riesman, D., Glazer, N. and Denney, R. (1950) *The Lonely Crowd: A Study of the Changing American Character.* Princeton: Yale University Press.

Sabini, J. and Silver, M. (1997) 'In Defense of Shame in the Context of Guilt and Embarrassment', *Journal for the Theory of Social Behaviour,* 27(1): 0021–8308.

Sherman, L., Strang, H., Barnes, G., Braithwaite, J., Inkpen, N. and Teh, M. (1998) *Experiments in Restorative Policing: A Progress Report to the National Police Research Unit on the Canberra Reintegrative Shaming Experiment.* Canberra: Australian National University.

Tangney, J. (1991) 'Moral Affect: The Good, the Bad and the Ugly', *Journal of Personality and Social Psychology,* 61(4): 598–607.

Tangney, J. P., Wagner, P. E., Fletcher, C. and Gramzow, R. (1992) 'Shamed into Anger? The Relation of Shame and Guilt to Anger and Self-Reported Aggression', *Journal of Personality and Social Psychology,* 62(4): 669–75.

Tangney, J. P., Wagner, P. E., Hill-Barlow, D., Marshall, D. E. and Gramzow, R. (1996) 'Relation of Shame and Guilt to Constructive Versus Destructive Responses to Anger Across the Lifespan', *Journal of Personality and Social Psychology,* 70(4): 797–809.

Taylor, G. (2000) 'Guilt, Shame and Shaming'. Paper presented at a Symposium 'Punishing Children', Utrecht, 8–9 June 2000.

Thomas, A. (1999) 'Remorse and Reparation: A Philosophical Analysis' in M. Cox (ed.) *Remorse and Reparation.* London: Jessica Kingsley Publishers.

Tomkins, S. S. (1987) 'Shame' in D. L. Nathanson (ed.) *The Many Faces of Shame.* New York: The Guilford Press.

Vagg, J. (1998) 'Delinquency and Shame: Data from Hong Kong', *British Journal of Criminology,* 38: 247–263.

Walgrave, L. and Aertsen, A. (1996) 'Reintegrative Shaming and Restorative Justice', *European Journal on Criminal Policy and Research,* 4(4): 67–85.

Young, R. and Goold, B. (1999) 'Restorative Police Cautioning in Aylesbury – from Degrading to Reintegrative Shaming Ceremonies?', *Criminal Law Review,* 126–38.

Chapter 14

Peacemaking and community harmony: lessons (and admonitions) from the Navajo peacemaking courts[1]

L. Thomas Winfree Jr.

Introduction

World-wide interest in restorative justice has generated a remarkable body of literature in a relatively short time.[2] Proponents cite existing programmes and practices with deep roots in long-standing Western and non-Western cultural traditions. For example, Braithwaite (1999) describes the grounding of restorative justice concepts in the justice practices of the ancient Arabs, Greeks, Romans, and the Germanic peoples after the fall of Rome. He also notes that various religions, including Buddhists, Indian Hindus, Taoists and Confucianists, recognize the importance of restoring community harmony and balance after a wrongdoing or disruptive event. Braithwaite's insightful review of both the optimism and pessimism associated with restorative justice is essential reading for anyone seeking to understand this world-wide criminal-justice paradigm.

Others ground their descriptions of restorative-justice programmes in native or indigenous cultures, including North America's First Nations (Hoyle 1995; LaPrairie 1998, 1999; Linden and Clairmont 1998; Warhaft, Palys and Boyce 1999), the traditional inhabitants of New Guinea (Dinnen 1997), Australia's Aboriginal and Islander communities (O'Donnell 1995), and the Maori of New Zealand (Consedine 1995). Moreover, family conferencing practices in New Zealand, Australia and Canada also provide unique insights to the generalizability of restorative justice (Sarre 1999), as do many related programmes found in correctional settings (Bonta *et al.* 1998; Kurki 1999; Pranis 1997; Richardson and Galaway 1995). These extant programmes and practices, maintain the advocates of restorative justice, are more than a passing fad or temporary trend in justice administration. They are built on success models that have considerable potential for emulation by many different legal systems. Experimental and evaluative studies suggest that restorative justice may positively influence the lives of participants at all levels – victims, perpetrators, criminal-justice personnel and community members (cf., Bonta *et al.* 1998; Harris and Burton 1998; McCold and Wachtel 1998; Office of Juvenile Justice and Delinquency Prevention 1998; Richardson and Galaway 1995; Sherman *et al.* 1998).

One of the most interesting responses to restorative-justice pro-grammes derives from the cultural practices of Aboriginal peoples.[3] As Braithwaite (1999: 2) observes, 'Restorative justice has been the dominant model of criminal justice throughout human history for all the world's peoples.' This 'new' justice theory seeks to address the needs of the communities and victims through apology and reparation, with the ultimate goal being the reintegration of the offender into society. Gehm (1998), too, emphasizes the Aboriginal roots of a unique and distinct restorative justice theory. He notes that such groups, on many continents besides Europe and North America, 'have long held the view that conflicts such as criminal offences represent, foremost, a tear in the social fabric that must be healed' (Gehm 1998: 5). Gehm cites as examples the Maori's *wagga wagga* model and similar ones among the traditional Lakota and Dakota peoples of North America. He describes one form in detail:

> Victim and offender are brought together in the presence of one or more elders. The elder speaks first, discussing the rupture in the community that the offense represents, both symbolically and materially. All persons who have been affected in some way by the offense and its aftermath – friends, neighbors, relatives of the victim and of the offender – are allowed to speak, without interruption, both to others in the assembly as well as specifically to the victim and/or offender. Often, they describe the griefs they have suffered, their relationship to the parties, and finally, what they think ought to happen. Following these conversations, the larger group is invited to depart. In private, victim and offender must decide between themselves what is to be done to make things right. Once an understanding is reached, it is explained first to the community elders who then invite the larger group back into the meeting where the decision is announced jointly (Gehm 1998: 5).

The body of literature on Aboriginal practices and their connection to contemporary restorative justice is important for more than just the clarity of their humanistic philosophies about wrongdoing and wrongdoers. Indeed, many Aboriginal cultural practices address the restoration of harmony, balance or peace within a community. However, they also contain cautionary elements, ones that have been largely ignored by proponents of the restorative justice theoretical paradigm. For example, LaPrairie (1998) expresses concern that programmes of the 'new' restorative justice, based on Aboriginal models, are viewed as quick fixes for the problems created by mainstream society. Moreover, she fears that these approaches will be adopted promiscuously, with no real regard for the selection criteria. In fact, many discussions of Aboriginal restorative justice describe its unique and limited application to the communities that generated the paradigm, although even on this point ambiguity remains high (Warhaft *et al.* 1999). Dinnen (1997) describes attempts to control lawlessness and violence in Papua New Guinea, employing a method of restorative justice. These ideas, Dinnen notes, seem well fitted for the Melanesian social environment.

O'Donnell (1995) adds a key social control element to this discussion. In describing Australia's Aboriginal Mediation Initiative, she warns that the new ways must not 'bring about the loss of face or authority of key elders' (O'Donnell 1995: 100). The Aboriginal people have, O'Donnell further notes, responded 'enthusiastically to a procedure that resembles more, in its origins, traditional dispute resolution processes within Aboriginal society than Western legal traditions.' This cultural grounding and its sensitivity toward the role of elders is crucial. Citing Christie (1977), she goes on to say that Western legal traditions have 'stolen' conflicts from the people for whom they have great value, both as individuals and communities (O'Donnell 1995: 97). Traditional conflict resolution helps to define and hold together the community, as opposed to the Western tradition's view that conflicts fragment and destroy communities.

These analyses suggest that a more complete understanding of restorative justice lies in the indigenous values that originate, support, and orient them. This chapter reviews several key lessons derived from the restorative justice practices of one specific native American tribe, the Navajo Nation. These practices have been adequately described elsewhere (Bluehouse and Zion 1996; Tso 1996; Yazzie and Zion 1995). This chapter grounds the Navajo Peacemaker Courts within Western and Aboriginal legal thinking, and reflects on the promises and admonitions inherent in this unique restorative-justice practice. This focus seems warranted given the world-wide interest in this paradigm. Researchers suggest that Aboriginal peoples prefer restorative justice models grounded in their respective cultures (see, e.g., Hoyle 1995; O'Donnell 1995, *inter alia*). What does this statement suggest about employing restorative-justice models, with Aboriginal cultural roots (see, e.g., Bazemore 1998; Braithwaite 1999), in communities where the dominant legal tradition has strong ties to traditional Western legal traditions?

Underlying Aboriginal ideas and philosophy

Before moving to a discussion of the Navajo peacemaking court's philosophy, practice and purpose, a brief review of general North American Aboriginal ideas and philosophy seems prudent. Also, a *caveat* is in order: North America contains more than 500 different Aboriginal tribes and groups, and while they share many common beliefs, it would be a grave mistake to view them as a monolithic group.[4] Nonetheless, they share important views on spirituality, tribal will and certain customs and traditions, especially about their group ties to a Creator or higher spiritual being. All of these ideas help to shape their views on conflict and its resolution.

The exercise of power: comparisons and contrasts

A useful point of comparison is between what for the purposes of this chapter are called Euro-Western Socio-political traditions (hereafter referred to as Western traditions) and Aboriginal-Native American traditions (hereafter referred to as Aboriginal traditions).[5] For example, in Western traditions, authority refers to the power to act, judge and command. It is derived largely from the European system of feudalism, especially the latter's emphasis on the fundamental inequality of man (Boldt and Long 1984: 541). Authority was necessary to protect society against rampant self-interest. However, in the Aboriginal traditions, all tribal members are viewed as equals, a belief derived from the tribe's founding Creator. That is, the tribe's peace and harmony is the handiwork of the Creator, not the result of any individual or even the tribe itself. On the formulation of good governance, the two models are in fundamental disagreement as to its origin and application.

The two models' respective views on the origins of power clarify this basic disagreement about governance. Western traditions emphasize pyramidal hierarchy. Those at the top (or those with the most power) provide leadership. They are the ruling body, and they make the rules and enforce them. Those at the bottom (or those with the least power) are ruled with or without their consent. This arrangement is necessary to ensure distribution of privileges and the maintenance of social order. In contrast, Aboriginal traditions endorse the idea of the tribal will, a consensual approach to the application of customs and traditions solutions. This approach encompasses day-to-day issues and problems and, even larger, extraordinary situations that may threaten the entire tribe. The solutions flowed from the Creator in the form of customs and traditions, but it was up to the tribe as a whole to apply them. Enlightened Western traditions evolved the social contract as an egalitarian means to extend authoritative rule over the masses. Aboriginal traditions, with their emphasis on egalitarianism, recognized that no individual had dominion over the life of another. The tribe is held together, then, by a spiritual compact (Boldt and Long 1984: 542).

A third key comparative element involves the ruling entity. In Western traditions, those with the power rule and govern. Sovereign authority may be vested in a person (e.g., a monarch, chancellor, prime minister or president) or an impersonal entity (constitution or government) or both (Dumont 1996: 20). This arrangement is necessary to 'guarantee efficient distribution of wealth, property, and (with enlightenment) the equal benefit of accumulation of wealth and exercise of power along with the development of more egalitarian and humane political structures' (Dumont 1996: 20). According to Aboriginal traditions, the interests of the individual and the tribe are inseparable; self-interest is tribal interest. For example, individual tribal members, including healers, elders and even war chiefs, were given authority, but that power was typically limited and situationally defined, not broad and inclusive. Ceremonies which play a major role in the employment of rules also show a certain flexibility. Among the Navajos, for example, the Enemy Way ceremony was originally intended as a response to infection caused by contact with foreigners in war; however, in more recent manifestations, this traditional prayer wards off infections caused by any foreign contacts (Gill 1981: 101).

These comparisons help provide a social context for why Aboriginal peoples prefer ceremonies and practices grounded in their indigenous cultures (see Table 14.1). However, they also imply something more critical. As Boldt and Long (1984: 540) point out, 'key ideas contained in the European–Western doctrine of sovereignty are incompatible with core values comprising traditional Indian culture.' Dumont (1996: 21) suggests that 'the most appropriate development of constructs and mechanisms of justice among Aboriginal people would appear to be best derived from a culture-based approach.' If Western traditions, and their accompanying justice practices, are incompatible with Aboriginal traditions, it seems plausible that problems may lie in the other direction as well. That is,

Table 14.1. Sovereignty in Euro-Western development and Aboriginal North American tradition

Euro-Western development	Aboriginal N.A. tradition
1. *Personal authority* – power to act; judge and command; derived from European system of feudalism and, later, social contract.	1. *Spiritual compact* – equality for all tribal members derived from 'Creator's' founding prescription; a means to provide community harmony that is derived from a source outside the individual and the tribe.
2. *Hierarchical relationships* – those at the top (most powerful) provide leadership or are the ruling body; those at the bottom (least powerful) are 'ruled' with or without consent; this is necessary to ensure distribution of privileges and the maintenance of social order.	2. *Tribal will* – a consensual view of the application of traditional solutions to day-to-day issues and problems and extraordinary situations.
3. *Ruling entity* – those with the power to rule and govern; authority may be vested in a person (e.g., monarch or president) and/or an impersonal entity (constitution or government).	3. *Customs/tradition* – historically evolved way of dealing with problems, issues, and other social constructions; viewed as derived from the 'Creator.'
4. *KEYS*: belief in the inherent inequality of human beings, and community held together by social contract.	4. *KEYS*: no individual was viewed as having control over the life of another; community held together by spiritual compact.

Source: Dumont (1996: 20–22)

lifting specific restorative practices out of one culture and grafting them into another, different one may be a mistake. At a minimum, a more complete understanding of the core values system underlying these customs and practices is needed.

Traditional values systems of North American aboriginal peoples

Dumont (1993, 1996), using the values system found among the Ojibwa tribe, provides an excellent synthesis of traditional values. Central to this system, as both a pedagogical device and philosophical symbol, is the circle.[6] At the centre of the circle is vision, a gift from the Creator to Aboriginal people.[7] Vision refers to two ideas. First, an Aboriginal person has a special way of seeing the world, different from that used by non-Aboriginal people. The sky, the earth, the waters all have special meanings for Aboriginal people, meanings that those lacking this vision would not understand. For the Navajo, and many other tribal groups, these elements of nature are relatives, brothers and sisters (Tso 1996: 177). This kinship is more than metaphysical; it is real for Aboriginal peoples steeped in traditional values and culture.

Second, the gift of vision allows Aboriginal people to see beyond the physical world; they have a capacity for all-around, *circular vision*, a metaphysical construct foreign to many Western traditions outside of, perhaps, a religious context. This vision enables them to see the interconnectedness of all things, which in turn, generates respect. That is, if you understand the totality of all things in the universe and their interconnectedness, you have respect for them. According to Dumont (1996: 23), this respect becomes a primary motivator for all values flowing from the primal gift of vision: 'Respect conditions all other values, thus engendering *a unique value system with a unique interpretation and prioritizing of each value*' (emphasis added).

For example, the Navajo people see the universe divided into good (*hózh*) and evil (*hóch*).[8] The Navajo *diyin dine'é*, or holy people, were both *hózh* and *hóch*, good and evil. The *diyin dine'é* included the Wind, the Thunder, the Sun and the Rain. These holy people have great power (*bidziil*) and associated danger (*báhádzid*), qualities also found in the *Diné*, what the Navajo people call themselves. In fact, the distinction between holy people and self often becomes blurred. This duality is often confusing to non-Aboriginal people, particularly those schooled in Western religious traditions. It nonetheless reflects the gift of vision.

Vision and respect influence the following eight primary Aboriginal values, most of which play roles in Aboriginal conceptions of restorative justice: honesty, sharing, strength, kindness, humility, wisdom, honour and bravery. Honesty refers to the actions that are characterized by integrity, dignity and autonomy in all relationships. The quality of sharing reflects the Aboriginal belief in the interdependence and interconnectedness of all life. Generosity and communal cooperation flow naturally from this sharing. Strength is often misinterpreted by non-Aboriginal people. In concordance with other values, strength refers to an all-encompassing view of kindness and respect for the integrity of oneself and others. The goal of strength is to provide for harmony, balance and well-being within oneself and the entire community. Recall that the concept of self should be indistinguishable from that of community. Strength should not be confused with power, since power is, for the Navajo people in particular, paired with danger: there can be no exercise of power without incurring risk (Farella 1984: 37). Kindness is the potential for 'caring and the desire for harmony and well-being in interpersonal relations' (Dumont 1996: 24). The value of humility reflects relationship between the self and the Creator. The individual, and all of life, are all sacred and equal parts of the Creator. Humility leads to a general desire for good relations and balance with life. The idea of the Elder embodies the value of wisdom. Wisdom is said to be present when a person embraces and reflects all of the other values present in the system. Crucially, their own gift of vision, as guided by respect, allows Elders to see that same quality in others. Honour is a complex set of attitudes and orientations toward other persons and what are called 'other-than-humans.' Specifically, all matter of entities, including the earth, the water and sky, must be honoured. Lastly, the value of bravery includes the idea of courage; however, it is broader than personal courage in battle or against adversity. Rather, bravery should lead to something beyond the individual, including security, peace, harmony and balance for the community or tribe.

Most non-Aboriginal people will recognize and may embrace similar if not identical values. What makes them unique to Aboriginal culture is the role of vision and respect in recognizing the role they play in everyday life (Dumont 1996: 23). For example, Aboriginal people view sharing as generosity and respect for all living things; sharing helps maintain or restore balance in the world, let alone the community. Among Western cultures sharing is often viewed as an obligation, something done because 'it is the right thing to do,' but it does not interfere with the individual's pursuit of personal achievements and success (Dumont 1996: 26). Honesty, too, means different things to Aboriginal people and non-Aboriginals. The Aboriginal value system providing for vision and respect mandates honesty in all relationships, an emphasis on truthfulness and integrity for its own sake. Among Western traditions, however, honesty reflects a merger of truthfulness and respectability.

Persons steeped in Aboriginal culture and values would, in all likelihood run into trouble with non-Aboriginal systems of justice. Among Aboriginal people, the purpose of justice is to restore peace and equilibrium within the community. They bring to bear all the other values, calling upon them to work for this restorative goal. In Western traditions, conversely, the emphasis is on law and procedures as the means to right a wrong. When these different values, different views of the same physical properties found in the world, move toward each other, zones of conflict emerge (Dumont 1996: 27, 28–32). For example, among Aboriginal people payment of compensation to the victim (or next of kin) by the offender (or their tribe/clan) represents an attempt to restore balance. Such compensation may include crimes as serious as murder, a practice recognized in tribal Europe as the *wergild*. In Western traditions, such practices, if allowed, would be merged with some other sentencing option, including retributive incarceration, rehabilitation. Also, a typical Aboriginal response to the law, when formally accused of a crime, is to plead guilty, owing to both a concern for the value of honesty or possibly non-confrontational acquiescence (Dumont 1996: 32). In most Western traditions, the expectation is that one will enter a plea of not guilty: the burden of proof is on the state and the accused is assumed to be innocent until proven guilty.

Navajo peacemaking court

The Navajo are unlike most other North American Aboriginal groups. A common refrain is that 'Navajos are different: they're not like other Indians' (Bailey and Bailey 1986: 5). Navajos themselves believe that they are different. During the 1950s, many American Indians tribes viewed tribal differences as secondary to their concerns as native Americans. The Navajos continued to view themselves not as Indians first, but as Navajos. For example, if one was queried about his or her status as an American Indian, a common reply would be 'No, I am a Navajo' (Bailey and Bailey 1986: 6–7; personal observations of the author).

Navajo history and culture: a brief overview

The Navajos are among the most studied of all American Indians. One anthropologist claims that they are 'probably the most studied group of people in the world' (Farella 1984: 3). While this may be hyperbole, we know a great deal about their philosophy of life (Farella 1984), religion (Gill 1981), history (Bailey and Bailey 1986) and political treaties (Mitchell 1973). Yet they remain, in many ways, an enigma, a polite but closed society.

How is this apparent paradox – a well studied, yet little understood group – possible? Geography plays a major role. The Navajo Nation is in three US states: New Mexico, Arizona (the Nation's largest physical part) and Utah. Moreover, the Navajo lead a life-style that emphasizes low-density living. More than 160,000 Navajos, organized into five regional agencies, more than 50 clans, and 110 chapter houses, are spread over an area twice the size of Belgium.[9] Over eighty percent live in rural settings, mostly miles from their nearest neighbour. One-third of all Navajo housing structures have no bedrooms, which means they are either traditional hogans – one room thatch and mud structures – or modernized versions of traditional hogans.

The language and history of the Navajo hold more clues to their unique status among North America's Aboriginal peoples. The Navajo language is part of the Na-Dené group of 22 languages. One linguistic subfamily, consisting of 20 separate languages, is Athabascan (or Athapascan). Navajo is the largest Athabascan subgroup. Seventy-five percent of all Navajos speak their native language, and nearly half indicate that they do not speak English 'very well'. Socio-linguistically, the Navajos are linked to the Apachean group. They are also linguistically tied to other Athabascan groups in the Canada's Northwest Territory and the Yukon, and isolated Aboriginal groups in California, Oregon and Alaska in the United States.

The history of the Navajos before the Spanish is largely a matter of conjecture. Anthropologists who study Aboriginal migration patterns in North America cannot agree on the date of their arrival in the south-western region of North America. Sometime between 800 and 1550, Athabascan speakers occupied most of what is today Arizona and New Mexico. The name Navajo was apparently a place name, Nabajú, assigned to the *Diné* by Fray de Zárate Salmerón around 1626 (Bailey and Bailey 1986: 12). Sometime before the Pueblo Revolt against the Spanish in 1680, the Navajos were still semi-nomadic hunter–gatherers and occasional farmers. By the time the Spanish re-established control over New Mexico in 1696, the Navajo economy began shifting to herding livestock.

The Navajos, like their Apache brethren, were also warlike raiders, directing their wrath largely against the Spanish settlements. Alternating periods of war and peace characterized the eighteenth century, but raiding was always a constant. Sometime late in that century, the Navajos abandoned their traditional homelands, the *Dinetah*, heading west to what is today the Four-Corners area of Arizona, Utah, Colorado and New Mexico. They actively raided the non-Indian settlers in the area, seeking livestock. The Navajo, in turn, were raided by Utes and Comanches. Throughout this period, the Navajos continued to grow as a nation, expanding from a relatively stable population of 3,000 to 4,000 in the seventeenth and eighteenth centuries or so to between 8,000 and 12,000 in 1860 (Bailey and Bailey 1986: 19).

The Navajo War of 1863–64 broke the link between raiding and herding. Their size as an Indian nation and ferocity as raiders may well have contributed to the attention the Navajo received from the US Army. Largely abandoned at the start of the Civil War, the Army returned to the Territory of New Mexico in 1863, and immediately began an aggressive campaign against the Navajos. Led by Kit Carson, soldiers and armed civilians – aided by Ute and Pueblo Indians – butchered or stole over a quarter of a million Navajo sheep, cattle and horses, and killed or captured all the Navajos they could find (Bailey and Bailey 1986: 9–25; Mitchell 1973: 90).

Beginning in early spring of 1864, the first of more than 7,500 Navajo men, women and children began the 400-mile Long Walk to Bosque Redondo (Mitchell 1973: 74). The US government believed that the Navajos could be pacified on the arid and desolate reservation near Fort Sumner. To make matters worse, the Bosque had been taken from the Comanches, whose name in Navajo meant 'Many Enemies' (Mitchell 1973: 82). The current Navajo position on the Long Walk is that their troubles began because 'many of the people began to disrespect the traditional teachings and the need to live in harmony… As a result, the views and priorities of those that did not fully respect tradition took precedence and began to take on the leadership of the *Diné*' (Navajo Nation, 2000: 1).[10] The war and Long Walk were the result.

In 1868, after four years of virtual captivity, the death of many Navajos, and yearly costs exceeding one million dollars, the US government agreed that the Bosque Redondo resettlement was a failure. They signed the Treaty of 1868 which gave the Navajos reservation lands; in return, the Navajo adopted a peaceful way of life and abstained from raiding (Mitchell 1973). The US government, however, continued to control the social and legal lives of the Navajo Nation through the Bureau of Indian Affairs (BIA), a bureaucratic organization first organized under the Department of the Army and eventually transferred to the Department of the Interior.[11]

The evolution of Navajo courts details the extent of this control, and, provides a backdrop for the development of Navajo Peacemaker Courts. The first Indian courts in the US, called the Court of Indian Offenses, were created in 1883. Their specific purpose was to destroy Indian law and replace it with one controlled by the US government. Nine years later, the BIA created the Navajo Court of Indian Offenses (Aberle 1982). This court introduced to the Navajos the foreign idea that a judge, who is personally disinterested in the affairs before him, reacts to the events rather than guides them. Since Navajos, like many Aboriginal peoples, believed in community consensus, the Western concept of the judge was counter-intuitive and against their cultural mandates (Ladd 1957). By the 1940s, Navajo judges had 'adapted adjudication to the traditional method of discussing legal problems as a group' (Yazzie and Zion 1995: 68). A few years before, in 1934, the Roosevelt Administration offered to allow tribes the power to create their own courts; however, the Navajo Nation, having only been formally organized in 1923, elected to keep the BIA-controlled courts.

Beginning in the late 1950s, a sequence of events began a 30-year shift toward traditionalism for the Navajo courts. In 1958, the BIA issued an opinion that the Navajo Nation could not appoint or supervise judges; moreover, the state of Arizona moved to assert legal jurisdiction over criminal and civil actions on Navajo lands (Yazzie and Zion 1995: 68). The Navajo Nation Council, their governing body, created the Courts of the Navajo Nation, a judicial branch that to this day resembles the state courts in New Mexico, Arizona and Utah. However, in 1981, the leaders of the Navajo Nation expressed concern that the courts had adopted far too many non-traditional approaches to justice. A year later the Navajo Judiciary Committee created the Navajo Peacemaker Court (Yazzie and Zion 1995: 69). The next step toward increased traditionalism in judicial matters occurred in 1991, when Navajo judges adopted the Navajo Nation Code of Judicial Conduct. This code encourages them to use Navajo ethics and values regarding consensual agreement through discussion to conduct informal hearings. As Navajo Chief Justice Tom Tso (1996: 172), observes, prior to 1868 and the subjugation of the Navajo people, disputes were resolved by mediation. By 1991, the Navajo courts had come full circle, returning in principle to the idea of restoring justice by traditional values and methods.

Basic Navajo ideals and values

The purpose of the Navajo Peacemaker Courts was, in traditional terms, to 'slay the monsters'. To understand this idea, several other terms are important. First, beauty, harmony or balance is called *hózh*, although the term defies direct translation, as it also includes community peace and clan solidarity; its opposite construct, disharmony or chaos, is *hóch* (Farella 1984: 31–33; Gill 1981: 54–5). Disharmony occurs when things are not as they should be, and includes any form of conflict, injuries, slights or other wrongs. Given disharmony, the Navajo community must engage in a healing, or peacemaking, ceremony to restore itself to a state of *hózh*. This link between healing and peacemaking is crucial and signals a unique values system at work.

The idea of monsters, or *nayéé*, is crucial to Navajo philosophy and tradition. *Nayéé* represent any threat to individual or group harmony. 'It refers more to the subjective than to the objective, more to the internal than to the external' (Farella 1984: 51). As such they include such social problems as physical illness, worry, marital problems, poverty, depression, delinquency and crime. Monsters first emerged in the Navajo creation story (Zolbrod 1984). Life in the underworld, before First Man and First Woman appeared on the surface, was nasty, brutish and generally unpleasant; moreover, the sexes were separated. The *nayéé* were the offspring of women's acts of masturbation (Farella 1984: 53). As evil beings, they set about to destroy the holy people, or *diyinii*. Later, Changing Woman, the progeny of the primal couple, had twins by a *diyinii*, one of whom became *nayéé' neezghání*, or 'Monster Slayer' (Farella 1984: 53).

The significance of this element of the Navajo creation story is more than as a cultural artefact. For the Navajo, the monsters are both metaphorical or heuristic devices and intrapsychic processes or diseases. Many Singers, those entrusted with the ceremonies essential to eliminating disharmony, do not make this distinction, seeing all *nayéé'* as requiring identification and removal. An important part of the process of 'slaying the monster' is to learn the names, ways and habits of the monsters. In traditional methods, knowing the monster's identity helped direct the Singer to the correct ceremonial prayer (Farella 1984; Zolbrod 1984).

According to Yazzie and Zion (1995: 71–2), contemporary Navajo have come to realize that the work of the Navajo Nation trial courts reflects the monsters among them, including alcohol-related offences and personal violence. Learning the ways and habits of the monsters translates into the theories about alcoholism and domestic violence. A key element in this process is to address denial, the belief that nothing is wrong, that there is no problem (Yazzie and Zion 1995: 77). The person who helps the offending person overcome this denial must be a *naat 'annii*, a Navajo civil leader.

Also present in this equation is an underlying fundamental tenet of Navajo customary or common law.[12] Specifically, the *nalyeeh* addresses the victim's rights. This term refers to the demand that the injured party be made whole for an injury. The *nalyeeh* is also a process for reconciliation between the offender and the victim, 'whereby people in ongoing family, clan, and community relationships "talk out" their problems for resolution' (Yazzie and Zion 1995: 81).

Traditional Navajo justice

These elements – the monsters and monster slayer, the ceremonial prayer and the civil leader, and the *nalyeeh* – are at the core of the Navajo

Peacemaker Courts. They operate within a Navajo traditional justice model, one that is closely tied to the Navajo family structure. For example, mediation is a horizontal system, just as is the Navajo common-law legal system. Both are based on clan relationships.

The Navajos are matrilineal. All Navajos are members of their mother's clan ('born to'), but also have strong ties to their father's clan ('born for'). Family and clan members help resolve disputes through the employment of two forces. The first is k'e, a term that refers to a complex of values, including compassion, cooperation, unselfishness, peacefulness and other positive values (see Table 14.1). These values create an intense, diffuse, and enduring solidarity among clan and community members. The second force, k'ei, refers to the clan system of descent relationships and groups of relatives to whom a person is connected. What holds them together is the k'e. Hence, these two sets of forces, an internal and pervasive sense of solidarity and an extended-family system that is held together by the former, provide a strong moral base for the traditional justice model.

Any movement toward hóch (disharmony) is called hashkeeji, while hozhooji is movement toward hózh (harmony). The person who traditionally listens to disputes, trying to employ hozhooji, is called the naat'annii, an elder or person who speaks wisely and well. The idea of a Navajo 'talking' is well grounded in their traditions. As Tso (1996: 176) observes about those subjected to it: 'There were usually no repeat offenders. Only those who have been subjected to a Navajo "talking" session can understand why this worked.' Perhaps this is due to the fact that in the Navajo culture, words have far more connotative force than in English, the other language to which they are commonly subjected. More-over, how the words are said is just as important, hence the importance of the naat'annii.

These practices and beliefs are combined in the Navajo Peacemaker Court. The modern Navajo name for the peacemaker is the hozhooji naat'annii. The literal translation of this title is 'Peace and Harmony Way Leader.' This person is not a judge, at least not in the formal sense of the word. Today, the Peacemaker Courts operate in each of the Navajo Nation's seven Judicial Districts. Under each District Court is a Family Court. The Peacemaker Courts are a division of these Family Courts.

Peacemaking ceremony

The Peacemaking Court ceremony typically lasts between four to six hours. The hozhooji naat-annii (hereafter called the Peacemaker) relies on the Navajo concepts of illness and healing. The ceremony itself employs two main processes. First, the Peacemaker uses suggestive words and symbols to purify the 'patients,' or conflicting parties. Second, there is a reaffirmation of solidarities with the community and the deities. This second process makes the patients the centre of goodwill and reintegration within the group. Supernatural powers are invoked, first through the opening prayer and then by embarking on the *hozhooji* in an effort to drive out the evil forces causing the disharmony (*hóch*). The Peacemaker relies heavily upon the forces of *k´e*, meaning that this belief system must be a part of the participants' individual and collective world view. It is also important to observe at this point that there is no separation of church and state in Navajo traditional culture, nor in the Peacemaker Court.[13]

The ceremony moves through distinct stages. Peacemakers may not use coercion, but resort instead to authoritative persuasion. The first stage is an opening prayer, intended to summon the aid of the supernatural. This is followed by the diagnosis, which consists mainly of a verification or identification of the disharmony. The diagnosis stage allows the Peacemaker to explore the relative positions of the parties in the universe. The Peacemaker may next employ allegories and other lessons to teach Navajo values. These examples are not meant to shame the individual, but rather demonstrate politely how the parties have violated Navajo ways, breached solidarity, broken with *hózh* (harmony), and moved themselves and perhaps the entire community to a state of *hóch* (disharmony). The emphasis at this stage is on practical and pragmatic lessons. The next stage involves the plan, or *hozhoojigo*, which literally means 'to do things in a good way' or 'go in the right way'. Plans are very important cultural artefacts for Navajos.[14] The plan should be consensual and guide the participants on the path to harmony, through the process of *hozhooji*. To demonstrate the sanctity of the ceremony, the peacemaker offers a prayer at its conclusion (Bluehouse and Zion 1996: 185).

The significance of the opening and closing prayers cannot be overstated. The peacemaking ceremony has been likened to the Beautyway ceremony, a part of the general class of prayers called Holyway prayer acts (Gill 1981: 128–29). The phrase *'hózh hasahsdli'* is repeated four times during the ending prayer, meaning, roughly, 'the world is *hózh* (in harmony) again' (Farella 1984: 167). These statements reinforce the idea of healing and wholeness within a cultural context clearly understood by the participants.

Using the Peacemaking Court: a postscript

The extant literature on Peacemaker Courts suggest that the court is used for domestic or family issues, and includes domestic violence and incest, youth-gang activities, and alcohol-related problems (Bluehouse and Zion 1996; Yazzie and Zion 1995). Court statistics are difficult to find. In Fiscal Year 1993, the Family Court Domestic Relations caseload included 41 Peacemaker actions, 'which covered a wide variety of family disputes' (Yazzi and Zion 1995: 74). This was 2.2 per cent of the Family Court's business for that year.[15] Four years later, largely due to a federal grant to implement alternative dispute resolution programmes, the Navajos reported that its seven tribal court districts handled nearly 3,000 Peacemaking cases (Meyer and Zion 2000: 111).

The reluctance of the Navajo Nation to share a detailed accounting of their Peacemaker Court activities is understandable on several levels. First, recall that church and state are not separate entities; hence, the Peacemaking process involves sacred religious philosophy and practice. Thus, it is not something to be shared in great detail with outsiders. Second, the Navajos are a reticent and proud people. Sharing this kind of information would not be in their character.

A third generic reason may help understand the reticence of many Aboriginal peoples. Recently, many US Aboriginal groups have felt under siege on several fronts. For example, physical anthropologists, after reviewing skeletons found in Nevada and Oregon, initially stated that non-Indians may have settled in the region 9,000 years ago. Many tribes take this suggestion as an insult to their cultures and origin stories. Traditionalists also view the exhumation and analysis of human remains as a violation of their culture and rights.[16] In August, 2000, the US Bureau of Land Management made a preliminary determination that the Nevada remains, called Spirit Cave Man, were those of a Native American; however, as cultural affiliation cannot be determined, the remains stay in federal custody (Bureau of Land Management 2000). In September, 2000, the US Interior Department ruled that Oregon's Kennewick Man belong to five American Indian tribes; however, physical anthropologists threatened to sue the government to stop the return and secret reburial of the remains (Las Cruces *Sun-News*, September 26, 2000: A8). In southwestern Colorado, anthropologists completed a study of human bones found in an Anasazi dwelling. This dwelling provides the strongest evidence to date that, as the headline proclaimed, 'Some Ancient Indians tasted human meat' (Las Cruces *Sun-News*, September 7, 2000: A6). The Pueblo Indians of New Mexico, who are believed to be descendants of the Anasazi, view cannibalism as a horrific taboo.

They also view these anthropological queries as direct attacks on their culture.

We do have a partial window on Peacemaker Court practices. This comes from a study of Navajo police officers (Gould 1999). The Navajo Nation operates its own police force. They also have their own police academy, the only US Indian tribe with one. As of 1999, there were approximately 300 commissioned officers and 200 civilian support staff. Gould (1999) interviewed 25 commissioned officers of the Navajo Nation Police Department. He found two types of officers: those who are 'not Navajo enough' and those who are 'too Navajo'. In general terms, the former employ a Western Tradition in their work, while the latter express higher levels of traditional values and spirituality. He also found that both types relied upon European-type law more than Navajo Common Law. However, the officers who were 'too Navajo' also expressed strong interest in Peacemaking and other traditional methods of social control (Gould 1999: 68). This finding is not inconsequential since police officers at the scene could make recommendations about the use of Peacemakers for victims, offenders and family members of both. Tso (1996: 176) also shares the opinion that the Navajo's Anglo-based law enforcement system may be part of the problem rather than part of the solution, especially if its does not value traditional means. The police are, after all, a primary gatekeeper in the criminal justice process.

Summary

What can we learn from Aboriginal restorative justice? First, the restorative justice systems of Aboriginal peoples in North America, what we have called peacemaking, appears to be heavily grounded in unique cultural beliefs. These beliefs, their supporting values and norms, may make translation of peacemaking to non-Aboriginal people a difficult task (see, too, Braithwaite 1999: 82; Umbreit and Coates 2000). For example:

- aboriginal people emphasize solidarity and consensus; a spiritual compact between the People and the Creator;

- supernatural elements play important roles, as in prayers, sacred ceremonies and symbols, and pre-human creation stories;

- western justice concepts of independent and impartial judges are foreign to Aboriginal people, who prefer an involved elder as a guide, not a judge;

- there are strong ties between concepts of healing and peacemaking, ideas that are very similar to the 'medical model' in criminology that views crime as an illness and corrections as a treatment;

- the method seems best reserved for family-centred problems that can take advantage of family, clan and local community as support systems.

Second, some elements of peacemaking may be translated into non-Aboriginal communities. For example:

- the use of horizontal, rather than vertical, mediation systems places all participants on an equal footing and appeals to those espousing equality of treatment and power;

- the use of 'lay judges' – as is the case in Peacemaker Courts – may be both an economic and social plus: the practice costs less and it involves a wider segment of the community in the justice-seeking, peacemaking process;

- the emphasis on the victim's well-being fits into the current world-wide movement toward greater consideration of victim's rights;

- the emphasis on Peacemaker Courts for domestic and family issues fits well with many of the same problems confronting contemporary non-Aboriginal peoples;

- the emphasis on reintegration may assist the perpetrator, the victim and the larger community at this crucial juncture.

Ultimately, the strongest reasons to study this form of restorative justice may lie in two areas. First, peacemaking places the restorative justice concepts (e.g., harmony–disharmony, balance, peacemaking–healing) in an historical and cross-cultural context. It may be fruitful to consider similar analyses of other Aboriginal restorative-justice practices. Second, the Navajo judges view peacemaking as having macro-legal and micro-legal applications, both of which are unique and should be recognized. At the macro-level, the mere presence of these courts give credence to their culture, their way of living, and their system of common-law justice. It allows peacemakers to pass on these values, as teachers, to the Navajo nation through its applications to everyday life. At the micro-level, its use to help heal families, clans and communities also serves to make for a strong Navajo Nation. These goals are no less important in non-Navajo, non-Aboriginal societies. They are the goals of all legal systems.

Notes

1. The author would like to thank Finn-Aage Esbensen and Elmar G. M. Weitekamp for their help in preparing an earlier version of this work. Also, the editorial comments of James Maupin are acknowledged. Finally, the chapter was reviewed by an anonymous member of the Navajo Nation, the goal being to avoid embarrassing the author and the Nation by mistakes or misstatements. Ultimately, any errors are those of the author.
2. *Criminal Justice Abstracts*, a computer-based reference system, lists 47 separate entries under restorative justice, the first published in 1994 and the most recent in 1999. Even this list underestimates the number of publications. Several of the citations are edited works, including Bazemore and Walgrave (1999), Boutellier *et al.* (1996), Bowen and Consedine (1999), Burnside and Baker (1994), Sullivan and Tifft (1998), Eggleston (1999), Immarigeon *et al.* (1997), Jaccoud and Walgrave (1999), Jackson (1998); Sullivan *et al.* (1998), Walgrave (1998), and Zehr *et al.* (1997). Collectively, these 12 works contain more than 90 essays on restorative justice published in a six-year period.
3. Aboriginal means, quite literally, the first or original, and is often used to refer to the first human inhabitants of a given geographical area. As used in this chapter, the term is used instead of several optional terms for the Aboriginal peoples of North America, including First Peoples, Native Americans, and American Indians as those terms have other meanings as well. Which term do these first inhabitants of North America prefer? Actually, many prefer their tribal and clan names above all others.
4. Beyond the 500-plus tribes recognized by the United States government, others are seeking recognition. Adding those in Canada and Mexico pushes this figure significantly beyond 500 tribes.
5. This discussion owes much to the work of Boldt and Long (1984) and Dumont (1993, 1996).
6. Most Western–European cultures think linearly, as in 'we shall never pass this place again.' Many Aboriginal cultures visualize time and life, among many cultural elements, as a circle, with no beginning and no end.
7. Dumont (1996: 22, 23) also notes that the Ojibwa believe that the Creator gave the other 'colors of man' gifts as well. For example, white people received movement, black people were given knowledge, and yellow people were gifted time.
8. This discussion of Navajo beliefs and philosophy is taken from Farella (1984: 31–68).
9. By most estimates, the Navajos are the largest American Indian tribe in the United States.
10. The Navajo history of this time also notes that at their low ebb in the Bosque Redondo, the *Diné* held a traditional ceremony, which foretold of their return to the sacred homelands. A treaty was soon signed, the history continues, and upon their return home the crops were bad. The traditional religious leaders held a *Ndaa'* (Enemy Way) ceremony to remove the infection from outsiders. Soon after, harmony was restored and the crops were bountiful.

11. The Bureau of Indian Affairs was created in 1824 as part of the War Department, where it remained until 1849, when it was moved to the Home Department of the Department of the Interior. Today most positions within the BIA are staffed by American Indians.
12. By act of the Navajo Nation Supreme Court, the Navajos use the term 'common law' to refer to rules based on traditional philosophy and practices, or customary law (Tso 1996: 175).
13. Perhaps this observation helps us to understand the role of organized religion in establishing various restorative justice programmes throughout the world.
14. Navajo society recognizes, among others, war planners (*hashkeeji naat'aah*) and peace planners (*hozhooji naat'aah*). While these terms have other meanings (e.g., *hashkeeji naat'aah* can also be translated as war leader), the emphasis on planning is consistent with Navajo culture.
15. In 1994, the Navajo Nation initiated an aggressive anti-violence programme entitled 'Slay the Monster,' using Navajo and Federal funds. Hence, it is possible that Peacemaker Courts are used more frequently in the wake of this programme.
16. The US government is returning archaeological Aboriginal remains to their tribal descendants under the Native American Graves Protection and Reparation Act of 1990, although this process is slow and complicated. Moreover, those found prior to the enactment of federal legislation are very difficult to secure, especially if they are in private hands.

References

Aberle, D. F. (1982) *The Peyote Religion Among the Navajo.* Chicago: University of Chicago Press.

Bailey, G. and Bailey, R. G. (1986) *A History of the Navajos: The Reservation Years.* Santa Fe: School of American Research Press.

Bazemore, G. (1998) 'Restorative Justice and Earned Redemption: Communities, Victims and Offender Reintegration,' *American Behavioral Scientist,* 41(6): 768–813.

Bazemore, G. and Walgrave, L. (eds) (1999) *Restorative Juvenile Justice: Repairing the Harm of Youth Crime.* Monsey, NY: Criminal Justice Press.

Bluehouse, Ph. and Zion, J. (1996) 'Hozhooji Naat'Aanii: The Navajo Justice and Harmony Ceremony' in M. A. Nielsen and R. A. Silverman (eds) *Native Americans, Crime and Justice.* Boulder, CO: Westview.

Boldt, M. and Long, T. A. (1984) 'Tribal Traditions and European-Western Political Ideologies: The Dilemma of Canada's Native Indians,' *Canadian Journal of Political Science,* 17: 3–30.

Bonta, J., Wallace-Capretta, S. and Rooney, J. (1998) 'Restorative Justice: An Evaluation of the Restorative Resolutions Project'. Ottawa, Canada: Solicitor General of Canada.

Boutellier, H. *et al.* (1996) 'Special Edition: Restorative Justice and Mediation', *European Journal on Criminal Policy and Research,* 4(4): 7–130.

Bowen, H. and Consedine, J. (eds) (1999) *Restorative Justice: Contemporary Themes and Practice*. Lyttleton, NZ: Ploughshares Publications.

Braithwaite, J. (1999) 'Restorative Justice: Assessing Optimistic and Pessimistic Accounts' in M. Tonry (ed.) *Crime and Justice: A Review of Research*. Chicago, Illinois: University of Chicago Press.

Bureau of Land Management (2000) 'BLM Makes Spirit Cave Man Determination.' Release Number: 2000–79, available at www.nv.blm.gov/News.Releases/Press_Releases/fy_2000/PR_00-79.html

Burnside, J. and Baker, N. (eds) (1994) *Relational Justice: Repairing the Breach*. Cambridge, UK: Waterside Press.

Christie, N. (1977) 'Conflicts as Property.' *The British Journal of Criminology*, 17, 1–26

Consedine, J. (1995) *Restorative Justice: Healing the Effects of Crime*. Lyttleton, NZ: Ploughshares Publications.

Dinnen, S. (1997) 'Restorative Justice in Papua New Guinea', *International Journal of the Sociology of Law*, 25(3): 245–62.

Dumont, J. (1993) *Aboriginal Peoples and the Justice System*. Ottawa, Canada: Ministry of Supply and Services.

Dumont, J. (1996) 'Justice and Native Peoples' in M. A. Nielsen and R. A. Silverman (eds) *Native Americans, Crime and Justice*. Boulder, CO: Westview.

Eggleston, C. (1999) 'Special Edition: Restorative Justice in Correctional Education', *Journal of Correctional Education*, 50(2): 38–71.

Farella, J. R. (1984) *The Main Stalk: A Synthesis of Navajo Philosophy*. Tucson, Arizona: The University of Arizona Press.

Gehm, J. R. (1998) 'Victim–Offender Mediation Programs: An Exploration of Practices and Theoretical Frameworks.' Western Criminological Review 1 (1). [Online], available at wcr.sonoma.edu/v1n1/gehm.html

Gill, S. D. (1981) *Sacred Words: A Study of Navajo Religion and Prayer*. Westport, Connecticut: Greenwood Press.

Gould, L. (1999) 'The Impact of Working in Two Worlds and its Effect on Navajo Police Officers', *Journal of Legal Pluralism*, 44: 53–71.

Harris, N. and Burton, J. B. (1998) 'Testing the Reliability of Observational Measures of Reintegrative Shaming at Community Accountability Conferences and at Court', *Australian and New Zealand Journal of Criminology*, 31(3): 230–41.

Hoyle, M. L. (1995) '"A Fitting Remedy": Aboriginal Justice as a Community Healing Strategy' in K. M. Hazlehurst (ed.) *Popular Justice and Community Regeneration: Pathways of Indigenous Reform*. Westport, CT: Praeger.

Immarigeon, R. *et al.* (1997) 'Special Issue: Restorative Justice – Part 2', *ICCA Journal on Community Corrections*, 8(2): 13–50.

Jaccoud, M. and Walgrave, L. (eds) (1999) 'Special Edition: Restorative Justice', *Criminologie*, 32(1): 3–160.

Jackson, P. (ed.) (1998) 'Special Issue: Restorative Justice: Theory Meets Practice', *Western Criminology Review*, 1(1): 1–140.

'Kennewick Man Skeleton Belongs to Indian Tribes.' (September 26, 2000). Las Cruces *Sun-News*. A8.

Kurki, L. (1999) 'Incorporating Restorative and Community Justice into American

Sentencing and Corrections', *Sentencing and Corrections: Issues for the 21st Century*. Washington, DC: Department of Justice.

Ladd, J. (1957) *The Structure of Moral Code: A Philosophical Analysis of Ethical Discourse Applied to the Ethics of the Navaho Indians*. Cambridge: Harvard University Press.

LaPrairie, C. (1998) 'The 'New' Justice: Some Implications for Aboriginal Communities', *Canadian Journal of Criminology*, 40(1): 61–79.

LaPrairie, C. (1999) 'Some Reflections on New Criminal Justice Policies in Canada: Restorative Justice, Alternative Measures, and Conditional Sentences', *Australian and New Zealand Journal of Criminology*, 32(20): 139–152.

Linden, R. and Clairmont, D. (1998) *Making It Work: Planning and Evaluating Community Corrections and Healing Projects in Aboriginal Communities*. Ottawa, Canada: Solicitor General of Canada.

McCold, P. and Wachtel, B. (1998) *Restorative Policing Experiment: The Bethlehem, Pennsylvania Police Family Group Conferencing Project*. Bethlehem, Pennsylvania: Real Justice.

Meyer, Jon'a F. and Zion, J. (2000) 'Navajo Nation' in G. Barak (ed.) *Crime and Crime Control: A Global View*. Westport, CT: Greenwood Press.

Mitchell, M. (1973) *The Navajo Peace Treaty 1868*. New York: Mason Lipscomb Publishers.

Navajo Nation (2000) 'The Long Walk', available at navajo.org/lwalk.html

O'Donnell, M. (1995) 'Mediation within Aboriginal Communities: Issues and Challenges' in K. M. Hazlehurst (ed.) *Popular Justice and Community Regeneration: Pathways of Indigenous Reform*. Westport, CT: Praeger.

Office of Juvenile Justice and Delinquency Prevention (1998) 'Implementing the Balanced and Restorative Justice Model'. Washington, DC: National Institute of Justice.

Pranis, K. (1997) 'Peacemaking Circles', *Corrections Today*, December, 72, 74, 76, 122.

Richardson, G. and Galaway, B. (1995) 'Evaluation of the Restorative Resolutions Project of the John Howard Society of Manitoba: Final Report'. Winnipeg, Canada: University of Manitoba.

Sarre, R. (1999) 'Family Conferencing as a Juvenile Justice Strategy', *Justice Professional*, 11(3): 259–96.

Sherman, L. *et al.* (1998). 'Experiments in Restorative Policing: A Progress Report to the National Police Research Unit'. Canberra, Australia: Australian National University.

'Some Ancient Indians Tasted Human Meat' (September 7, 2000), Las Cruces *Sun-News*, A6.

Sullivan, D. and Tifft, L. (eds) (1998) 'Special Issue: Criminology as Peacemaking', *Justice Professional*, 11(1–2): 5–212.

Sullivan, D., Tifft, L. and Cordella, P. (eds) (1998) 'Special Issue: The Phenomenon of Restorative Justice', *Contemporary Justice Review* 1(1): 1–66.

Tso, Chief Justice Tom (1996) 'The Process of Decision Making in Tribal Courts' in M. A. Nielsen and R. A. Silverman (eds) *Native Americans, Crime and Justice*. Boulder, CO: Westview.

Umbreit, Mark S. and Coates, R. B. (2000) *Multicultural Implications of Restorative*

Justice: Potential Pitfalls and Dangers. Washington, DC: Office for Victims of Crime.

Walgrave, L. (ed.) (1998) *Restorative Justice for Juveniles: Potentialities, Risks and Problems*. Leuven, Belgium: Leuven University Press.

Warhaft, E. B., Palys, T. and Boyce, W. (1999) 'This Is How We Did It: One Canadian First Nation Community's Efforts to Achieve Aboriginal Justice', *Australian and New Zealand Journal of Criminology*, 32(2): 168–81.

Yazzie, R. and Zion, J. W. (1995) '"Slay the Monsters" Peacemaker Court and Violence Control Plans for the Navajo Nation' in K. M. Hazlehurst (ed.) *Popular Justice and Community Regeneration: Pathways of Indigenous Reform*. Westport, CT: Praeger.

Zehr, H. *et al.* (1997) 'Special Issue: Restorative Justice', *Corrections Today*, 59(7): 68–114.

Zolbrod, P. G. (1984) *Diné Bahanè: The Navajo Creation Story*. Albuquerque, New Mexico: University of New Mexico Press.

Chapter 15

From philosophical abstraction to restorative action, from senseless retribution to meaningful restitution: just deserts and restorative justice revisited

Ezzat A. Fattah

The current rhetoric of just deserts is a curiously abstract, formal doctrine, divorced from social context and from any vision of social objectives beyond 'law and order', which it does not obviously or easily achieve ... If we divorce the notion of proportionate penalties from social context and social purpose, we are left with little more than punishment (or as Christie (1982) reminds us, the graduated infliction of harm or pain) without any clear vision of what it is trying to achieve.

Peter Taynor (1997: 255)

Introduction

What could be a better time than the beginning of a new millennium to re-examine and assess society's sacred cows and other social institutions that have been in place for hundreds of years? One of those archaic and antiquated institutions is the current criminal justice system, a vestige from a bygone era. There is a consensus that the system is not achieving its goals. And what better proof of its dismal failure in preventing crime and deterring potential offenders than the record numbers of people in prison in many countries? As a result of ridiculously low clearance rates and of the attrition in the criminal justice process, only a tiny fraction of all those who commit crimes, particularly property offences, face charges before the courts and even a smaller fraction end up being punished (Fattah 1997). Estimates of the size of the latter group range from as low as 1 per cent to an optimistic estimate of 10 per cent. Something must be terribly wrong with a system that promises victims to punish their offenders and fails to deliver nine times out of ten. So what exactly is wrong with the system? One of the major problems is the system's notorious resistance to change.

In the nineteenth century, philosophy gave birth to a new group of sciences: the social sciences. The emergence of those sciences signalled not only a significant scholarly progress, but also the move from the abstract to the concrete, from fiction to reality, from the speculative to the empirical, from the theological to the sociological, and from the metaphysical to the psychological and criminological. Although the evolution of the social sciences has been quite remarkable, the criminal law and the criminal justice system remained somehow frozen in time. They continued to be based on, and to operate according to, the abstract philosophical and metaphysical notions of the Age of Enlightenment. They remained largely impenetrable to the theories and research findings of the new sciences. The abstract, philosophical goals of expiation, atonement and retribution remained paramount, and little or no attempt was made to gear the criminal-justice system toward the achievement of social objectives such as reconciliation, restoration, reparation and reintegration. Rather than seeing justice as the means by which peace and social harmony are restored, by which the social ties and bonds severed by the offence are rebuilt and reinforced, 'justice' continued to dispense punishment according to divine criteria and to pursue abstract and unattainable goals.

But like everything else, justice paradigms have to change because they are neither permanent, immutable nor transcendental. Justice paradigms have to change with social evolution in order to remain in harmony with the prevailing belief systems and to take stock of whatever advances and discoveries are achieved in the fields of criminology, victimology and penology. The goals of expiation and atonement, borrowed directly from theology, are no longer in tune with the realities and the beliefs of the secular, technological, post-industrial society of the twenty-first century. No wonder that the notions of malicious intent, *mens rea* and pre-meditation have been abandoned in entire sectors of the criminal code to be replaced by modern notions such as negligence, recklessness, endangerment etc. Slowly but surely, the criminal law is shifting from a guilt orientation to a consequence orientation (Fattah 1993, 1995). According to Wooton (1963), ninety per cent of the offences that come before the criminal courts no longer require intent but are strict liability offences. In modern secular societies, the notions of risk and harm are gradually replacing those of evil, wickedness and malice, and are bound therefore to become central concepts in the social and crime policies of the future. Future policies of crime control will be largely based on risk assessment, risk management, risk coverage, risk reduction and risk prevention. The primary aims of such a response will be redress, reparation and compensation. My guess is that the arbitrary and artificial distinction between crimes and civil torts will disappear, and that the artificial boundaries that have been erected over the years between criminal courts and civil courts will be removed. All harmful actions will generate an obligation to redress coupled with endeavors to prevent their future occurrence. This will be the era of restorative justice (Fattah 1998, 1999a, 1999b, 2000a, 2000b).

Restorative justice is justice that has redress to the victim as one of its primary goals, whether or not the offender has been detected, arrested or charged. It is justice that stipulates that it is society's obligation, the society that has failed to protect the victim or to find the culprit, to redress the harm done to the victim. It is justice for victims with the active partici- pation of those victims. It is justice that recognizes their plight and affirms their rights. It is justice that ensures that their wishes are respected, their needs are met and their expectations are fulfilled. But rather than moving in this progressive direction and attempting to achieve a truly sociological justice, the last two decades of the twentieth century were characterized by certain reactionary trends.

Under the influence of conservative politicians, supported by a few academics, the so-called utilitarian goals of punishment were practically abandoned. Punishment, under the attractive, but deceiving, label of 'just deserts' is being meted out for the sole purpose of inflicting pain and suffering on offenders, who, more often than not, are victims themselves. Even the Scandinavian countries, whose tolerance and readiness to forgive used to be the envy of other nations and who were the front- runners in penal reform, did not seem to be immune to the punishment wave that was sweeping the Western world. They reluctantly followed the popular trend and with no positive results to show for the heavy human, social and material sacrifices that are being made in the name of punishment (Fattah 2000a).

It is not difficult to show that punishment in the present day has no utilitarian purpose. It is punishment for the sake of punishment. It is punishment devoid of context, purpose or vision. How effective is punish- ment in deterring or preventing crimes of negligence or recklessness? Does it make sense to punish strict liability offences in the absence of any empirical evidence showing that punishment can and does reduce the incidence of those offences? One has to wonder about the utility, or rather the futility, of imposing retributive sanctions, whether a prison sentence or a penal fine destined for the public treasury, on those guilty of un-intentional offences? Wouldn't restorative justice solutions be a much better alternative to those retaliatory sanctions?

How surprising it is, therefore, to hear in the twentieth and twenty-first century, eminent scholars defending the penal philosophy of the eighteenth century. What could be more regressive than to try in this day and age to promote the notion of 'retributive justice' and sentencing principles such as 'just deserts', when thousands of years ago Greek philosophers like Plato, Aristotle and Socrates denounced vengeful punishment and insisted that punishment can only be inflicted to achieve utilitarian goals. What redeeming value does 'just deserts' have, and what useful or utilitarian purpose does it serve other than providing a euphemism for institutional revenge?

Proponents of 'just deserts' who criticize the principles and practices of restorative justice for allegedly undermining the theological doctrine of retribution, are not too different from Pope Pius IX. Pius IX in a 'Syllabus of Errors' (published in 1864) condemned the development of what he called the 'false principles' of the Liberal Age, which he believed were undermining the Catholic faith. Among the 'false principles' he cited was the 'freedom of religious thought and expression, freedom of conscience and the separation of Church and State'. How similar is his position to that of the high priests of 'just deserts' who stubbornly defend an outdated, anachronistic and discredited doctrine. How similar is his position to that of those who stubbornly continue to support the archaic, barbaric and paganistic ritual of the death penalty, claiming that its abolition will undermine respect for law and order!

Surprisingly, many of those who oppose the notion of restorative justice and continue to demand retribution, even for non-violent crimes, have no problem accepting administrative or civil remedies for various types of corporate, white collar and professional crimes, and voice no objection to the civil regulation of corporate wrongdoing.

Unfortunately for society, most influential people – politicians, policy-makers, bureaucrats, and even scholars and academics – prefer to live in the past and to cling to the false security of conventional practices. Many suffer from misoneism, the fear of everything that is new or different. For them, every innovation is threatening, every new idea is a dangerous idea, and every new paradigm is an unwelcome change. This resistance to change, sad to say, is endemic in criminal justice circles. Worse still is the prevailing lack of vision, the reluctance or outright refusal to re-examine, re-evaluate and rethink the system's underlying values, principles and philosophy, or to contemplate a radical and sweeping reform.

Luckily, however, there are those few who are able to look into the future and envision something totally different, something far better, a world without punishment, without prisons and with much less suffering. A world where the commitment to freedom renders imprisonment, by definition, a cruel and unusual punishment. They envision a society where social norms and moral values are not coercively enforced but are readily accepted and willingly respected. They envision a state that does not take a life for a life, does not deliberately inflict pain on wrongdoers, and does not treat those who violate existing laws as human waste or social junk. They envision a state that does not base its prevention policy on fear, threats and intimidation, a state that does not base its penal policy on elimination, segregation, incapacitation and incarceration.

Is a theory of justice possible?

Recent literature on justice models and paradigms is replete with new and old terminology. Among the terms used one finds: retributive justice, restorative justice, peace-making justice, transformative justice, informal justice, healing justice, satisfactory justice, real justice, relational justice, positive justice, etc., etc. Authors go to great length trying to define, describe and explain each adjective, but hardly any effort is made to explain the noun itself, as if justice can be universally defined or uniformly applied, as if the term is self-evident or self-explanatory.

This is surprising because to my knowledge there is no agreed-upon definition of justice. What is justice? Is there such a thing as 'natural justice'? Is justice a universal concept? Do people in different cultures share the same understanding of what justice is? Are there cultural variations in the perceptions of justice and in defining its requirements? How exactly do groups and communities that have escaped the influence of Western theological and moralistic teachings understand the word 'justice'? Do they, in fact, have in their native language a term equivalent to the Western term 'justice'?

What is badly needed are sociological and cross-cultural studies aimed specifically at discovering the notions, the conceptions and the ideas of justice among various communities, in particular communities that are as close to the state of nature as can be. How surprising it is that studies of the notion of justice among the indigenous communities in Australia, New Zealand, Papua New Guinea, or among Canada's First Nations are so hard to find, despite the geographical proximity of those communities to many of the scholars who are interested in, and advocating, restorative justice. And yet it can be argued that justice is neither a theological nor a philosophical concept, but a sociological concept in the true sense of the word.

Despite the lack of those fundamental studies, many authors have been talking about, or even proposing, a theory of justice, essentially a Western ethnocentric justice theory (Rawls 1971). But is it correct to speak of a 'justice theory'? Is it possible to formulate a theory of justice? A theory is a scholarly construct aimed at explaining a natural, social or behavioural phenomenon. It is a construct that lends itself to empirical testing and validation. According to Webster's Twentieth-century Dictionary, 'a theory is a formulation of apparent relationships or underlying principles of certain observed phenomena which has been verified to some degree.' A theory requires a valid proof of its acceptance and this is what distinguishes theory from a hypothesis or mere speculation. It is possible therefore to talk about a criminological theory formulated to explain crime or delinquency or a penological theory such as 'deterrence theory' which maintains that the fear of punishment or the actual experience of punishment does deter people from committing crime.

Justice, however, is neither a phenomenon nor a theory. It is an idea, or better still, an ideal. Justice is a subjective feeling, and this is precisely why a theory of justice seems no more possible or feasible than a theory of love or hate. This is not to say that it is not possible to study and to analyse methods of conflict resolution and dispute settlement in different communities. It is not to deny the possibility of discovering what may be described as a philosophy of justice, or developing a justice paradigm or a justice model. But to call retribution or 'just deserts' a theory is an affront to our intelligence and to our scholarly understanding of what constitutes a theory. Retribution is not a theory! It is nothing more than a philosophical justification for the deliberate infliction of pain and suffering on a fellow human being. And the justification is not only ethically flawed, it is also morally indefensible. Others may agree or disagree, but in my humble opinion there is a huge difference between philosophizing and theorizing. Academics, however, are fond of theory and always want to believe that they have invented one that will withstand the test of time. In the 1960s, an American professor published a criminology textbook in which he offered what he surely believed was the criminological equivalent to Einstein's theory of physics: a theory of relativity. What he called a theory was nothing more than a number of disjointed, banal and rather axiomatic statements about crime.

The field of restorative justice has also suffered from some misguided, though well-intentioned, attempts to develop a theory. Those endeavours could better be described as armchair philosophizing than genuine efforts to explore the various sociological and cultural meanings of justice. The result was something akin to a normative theory of justice. A normative theory of justice is a contradiction in terms because it does not fit, and is in fact at odds with, the true definition of what a scientific theory is all about. While normative theory is not really a theory for the reasons mentioned above, it is always possible to develop a theory of norms, that is, a theory that seeks to explain the origins of social and cultural norms, the functions of those norms, their changeability over time, their variability in space, etc. In other words, there is a difference between the setting of norms, which is a normative exercise, similar to what the penal code does, and the sociological study and analysis of norms, which is a scientific enterprise. Setting norms does not a theory make. Anomie theory, for example, is a theory about norms but is not a normative theory. The same is true of a theory of social reaction to crime and deviance or a theory of social control. But a normative theory is no more possible than an ethical theory. Formulating ethical, moral or legal principles is different from formulating a scientific theory. The ten ethical principles, with which I concluded my paper at the 10th Victimology Symposium in Montreal (Fattah 2001) are just that: principles. They are not a theory; they are nothing more than ethical desiderata.

Is fair and just punishment feasible?

Whether one refers to the writings of classical retributivists like Kant and Hegel or contemporary retributivists such as H. J. McClosky, C. W. K. Mundle, or J. G. Murphy, they all insist that for punishment to be just it has to be efficacious, profitable and necessary. It also has to be within limits and proportional to the offence being punished. None of those conditions is met by the punishments being meted out by the criminal courts in our countries at present.

It would be foolhardy to challenge, or to argue against, the overwhelming empirical and historical evidence and to maintain that punishment is effective. And it would simply be ludicrous to claim that punishment is profitable. Punishment might have been profitable at the time of penal servitude or when convicts were forced to perform horrendous tasks in exchange for bread and water. Punishment cannot be profitable when the average annual cost of keeping an inmate in a Canadian maximum-security institution is close to 100,000 DM.

Is punishment necessary? The onus of proof rests upon those who claim it to be; they are the ones who have to show that there is no viable alternative, that punishment is the only way, or the best way. This is because punishment is the deliberate infliction of pain, and inflicting pain, as Nils Christie (1982) pointed out, is a serious matter that is often at variance with cherished values such as kindness and forgiveness. And it is for this reason that philosophers, since ancient times, have industriously engaged their brains and exhausted their wits trying unsuccessfully to come up with some valid justification for punishment.

As none of the conditions required by the philosophers and retributivists is being met, the inevitable conclusion is that the punishments that are daily dispensed by the criminal justice system are unjust, and thus cannot be ethically condoned or morally defended.

And while the requirements of efficacy, profitability and necessity do not withstand any empirical test, it is the condition of proportionality that can never be met by punitive sanctions, particularly imprisonment. Almost two decades ago, in an article published in the *Canadian Journal of Criminology* (Fattah 1982), I went to great length to explain how impossible it is to make a prison sentence proportional to the offence being punished. And yet, imprisonment continues to be used as the primary means of retribution. This despite the fact that it is totally impossible to rationally or equitably determine what prison term is a fair expiation for an attack on property, or to create an equitable balance between physical and sexual assaults and a given number of days, months or years in prison. Despite well-meaning attempts such as 'the justice model', 'the principle of commensurate deserts', 'the presumptive sentence', the arbitrariness of such equation is both evident and inevitable. Yes, it is possible to grade various criminal offences according to their objective and/or perceived seriousness. However, to come up with a prison term equivalent to theft or robbery, to assault or rape, is inevitably arbitrary, capricious and despotic. As the inherent problem of equating the amount of deprivation of liberty with the degree of moral guilt of the offender, or with the extent of the harm done, has never been solved, the capricious determination of the length of imprisonment is left either to the arbitrariness of legislators or the discretion of sentencing judges, with all the disparities and inequities that ensue. That we continue to accept and to apply a punishment that poses such insoluble ethical, fairness and equity problems is, sad to say, a clear indication that we are more committed to the justice principles of the eighteenth century than we are to the egalitarian and human rights principles of the twentieth century.

Suppose it is argued that punishment will be proportionate not to the seriousness of the offence but to the moral responsibility of the offender. Could this proposition serve as a basis for a more equitable system of punishment? The answer, needless to say, is a categorical *no*. This is because the degree of moral responsibility of the offender, which is unique for every accused, can never be quantified or measured. It is therefore a serious scientific error to advocate a sentencing system which supposedly will dispense varying dosages of punishment on the basis of an abstract notion (moral responsibility) that is neither susceptible to quantification nor measurement (Fattah 1992: 78).

Nor is fairness and equality achieved when the determination of punishment is made solely on the basis of the nature and the seriousness of the offence being punished. It is neither fair nor equitable to give those found guilty of identical or similar crimes identical prison sentences. The same prison term does not entail the same amount of pain and suffering, does not involve identical deprivations, and does not carry with it the same consequences to different offenders. The pains and consequences of imprisonment are far different even when offenders are kept in the same institution, in similar conditions, for the same length of time. As long as it remains impossible to measure the pains of imprisonment (Sykes 1971) and to weigh the sufferings and deprivations resulting from it for each individual offender, the use of incarceration as a retributive sanction will never ever be justified in a democratic and just society.

The inherent unfairness and arbitrariness of a sentencing system based on the questionable premise of just deserts was highlighted by Thomas Gabor (1998: 85) who pointed out that:

A sentencing system based on desert might not be so objectionable were commensurate or proportional sentences as readily quantifiable as justice-oriented sentencing guidelines suggest. These highly systematized schemes promote the illusion that there is a fairly precise penalty fitting each type of offence.

Like the philosophers of the classical school who were genuinely concerned with the abuses of the judicial system, proponents of models such as 'just deserts', 'determinate sentence', 'presumptive sentence' thought of them as a possible remedy to the appalling sentencing disparities and as a way of introducing some degree of fairness and equity into an inherently unjust system. Those contemporary scholars, however, were guided by the same naive conviction that led classical thinkers to believe that only a system of fixed punishments would eliminate the injustices and inequities of the old regime. The attempt to revive the simplistic ideas of classical thinkers was evident in the report of the Committee for the Study of Incarceration in the USA (von Hirsch 1976). Members of the Committee could not conceive of individualization without disparity and therefore retreated from the idea of individualized justice. Rather than suggesting solutions to the problem of sentencing disparities, they opted instead for a greater mechanization of justice. The basic problem, however, lies not in disparity but in having retribution as the goal of punishment. And to achieve the abstract goal of retribution mechanized justice is neither fairer nor more just than discretionary justice.

What is wrong with those well-meaning legal scholars is their inability to envision a society that does not punish. Nor are they alone in this thinking. The idea of doing away with punishment altogether is not acceptable even to most criminologists. But there are a few who believe that a punishment-free society is not only possible but is at hand, and that it may come into being sooner than we think. In her presentation of a feminist vision of justice, Harris (1991: 94) questioned the unshakeable faith in the necessity of punishment. She writes:

Indeed, we need to question and rethink the entire basis of the punishment system. Virtually all discussion of change begins and ends with the premise that punishment must take place. All of the existing institutions and structures – the criminal law, the criminal processing system, and the prisons – are assumed. We allow ourselves only to entertain debates about rearrangements and reallocations within those powerfully constraining givens … The sterility of the debates and the disturbing ways they are played out in practice underscore the need to explore alternative visions. We need to step back to reconsider whether or not we should punish, not just to argue about how to punish.

The Canadian Sentencing Commission

In the late 1980s, Canada had the misfortune of having a so-called 'Sentencing Commission' which I believe was set up by the conservative government of the time in order to move Canada in the same punitive/ retributive direction that had already been established in the UK and the United States. The Commission blatantly ignored the recommendations of critics of retribution, like myself, who wanted to use the opportunity to affirm the superiority of the restorative justice model, and issued a report that was reactionary, flawed and strongly biased in favour of one specific sentencing philosophy: 'just deserts'. Surprisingly, this was the time when the victim movement was in full swing and there was a growing awareness of victims' plight and of the need to recognize their rights. In such a climate favourable to victims' concerns, one would have expected the Sentencing Commission to affirm that the primary goal of sentencing is to repair the harm done to the victim by the offence and to prevent future harm. Instead, the Commission opted for some abstract goals characteristic of a right-wing philosophy of justice, goals that can only lead to the depersonalization and dehumanization of the justice system. It stated that

> ... the fundamental purpose of sentencing is to preserve the authority of, and promote respect for, the law through the imposition of just sanctions (Canada 1988: 151).

Not a mention of victims, their needs and/or their rights, not a word about providing redress to the victims, *nothing*! Some years later, the Commission's statement was adopted almost verbatim and became part of Section 718 of the Canadian Criminal Code declaring that sentencing has as its fundamental purpose 'to contribute ... to respect for the law and the maintenance of a just, peaceful and safe society by imposing just sanctions'.

In a brief I submitted to the *House of Commons Standing Committee on Justice and Solicitor General* in March 1988, I made some comments on the Sentencing Commission's report. I said:

> In an era meant to become the golden age of the victim, there seems to be a growing obsession with punishment, euphemistically called 'just deserts'. *Yet having punishment as the central focus of our criminal justice system is neither morally legitimate nor practically effective.* It can only act to the detriment of the victim. Dispute settlement, mediation, reconciliation, arbitration, reparation, are concepts foreign to a system based on punishment, a system that regards the crime not as a human action but as a legal infraction. The operation of such a system acts to intensify the conflict rather than solving it. And instead of bringing the feuding parties together it widens the gap that separates them. (Fattah 1988.)

The point I was trying to make, as far back as 1988, is that the philosophy of 'just deserts' neither serves the interests of crime victims, nor does it satisfy their most obvious needs. Years later, Clear (1994) expressed a similar view when he affirmed that penal harm does not help the victim and cannot make the victim whole again. Instead, the focus on getting even with the offender could in some ways divert the victim from his/her personal path of recovery. Clear adds:

> In this way, the emphasis on penal harm may actually be a disservice to the victim, in that it promises that if the State is only able to impose a penalty severe enough, the victim will be able to overcome the crime. The focus is placed on what happens to the law violator, not

what happens with the victims. The victim's victory at sentencing is eventually exposed as a pyrrhic conquest, for the problem faced by the victim does not center on the offender. (1994: 173).

Conclusion

Every discipline, every movement, every profession needs a critical voice that acts as its conscience, pointing to its weaknesses, its shortcomings, to what it is not doing right, to how it can improve, better itself and correct its shortcomings. To try to silence this critical voice, as often happens, can, in science as in politics, be a recipe for disaster. Many years ago, I decided, at the risk of antagonizing friends and upsetting colleagues, to assume this unpopular but essential role. As I have done with regard to the victim movement, I have tried to offer constructive criticism of the restorative justice movement. Despite my criticism, I have always been, and will always remain, a strong believer in, and ardent supporter of, restorative justice, and someone who cares deeply about victims of crime. But we would be doing the restorative justice movement and ourselves a disservice if we offered it our blind and unconditional support.

The main reason for supporting and adopting the restorative justice paradigm should not be the desperation to find a viable alternative to a system that has dismally failed, but only because of scientifically-based conviction of its merit, its potential, its strength, its vitality, and its viability as a justice paradigm for the twenty-first century.

And before ideologically committing ourselves to the restorative justice model because we see it as a positive, constructive alternative to the negative, destructive and wasteful model of punishment, we need to conduct objective and impartial empirical research aimed at finding out what works best for the victim, for the offender, for the community and for society at large.

To be able to identify, define and delineate the most urgent areas of this research, there is a need for healthy, constructive and critical debates on the paradigm itself and on the practices of restorative justice in various communities including our own. When participating in those healthy debates, and when conducting such necessary research, let us not be more preoccupied with rules than with principles, with form than with substance, with theory than with practice, with procedures and technicalities than with actual outcomes. And above all, let us not confound the paradigm itself with the practical problems of its implementation. Let us distinguish the principles from the potential difficulties in their adoption, and let us separate the goals and objectives of restorative justice from the possible hurdles and obstacles in the way of their attainment.

The challenge is a formidable one and there are enormously tough tasks that lie ahead. But it is always exciting to join forces to overcome the obstacles, to solve the problems and to defy the odds. There is a pressing need to work together to find better and more humane ways of dealing with harmful, injurious acts, to find more constructive and less destructive means of doing justice, and of dealing with those who intentionally or unintentionally do harm to others. There is an urgent need to find peaceful, non-violent and more personalized means of dispute settlement and conflict resolution. Retributive justice and just deserts, under different names and in varying forms, have been practised for centuries. Society has responded to evil with evil, to violence with violence, has inflicted immeasurable volumes of pain and suffering, and in the process has destroyed too many lives, too many families and caused enormous waste of human and social potential.

So all I am saying is give restorative justice a chance.

References

Canada (1988) *Sentencing Commission Report.* Ottawa.

Christie, N. (1982) *Limits to Pain.* Oxford: Martin Robertson.

Clear, T. R. (1994) *Harm in American Penology. Offenders, Victims and Their Communities.* Albany: State University of New York Press.

Council of Europe (2000) *Mediation in Penal Matters.* Recommendation no. R(99) and Explanatory Memorandum. Strasbourg: Council of Europe.

Dittenhoffer, T. and Ericson, R. (1983) 'The Victim/Offender Reconciliation Programme: A Message to the Correctional Reformers', *University of Toronto Law Journal,* 315–47. Reprinted in E. A. Fattah (ed.) *Towards a Critical Victimology.* London: Macmillan. New York: St. Martin's Press.

Fattah, E. A. (1982) 'Making the Punishment Fit the Crime. Problems Inherent in the Use of Imprisonment as a Retributive Sanction', *Canadian Journal of Criminology,* 24(1): 1–12.

Fattah, E. A. (1988) *On Victims, Parole, and the Sentencing Commission.* Brief submitted to the House of Commons standing Committee on Justice and Solicitor General, March, 1988.

Fattah, E. A. (1992) 'Beyond Metaphysics: The Need for a New Paradigm – On Actual and Potential Contributions of Criminology and the Social Sciences to the Reform of the Criminal Law' in R. Lahti and K. Nuotio (eds) *Criminal Law Theory in Transition – Finnish and Comparative Perspectives.* Helsinki: Finnish Lawyers Publishing Company.

Fattah, E. A. (1993) 'From a Guilt Orientation to a Consequence Orientation: A Proposed New Paradigm for the Criminal Law in the 21st Century' in W. Kuper and J. Welp (eds) *Beiträge zur Rechtswissenschaft*. Heidelberg: C. F. Müller Juristischer Verlag.

Fattah, E. A. (1995) 'Restorative and Retributive Justice Models: A Comparison' in H.-H. Kühne (ed.) *Festschrift für Koichi Miyazawa*. Baden-Baden: Nomos Verlagsgesellschaft. Reprinted in E. A. Fattah and T. Peters (eds) *Support for Crime Victims in a Comparative Perspective.* (1998) Leuven: Leuven University Press, Belgium.

Fattah, E. A. (1997) *Criminology: Past, Present and Future.* London: Macmillan, New York: St. Martin's Press.

Fattah, E. A. (1998) 'Some Reflections on the Paradigm of Restorative Justice and its Viability for Juvenile Justice' in L. Walgrave (ed.) *Restorative Justice for Juveniles: Potentialities, Risks and Problems for Research.* Leuven: Leuven University Press.

Fattah, E. A. (1999a) *Mediation in Penal Matters.* Report for Correctional Services Canada.

Fattah, E. A. (1999b) 'Victim Redress and Victim–Offender Reconciliation in Theory and Practice – Some Personal Reflections', *Hokkaigakuen Law Journal*, 35(1): 155–82.

Fattah, E. A. (2000a) 'How Valid are the Arguments Frequently Made Against Mediation and Restorative Justice?' in H. Giertsen (ed.) *Albanian and Norwegian Experiences with Mediation in Conflicts.* Oslo: Institute of Criminology.

Fattah, E. A. (2000b) *Preventing Repeat Victimization as the Ultimate Goal of Victim Services.* Keynote address, Conference on Services for Victims of Crime. Melbourne, Sept. 7–9, 2000.

Fattah, E. A. (2001) 'Does Victimology Need Deontology? Ethical Conundrums in a Young Discipline'. *Proceedings of the 10th International Symposium on Victimology,* 2001.

Gabor, T. (1998) 'Looking Back or Moving Forward: Retributivism and the Canadian Sentencing Commission Proposals' in T. F. Hartnagel (ed.) Canadian Crime Control Policy – Selected Readings. Toronto: Harcourt Brace.

Harris, K. M. (1991) 'Moving Into the New Millennium. Toward a Feminist Vision of Justice' in H. E. Pepinsky and R. Quinney (eds) *Criminology as Peacemaking.* Bloomington: Indiana University Press.

Rawls, J. (1971) *A Theory of Justice.* Cambridge, MA: Belknap Press.

Raynor, P. (1997) 'Some Observations on Rehabilitation and Justice', *The Howard Journal*, 36(3): 248–62.

Sykes, G. M. (1971) 'The Pains of Imprisonment' in L. Radzinowicz and M. E. Wolfgang (eds) *Crime and Justice* (vol. 3). *The Criminal in Confinement.* New York: Basic Books.

von Hirsch, A. (1976) *Doing Justice – The Choice of Punishment.* Report of the Committee for the Study of Incarceration. NY: Hill and Wang.

Wooton, B. (1963) *Crime and the Criminal Law: Reflections of a Magistrate and Social Scientist.* London: Stevens and Sons.

Chapter 16

Restorative justice: present prospects and future directions

Elmar G. M. Weitekamp

Almost exactly ten years ago, I wrote a chapter for a book evaluating the development of restorative justice in the Unites States of America and Canada and concluded that the criminal justice systems again managed to bury this unique, innovative, and ancient form of handling and solving conflicts (Weitekamp 1991). I gladly admit that I seem to have been wrong and only a year later, in 1991, I participated in a conference in Il Ciocco in Italy, at which some fifty international scholars discussed for the first time various forms of victim–offender mediation schemes all over the world. Ever since, many conferences and workshops have been held on the topic of restorative justice. That these meetings gain in importance can be seen in the fact that at the Tenth United Nations Congress on Crime Prevention and Treatment of Offenders, very successful ancillary meetings on restorative justice were organized.

It is interesting to note that in the historical background and development of restorative justice the terms restitution, reparation, compensation, atonement, redress, community service, mediation and indemnification have been used interchangeably in the literature. The term restorative justice is a fairly new one and restorative justice means different things, depending on the country, state and community where such programmes exist. Restorative justice is, so to speak, an umbrella term for all sorts of ways to undo the wrong caused by crimes or offences. According to Walgrave (1998), restorative justice is a distinct and unique response to crime and has to be distinguished clearly from retributive and re-habilitative responses to crime. Restorative justice focuses on losses, repairs the damage inflicted, seeks satisfied parties and views the victim as the central person of the whole process.

The old concepts and responses to crime, such as the retributive and rehabilitative ones, no longer work appropriately, and criminal justice systems are at breaking point. Complaints about the ability of current systems of justice to secure and make life worthwhile are universal. In addition to the failure of justice systems, according to Currie (1997), the socio-cultural syndrome of individualistic and hedonistic value patterns, the neglect of collectivistic orientations, and the erosion of the social embeddedness of individuals are responsible for rising crime rates in western and consumer societies. Cultural and structural individualization lead to disintegration and affect mainly families, neighbourhoods and communities. In addition, social disintegration reduces participation in and attachment to the institutions of society. Many scholars, among them Walgrave and Geudens (1996) for instance, believe that a way out of this dilemma could be found in developing a restorative paradigm as a fully-fledged alternative to both the rehabilitative and retributive approaches to justice. The restorative justice philosophy is based on the ancient concepts such as those developed by the Inuit, Maori, Native Indians of America, Africans and Aboriginals and can be found in its various forms from Alaska via California to New Zealand and Australia, in Africa, Asia, South America and Europe. Many countries are now looking at and implementing such programmes and concepts, having realized, according to Fattah (1998), that what criminal justice systems need in times of growing complexity is: decentralization, de-formalization, downscaling, restructuring, de-specialization and decriminalization; or, in other words, a criminal justice system based on restorative justice.

The importance of restorative justice philosophy can be seen in the fact that it has been incorporated in newer concepts of policing, prevention programmes, and within the context of justice systems.

The traditional style of policing was to keep public peace and order, to enforce laws, make arrests, and provide short-term solutions to problems which occurred. It ignored the old principles and aspects of the community's and citizens' welfare and their working together with the police. Dissatisfaction with the traditional policing style led to the development of community- and problem-oriented policing. The philosophy of community- and problem-oriented policing is proactive and promotes long-term concepts for solving problems that are criminal, produce victims in a given community, affect our quality of life or increase our fear of crime, as well as relate to other community issues. Community-

and problem-oriented policing imply a special cooperation between the police, the citizens and the community for crime prevention. The concepts try to involve every citizen of a whole community in the activities to reduce and control acute crime problems, victimization, drug markets, fear of crime and the decline of the neighbourhood, in order to improve the quality of life in the community.

These new forms of policing fit very well into the restorative justice paradigm and its philosophy: one of the key elements in Marshall's (1996: 37) definition is that 'all parties with a stake in a specific offence come together to resolve collectively how to deal with the aftermath of the offence and its implication for the future'. If one substitutes the words 'stake in a specific offence' with 'stake in a specific community' and considers as the key players in the community its citizens, potential offenders and victims, the police officers and other interested parties, one truly has a restorative justice model. In examining the views of citizens and citizens' expectations with regard to policing, we concluded in a study in Tübingen (Weitekamp *et al.* 1996) that: (1) citizens want a strong police force with a high visibility in their neighbourhood and (2) that citizens want police officers who are their friends and helpers and are prepared and willing to handle all kinds of problems within the community. We concluded that these expectations can best be accomplished by adding the offenders as an important party and, even more importantly, the victims of crimes, to the existing concepts of problem- and community-oriented policing. By introducing such a balanced restorative justice model, this approach includes all aspects in an integrated manner, such as crime, fear of crime, crime prevention and the improvement of the quality of life for all people who are involved.

A quite similar approach is taken by the preventive model of 'communities that care' developed by Hawkins (1993) and his colleagues in Seattle. Three conditions are essential for their model: (1) risk factors have to be identified in a reasonable way, especially for groups such as the child and the family, and for the environment; (2) matters are available which have to be proven to be effective; and (3) consistent and stable prevention policy, in a joint effort by the involved agencies who conduct a concerted action, is needed, in which collaboration is essential. In order to create such communities, the authors worked out nine steps to create successfully such communities that care.

Again, the conditions and steps of the 'community that care' programme have a lot in common with the restorative justice paradigm in that they get together all the parties involved and try to heal a situation or to improve the quality of life in the community by reducing fear of crime and avoiding victimization of its citizens.

Looking at the newest developments of restorative justice within the context of existing justice systems, one finds that they resemble in fact very old and ancient forms of restorative justice as used in acephelous societies and other forms of humankind: family group conferences, family conferences, peace circles, community circles, or circle hearings as used by indigenous people such as the Aboriginals, Maori, Inuit, the Native Indians of North America and African peoples. The new concepts and models treat crime as an offence against human relationships, recognize that crime is wrong and when it happens can further alienate the community, the family of the victim and the offender and lead to damage, disrespect, disempowerment and feelings of insecurity. The chance of the restorative justice approach is to recognize the injustice, so that in some form, equity will be restored, thus leading the participants of this process to feel safer, more respected and more empowered.

It is somewhat ironic that, at the beginning of the new millennium, we have to go back to methods and forms of conflict resolution which were practised some millennia ago by our ancestors. However, these examples clearly indicate that the restorative justice paradigm in the areas of policing, crime prevention, community building and justice itself is very powerful and seems to conquer areas which advocates of restorative justice for a long time had dreamed of, but were sceptical about whether the restorative justice approach could ever achieve them. We have heard of restorative justice approaches in cases of corporate crime, in cases of family violence and partner violence, in cases of adults as well as of juveniles, and to solve problems among young students. We have learned about new and exciting models of restorative justice such as peacemaking circles, circle sentencing, community sentencing, and a host of forms of family group conferences and group mediation. The message is crystal clear: the restorative justice movement is on the move, but a crucial question is, where is it now and where might it go?

Despite these positive and exciting new developments, it has to be pointed out that so far only very little has been achieved by restorative justice. The majority of crimes in the world go undetected and, as Braithwaite (1999) pointed out, 90 per cent of victims will always be untouched by restorative justice processes since most victims are victims of white-collar crime without even realizing that they have been victims of crime. In addition, Fattah (1998) has pointed out that as a result of gross under-reporting, a very high percentage of serious crimes are never reported to the criminal justice systems and are dealt with without recourse to the system. Everybody seems to talk about restorative justice, but in reality one finds such approaches only here and there, and most crimes, if coming into the remit of criminal justice system at all, are still handled in a retributive style; the era of a restorative justice paradigm as a fully-fledged alternative to both rehabilitative and retributive approaches remains very distant.

Even if we could come close to achieving such a system, the important question remains whether we still need parts of the current justice system in order to guarantee the rights of offenders, and in particular the rights of victims who do not want to participate in programmes of restorative justice. It has been pointed out here by numerous critics that it is of utmost importance that procedural safeguards and standards are developed for restorative justice. That is true and necessary, but it is interesting to note that these persons base their arguments on the philosophies of more punitive/retributive criminal justice systems, systems that have, according to Fattah (1998), done a lousy job, since those systems promise crime victims that they will punish the perpetrator of the crime against them but fail nine times out of ten, since 10 per cent of all criminal cases is the maximum number of cases which make it to the courts. Hulsman (1986) points out in this context that there exist no intrinsic differences between people who are directly involved in criminal events and those involved in other unpleasant events. While most of those unpleasant events are solved within the social context in which they take place, such as the family, the trade union or the neighbourhood, this is not done with criminal cases in which, according to Christie (1978), the criminal justice system takes the conflict away from the people who are involved in it, thus handling the conflict outside their social context and environment.

We will have also to face offenders for whom the restorative justice approach will not work and who have to be incarcerated in order to protect citizens, communities and societies. However, the state and its institutions should in these cases also apply a restorative justice approach as far as possible and base its response on a restorative justice philosophy. A good example showing that a restorative justice approach can be applied at all levels is the Belgian experience; there, according to Tony Peters, in the prison system there are always ways to start a healing process between the offender and victim in very serious cases. The work of Mark Umbreit (see, e.g., Umbreit 1999) demonstrates that a restorative justice approach can also be used even in cases of homicide.

However, while restorative justice models appear and sound very promising in theory and achieve much better levels of satisfaction for victims, offenders and all other persons involved in such programmes, evaluations of these programmes reveal that they are usually plagued by one or more of the following shortcomings:

(1) despite a tremendous amount of legislative activity in introducing and reinforcing restorative justice models and programmes, they are applied in a very unsystematic manner and have not, with maybe the exception of New Zealand and Austria, gained a major role in any justice system;

(2) restorative justice models often do not serve as alternatives to incarceration, and often lead to stronger, wider and different nets of social control;

(3) restorative justice models often admit only a small number of minorities and a disproportionately high number of juveniles, first time offenders and property offenders;

(4) competing agencies, with unclear missions, who have different stakes in restorative justice and often compete or contradict restorative justice, harm the movement more than doing restorative justice a favour;

(5) poor planning, unsystematic implementation and, even more importantly, the short-sighted evaluations of restorative-justice programmes constitute a major problem and are responsible for the often trivial results achieved by existing programmes.

In addition to these shortcomings, we also find a number of paradoxes in the field of restorative justice: Germany, for example, is the only country in the world which does not use the terminology of victim–offender mediation. If one looks at texts written in English one always finds the notion that Germany has victim–offender mediation programmes. However, the German term used in law, literature and practice is 'Täter-Opfer Ausgleich' which, if correctly translated into English, is 'offender–victim mediation'. One wonders why this is the case. Maybe a look at another German-speaking country, namely Austria, helps to clarify the situation. Austria uses the terminology 'Aussergerichtlicher Tatausgleich' which translates as out-of-court settlement (mediation). While the Austrians use a rather neutral terminology, all other countries point out that in their mediation schemes the victim comes first in the restorative justice process and in victim–offender mediation schemes as well. This seems to be correct and is supported by restorative justice philosophy.

If, on the other hand, the focus or the central person of the whole process should be the offender, one should logically call that process offender–victim mediation, which clearly implies that the offender comes first and the victim last. If one takes this matter seriously, as one should do in our opinion, one has to question the German approach towards restorative justice, since the terminology indicates that there is a lack of understanding of the basic philosophical roots of restorative justice and victim–offender mediation.

A second paradox in this context can be found in Spain and France. As Trujillo (2000) points out, France and Spain use the terminology penal mediation. Penal mediation was introduced in France as a process in which the victim, the offender and a mediator act under the control of the prosecutor. However, this constitutes a paradox, since the terms penal, which stands for punishment, and mediation, which stands for restoration, which this term brings together, contradict each other. Again, one should be careful and not mix up different concepts.

The local structure usually determines whether restorative justice schemes exist and, if so, in which ways they are applied and how extensive the volume of cases being handled is. In order to illustrate this, let us consider the following happenings in one of the States of Germany. The Ministry of Justice of that particular State wanted to push and extend existing victim–offender mediation programmes and provided some millions of German marks to fifteen cities in order to start new victim–offender schemes for adults. In one of those cities, the Minister of Justice and the Prosecutor General of that State came in person to the opening of the new mediation service and pointed out how important it was to establish such services and that victim–offender mediation was such a valuable tool to resolve conflicts caused by crimes. One should expect, with such publicity and support on the highest level of the state executive, that this programme would flourish in no time and become a major role player in the local infrastructure of the criminal justice system, but this was not at all the case. According to the legality principle, the majority of cases in Germany is referred to mediation by the prosecutor's office and a smaller part by the judges. The local prosecutor's office in that particular city strongly opposed victim–offender mediation, and the judges were not much in favour of it either, and they boycotted the newly established victim–offender mediation office. This led to the two full-time mediators and one secretary sitting around for over a year with no cases referred to them by the prosecutor's office or the judges.

Another paradox which one can find in evaluating the development of restorative justice and victim–offender mediation worldwide is the fact that in countries in which a strong victim support system exists, restorative justice and victim–offender mediation programmes are developed in an unsystematic way, vary greatly from region to region and have almost no importance, while countries with a poor or no victim support system seem to be a more fruitful ground for the restorative justice movement.

It is in our opinion a paradox that we have countries with well developed and influential victim support and with a mediocre restorative justice movement and, on the other hand, weak or bad victim support and a better and stronger restorative justice movement; nevertheless, this does make some sense. We (Weitekamp 1999b) pointed out that one of the factors in the rediscovery of restorative justice in the twentieth century was that the victims of crimes were completely left out by existing criminal justice programmes and procedures and were the big losers in the justice process. Before victim–offender mediation and other forms of restorative justice were rediscovered, Fry (1951) asked if our ancestors were not wiser with reference to the extensive use of restorative justice approaches to solve problems. Fry argued (Weitekamp 1989, 1999a) both for restitution and restorative justice schemes as well as for state-administered compensation schemes. She argued that victim compensation should be seen as an integral part of an enlightened social policy similar to workers' compensation programmes. Her proposal neither precluded the possibility of restorative justice measures being imposed by the courts, nor ruled out civil court actions by the victim. She realized, however, that restorative justice could not reach all victims equally and suggested a combined approach, with restorative justice whenever possible and state compensation whenever needed (Geis 1977). Her efforts ultimately led to the creation of state victim compensation programmes in New Zealand and Britain, which served as models for many other countries.

Margery Fry symbolizes in our opinion the ideal combination of victim support and restorative justice, since her model includes all victims of crimes. Ideally, restorative justice measures, in which the victim is the most important and central person and the offender has to take over responsibility by undoing the wrong, will take place when an offender is available, and in cases where no offender is available society at large compensates the victim. The latter question is often neglected even by the most vivid restorative justice advocates. It is interesting to note that the victim support–restorative justice paradox developed after Margery Fry had called for this almost ideal combination between the two movements. State compensation programmes developed earlier than mediation and restorative justice schemes, but one has to wonder why victim support reached such a prominent place in countries like Great Britain and the Netherlands, while in other countries it never blossomed at all. And, on the other hand, why restorative justice and mediation gained some influence in some countries, and one hears almost nothing about victim support in those countries. Probably one, if not the best victim support system exists in the State of Victoria, Australia, but family group conferencing as a form of restorative justice which, besides New Zealand, Australia is famous for, is almost never applied in Victoria.

This gap between victim support and restorative justice constitutes in a way a dilemma and a good way out; and the best way to enhance the victim would be if both movements joined forces. Vanfraechem (2000) was one of the first to point out that both movements could and should join forces since both would benefit from it. While victim support sometimes receives victims who are unwilling to go through the judicial process, they could easily refer them to restorative justice programmes which do not necessarily handle cases completely outside of the judicial system, but certainly do not represent the judicial system. On the other hand, victim support also has a lot to offer the restorative justice movement, since it provides services which cannot be provided by mediators or conference facilitators. One of the worst scenarios which could happen is that those two movements would start to compete with each other and for conflict to develop over who is more important. The losers of this battle would clearly be the victims of crimes.

While the restorative justice movement is at this point in time stronger than ever and has so far achieved a great deal, we would like to point out that important additional improvements can be achieved in the following areas:

(1) Natural or true experiments are urgently needed in order to determine if victim–offender mediation and restorative justice schemes actually work better than the traditional judicial procedures. The RISE program in Canberra, Australia, in which cases are randomly assigned either to family group conferences or to court, could be used as a role model for such research endeavours; however, these might also be difficult or impossible to conduct.

(2) Although we have some indication that the recidivism rate is not worse and likely to be better if people participate in victim–offender mediation programmes and restorative justice schemes, we need better studies in order to find out more about this important aspect. Research on this topic is usually based on too small samples and the time period for recidivism is usually too short as well. This often reflects the experimental character of the programmes, which are usually small and do not serve high numbers, and the fact that the more interesting programmes exist only for short periods of time.

(3) We do know quite a bit about levels of satisfaction of victims, offenders and other people involved in victim–offender mediation programmes and restorative justice schemes. However, this knowledge comes almost exclusively from Australia, New Zealand, and North America. Such studies seem to be almost non-existent in Europe; in Germany, for

instance, one will look in vain for such a study. Without those studies, which should be qualitative as well as quantitative, we cannot determine how to improve our programmes and might make some fatal mistakes in the application of programmes.

(4) We also know almost nothing about the long-term effects of mediation or restorative practices on the victims, offenders and all other people who are involved or excluded from such processes. Longitudinal studies could be of essential value in order to find out more about these effects and what they are.

(5) Countries should set up national offices in order to monitor what is going on in their respective countries with regard to victim–offender mediation programmes and restorative justice schemes. It is of course extremely difficult to do so, since one has to rely on the cooperation of the practitioners, who often feel that research is burdening them with more work rather than providing something from which they will benefit. The creation of such data bases can be of great value if one wants to find out what is going on, if progress is being made or if restorative justice will only play a minor role later on.

(6) Further surveys should be conducted on the development of the practice of victim–offender mediation programmes and restorative justice schemes. It is, for instance, important to know if organizations or institutions which offer such programmes become more professional, use innovative methods, how their mediators and conference facilitators are trained, and what kind of cases they handle. Progress or decline could be determined through such studies.

(7) We should invent some form of quality control for restorative justice programmes, as well as for laws dealing with these matters, and assess after a certain amount of time if they work and should be continued, if they should and could be improved, or if they should be terminated. So far, we seem to be doing a very poor job in this regard even though we are so used to controlling the standards and the functioning of things on a regular basis in all sorts of aspects of life. Laws, rules, regulations and programmes of victim–offender mediation and restorative justice programmes should definitely not be excluded from such quality control.

So where might the restorative justice movement go from here? While we have so far concentrated our attention on the potential, problems, paradoxes and how restorative justice could be improved, we will now look into the promises of this movement. We think that the development of restorative justice, some 20 years after the rediscovery and the first implementation of such schemes, is ripe for change and for an extension beyond what is existing currently. Today we find the more advanced restorative justice approaches and programmes outside of Europe, and they have a lot to offer. We find such advanced schemes as circle sentencing and community circles in Canada and Alaska, peace circles in the United States of America, healing circles in Canada and South Africa, and family group conferences in Australia and particularly in New Zealand. While we can now find the first pilot projects of family group conferences in Europe in the Thames Valley in England, some in Scotland, and plans to establish one in Belgium, these new forms of restorative justice are often not or not well known in many countries.

The underlying philosophy and applied practice of the New Zealand model of family group conferences can be seen as a model for the rest of the world in order to deal with more complicated cases, in particular for the developed countries and countries in transition with immigrant groups which are often marginalized and living in segregated areas of cities. The family group conference seems to be a promising and more suitable way than victim–offender mediation to promote justice, to improve the role of victims, and to lead to peaceful solutions, since it takes the cultural background and values of immigrants better into account and focuses more on family and clan traditions.

Family group conferences as introduced in New Zealand in 1989 could be the answer, having major advantages compared to traditional justice procedures and extending the rather restricted approach of victim–offender mediation and entailing the following ingredients: the central idea of family group conferences is that children and families have a fundamental right and responsibility to participate in decisions that affect them. One of the key assumptions is that families are competent to make decisions, rather than the more traditional view that they are 'pathological', 'dysfunctional' or 'deficient' in some way. Sensitivity and practical recognition of culture and cultural identity is another principle of family group conferencing. The affirmation of the values of indigenous people and the enabling of these values to be reflected in the decision-making context are of great importance. Family group conferencing is a restorative, not a retributive approach and concerned with the broader relationships between offenders, victims, their families and the communities. A crime in this context is considered to be more than a simple violation of a law, and the key to this approach is to focus on the damage and injury done to victims and communities and to restore peace in the social context in which this happened. While family group conferences are almost unknown in many countries, they could be a major development in building safer societies and the more effective integration of immigrant communities.

Let us turn now to the situation of youth and youth groups and the development of youth violence. Pfeiffer (1998) found that since the middle of the 1980s, we have been experiencing an increase in youth violence in Europe. This rise in violence indeed exists, and one has to ask what its social features are, based as it is on a collective character, and the ways in which gang structures are being developed in Europe. James (1995), for one, argues in this context that one of the legacies of recent developments toward economic rationalism is the creation of a 'winner/loser culture' which creates profound disparities between those who are economic winners in the present financial and public policy climate, and those who are left stranded at the bottom of the economic heap, the losers.

Polk and Weitekamp (1999) speak in this context of juveniles or a group of young people who are abandoned. One of the most critical factors of the emergence of a 'winner/loser' culture is how the life circumstances have changed for those who are located socially at lower points in the social structure. Boys and girls who are 'losers' are caught in a dreadful developmental trap. Historically, virtually all young people, regardless of their place in the class structure, could look forward to a process which would move them from childhood, through schooling, into adulthood with some combination of work and family roles. The trajectories were quite different at different class levels, to be sure, so that those lower in the class structure historically would exit school much earlier than high-status students who might stay on through university and further professional studies before leaving to enter work. Full-time jobs have virtually disappeared in the space of one generation, so that it is now being estimated that there will be literally no full-time jobs available to teenagers. Wilson (1996) speaks in this context of work that has disappeared, especially in the new, urban areas. Forced out of the education streams by selection criteria which either reject or discourage their continuation, these young people leave school and enter into a world where there are neither jobs nor economic support to sustain them: they are being, in short, abandoned.

The situation of abandoned youth thereby places them under a number of forms of stress, which are likely to increase their willingness to use violence. Their entrapment in a social no-mans-land outside of the conventional pathways leading to adulthood means that they do not have available the traditional structural supports for their identity as males. There is a resultant economic and social status ambiguity that demands to be addressed. Caught in conflicts with other males, the abandoned young person cannot fall back on a wide network of other definitions of self as a way of asserting a self-concept which says, 'this is who I am as a man.'

Violence is an apparent low-cost alternative and forming of gangs can be of great attraction. The gang and the status it brings can change the rules of the game and turn a loser into a winner.

World-wide, we find at the moment many signs of this emergence of 'winner/loser cultures', which present a fertile ground for the formation of gangs whose members use violence as an expression of their masculinity. In Germany, for example, we have a group of Russians of German descent, who form one of the groups which feels abandoned by their 'new' society. These immigrants receive German citizenship immediately after coming to Germany. Culturally speaking, however, they are double losers, since in the former Soviet Union they were treated as a minority group and labelled as German fascists. Shortly after arrival in their new society, they experience again the status of a minority group and are labelled as Russians, even though they have German citizenship. In addition to belonging to a minority group, they have language problems, difficulties in schools and jobs. The schooling and job skills they acquired in the former Soviet Union are worth nothing and block legal opportunities for establishing themselves, thus marginalizing them and leading to social exclusion. The language problems and cultural differences lead to isolation, so that the 'Russians' only deal with other 'Russians'. The group, clique and clan represent the social environment in which they feel good, and the German culture and environment become dangerous worlds and can lead to the formation of gangs. The gang gives them a feeling of belonging in which they can develop an identity. The reliance on group activities and groups as resorts of belonging in an 'enemy state' or in an 'enemy society' are behaviours the Russians of German descent had learned and were accustomed to in the former Soviet Union, where they were needed in order to survive. Their experience at the moment, for the second time, is that the German state and society are 'enemies' and that they have to rely on their minority group. The blocking of legal means to succeed in the new society leads of course to the formation of gangs and criminal behaviour. Hand in hand with their isolation goes the fact that they treat the state and its representatives as the enemy, meaning there exists a great distrust towards all official institutions, especially towards the police, justice and the criminal justice system. They consider the German police officers as 'sissies', since they ask 'how can I help you' rather than beating up people as they experienced it in the former Soviet Union. The sentences imposed by courts are considered to be too lenient and time in prison is sometimes considered to be a vacation. Similarly marginalized and socially excluded groups one can find in almost all countries, and the increasing mobility creates more such problems.

It becomes quite clear in this context that we do not reach these people with our traditional forms of court hearings and forms of justice, and the new forms of restorative justice – group mediation, peace circles, circles sentencing, community sentencing, healing circles and family group conferencing – seem to be the right answer. The reason why everything speaks for the fact that the newer forms of restorative justice will work much better than the traditional systems is that they take the traditions and values of the clan or group into account and involve family, clan members and the community more in the process. If we want to tackle youth abandonment more successfully than we are doing now, especially for immigrant and minority groups, and if we want to improve justice, we have to rely more on the newer forms of restorative justice and abandon retributive justice. In order to achieve this, we need to experiment much more with all forms of mediation and restorative justice and to overcome existing problems and solve existing paradoxes. Despite my concerns and problems with the restorative justice movement, the speed of the developments, both in theory and practice, all over the world shows the deep disenchantment with traditional criminal justice and the punishment paradigm. One of the biggest successes of the restorative justice movement so far is that the Commission of the United Nations Congress adopted a draft set of Basic Principles on the Use of Restorative Justice Programs in Criminal Matters. We have heard exciting news about the newest developments in the field of restorative justice, and they all have one thing in common: any social intervention should redress the harm done by offences, start a process of healing, and restore peace among people, in the community and society at large.

So where are we now and where might we go? It will certainly not rain every time after a rain dance, but it does, contrary to Andrew von Hirsch, already rain sometimes after a rain dance; and if we work hard and advance restorative justice further, it will even rain more often after a rain dance.

References

Bazemore, G. and Walgrave, L. (1999) *Restorative Juvenile Justice: Repairing the Harm of Youth Crime.* Monsey, NY: Criminal Justice Press.

Braithwaite, J. (1999) 'Restorative Justice: Assessing Optimistic and Pessimistic Accounts' in M. Tonry (ed.) *Crime and Justice: A Review of Research.* Chicago: The University of Chicago Press.

Brienen, M. E. I. and Hoegen, E. H. (2000) *Victims of Crime in 22 European Criminal Justice Systems.* Nijmegen: Wolf Legal Productions.

Christie, N. (1978) 'Conflicts as Property' in *British Journal of Criminology*, 17: 1–15.

Currie, E. (1997) 'Market, Crime, and Community. Toward a Mid-Range Theory of Postindustrial Violence' in *Theoretical Criminology*, 1: 147–172.

Fattah, E. (1998) 'Some Reflections on the Paradigm of Restorative Justice and its Visibility for Juvenile Justice' in L. Walgrave (ed.) *Restorative Justice for Juveniles: Potentialities, Risks and Problems*. Leuven: Leuven University Press.

Fry, M. (1951) *Arms of the Law*. London: Victor Gollancz.

Geis, G. (1977) 'Restitution by Criminal Offenders: A Summary and Overview' in J. Hudson and B. Galaway (eds) *Restitution in Criminal Justice*. Lexington: DC Heath Company.

Hawkins, D. (1993) *Communities that Care. Risk and Protective Factor-Focused Prevention Using the Social Development Strategy*. Development Research and Programs Institute, Seattle, USA.

Hulsman, L. H. C. (1986) 'Critical Criminology and the Concept of Crime' in *Contemporary Crises*, 10(1): 63–80.

James, O. (1995) *Juvenile Violence in a Winner-Loser-Culture: Socio-Economic and Familial Origins of the Rise of Violence Against the Person*. London: Free Association Books.

Marshall, T. (1996) 'The Evolution of Restorative Justice in Britain' in *European Journal on Criminal Policy and Research*, 4: 21–43.

Pfeiffer, C. (1998) 'Juvenile Crime and Violence in Europe' in M. Tonry (ed.) *Crime and Justice: A Review of Research*. Chicago: University of Chicago Press.

Polk, K. and Weitekamp, E. G. M. (1999) *Emerging Patterns of Youth Violence*. Paper presented at the American Society of Criminology Meetings, Toronto.

Reeves, H. (2000) *New Developments of Victim Support in Great Britain*. Paper presented at the 15th International Course on Victimology, Victim Assistance and Criminal Justice, Dubrovnik, Croatia.

Reich, K., Weitekamp, E. G. M. and Kerner, H.-J. (1999) 'Jugendliche Aussiedler: Probleme und Chancen im Integrationsprozess' in *Bewährungshilfe*, 46(4): 335–59.

Stoll, F. (1999) 'Von Russland nach Württemberg: Eine Studie zur Integration jugendlicher Spätaussiedler'. Unpublished Master's Thesis. Faculty of Social and Behavioral Sciences, University of Tübingen.

The European Forum of Victim–Offender Mediation and Restorative Justice (2000) *Victim–Offender Mediation in Europe: Making Restorative Justice Work*. Leuven: University of Leuven Press.

Trujillo, J. (2000) 'Mediation: Would It Work In Spain Too?' Unpublished Master's Thesis. Faculty of Law, University of Leuven.

Umbreit, M. (1999) 'Avoiding the Marginalization and "McDonaldization" of Victim–Offender Mediation: A Case Study in Moving Towards the Mainstream' in G. Bazemore and L. Walgrave (eds) *Restorative Juvenile Justice: Repairing the Harm of Youth Crime*. Monsey, NY: Criminal Justice Press.

Vanfrechem, I. (2000) 'Victim's Role in Restorative Justice: Is it Worth While for Them?' Unpublished Master's Thesis. Faculty of Law, University of Leuven.

Van Ness, D. and Heetderks Strong, K. (1997) *Restoring Justice*. Cincinnati, OH: Anderson.

Walgrave, L. (1994) 'Beyond Rehabilitation. In Search of a Constructive Alternative in the Judicial Response to Juvenile Crime' in *European Journal on Criminal Policy and Research*, 2: 129–54.

Walgrave, L. (1995) 'Restorative Justice for Juveniles: Just a Technique or a Fully Fledged Alternative?', *The Howard Journal*, 34(3): 228–49.

Walgrave, L. and Geudens, H. (1996) 'The Restorative Proportionality of Community Service for Juveniles', *European Journal of Crime, Criminal Law and Criminal Justice*, 4: 361–80.

Walgrave, L. (1998) *Restorative Justice for Juveniles: Potentials, Risks and Problems*. Leuven: University of Leuven Press.

Wandrey, M. and Weitekamp, E. G. M. (1998) 'Die organisatorische Umsetzung des Täter-Opfer-Ausgleichs in der Bundesrepublik Deutschland – eine vorläufige Einschätzung der Entwicklung im Zeitraum von 1989 bis 1995' in D. Dölling *et al.* (eds) *Täter-Opfer Ausgleich in Deutschland: Bestandsaufnahme und Perspektiven*. Bonn: Forum Verlag Godesberg.

Weitekamp, E. G. M. (1989) *Restitution: A New Paradigm of Criminal Justice or a New Way to Widen the Net of Social Control?* Ann Arbor: University Microfilms.

Weitekamp, E. G. M. (1991) 'Recent Developments on Restitution and Victim–Offender Reconciliation in the USA and Canada: An Assessment' in G. Kaiser, H. Kury and H.-J. Albrecht (eds) *Victims and Criminal Justice*. Freiburg: Max-Planck-Institut für Ausländisches und Internationales Strafrecht.

Weitekamp, E. G. M. (1993) 'Restorative Justice: Towards a Victim Oriented System', *European Journal on Criminal Policy and Research*, 1(1): 70–93.

Weitekamp, E. G. M. (1995) 'From "Instant" Justice till Restorative Justice: In Search of New Avenues in Judicial Dealing with Crime' in C. Fijnaut, J. Goethals, T. Peters and L. Walgrave (eds) *Changes in Society, Crime and Criminal Justice in Europe* (vol 1), *Crime and Insecurity in the City*. The Hague: Kluwer Law International.

Weitekamp, E. G. M. (1998) 'Calculating the Damage to be Restored: Lessons from the National Survey of Crime Severity' in E. Fattah and T. Peters (eds) *Support for Crime Victims in a Comparative Perspective. A Collection of Essays dedicated to the Memory of Professor Frederick McClintock*.

Weitekamp, E. G. M. (1999a) 'The History of Restorative Justice' in G. Bazemore (ed.) *Restorative Juvenile Justice: Repairing the Harm of Youth Crime*. Monsey, NY: Criminal Justice Press.

Weitekamp, E. G. M. (1999b) 'The Paradigm of Restorative Justice: Potentials, Possibilities, and Pitfalls' in J. J. M. Van Dijk, R. G. H. Van Kaan and J.-A. Wemmers (eds) *Caring for Crime Victims: Selected Proceedings of the 9th International Symposium on Victimology*. Monsey, NY: Criminal Justice Press.

Weitekamp, E. G. M. (2000) 'Research on Victim–Offender Mediation. Findings and Needs for the Future' in *Victim–Offender Mediation in Europe: Making Restorative Justice Work*. Leuven: University of Leuven Press.

Weitekamp, E. G. M. and Herberger, S. M. (1995) 'Amerikanische Strafrechtspolitik auf dem Wege in die Katastrophe: Von selektiver Inhaftierung, der

Implementierung fixierter Strafen, dem Ausbau der Gefängnisse, dem Start eines Drogenkrieges, der Ausweitung der Todesstrafe und der Verabschiedung des Violent Crime Control and Law Enforcement Act of 1994', *Neue Kriminalpolitik*, 7(2): 16–22.

Weitekamp, E. G. M. and Tränkle, S. (1998) 'Die Entwicklung des Täter-Opfer-Ausgleichs in der Bundesrepublik Deutschland: Neueste Ergebnisse und Befunde' in F. E. S. L. Brandenburg (ed.) *Der Täter-Opfer-Ausgleich. Moderner Beitrag zur Konfliktregelung und zur Sicherung sozialen Friedens*. Potsdam.

Weitekamp, E. G. M., Kerner, H.-J. and Meier, U. (1996) 'Problem Solving Policing: Views of Citizens and Citizens Expectations' in P.-O. Wikstroem, L. Sherman and W. Skogan (eds) *Proceedings of the International Conference and Workshop on Problem, Solving Policing as Crime Prevention*, Stockholm, Sweden, September 1996 (forthcoming).

Wilson, W. J. (1996) *When Work Disappears: The World of the New Urban Poor*. New York: Vintage Books.

Zehr, H. (1990) *Changing Lenses: A New Focus for Crime and Justice*. Scottdale, PA: Herald Press.

Index

abandoned youth, 333
Aboriginal domain, 43–4
Aboriginal Mediation Initiative, 287
Aboriginal peoples
    exercise of power, 288–90
    ideas and philosophy, 288
    restorative justice, 286–8, 301–2
    see also North American Aboriginal
      peoples
acceptance of alternative approaches,
    inclusion, 6
accountability, US conferencing, 192
acknowledgement of interests,
    inclusion, 5
action, guilt through, 255–6
admissions of guilt, 58–9
affect theory, 270
aggression, consequence of shame,
    271–2
agreements, 3, 7, 56–7
alienation, 21
allegoric personification, justice, 224–8,
    243–5
amende honorable, 251

amends, 3–4, 8t
Anasazi, 300
ancient societies
    divine intervention, 258
    experience of guilt, 257
anger, expression of, 57–8
anthropology, 248
anxiety
    dealing with through sacrifice,
      255
    victim participation, 53
apologies, 4, 8
Aristotelian doctrine of justice, 227
assythment, 263
Australia
    restorative justice programmes,
      32–3, 47
    violation of rights, 47
authority
    institutionalized violence, 253
    Western and Aboriginal traditions,
      288
availability of community, 76
avoidance, 271

BAS, 15
Bauman, Zygmunt, 37
Beccafumi, Domenico, 243, 244f
Beerntsen, Penny, 23, 24
Belgium
    children's rights, 207–8
    restitution funds, 211
belonging see journey to belonging
BIA see Bureau of Indian Affairs
bifurcated justice systems, 47–8
blindfolded Justice, 224–6
bloodfeuds, 256, 259, 263
Bosque Redondo resettlement, 295
Braithwaite, on crime, shame and
    reintegration, 275–6
bravery, Aboriginal value systems, 292
breach of the peace, 249
Broken April, 256
Bureau of Indian Affairs (BIA), 295,
    296
Bureau of Land Management (US), 300

Calasso, Roberto, 247, 252, 254
Canada
    circle sentencing, 45
    Sentencing Commission, 316–18
Canadian Journal of Criminology, 314
cannibalism, 300–1
capacity building, 158t
capital execution, 249
catharsis, 255
chain gangs, 61
changed behaviour, 4
Changing Lenses, 66, 67
charge types, US conferencing, 187
Charila, 247, 252, 262
childhood dilemmas, 269
children, restorative justice, 204–20
    influence on criminal justice
        proceedings, 215–20
    procedural safeguards
        content of, 209–14
        need for, 205–9
        in search of, 220
Choes Festival, 259
Chrysanthemum and the Sword, The, 269

circle, Ojibwa tribe value system, 291
circle sentencing, 45, 332
circular vision, 291
civil society, promises of, 94
Claassen, Ron, 14
client satisfaction surveys, 57
Cohen, Stan, 39–40
collaboration hypothesis, 117
collective efficacy, 159, 195
collective solidarity, calculating, 100–4
colonial policies, 41
communicative nature, of mediation,
    232–4
communitarianism
    in the constitutional democracy,
        82–4
    ethics, 80
    ideals, 77–8
    inclusion into the democratic state,
        78–9
    revival of community, 74
    shame, 276
communities that care, 324
community
    involvement, US conferencing,
        193–5
    promise of, 99–104
    restorative justice thinking
        centrality of, 71–3
        problems with, 74–7
    role, youth crime, 151
    space and, 38–40
Community Accountability Boards
    (CABs), 182
community agencies, support from, 94
community group conferencing, 75,
    125, 126t
community guides, 162
community healing, 158t
community punishment, 61
community restorative panels, 182
community service, 61
community service orders, 61
Community Without Unity, 102
commutative justice, 227
companionship, 80

compensation, 52, 261
composition, 250
conferencing *see* restorative
  conferencing
confession, 259
conflict resolution
  role of mediator, 236–8
  through restorative justice, 93–4
  traditional approaches, 264
Connell, Bob, 33–4
consistency, 55
control, social discipline, 112
Court of Indian Offenses, 295
court process
  avoidance of, diversion policy, 147
  stigmatization, 148
Courts of the Navajo Nation, 296
crime
  Braithwaite on, 275–6
  building local community capacity,
    194–5
  public intervention, 84
  punishment, 252
  restorative justice lens, 154
  as stolen conflict, 159
  undetection, 325
crime control, 39, 309
Crime and Disorder Act (1998), 51, 54,
  58, 61, 63
Crime, Shame and Reintegration, 26, 267
criminal behaviour, explanations of,
  253
criminal justice
  negative impact of interventions,
    159
  place of spirit, 263
  republican theory, 82–3
Criminal Justice and Court Services
  Act (2000), 61
criminal justice system
  citizenship and criminality, 38–9
  expansion of, 156
  history of colonization, 46–7
  indigenization, 44
  information and explanation, 52
  resistance to change, 308–9

restorative practices in, 13–17
retributionism, 82
subordination of minority groups,
  36
criminal responsibility, mediation, 212
criminalization, racialization, 36, 39
crisis of Kelsen's paradigm, 240
culture, emotional sanctions, 270
customary law, 45–6

Dahrendorf, R., 233
damage repair, 214
dead, influence of the, 258–9
death penalty, 251
decision-making, non-colonial, 44
decolonization, restorative justice,
  32–48
deep colonising effects, 41
deliberative justice, 94
Derrida, J., 98–9, 101, 102, 103
dialectic, concept of, 229–30
dialectic process, mediation as, 232–4
direct stakeholders, 114
disapproval, 275
Discipline and Punish, 251
disconnect, in restorative justice, 166
distributive justice, 227
diversion
  as policy and programme, 146–51
  reframing, 163–6
  restorative justice lens, 154–7
  rise of interventionism plus, 151–3
  US experience, 145–6
diversion panels, 182
diversion policy, 144
diversionary conferencing, 277
diyinii, 297
dominion
  defining, 82
  pursuit of, 83–4
dual-track model, 15–16
due process, 65

education, for offenders, 58
Elders, Aboriginal tribes, 292
embarrassment, 271

emotion
  in encounters, 3
  shaped by socialization, 270
emotional sanctions, 270
empirical research, shame, guilt and
  remorse, 268–9, 274
empowerment hypothesis, 117
encounters, restorative justice, 3, 7, 8t
Enemy Way, 289
energy theory, 158t
England and Wales, victim assistance
  perspective, 51–3
Enlightenment thought, 33, 309
entre-deux space, 231, 236, 241
ethics, restorative justice, 79–81
ethnic groups, criminality, 36, 38–9
European Court of Human Rights,
  207
European Recommendation on
  Mediation in Penal Matters, 210,
  214
exclusion
  colonized peoples, 46
  through community, 40, 99–100
  see also inclusion
exclusivism, of communities, 76–7
expectations, of mediation, 58
explanation, victims' right to, 52

false principles, 311
family group conferences
  New Zealand, 91, 110, 279, 280,
    332–3
  referrals, 164–5
Fanon, Franz, 35
feasting, associated with mortuary
  rites, 259
federal funding, diversion
  programmes, 150
female figure, portrayal of justice, 224
festive elements, punishment, 250
forgiveness, motivation for mediation,
  57
formal controls, over-reliance on, 161
formalism, need for, 205
Foucault, M., 33, 97, 251

France, mediation, 229, 328
Frankel, Viktor, 24
Fresno Victim–Offender Reconciliation
  Program, 14
fully restorative programmes
  offender fairness, 124t
  offender satisfaction, 123t, 130, 131,
    132
  victim fairness, 122t
  victim satisfaction, 121t, 125, 126t,
    128, 129t
fully restorative systems, 7, 10, 11t, 15,
  16
funding, US conferencing, 185–6
Furies, the, 253

gangs, 334
gender
  decolonization, 41
  social space, 36
Genealogy of Morals, The, 249
generosity, amends, 4
Germany
  immigrant gang, 334
  restorative justice, 327–8
'get tough' initiatives, 152
ghosts, settling bloodfeuds, 259
Giustizia, La, 243, 244f
globalization, 33–4, 37–8, 40
Gods
  repositories of guilt, 255
  in sacrifice, 259
good practice, standards for, 218–20
government programmes, 150
government support, assisting victims,
  53
guilt, 27
  admission, before mediation, 58
  Braithwaite on, 275
  culture and individual differences,
    270
  in developmental hierarchy, 269–70
  distinguishing from shame, 270–1
  empirical research, 268–9
  linguistic analysis, 268
  meaning of, 254–7

as misfortune, 261–2
national character, 269

Habermas, J., 78–9, 233
Halbert, Ellen, 27
harms
    repairing, US conferencing, 190
    restorative justice practices, 97
hashkeeji, 298
healing, for victims, 58
healing circles, 332
Hearn, Lafcadio, 248
Hegel, 229, 234
H.M. Advocate v McKenzie, 52
hóch, 296, 298
honour, journey towards, 26–8
hospitality, collective solidarity,
    102–4
hózh, 296, 298, 299
hózh hasahsdli, 299
hozhooji, 298
hozhoojigo, 299
human rights approach, 220
humiliation, 26, 27
humility, Aboriginal value systems,
    292
hybrid model, 16
hybridization, US conferencing
    programmes, 184–5
hyperdialectic, 231
hypotheses, restorative justice theory,
    117–18

iconography, justice, 224
identity, journey to, 21–2
ideology, portrayal of justice, 226–8
Implementing Restorative Justice
    Principles in Your Agency, 14
imprisonment
    pains and consequences of, 315
    retribution, 314–15
    trauma from, 22
inclusion
    restorative value, 5–6, 9–10
    see also exclusion
indigenization, 44

indigenous peoples, restorative justice,
    32–48
indirect stakeholders, 114
individual development, shame in,
    269–70
individual differences, emotional
    sanctions, 270
informal community networks, 162
informal social control, 156, 161
informality, 205
information, victims' right to, 52
informed consent, 213
inner directed people, 269
innocence, presumption of, 217–18
Institutiones, 228
intent, 219
intention, 63
International Convention on
    Children's Rights, 207
Internet search, restorative
    conferencing, 179
interpersonal dialogue, 158t
interpretation, mediation, 237
intersubjective space, 231, 236, 241
intervention
    emerging restorative justice
        theories, 158t
    negative impact of criminal justice,
        159
    public, 84
    theory, 145
    see also non-intervention
interventionism plus, 151–3
interventionist lens, diversion, 148–51
invitation, to participate, 5
involvement hypothesis, 118–25
Italy, mediation in, 228

Japanese railway station, 248–9
journey to belonging, 21–30
judgement, journey towards, 25–6
judges
    juvenile, 216–17
    Navajo, 295–6
judicial instrument, need for, 208
judicious non-intervention, 147

juridical theory
    guilt, 254
    Kelsen's, 240
jurisprudence, 244
just deserts, 65, 310, 311
justice
    allegoric personification, 224–8,
        243–5
    Navajo people, 297–8
    paradigms, social evolution of, 309
    see also criminal justice; juvenile
        justice; restorative justice
justice systems
    bifurcated, 47–8
    community role, 151
    restorative justice, 325
    see also criminal justice systems
juvenile judges, 216–17
juvenile justice, 143–69
    diversion as policy and
        programme, 146–51
    diversion programmes, 144, 151–2
    interventionism plus, 151–3
    modern diversion (US), 145–6
    restorative justice, 143
        building social capital, 157–63
        citizen involvement, 168–9
        implementation, 167–8
        incorporating principles and
            practice, 1–2
        objective of, 166
        principles for a new informalism,
            154–7
        reframing diversion, 163–6
    target populations, 206
juvenile protection, 205–7
juveniles, restorative conferencing,
    177–200

Kennewick Man, 300
kindness, Aboriginal value systems,
    292
knowing subject, 230, 231, 237
knowledge
    concept of, 230–2
    mediation, 232–4

knowledge/power relationship, 33
Kuhn, Thomas, 66

language
    expression of interpretation, 237
    in mediation, 233
    Navajo people, 294
Laws, The, 260
legal assistance, right to, 213–14
legal institutions, replacement of, 95–9
legal process, expression of anger, 58
legal rights, lack of, child protection,
    206, 207
legal traditions, impact on gender
    relations, 41
'less meant more' policy, 149
letter of slainis, 264
libertarian lens, diversion, 146–8
libertas, 84
life sentence, 249
liminal spaces, 42
linguistic analyses, shame, guilt and
    remorse, 268, 274

macro dimension, conflict resolution,
    94
Magnesia, 260
Making Democracy Work, 85
mana, 273–4
Man's Search for Meaning, 24
Maori people
    cultural importance of shame,
        273–4
    wagga model, 286
material assistance, reintegration, 5, 9
meaning, journey towards, 23–5
measures of restorativeness,
    hypothesis test, 120
mediation, 52
    admission of guilt, 58–9
    criminal responsibility, 212
    definitions, limits of current, 228–9
    as a dialectical process, 232–4
    dispute settlement, 260–1
    disservice to victims, 57
    foundations of, 229–32

goals of, 56
law, 238–43
in modern societies, 263
net-widening, 64, 211–12
public prosecutors, 212
unequal distribution of property, 62
unsuccessful, 216
see also offender–victim mediation;
victim–offender mediation
mediators
early Scottish, 263
middle-class-ness, 60
monitoring of, 57
role of, 234–8
Toba-Batak tribe, 262–3
US conferencing, 186
medium level, conflict resolution, 94
meetings, in encounters, 3, 7
memories, repressed, 24–5
micro level, conflict resolution, 93–4
middle class values, juvenile
protection, 207
middle-class-ness, mediators, 60
mind, decolonization of, 35
minimally restorative systems, 12, 13t
minor offenders
restitution from, 211
voluntary participation, 212–13
moderately restorative systems, 10–11,
12t
monsters, Navajo philosophy, 296–7
moral direction, reintegration, 5
'more-is-better' perspective, 149
mostly restorative programmes
offender fairness, 124t
offender satisfaction, 123t, 129–30,
131, 132
victim fairness, 122t
victim satisfaction, 121t, 125, 126–7t,
129t
motivation, to punish, 250

naat' annii, 297
narrative, encounters, 3
national character, shame and guilt,
269

Navajo Court of Indian Offenses, 295
Navajo Judiciary Committee, 296
Navajo Nation Council, 296
Navajo Peacemaker, 298, 299
Navajo peoples
Enemy Way, 289
history and culture, 293–6
ideals and values, 291, 296–7
peacemaking ceremony, 298–9
power, 292
traditional justice, 297–8
using the Peacemaking Courts,
300–1
Navajo War, 294–5
nayée, 296–7
negative thought, 230
neglectful approach, social discipline,
113
Neighbourhood Accountability Boards
(NABs), 182
net-widening
diversion programmes, 149–50, 155,
164
mediation, 64, 211–12
restorative justice, 96
use of proportionality, 211
new interpretation, mediation, 237
new medical establishment, 153
New Zealand, conferencing in, 279–80
Nietzsche, 249, 250, 251, 252, 255, 256
non-intervention, policy of, 147–8
see also intervention
non-restorative programmes
offender fairness, 124t
offender satisfaction, 123t, 129, 131,
132
victim fairness, 122t
victim satisfaction, 121t, 125, 127t,
128, 129t
normative theory, restorative justice,
144–5, 154
norms, validity of, 233
North American Aboriginal peoples
value systems, 290–3
see also Navajo peoples
Nuer tribe, 259, 262

oaths, 258
O'Connell, Terry, 14–15
offender fairness, 124t
offender perceptions, 129–36
offender satisfaction, 123t, 129–36
offender–victim mediation, 327
offenders
    concerns, 55–9
    education, 58
    experience of trauma, 22–3
    learning about, 61–2
    role, US conferencing, 192, 193t
    see also minor offenders
Ojibwa tribe, 290–1
order, restorative justice, 17
Orientalism, 33
Osiris, Khallil, 25
other directed people, 269
outlawry, 249
overlapping consensus, 239
oversight, restorative systems, 17

Pacific peoples, cultural importance of
    shame, 273–4
paradoxes, restorative justice, 327–9
parent-teacher associations, 160
parochial control, 160, 161
parochial social support, 162–3
parsimony, 83, 84
peace, law as a structure for, 244–5
peace circles, 332
Peacemaker Courts (Navajo)
    origin of, 295–6
    using, 300–1
peacemaking ceremony, Navajo
    peoples, 298–9
penal mediation, 232–3, 234, 328
people presence, US conferencing, 188,
    189t
permissive approach, social discipline,
    112–13
Pius IX, Pope, 311
Plato, 260
police force
    Navajo, 301
    restorative conferencing, 277

policing
    restorative justice philosophy, 323–4
    subordination of minority groups,
        36
pollution, guilt associated with, 256
popular justice, promise of, 95–9
postcolonial justice, 42–3
power
    exercise of, 288–90
    Navajo peoples, 292
    relationships, spatial forms, 36
President's Commission on Crime,
    Law Enforcement and
        Administration of Justice, 147,
        148
prevalence, US restorative
    conferencing, 181–5
preventive model, communities that
    care, 324
primary intent, 219
private controls, 160, 161
private justice, 250
private social support, 162
private space, 37
procedural problems, restorative
    justice, 54
procedural safeguards
    content of, 209–14
    lack of, 63–5
    need for, 205–9
    in search of, 220
processing referral point, US
    conferencing, 187–8
proportionality, 83
    lack of, child protection, 206
    principle of, 210–12
protection, for victims, 52
psychological consequences, of shame,
    272
psychological meaning, of guilt, 254
public controls, 160, 161
public intervention, 84
public prosecutors, 212, 215–16
public/private space, 37
punishment
    assuaging anger through, 58

dispute resolution, 261
divine intervention, 258
feasibility of fair and just, 314–16
genealogy of, 249–54
goals of, 56
guilt and shame, 27, 256
social discipline, 112
utilitarian goals, 310
western legal form and customary
    law, 45
see also community punishment
punitive approach, social discipline,
    112, 113t, 114

racialization, 35–6, 36, 39
Rawls, J., 239
re-narration, of stories, 28
re-offending, 282
re-reading offences, 237–8
reality, 229, 230, 239–40
reciprocity, 28
reconciliation, inhibition of victim's
    anger, 57
Reeves, Dame Helen, 51
referral sources, US conferencing,
    186–7
rehabilitation, 56
reintegration, 4–5, 9
    Braithwaite on, 275–6
    remorse and, 280–1
    US conferencing, 192, 193t
reintegrative shaming, 157, 158t, 276,
    277–8
relation, and knowledge, 230
relationship-building, 155
religious movements, 72–3
remorse
    empirical research, 268–9
    linguistic analysis, 268
    reintegration, 280–1
repair, principle of, 154
repairing harm, US conferencing, 190
reparation
    community service, 61
    institutions associated with, 260
    uniformity of, 55

victim requests for, 54
reparation orders, 61
repressed memories, 24–5
republican theory, criminal justice,
    82–3
resistance
    decolonization, 42
    and rule, 43
    social space, 36
resources
    practising restorative justice, 54
    victim assistance and restoration,
        53–4
respect, 80, 81
    Aboriginal values, 291
    reintegration process, 5, 9
responsibility, 80, 81, 256
restitution, 4, 8
    funds, 211
    meals, 259–60
restoration, 29–30, 95
restorative approach, social discipline,
    113, 114
restorative conferencing, 278
    Australia, 32, 47
    models, 161
    New Zealand, 279–80
    programmes, offender perceptions,
        131
    reintegrative shaming, 277
    role of shame in, 278–9
    US study, 177–200
        findings, 181–90
        key stakeholder involvement,
            191–5
        limitations of research, 198–9
        methodology, 179–81
        summary and discussion, 195–8
    versions of, 277
    see also community group
        conferencing; family group
        conferences
restorative justice
    Aboriginal roots, 286–8, 301–2
    building social capital, 157–63
    central position of community, 71–3

challenges for, 79–84
for children, 204–20
criticisms of, 53–4
due process and just deserts, 65
expansion of, 17
future of diversion and informal
   social control, 143–69
governmental interest in, 1–2
journey to belonging, 21–30
new paradigms, 66–7
offenders' concerns, 55–9
politics of decolonization, 32–48
present prospects and future
   directions, 322–35
principles, 2
procedures, lack of formal
   safeguards, 63–5
promise of, 90–104
punishment, guilt and spirit in,
   247–64
putting into practice, 54–5
reinforcing the status quo, 59–62
role of shame, guilt and remorse,
   267–82
systems
   assessing character of, 6–13
   components of, 3–6
   models of, 13–17
theory, 110–39, 311–14
values, 2, 3–6
victim assistance perspective, 51–2
restorative practices
   difficulties in comparing, 118–19
   typology, 115–16
   theory validation, 116–39
restorativeness, US conferencing,
   189–90
retributive justice, 29–30
   community and the weakness of,
      72–3
   ethics of, 81–2
retributive limits, 210
rights and freedoms, 82–3, 84
rituals, 251
   criminal and penal systems, 277
   humiliation of offender, 263–4

Roman coins, portrayal of justice, 225f
Rowlands, Rosemary, 26
ruling entity, Western traditions, 289

sacred thinking, behind punishment,
   249
sacrifice
   Gods in, 259
   purpose of, 255
sacrificial slaughter, 251
safeguard model, 16
Sartre, Jean-Paul, 35, 229
satiability, 83
scales, portrayal of justice, 227, 243
secondary deviance, 147
secular contexts, spiritual in, 263
self for others, 234
self-blame, 271
self-correction hypothesis, 147
self-esteem, consequences of shame,
   276
sentencing, victim's right to a say in,
   52
sentencing circles, 110
Sentencing Commission, Canadian,
   316–18
services, right to, 52
shame
   consequences of, 271–2
   culture and individual differences,
      270
   distinguishing from guilt, 270–1
   empirical analysis, 268–9
   implementing, 277–80
   importance for Maori and Pacific
      peoples, 273–4
   individual development, 269–70
   linguistic analysis, 268
   national character, 269
   in restorative justice circles, 26–7
   restorative justice processes, 275–6
shaming, 254, 275
   see also reintegrative shaming;
      stigmatic shaming
shortcomings, restorative justice
   models, 326–7

sickness, experience of punishment, 252
social capital, 85, 159, 194–5
social change, 95, 96
social control
    decline in informal, 156
    indigenization of, 44
    types of, 160–1
Social Discipline Window, 112–14, 116, 117
social disintegration, 323
social order, community interest, 39
social sciences
    emergence of, 308–9
    restorative justice theory, 111
social space, 36
social support, 161–3
solidarity, 80, 81
sovereignty, 290t
space, and community, 38–40
Spain, penal mediation, 328
spatial dimension, of knowledge, 231
spatial forms, 35–7
spirit
    domain of, 257–60
    place in criminal justice, 263
Spirit Cave Man, 300
spiritual direction, reintegration, 5
staffing, US conferencing, 186
stakeholder needs, 114–15
stakeholder participation
    principle of, 154
    restorative justice, 115–16
    sense of community membership, 78
    US conferencing, 191–5
standards, for good practice, 218–20
Stanford Law Review, 55
state preferences, US conferencing, 183–4
stereotypes, 62
stigmatic shaming, 276, 277
stigmatization, court process, 148
stolen conflict, 159
strength, Aboriginal values, 292
strict liability, 262, 309, 310

Structure of Scientific Revolutions, 66
subjectivity
    of community, 74
    restorative justice, 34
subjects, hypothesis test, 120
support, social discipline, 112
sword, portrayal of justice, 227–8
Syllabus of Errors, 311
symbolism, allegoric personification of justice, 224, 226–8

testimony, term, 25
thought, European systems of, 35
Toba-Batak tribe, 252, 257, 258, 262–3
tondi, 257
tradition directed people, 269
traditional societies
    divine intervention, 258
    experience of guilt, 257
    strict liability for actions, 262
tragedy, journey to belonging, 22
transformation in community, 154
transformation hypothesis, 117
transformative potential, conflict, 93
trauma
    journey to belonging, 22–3
    journey to meaning, 23–4
Trauma and Recovery, 25
treatment, of victims and offenders, 60
Trobriand Islanders, 259
trust, 85
Truth and Reconciliation Commission, 24

UN Congress on the Prevention of Crime and the Treatment of Offenders, 204
UN Preliminary Draft Elements of a Declaration of Basic Principles on the Use of Restorative Justice Programmes in Criminal Matters, 210, 213, 214
uncoupling, offence and offender, 276
understanding, from encounters, 3, 7
unified model see fully restorative system

United States
   critique, offender concerns, 55–9
   modern diversion, 145–6
   restorative conferencing study,
      177–200
   stigmatic shaming, 277
   see also North American Aboriginal
      peoples

values
   Navajo peoples, 296–7
   North American Aboriginal
      peoples, 290–3
   restorative justice, 2, 3–6
   spiritual, 263
vengeance, 250
vengeful victims, 59–60
victim assistance perspective,
   51–3
victim fairness, 122t
victim participation, 51, 53, 191
victim perceptions, 125–9
victim personal statements, 53
victim satisfaction, 121t, 125–9,
   191–2
victim support, 329–30, 51
   five principles, 52
   integrated justice system, 66
   victim assistance funds, 53
victim–offender mediation, 52
   criticism of early projects, 54
   dialogue, 61–2, 182, 183
   offender satisfaction, 130
   relational process, 233
   victim satisfaction, 125, 126–7t
   victim as sentencer, 56
victim–offender reconciliation
   programmes, 3, 126–7t
victimization, 23, 26
vindication, 25, 28–9
*Violence: Reflections on a National
   Epidemic*, 22

violence
   institutionalized, 253
   need to reciprocate, 28
   re-enactment of trauma, 22
   victimization, 26
   youth groups, 333
virgin suicide, 247, 252, 262
vision, Ojibwa tribe, 291
Visions of Social Control, 39–40
voluntary participation, 212–13

wagga model, 286
Wales *see* England and Wales
welfare image, of justice, 92
West
   authority, 288–90
   knowledge/power relationship, 33
   legal traditions, impact on gender
      relations, 41
   quest for community, 39–40
whakamaa, concept of, 273–4, 281
Wiggins, Sharon, 25
winner/loser cultures, 333, 334
wisdom, Aboriginal value systems, 292
Witness Support Service, 52
Wittman, Denis, 14
Wretched of the Earth, The, 35
wrongs, redressing, 96

Youth Aid Panels, 182
youth crime
   community role, 151
   informal social control, 161
   non-intervention, 147–8
   non-response, 156
   social capital, 159
Youth Justice Board, 54–5
youth violence, 333
youths, as subjects of rights, 207–8

Zehr, Howard, 3, 66, 67
zero tolerance, 152, 153